# THE OFFICE IS A BEAUTIFUL PLACE WHEN EVERYONE ELSE WORKS FROM HOME

## Recent DILBERT® Books from Andrews McMeel Publishing

Eagerly Awaiting Your Irrational Response

Dilbert Turns 30

Cubicles That Make You Envy the Dead

Dilbert Gets Re-accommodated

I'm No Scientist, But I Think Feng Shui Is Part of the Answer

Optimism Sounds Exhausting

Go Add Value Someplace Else

I Sense a Coldness to Your Mentoring

Your New Job Title Is "Accomplice"

I Can't Remember If We're Cheap or Smart

Teamwork Means You Can't Pick the Side that's Right

How's That Underling Thing Working Out for You?

Your Accomplishments Are Suspiciously Hard to Verify

Problem Identified and You're Probably Not Part of the Solution

I'm Tempted to Stop Acting Randomly

14 Years of Loyal Service in a Fabric-Covered Box

Freedom's Just Another Word for People Finding Out You're Useless

Dilbert 2.0: 20 Years of Dilbert

This Is the Part Where You Pretend to Add Value

# THE OFFICE IS A BEAUTIFUL PLACE WHEN EVERYONE ELSE WORKS FROM HOME

DILBERT™
BY
SCOTT ADAMS
dilbert.com

Andrews McMeel
PUBLISHING®

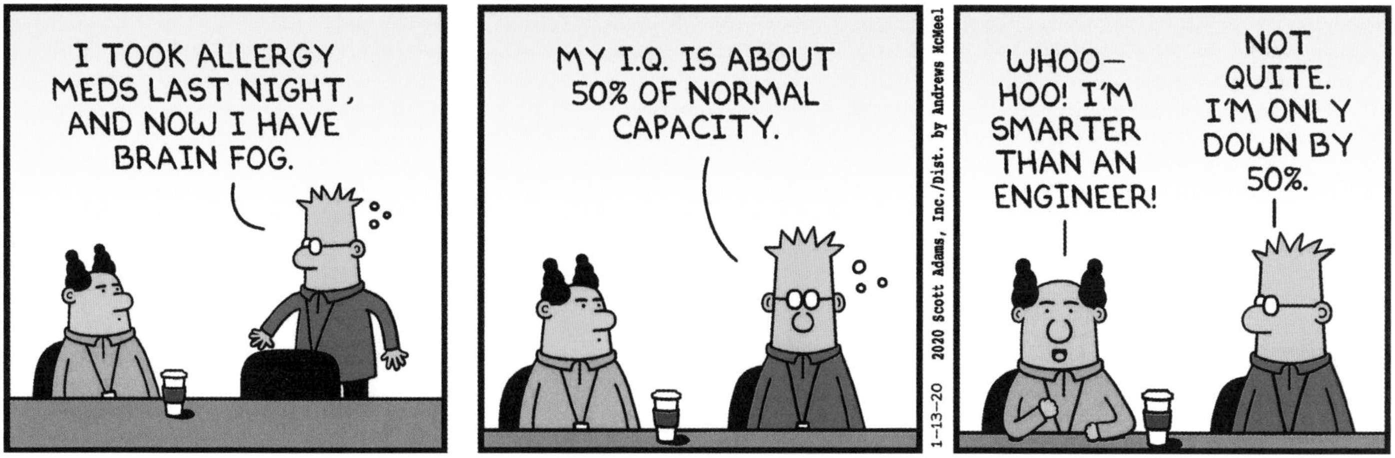
I TOOK ALLERGY MEDS LAST NIGHT, AND NOW I HAVE BRAIN FOG.
MY I.Q. IS ABOUT 50% OF NORMAL CAPACITY.
1-13-20 2020 Scott Adams, Inc./Dist. by Andrews McMeel
WHOO-HOO! I'M SMARTER THAN AN ENGINEER!
NOT QUITE. I'M ONLY DOWN BY 50%.

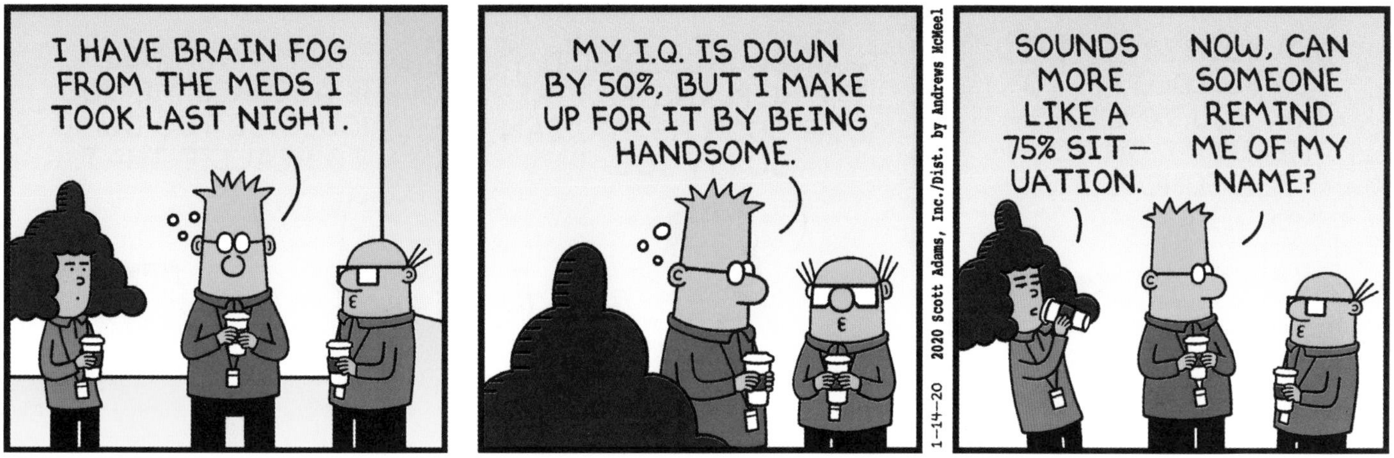
I HAVE BRAIN FOG FROM THE MEDS I TOOK LAST NIGHT.
MY I.Q. IS DOWN BY 50%, BUT I MAKE UP FOR IT BY BEING HANDSOME.
1-14-20 2020 Scott Adams, Inc./Dist. by Andrews McMeel
SOUNDS MORE LIKE A 75% SIT-UATION.
NOW, CAN SOMEONE REMIND ME OF MY NAME?

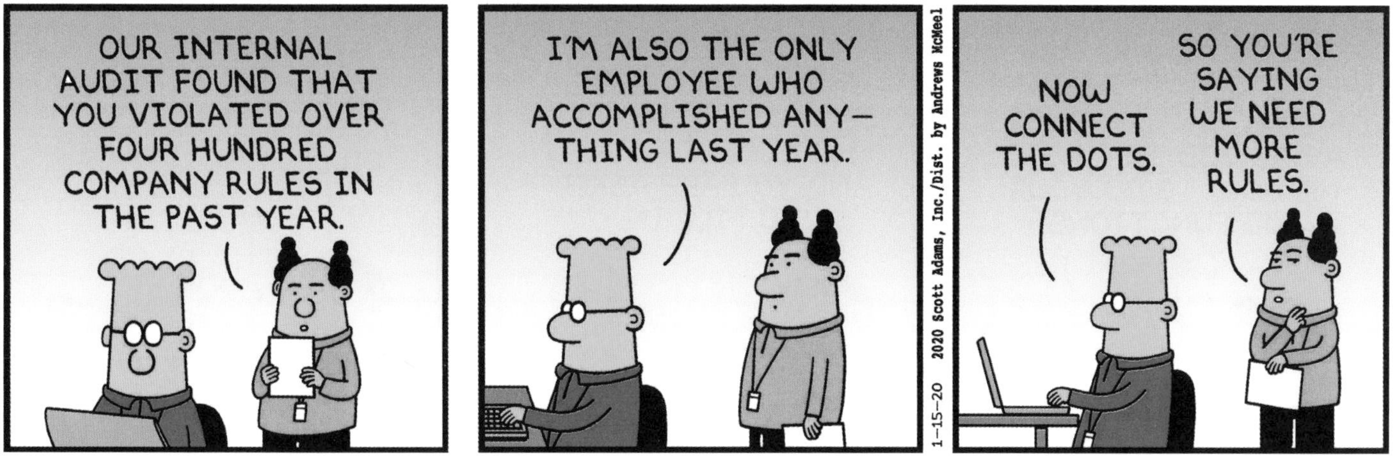
OUR INTERNAL AUDIT FOUND THAT YOU VIOLATED OVER FOUR HUNDRED COMPANY RULES IN THE PAST YEAR.
I'M ALSO THE ONLY EMPLOYEE WHO ACCOMPLISHED ANY-THING LAST YEAR.
1-15-20 2020 Scott Adams, Inc./Dist. by Andrews McMeel
NOW CONNECT THE DOTS.
SO YOU'RE SAYING WE NEED MORE RULES.

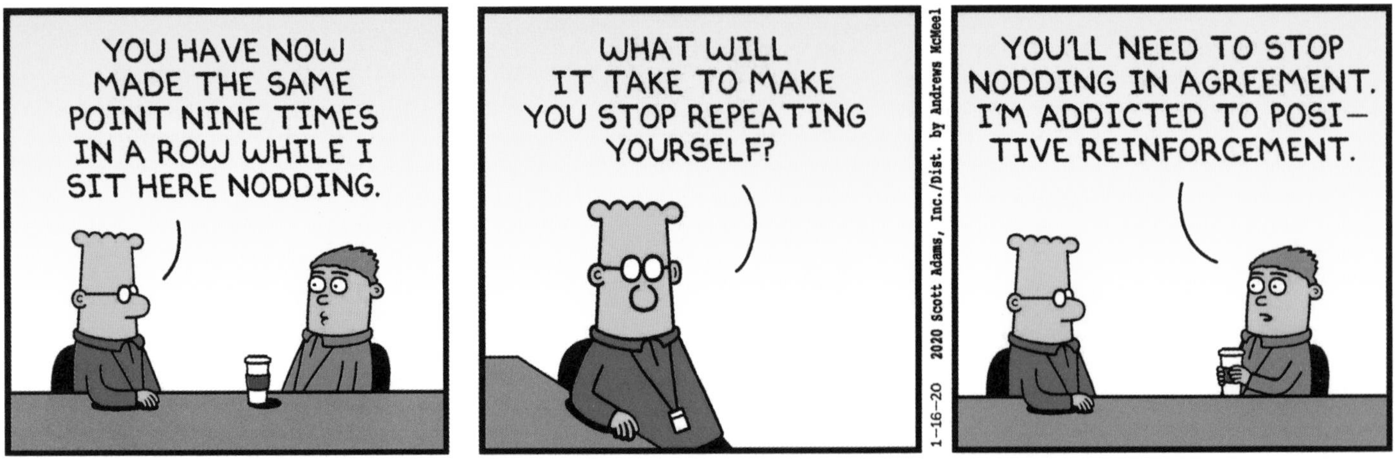
YOU HAVE NOW MADE THE SAME POINT NINE TIMES IN A ROW WHILE I SIT HERE NODDING.
WHAT WILL IT TAKE TO MAKE YOU STOP REPEATING YOURSELF?
1-16-20 © 2020 Scott Adams, Inc./Dist. by Andrews McMeel
YOU'LL NEED TO STOP NODDING IN AGREEMENT. I'M ADDICTED TO POSI-TIVE REINFORCEMENT.

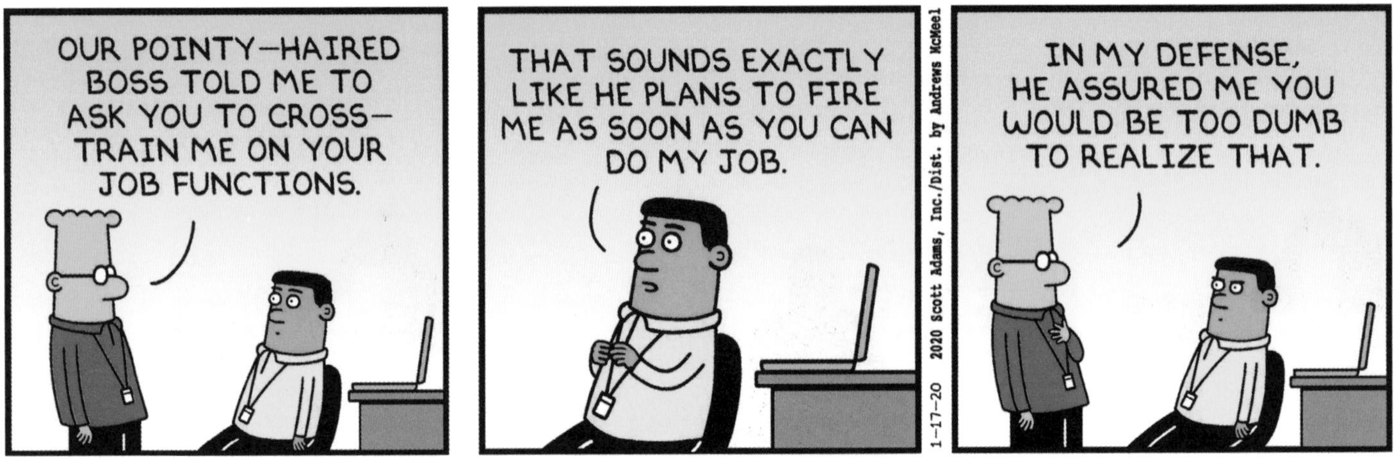
OUR POINTY-HAIRED BOSS TOLD ME TO ASK YOU TO CROSS-TRAIN ME ON YOUR JOB FUNCTIONS.
THAT SOUNDS EXACTLY LIKE HE PLANS TO FIRE ME AS SOON AS YOU CAN DO MY JOB.
1-17-20 © 2020 Scott Adams, Inc./Dist. by Andrews McMeel
IN MY DEFENSE, HE ASSURED ME YOU WOULD BE TOO DUMB TO REALIZE THAT.

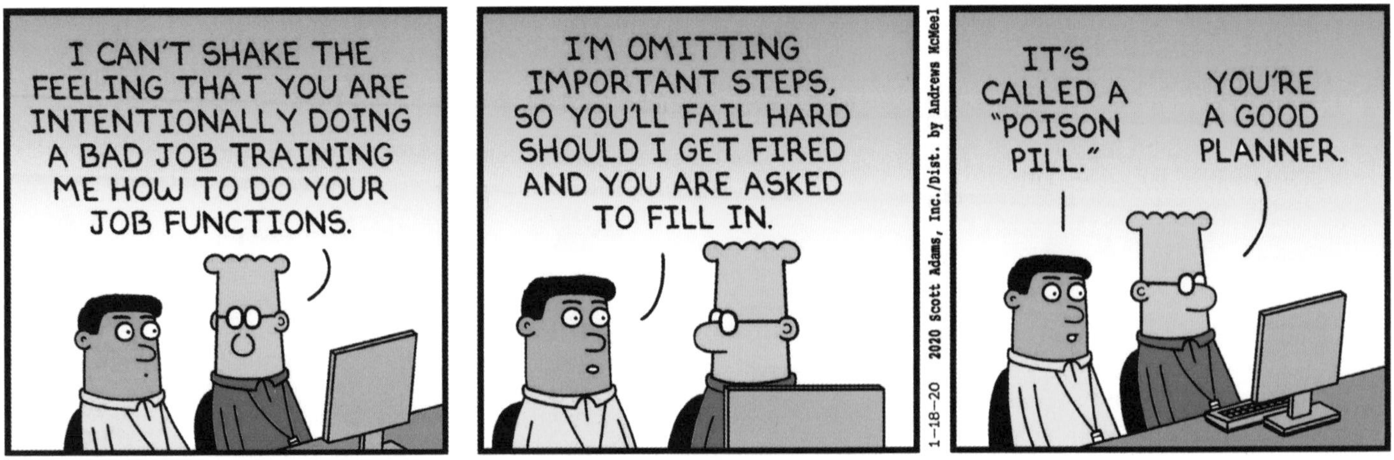
I CAN'T SHAKE THE FEELING THAT YOU ARE INTENTIONALLY DOING A BAD JOB TRAINING ME HOW TO DO YOUR JOB FUNCTIONS.
I'M OMITTING IMPORTANT STEPS, SO YOU'LL FAIL HARD SHOULD I GET FIRED AND YOU ARE ASKED TO FILL IN.
1-18-20 © 2020 Scott Adams, Inc./Dist. by Andrews McMeel
IT'S CALLED A "POISON PILL."
YOU'RE A GOOD PLANNER.

I'M PROMOTING YOU TO THE POSITION OF "MASTER ENGINEER."
I'M ALREADY A SENIOR ENGINEER.
NOW YOU'RE A MASTER ENGINEER.
WITH ALL OF THE RIGHTS AND RESPON– SIBILITIES THAT COME WITH IT.
SUCH AS. . . ?
WELL, FOR EXAMPLE, YOU CAN DO MORE KINDS OF WORK.
FOR MORE PAY?
NO, NO, NO!
YOU'RE THINKING OF "PLATINUM LEVEL" ENGINEERS. YOU'RE NOT ONE OF THOSE.
THAT COMES NEXT?!
OPTIMISM IS NOT AN ATTRACTIVE QUALITY.
© 2020 Scott Adams, Inc./Dist. by Andrews McMeel
1-19-20

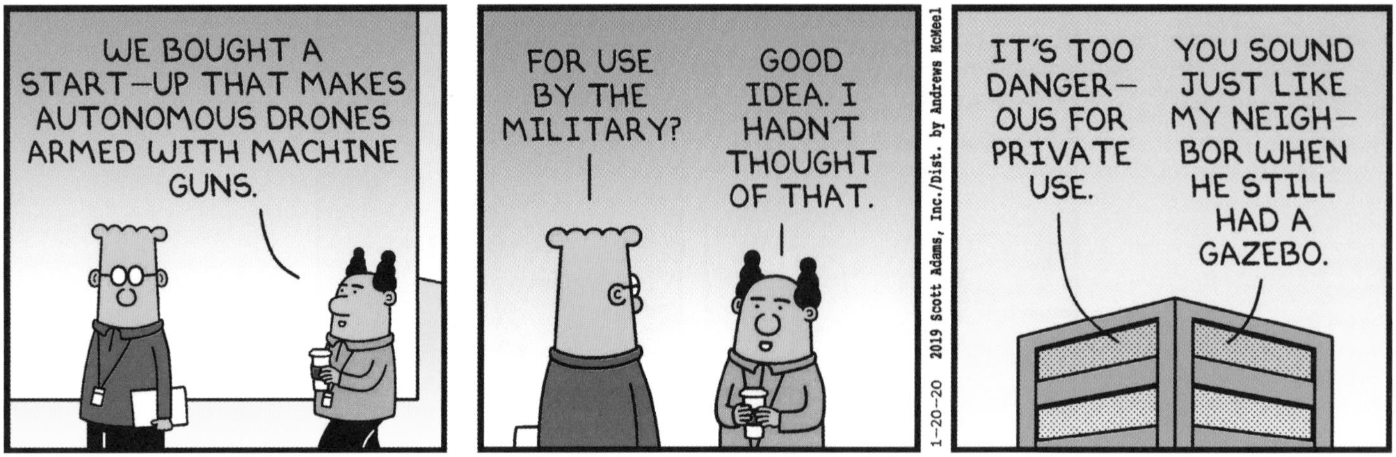
WE BOUGHT A START—UP THAT MAKES AUTONOMOUS DRONES ARMED WITH MACHINE GUNS.
FOR USE BY THE MILITARY?
GOOD IDEA. I HADN'T THOUGHT OF THAT.
IT'S TOO DANGER—OUS FOR PRIVATE USE.
YOU SOUND JUST LIKE MY NEIGH—BOR WHEN HE STILL HAD A GAZEBO.
1-20-20 2019 Scott Adams, Inc./Dist. by Andrews McMeel

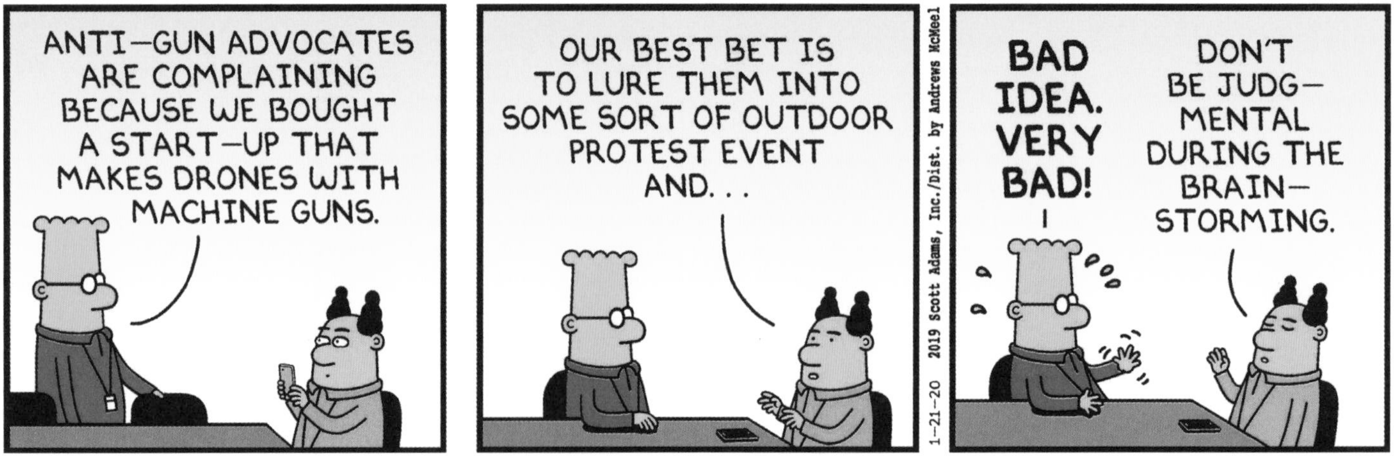
ANTI—GUN ADVOCATES ARE COMPLAINING BECAUSE WE BOUGHT A START—UP THAT MAKES DRONES WITH MACHINE GUNS.
OUR BEST BET IS TO LURE THEM INTO SOME SORT OF OUTDOOR PROTEST EVENT AND. . .
BAD IDEA. VERY BAD!
DON'T BE JUDG—MENTAL DURING THE BRAIN—STORMING.
1-21-20 2019 Scott Adams, Inc./Dist. by Andrews McMeel

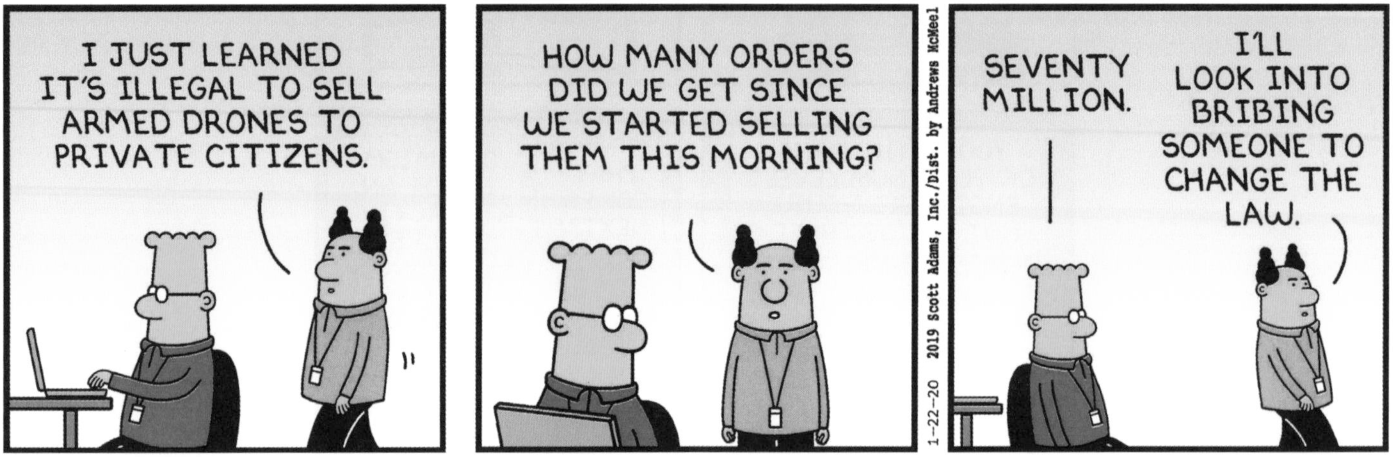
I JUST LEARNED IT'S ILLEGAL TO SELL ARMED DRONES TO PRIVATE CITIZENS.
HOW MANY ORDERS DID WE GET SINCE WE STARTED SELLING THEM THIS MORNING?
SEVENTY MILLION.
I'LL LOOK INTO BRIBING SOMEONE TO CHANGE THE LAW.
1-22-20 2019 Scott Adams, Inc./Dist. by Andrews McMeel

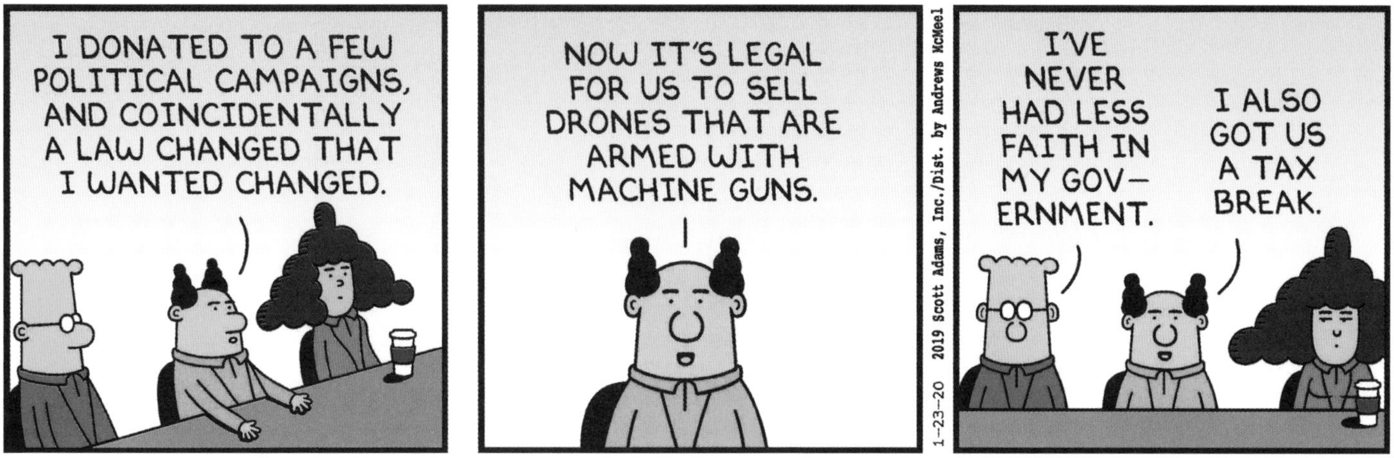
I DONATED TO A FEW POLITICAL CAMPAIGNS, AND COINCIDENTALLY A LAW CHANGED THAT I WANTED CHANGED.
NOW IT'S LEGAL FOR US TO SELL DRONES THAT ARE ARMED WITH MACHINE GUNS.
I'VE NEVER HAD LESS FAITH IN MY GOV– ERNMENT.
I ALSO GOT US A TAX BREAK.
1-23-20 2019 Scott Adams, Inc./Dist. by Andrews McMeel

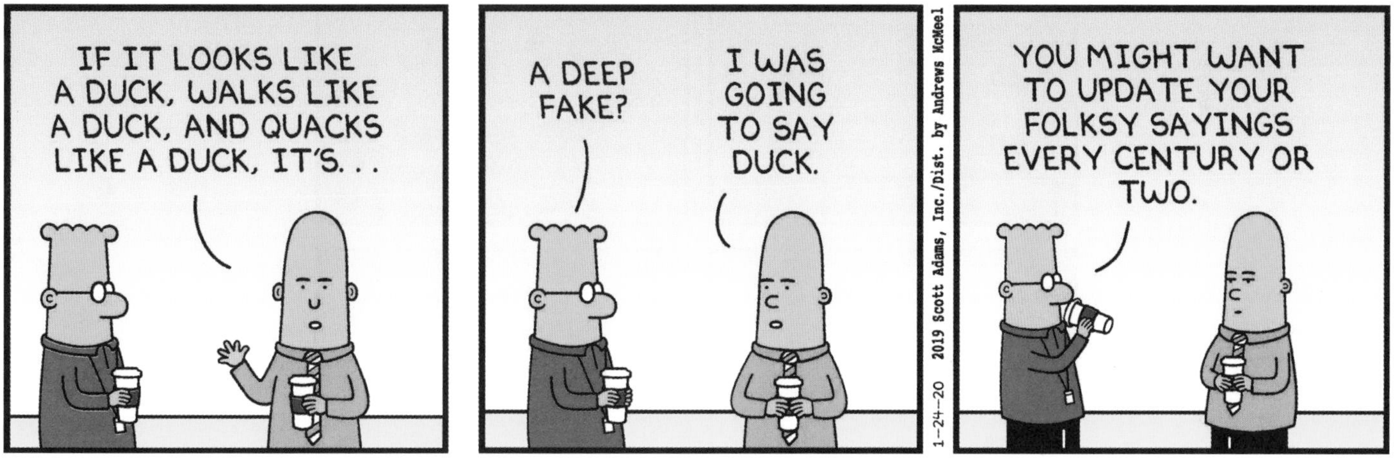
IF IT LOOKS LIKE A DUCK, WALKS LIKE A DUCK, AND QUACKS LIKE A DUCK, IT'S. . .
A DEEP FAKE?
I WAS GOING TO SAY DUCK.
YOU MIGHT WANT TO UPDATE YOUR FOLKSY SAYINGS EVERY CENTURY OR TWO.
1-24-20 2019 Scott Adams, Inc./Dist. by Andrews McMeel

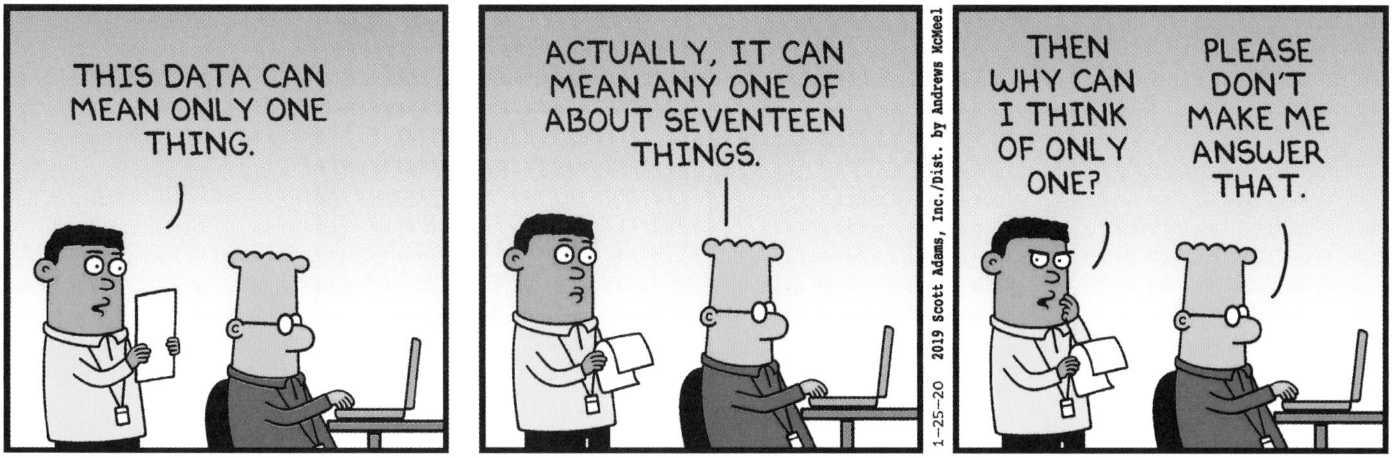
THIS DATA CAN MEAN ONLY ONE THING.
ACTUALLY, IT CAN MEAN ANY ONE OF ABOUT SEVENTEEN THINGS.
THEN WHY CAN I THINK OF ONLY ONE?
PLEASE DON'T MAKE ME ANSWER THAT.
1-25-20 2019 Scott Adams, Inc./Dist. by Andrews McMeel

A REPORTER FOR BUZZFLAWED WANTS TO INTERVIEW YOU.

I DON'T SEE ANY DOWNSIDE TO THAT!

MY FIRST QUESTION IS, DO YOU STILL CHEAT ALL OF YOUR SUPPLIERS?

© 2020 Scott Adams, Inc./Dist. by Andrews McMeel

NO! OF COURSE NOT.

SO, YOU'RE ADMITTING YOU CHEATED YOUR SUPPLIERS IN THE PAST?

GET OUT OF MY OFFICE, YOU EVIL MONSTER!

OKAY. I GOT WHAT I NEEDED.

ONE WEEK LATER

"THE PUDGY MISCREANT COULD NOT HIDE HIS GLEE WHEN BRAGGING ABOUT CHEATING HIS SUPPLIERS."

1-26-20

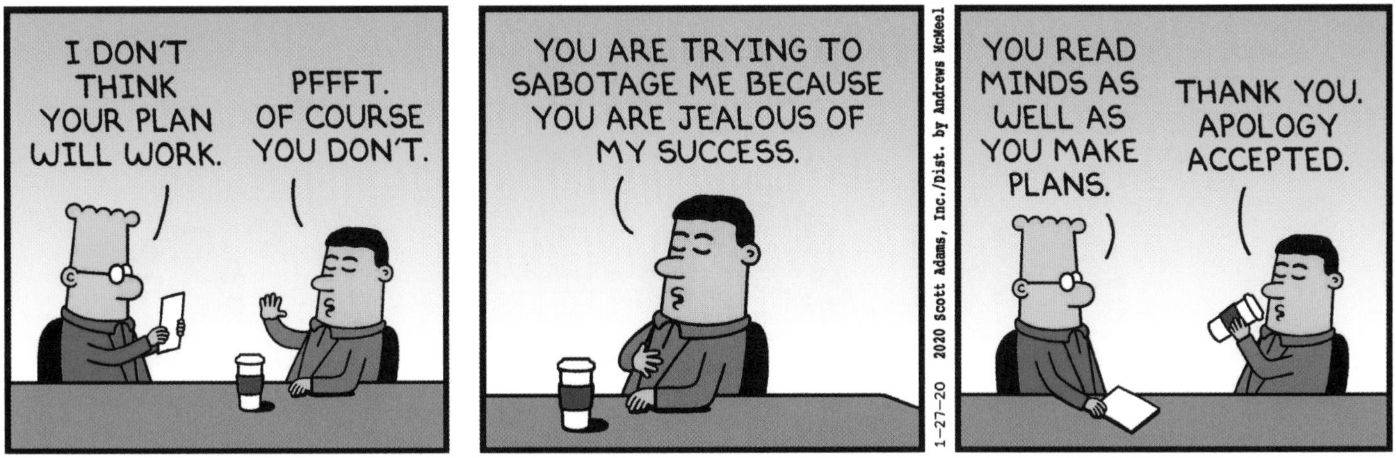
I DON'T THINK YOUR PLAN WILL WORK.
PFFFT. OF COURSE YOU DON'T.
YOU ARE TRYING TO SABOTAGE ME BECAUSE YOU ARE JEALOUS OF MY SUCCESS.
1-27-20 2020 Scott Adams, Inc./Dist. by Andrews McMeel
YOU READ MINDS AS WELL AS YOU MAKE PLANS.
THANK YOU. APOLOGY ACCEPTED.

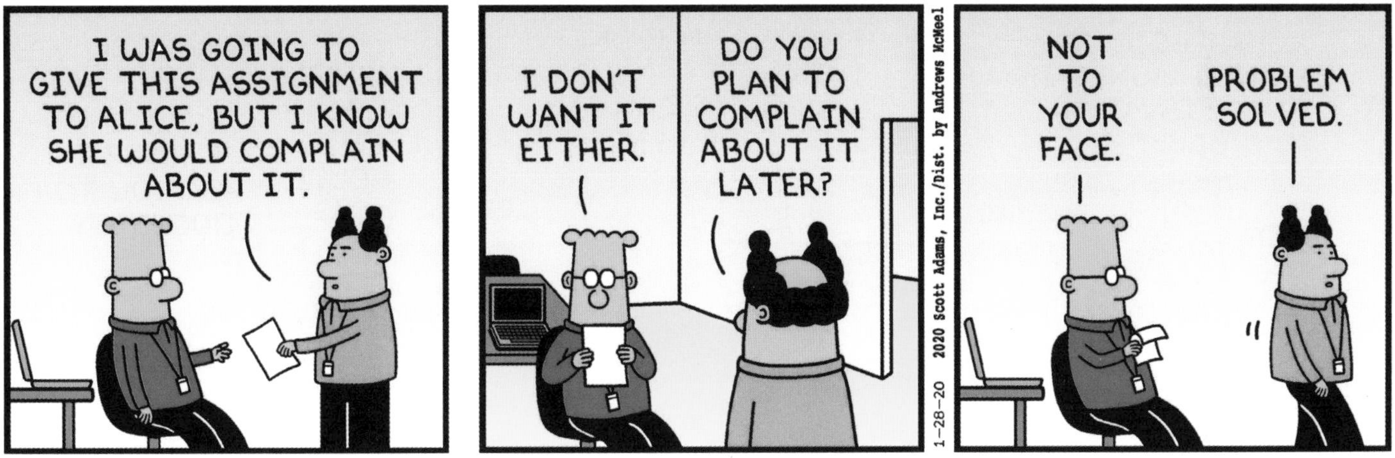
I WAS GOING TO GIVE THIS ASSIGNMENT TO ALICE, BUT I KNOW SHE WOULD COMPLAIN ABOUT IT.
I DON'T WANT IT EITHER.
DO YOU PLAN TO COMPLAIN ABOUT IT LATER?
1-28-20 2020 Scott Adams, Inc./Dist. by Andrews McMeel
NOT TO YOUR FACE.
PROBLEM SOLVED.

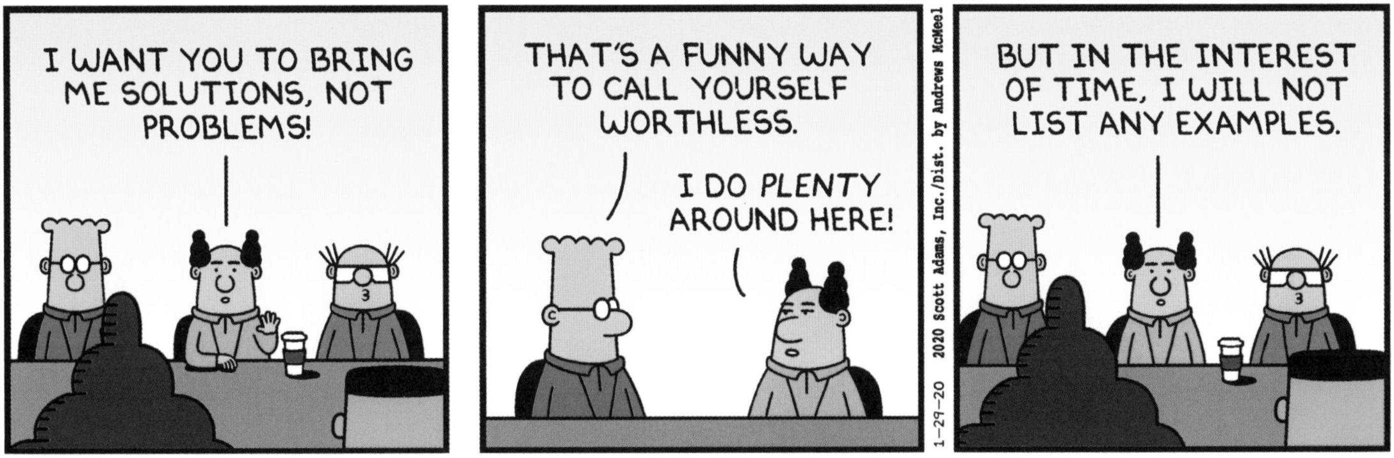
I WANT YOU TO BRING ME SOLUTIONS, NOT PROBLEMS!
THAT'S A FUNNY WAY TO CALL YOURSELF WORTHLESS.
I DO *PLENTY* AROUND HERE!
1-29-20 2020 Scott Adams, Inc./Dist. by Andrews McMeel
BUT IN THE INTEREST OF TIME, I WILL NOT LIST ANY EXAMPLES.

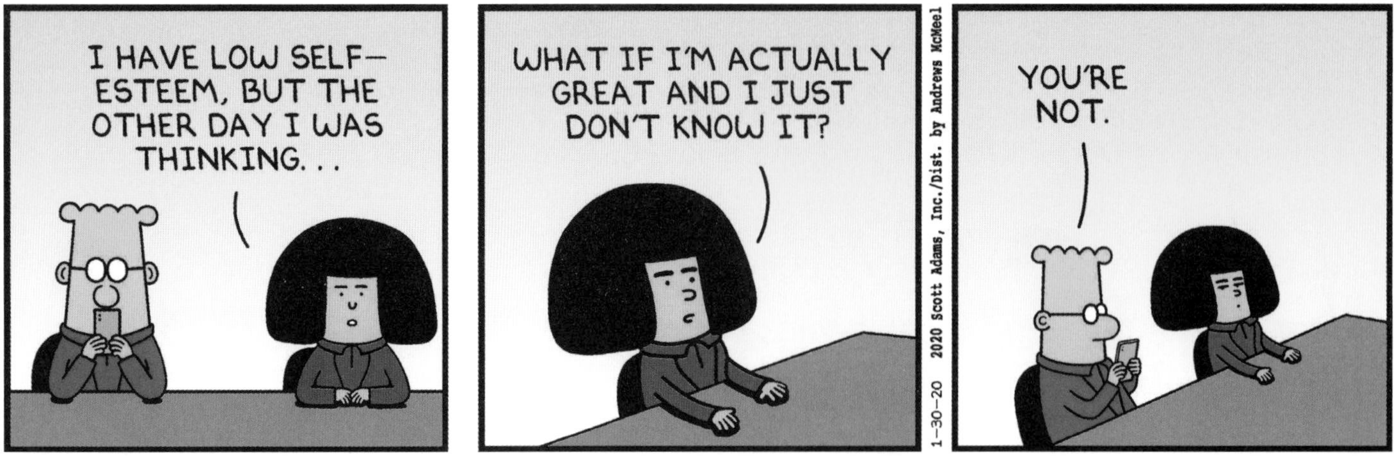
I HAVE LOW SELF–ESTEEM, BUT THE OTHER DAY I WAS THINKING. . .
WHAT IF I'M ACTUALLY GREAT AND I JUST DON'T KNOW IT?
1-30-20 2020 Scott Adams, Inc./Dist. by Andrews McMeel
YOU'RE NOT.

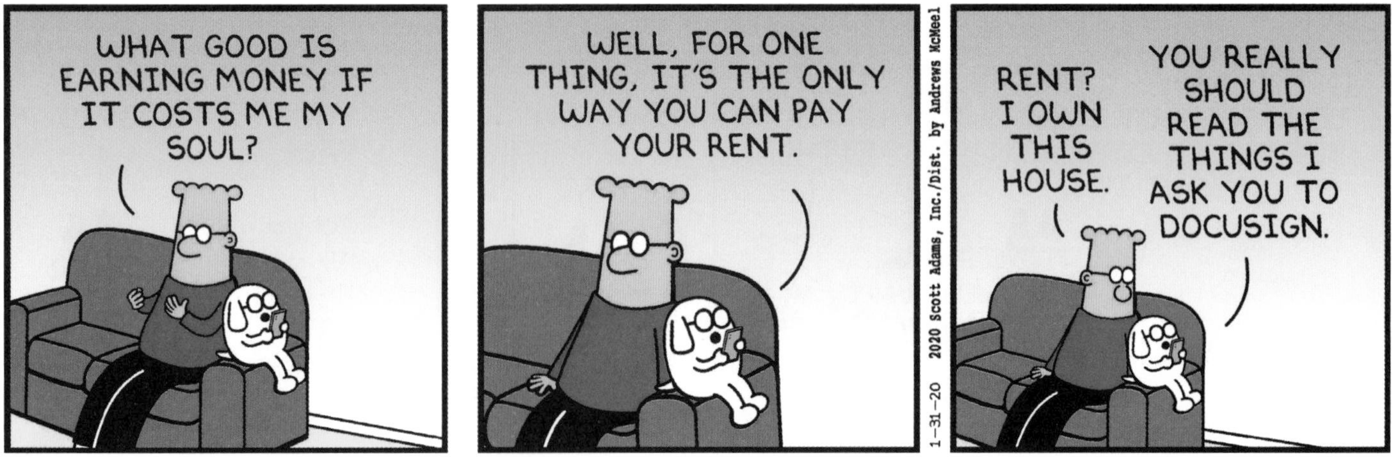
WHAT GOOD IS EARNING MONEY IF IT COSTS ME MY SOUL?
WELL, FOR ONE THING, IT'S THE ONLY WAY YOU CAN PAY YOUR RENT.
1-31-20 2020 Scott Adams, Inc./Dist. by Andrews McMeel
RENT? I OWN THIS HOUSE.
YOU REALLY SHOULD READ THE THINGS I ASK YOU TO DOCUSIGN.

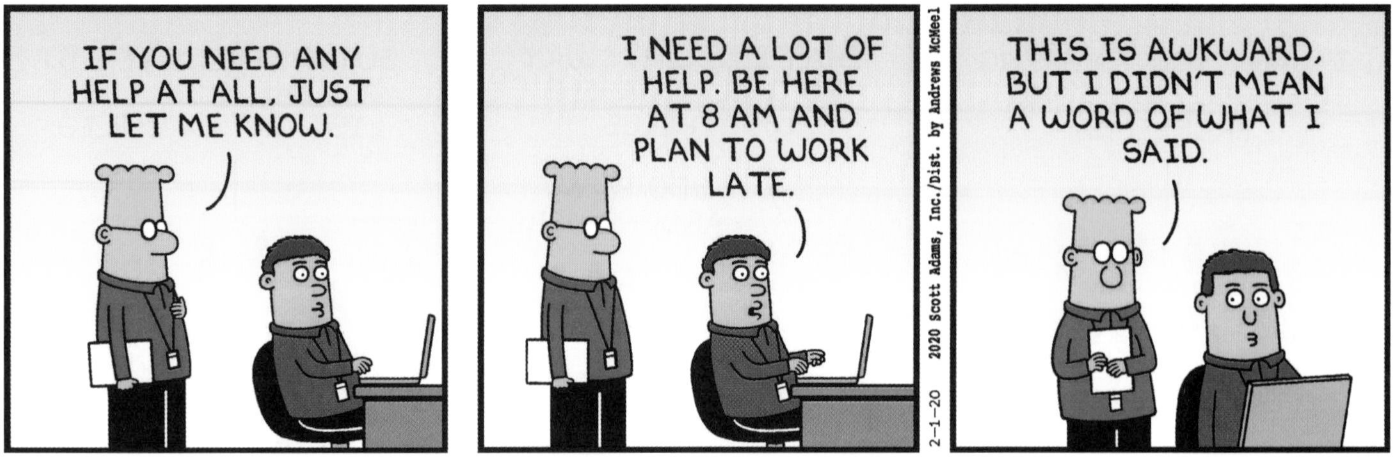
IF YOU NEED ANY HELP AT ALL, JUST LET ME KNOW.
I NEED A LOT OF HELP. BE HERE AT 8 AM AND PLAN TO WORK LATE.
2-1-20 2020 Scott Adams, Inc./Dist. by Andrews McMeel
THIS IS AWKWARD, BUT I DIDN'T MEAN A WORD OF WHAT I SAID.

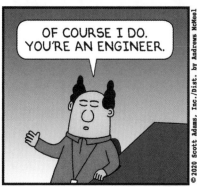

I CAN'T GIVE YOU A GOOD PERFORMANCE REVIEW BECAUSE YOU HAVEN'T PERFORMED UP TO EXPECTATIONS.
DO YOU EVEN KNOW WHAT MY JOB IS?
OF COURSE I DO. YOU'RE AN ENGINEER.
YES, BUT DO YOU KNOW WHAT PROJECTS I'M WORKING ON?
WELL, VARIOUS THINGS, AND SOME MISCELLANEOUS THINGS, TOO.
HOW CAN YOU DETERMINE MY JOB PERFORMANCE WHEN YOU DON'T KNOW WHAT MY JOB IS?
HAVE YOU HEARD OF HEURISTICS? YOU'RE BAD AT EVERYTHING I'VE OBSERVED, SO I ASSUME YOU ARE BAD AT EVERYTHING ELSE AS WELL.
YOU SHOULD HAVE STARTED WITH THAT.
© 2020 Scott Adams, Inc./Dist. by Andrews McMeel
2-2-20

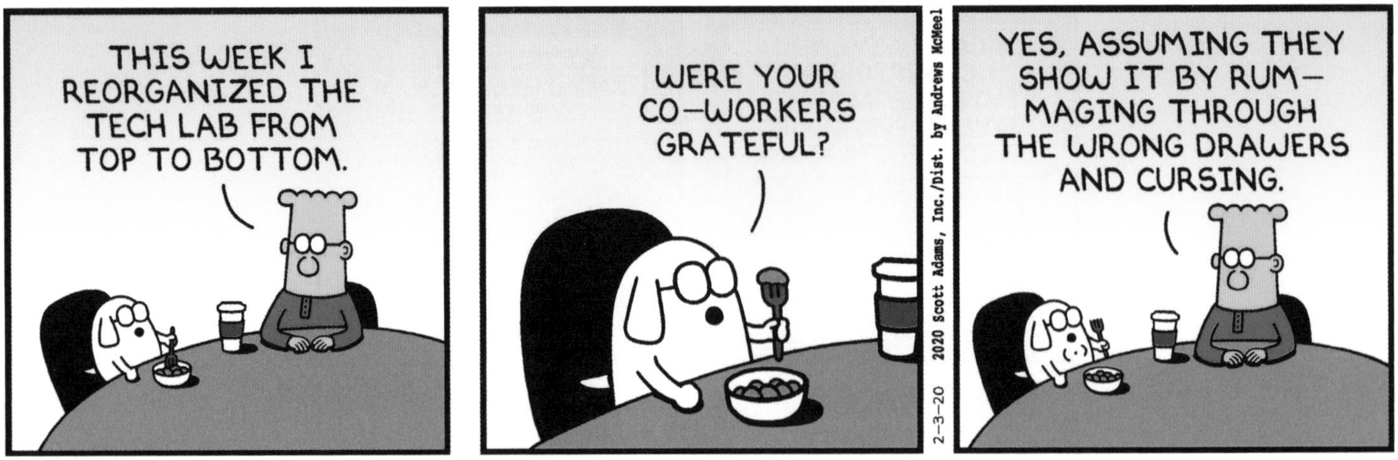
THIS WEEK I REORGANIZED THE TECH LAB FROM TOP TO BOTTOM.
WERE YOUR CO—WORKERS GRATEFUL?
2-3-20 2020 Scott Adams, Inc./Dist. by Andrews McMeel
YES, ASSUMING THEY SHOW IT BY RUM—MAGING THROUGH THE WRONG DRAWERS AND CURSING.

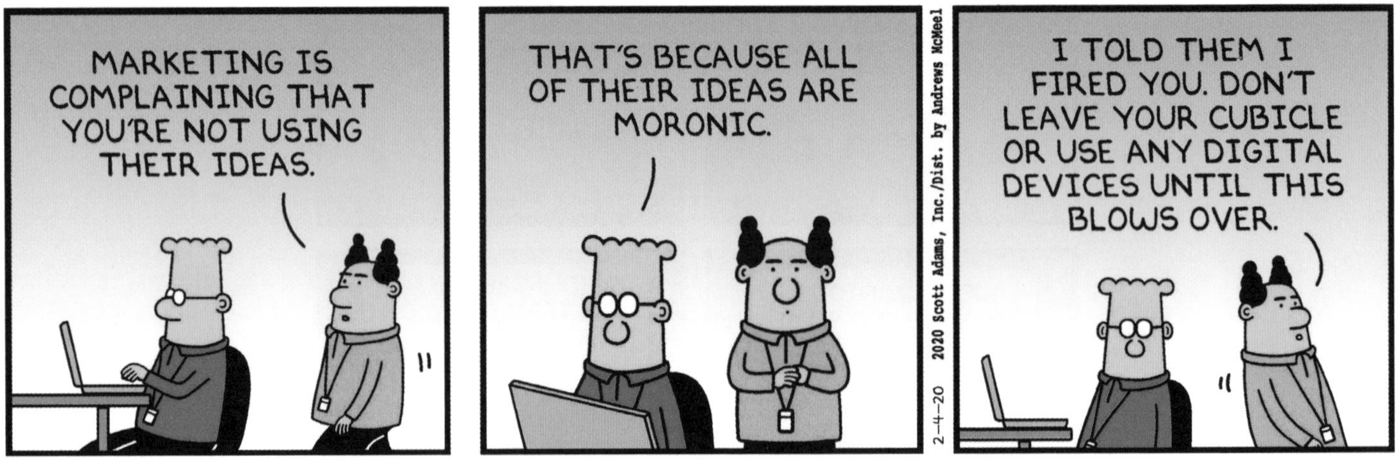
MARKETING IS COMPLAINING THAT YOU'RE NOT USING THEIR IDEAS.
THAT'S BECAUSE ALL OF THEIR IDEAS ARE MORONIC.
2-4-20 2020 Scott Adams, Inc./Dist. by Andrews McMeel
I TOLD THEM I FIRED YOU. DON'T LEAVE YOUR CUBICLE OR USE ANY DIGITAL DEVICES UNTIL THIS BLOWS OVER.

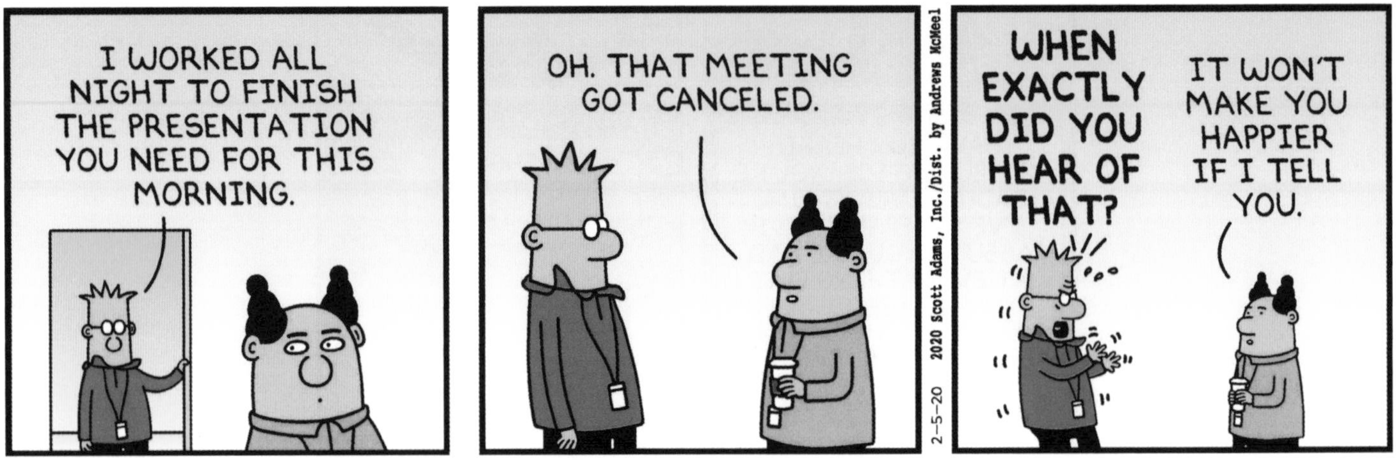
I WORKED ALL NIGHT TO FINISH THE PRESENTATION YOU NEED FOR THIS MORNING.
OH. THAT MEETING GOT CANCELED.
2-5-20 2020 Scott Adams, Inc./Dist. by Andrews McMeel
WHEN EXACTLY DID YOU HEAR OF THAT?
IT WON'T MAKE YOU HAPPIER IF I TELL YOU.

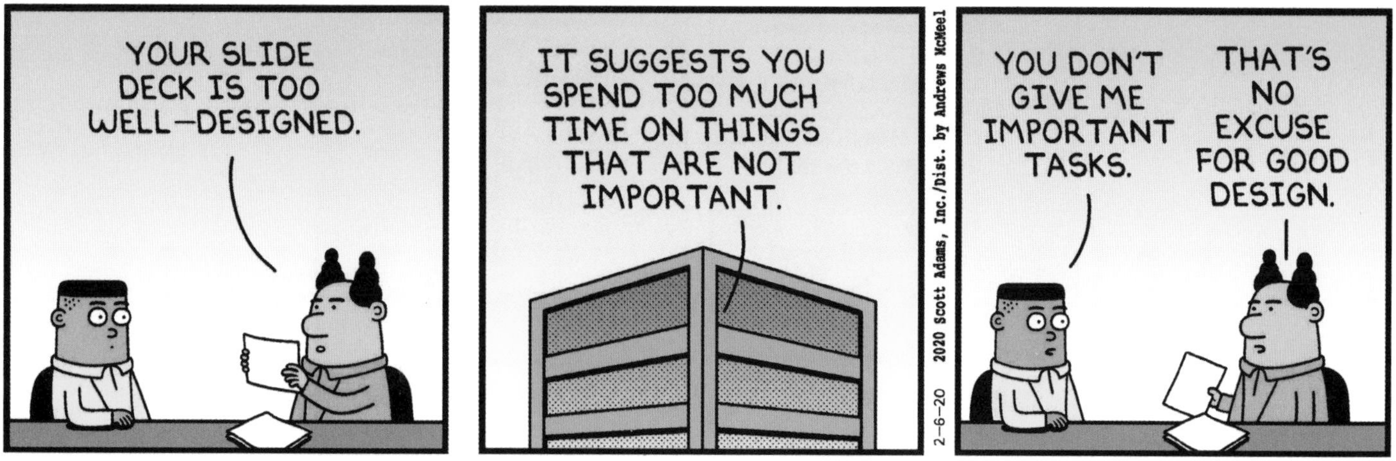
YOUR SLIDE DECK IS TOO WELL-DESIGNED.
IT SUGGESTS YOU SPEND TOO MUCH TIME ON THINGS THAT ARE NOT IMPORTANT.
2-6-20 2020 Scott Adams, Inc./Dist. by Andrews McMeel
YOU DON'T GIVE ME IMPORTANT TASKS.
THAT'S NO EXCUSE FOR GOOD DESIGN.

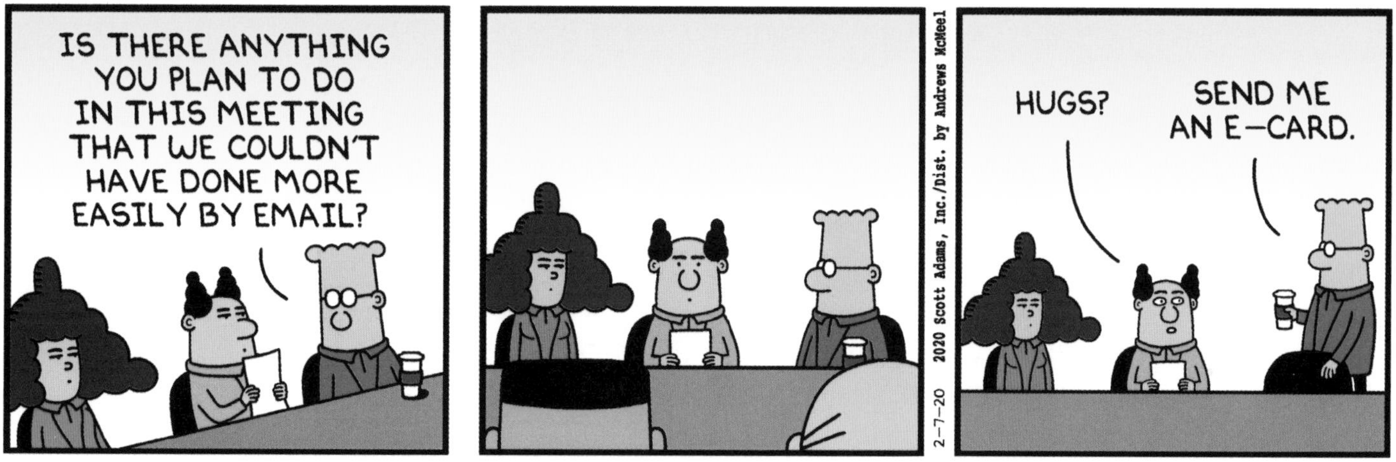
IS THERE ANYTHING YOU PLAN TO DO IN THIS MEETING THAT WE COULDN'T HAVE DONE MORE EASILY BY EMAIL?
2-7-20 2020 Scott Adams, Inc./Dist. by Andrews McMeel
HUGS?
SEND ME AN E-CARD.

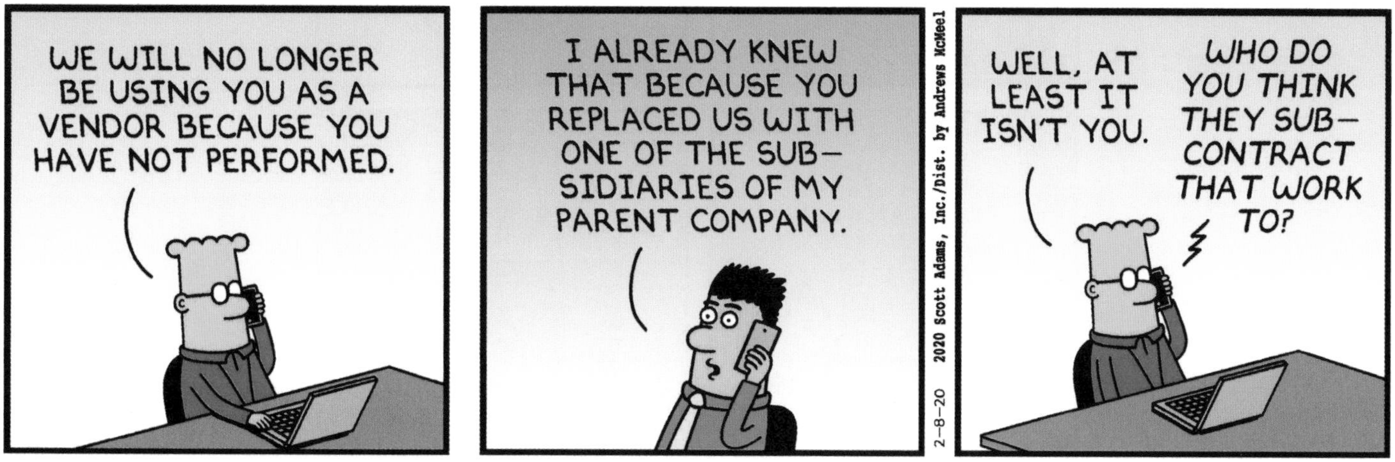
WE WILL NO LONGER BE USING YOU AS A VENDOR BECAUSE YOU HAVE NOT PERFORMED.
I ALREADY KNEW THAT BECAUSE YOU REPLACED US WITH ONE OF THE SUB-SIDIARIES OF MY PARENT COMPANY.
2-8-20 2020 Scott Adams, Inc./Dist. by Andrews McMeel
WELL, AT LEAST IT ISN'T YOU.
WHO DO YOU THINK THEY SUB-CONTRACT THAT WORK TO?

I DON'T WANT EMPLOYEES WHO ARE ONLY WORKING FOR THE MONEY.
I WANT EMPLOYEES WHO ARE WORKING TO MAKE THE WORLD A BETTER PLACE.
HOW DOES WORKING HERE MAKE THE WORLD A BETTER PLACE?
HALF OF OUR PRODUCTS CAUSE CANCER, AND THE OTHER HALF DON'T WORK AT ALL.
WE DON'T EVEN PAY TAXES.
ONE COULD ARGUE THAT EVERY DAY WE SPEND WORKING HERE MAKES THE PLANET A LITTLE BIT WORSE.
IS THAT WHY I NEVER SEE YOU DOING ANY WORK?
WHEN DID IT BECOME A CRIME TO CARE ABOUT PEOPLE? SHEESH!
© 2020 Scott Adams, Inc./Dist. by Andrews McMeel
2-9-20

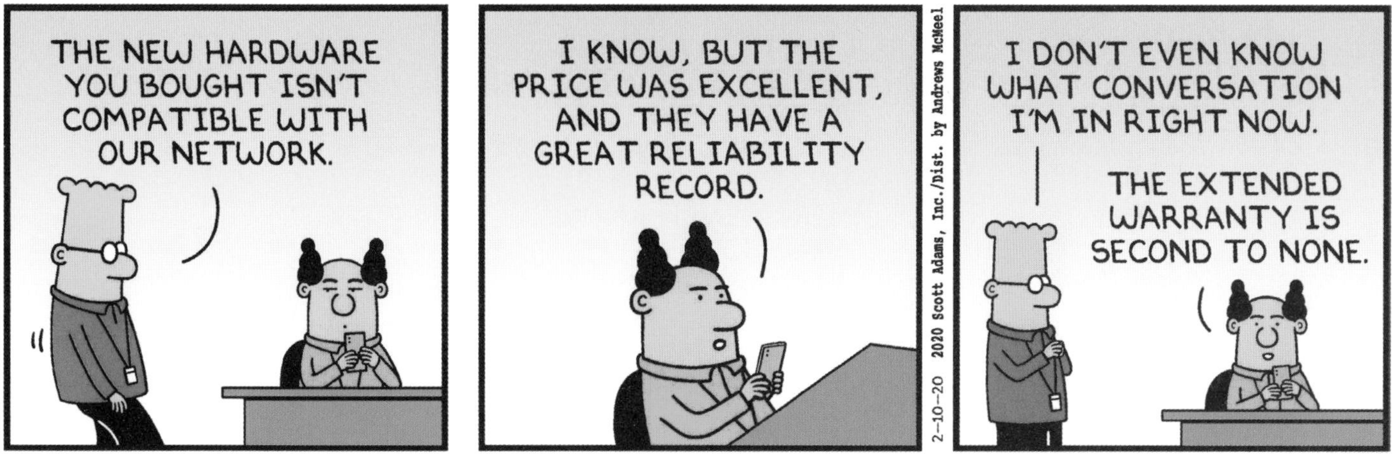
THE NEW HARDWARE YOU BOUGHT ISN'T COMPATIBLE WITH OUR NETWORK.
I KNOW, BUT THE PRICE WAS EXCELLENT, AND THEY HAVE A GREAT RELIABILITY RECORD.
2-10-20 2020 Scott Adams, Inc./Dist. by Andrews McMeel
I DON'T EVEN KNOW WHAT CONVERSATION I'M IN RIGHT NOW.
THE EXTENDED WARRANTY IS SECOND TO NONE.

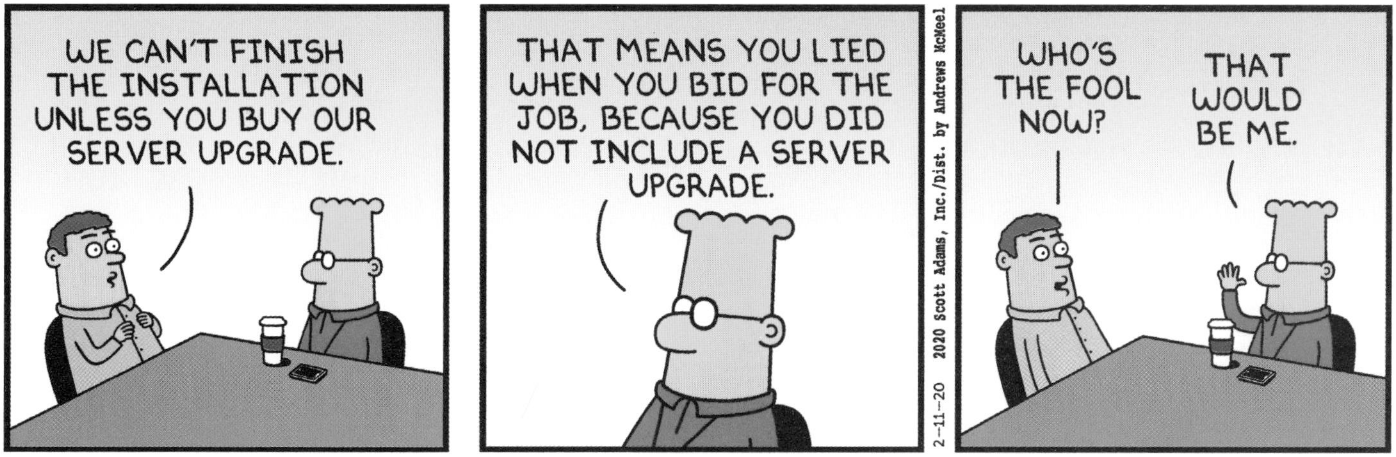
WE CAN'T FINISH THE INSTALLATION UNLESS YOU BUY OUR SERVER UPGRADE.
THAT MEANS YOU LIED WHEN YOU BID FOR THE JOB, BECAUSE YOU DID NOT INCLUDE A SERVER UPGRADE.
2-11-20 2020 Scott Adams, Inc./Dist. by Andrews McMeel
WHO'S THE FOOL NOW?
THAT WOULD BE ME.

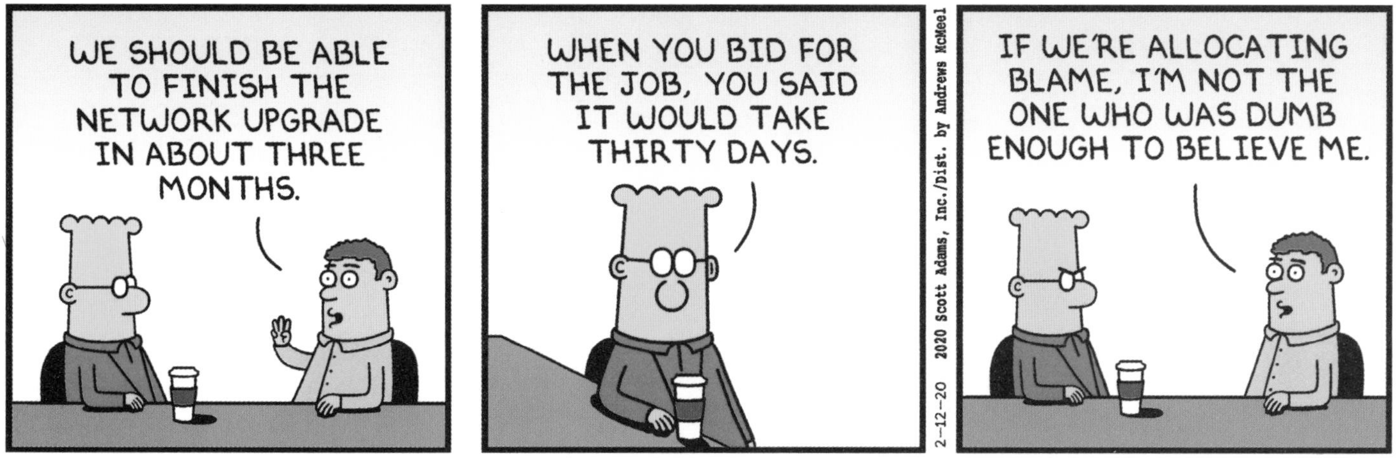
WE SHOULD BE ABLE TO FINISH THE NETWORK UPGRADE IN ABOUT THREE MONTHS.
WHEN YOU BID FOR THE JOB, YOU SAID IT WOULD TAKE THIRTY DAYS.
2-12-20 2020 Scott Adams, Inc./Dist. by Andrews McMeel
IF WE'RE ALLOCATING BLAME, I'M NOT THE ONE WHO WAS DUMB ENOUGH TO BELIEVE ME.

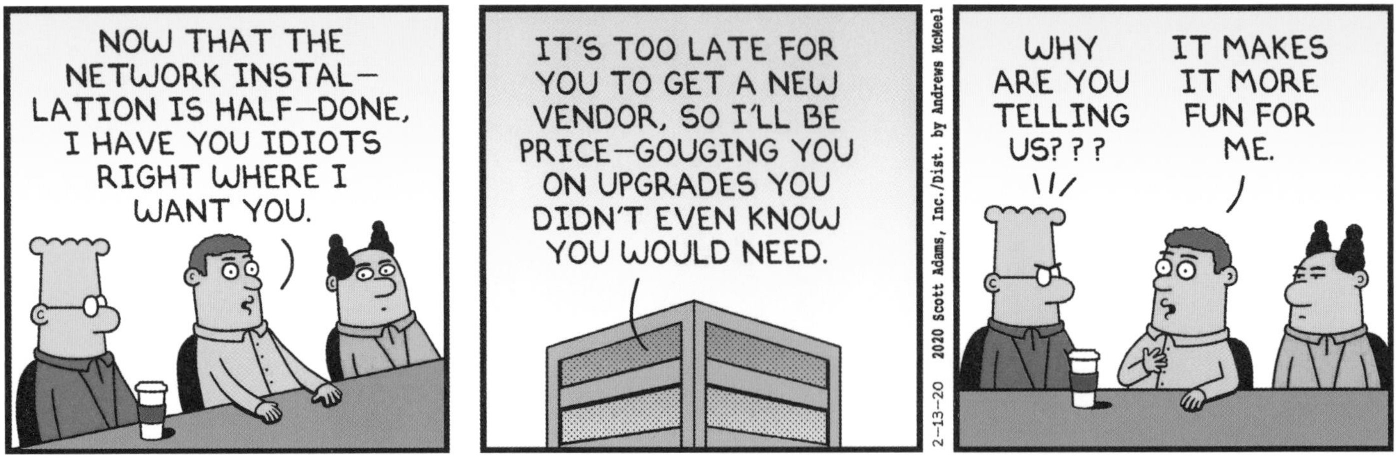
NOW THAT THE NETWORK INSTAL–LATION IS HALF–DONE, I HAVE YOU IDIOTS RIGHT WHERE I WANT YOU.
IT'S TOO LATE FOR YOU TO GET A NEW VENDOR, SO I'LL BE PRICE–GOUGING YOU ON UPGRADES YOU DIDN'T EVEN KNOW YOU WOULD NEED.
2–13–20 © 2020 Scott Adams, Inc./Dist. by Andrews McMeel
WHY ARE YOU TELLING US???
IT MAKES IT MORE FUN FOR ME.

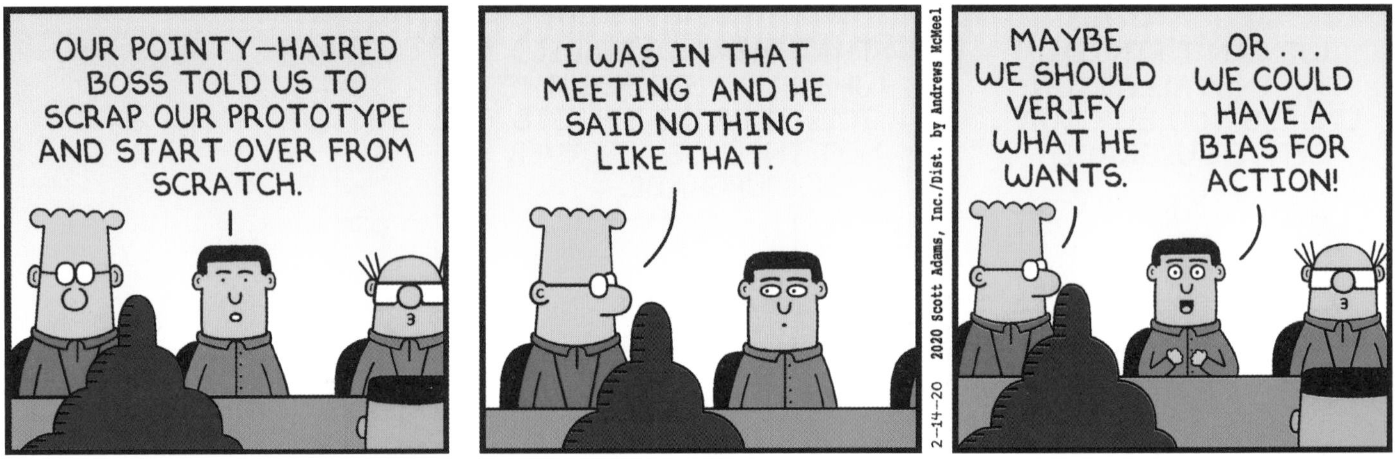
OUR POINTY–HAIRED BOSS TOLD US TO SCRAP OUR PROTOTYPE AND START OVER FROM SCRATCH.
I WAS IN THAT MEETING AND HE SAID NOTHING LIKE THAT.
2–14–20 © 2020 Scott Adams, Inc./Dist. by Andrews McMeel
MAYBE WE SHOULD VERIFY WHAT HE WANTS.
OR . . . WE COULD HAVE A BIAS FOR ACTION!

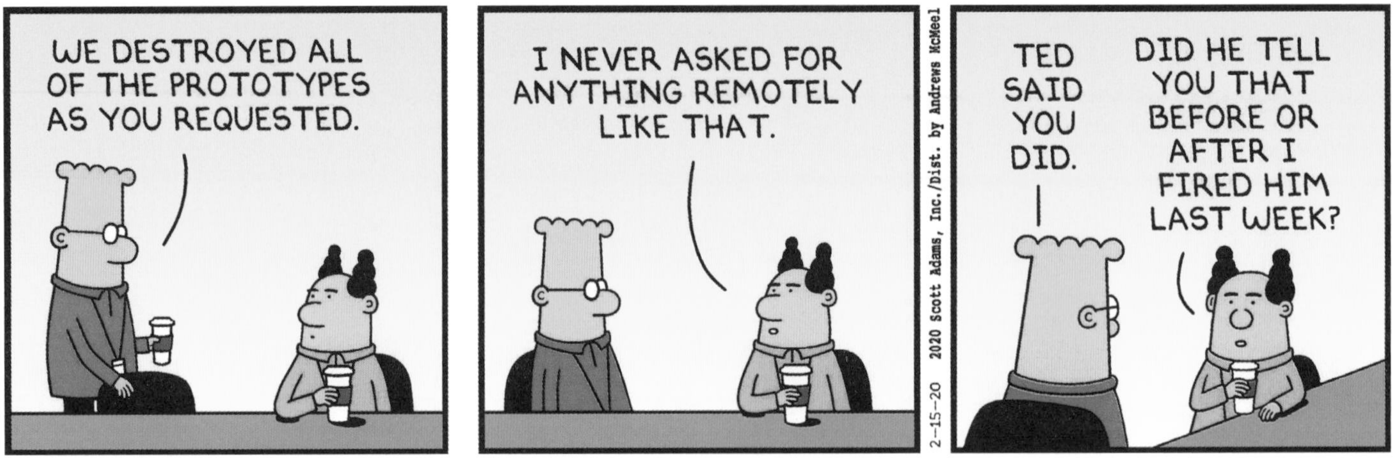
WE DESTROYED ALL OF THE PROTOTYPES AS YOU REQUESTED.
I NEVER ASKED FOR ANYTHING REMOTELY LIKE THAT.
2–15–20 © 2020 Scott Adams, Inc./Dist. by Andrews McMeel
TED SAID YOU DID.
DID HE TELL YOU THAT BEFORE OR AFTER I FIRED HIM LAST WEEK?

IT'S HARD TO FIND QUALIFIED ENGINEERS IN THIS JOB MARKET, SO I'M CASTING A WIDER NET.
IT SAYS HERE YOU HAVE EXPERIENCE AS A MORTUARY ASSISTANT AND A BAKER.
THAT'S NOT EXACTLY LIKE BEING AN ENGINEER, BUT I WANT TO STAY OPEN-MINDED.
TELL ME ABOUT A TIME YOU HAD TO DEAL WITH FAILURE AND WHAT YOU DID ABOUT IT.
WELL, ONE TIME I TOTALLY BOTCHED AN EMBALMING.
SO I USED A CHAIN-SAW TO REDUCE THE CORPSE TO FLUSHABLE PARTS.
I TOLD THE FAMILY HE CAME BACK TO LIFE AND RAN AWAY.
*OOOKAY.* AND WHY DID YOU BECOME A BAKER?
SO I COULD EAT MY MIS-TAKES.
© 2020 Scott Adams, Inc./Dist. by Andrews McMeel
2-16-20

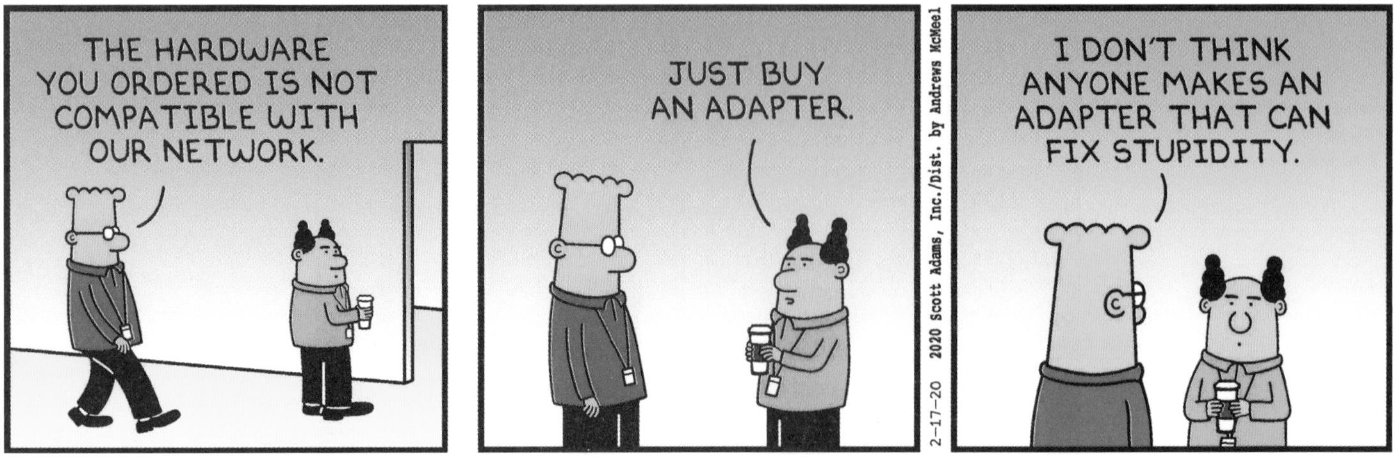
THE HARDWARE YOU ORDERED IS NOT COMPATIBLE WITH OUR NETWORK.
JUST BUY AN ADAPTER.
I DON'T THINK ANYONE MAKES AN ADAPTER THAT CAN FIX STUPIDITY.
2-17-20 2020 Scott Adams, Inc./Dist. by Andrews McMeel

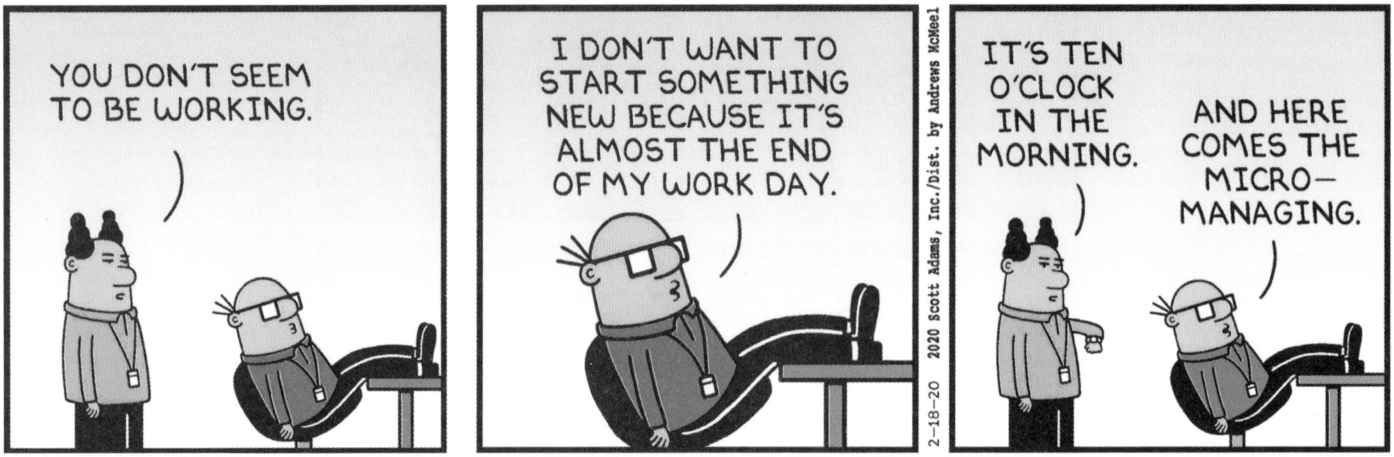
YOU DON'T SEEM TO BE WORKING.
I DON'T WANT TO START SOMETHING NEW BECAUSE IT'S ALMOST THE END OF MY WORK DAY.
IT'S TEN O'CLOCK IN THE MORNING.
AND HERE COMES THE MICRO—MANAGING.
2-18-20 2020 Scott Adams, Inc./Dist. by Andrews McMeel

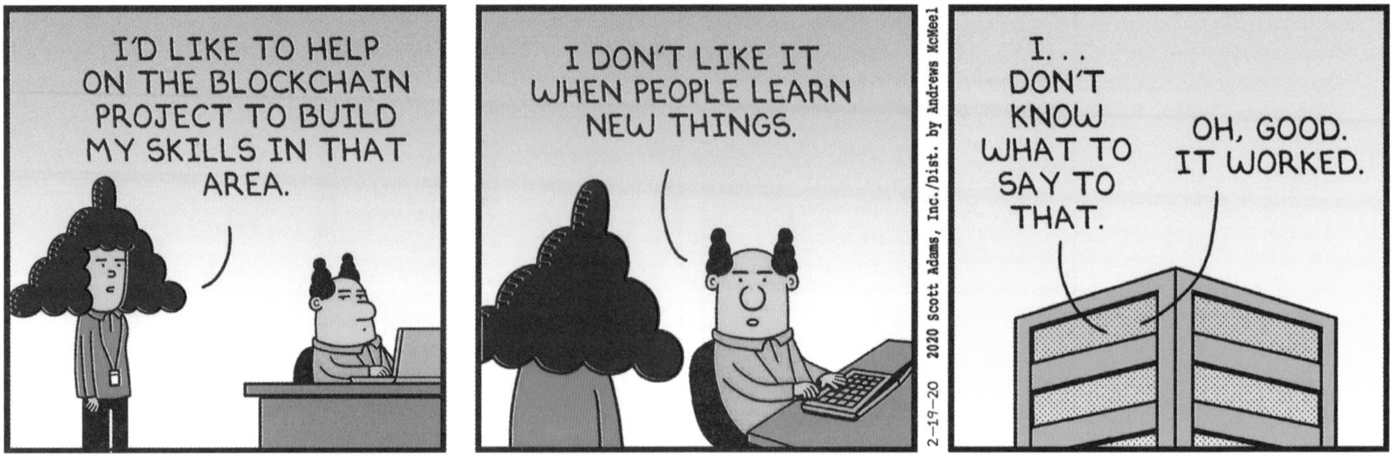
I'D LIKE TO HELP ON THE BLOCKCHAIN PROJECT TO BUILD MY SKILLS IN THAT AREA.
I DON'T LIKE IT WHEN PEOPLE LEARN NEW THINGS.
I... DON'T KNOW WHAT TO SAY TO THAT.
OH, GOOD. IT WORKED.
2-19-20 2020 Scott Adams, Inc./Dist. by Andrews McMeel

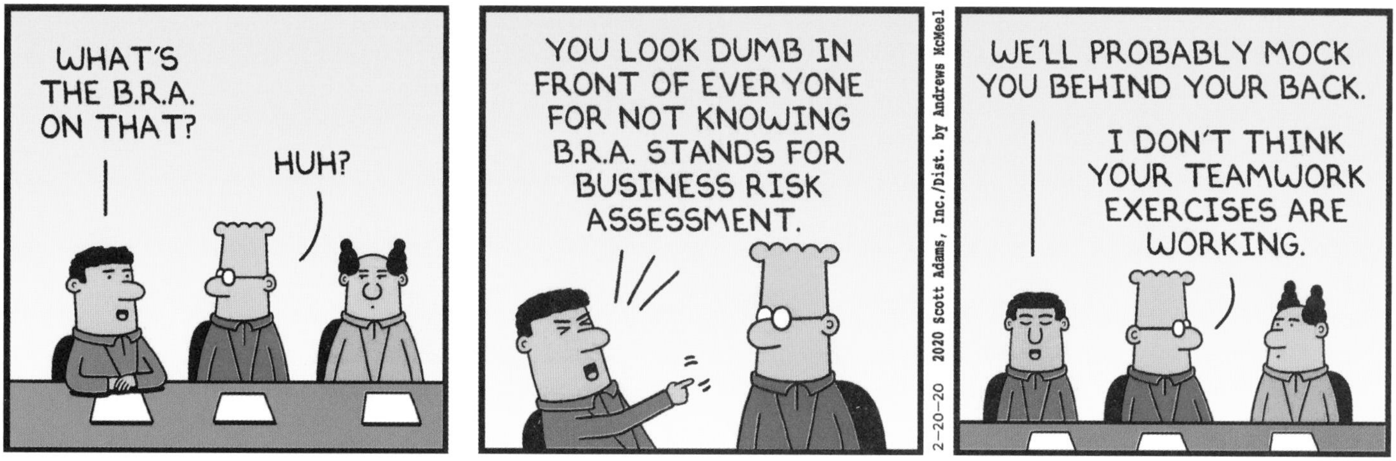
WHAT'S THE B.R.A. ON THAT?
HUH?
YOU LOOK DUMB IN FRONT OF EVERYONE FOR NOT KNOWING B.R.A. STANDS FOR BUSINESS RISK ASSESSMENT.
2-20-20 2020 Scott Adams, Inc./Dist. by Andrews McMeel
WE'LL PROBABLY MOCK YOU BEHIND YOUR BACK.
I DON'T THINK YOUR TEAMWORK EXERCISES ARE WORKING.

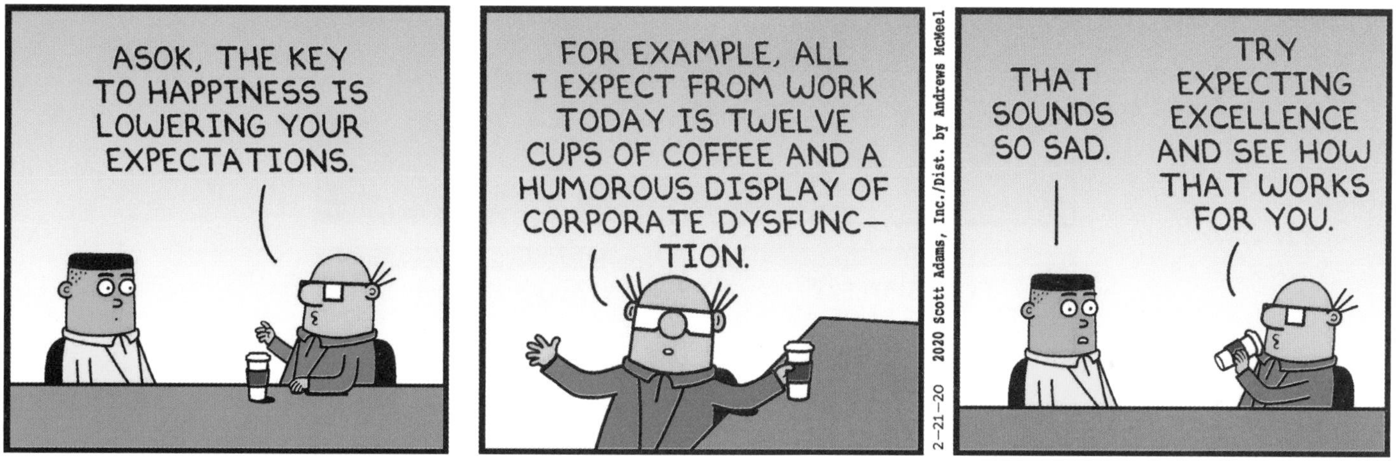
ASOK, THE KEY TO HAPPINESS IS LOWERING YOUR EXPECTATIONS.
FOR EXAMPLE, ALL I EXPECT FROM WORK TODAY IS TWELVE CUPS OF COFFEE AND A HUMOROUS DISPLAY OF CORPORATE DYSFUNC-TION.
2-21-20 2020 Scott Adams, Inc./Dist. by Andrews McMeel
THAT SOUNDS SO SAD.
TRY EXPECTING EXCELLENCE AND SEE HOW THAT WORKS FOR YOU.

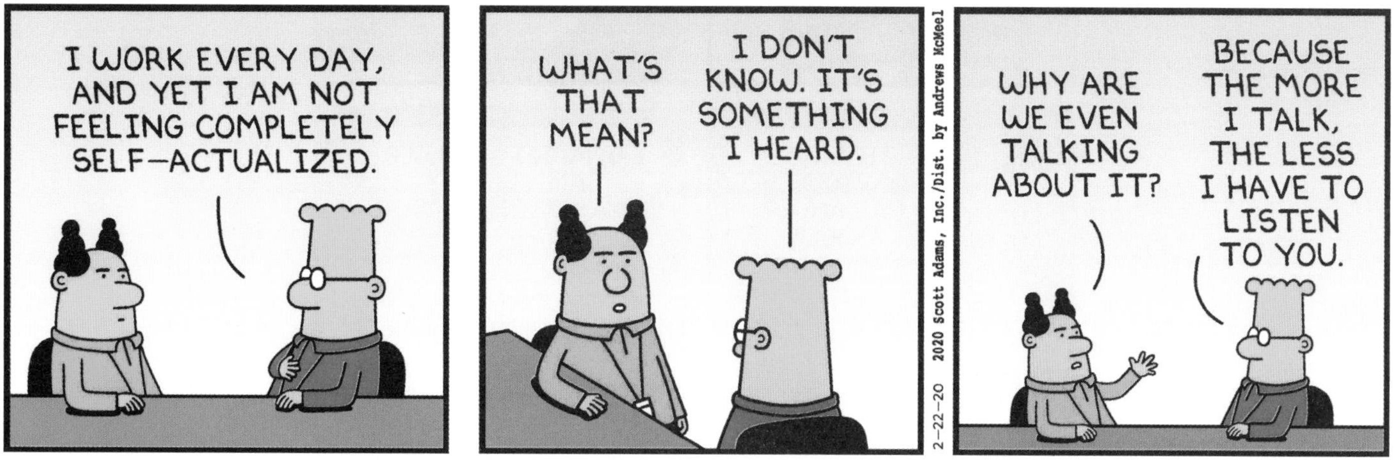
I WORK EVERY DAY, AND YET I AM NOT FEELING COMPLETELY SELF-ACTUALIZED.
WHAT'S THAT MEAN?
I DON'T KNOW. IT'S SOMETHING I HEARD.
2-22-20 2020 Scott Adams, Inc./Dist. by Andrews McMeel
WHY ARE WE EVEN TALKING ABOUT IT?
BECAUSE THE MORE I TALK, THE LESS I HAVE TO LISTEN TO YOU.

I CAN'T SUPPORT THIS PROJECT BECAUSE YOU'RE ALL A BUNCH OF CORRUPT, GODLESS COMMUNISTS.
JUST OUT OF CURIOSITY, WHERE DID YOU GET YOUR EDUCATION?
I LEARNED EVERYTHING I NEED TO KNOW ON SOCIAL MEDIA.
HOW DOES THAT HELP YOU EVALUATE A TECHNICAL PROPOSAL?
© 2020 Scott Adams, Inc./Dist. by Andrews McMeel
IT'S SIMPLE. I TAKE ONE LOOK AT ALL OF YOUR JERKY FACES, AND I KNOW EVERYTHING I NEED TO KNOW.
I MEAN, LOOK AT THIS GUY'S FACE. HE'S OBVIOUSLY A GRIFTER.
LUCKY GUESS.
THIS ONE OBVIOUSLY HAS ANGER ISSUES.
I DEMAND A LARGER SAMPLE SIZE!
WHATEVER, GEEKFACE.
2-23-20

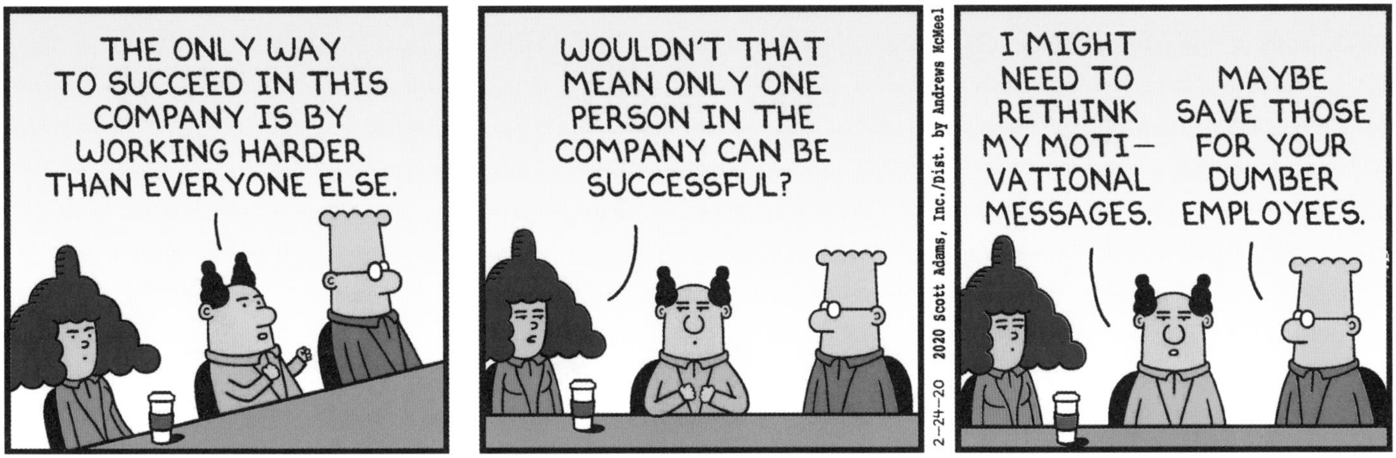
THE ONLY WAY TO SUCCEED IN THIS COMPANY IS BY WORKING HARDER THAN EVERYONE ELSE.
WOULDN'T THAT MEAN ONLY ONE PERSON IN THE COMPANY CAN BE SUCCESSFUL?
2-24-20 2020 Scott Adams, Inc./Dist. by Andrews McMeel
I MIGHT NEED TO RETHINK MY MOTI– VATIONAL MESSAGES.
MAYBE SAVE THOSE FOR YOUR DUMBER EMPLOYEES.

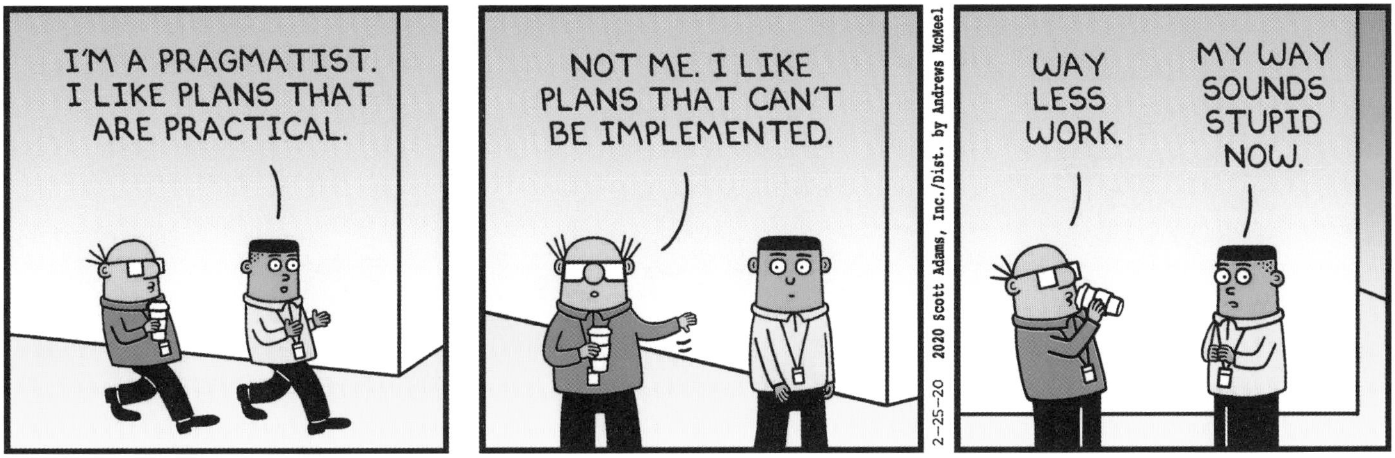
I'M A PRAGMATIST. I LIKE PLANS THAT ARE PRACTICAL.
NOT ME. I LIKE PLANS THAT CAN'T BE IMPLEMENTED.
2-25-20 2020 Scott Adams, Inc./Dist. by Andrews McMeel
WAY LESS WORK.
MY WAY SOUNDS STUPID NOW.

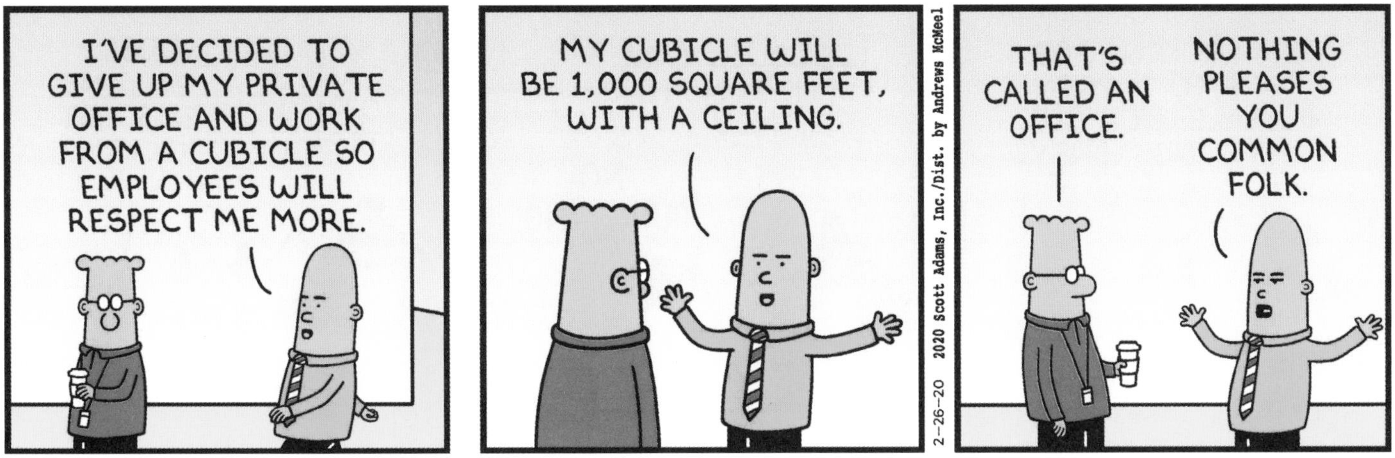
I'VE DECIDED TO GIVE UP MY PRIVATE OFFICE AND WORK FROM A CUBICLE SO EMPLOYEES WILL RESPECT ME MORE.
MY CUBICLE WILL BE 1,000 SQUARE FEET, WITH A CEILING.
2-26-20 2020 Scott Adams, Inc./Dist. by Andrews McMeel
THAT'S CALLED AN OFFICE.
NOTHING PLEASES YOU COMMON FOLK.

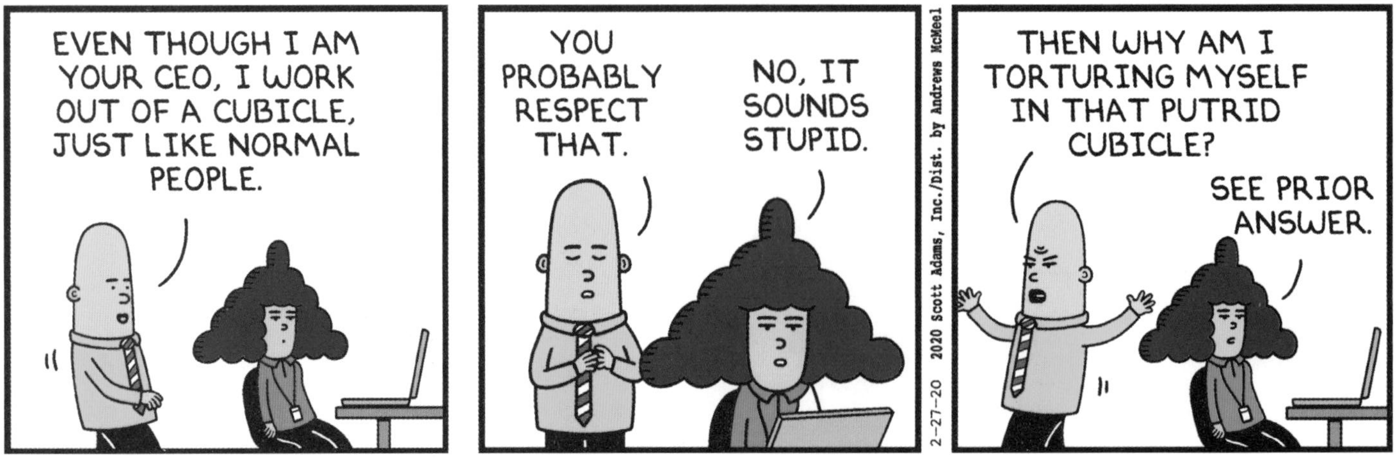
EVEN THOUGH I AM YOUR CEO, I WORK OUT OF A CUBICLE, JUST LIKE NORMAL PEOPLE.
YOU PROBABLY RESPECT THAT.
NO, IT SOUNDS STUPID.
THEN WHY AM I TORTURING MYSELF IN THAT PUTRID CUBICLE?
SEE PRIOR ANSWER.
2-27-20 2020 Scott Adams, Inc./Dist. by Andrews McMeel

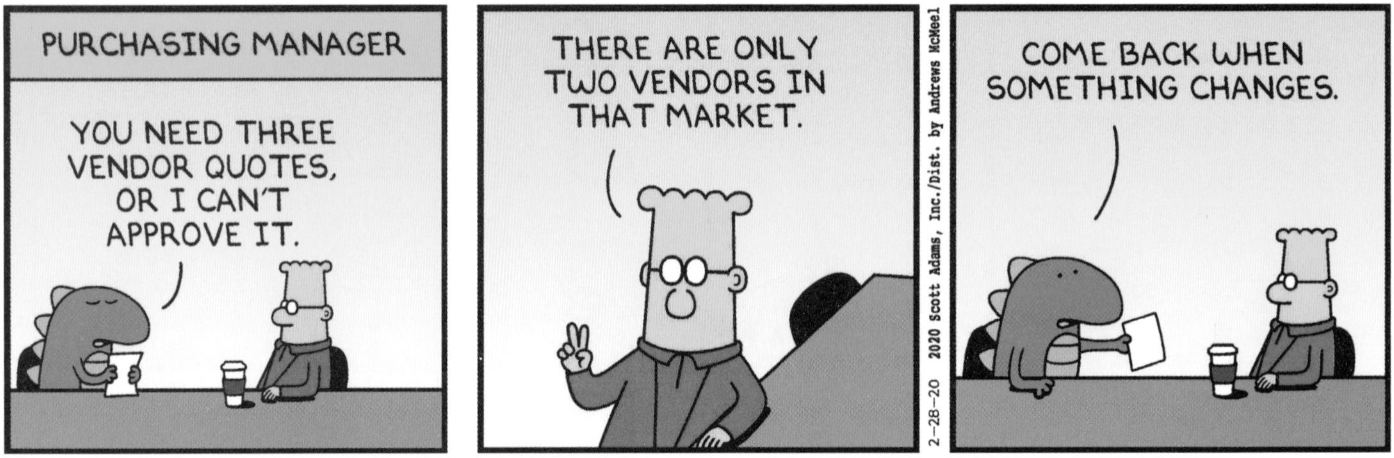
PURCHASING MANAGER
YOU NEED THREE VENDOR QUOTES, OR I CAN'T APPROVE IT.
THERE ARE ONLY TWO VENDORS IN THAT MARKET.
COME BACK WHEN SOMETHING CHANGES.
2-28-20 2020 Scott Adams, Inc./Dist. by Andrews McMeel

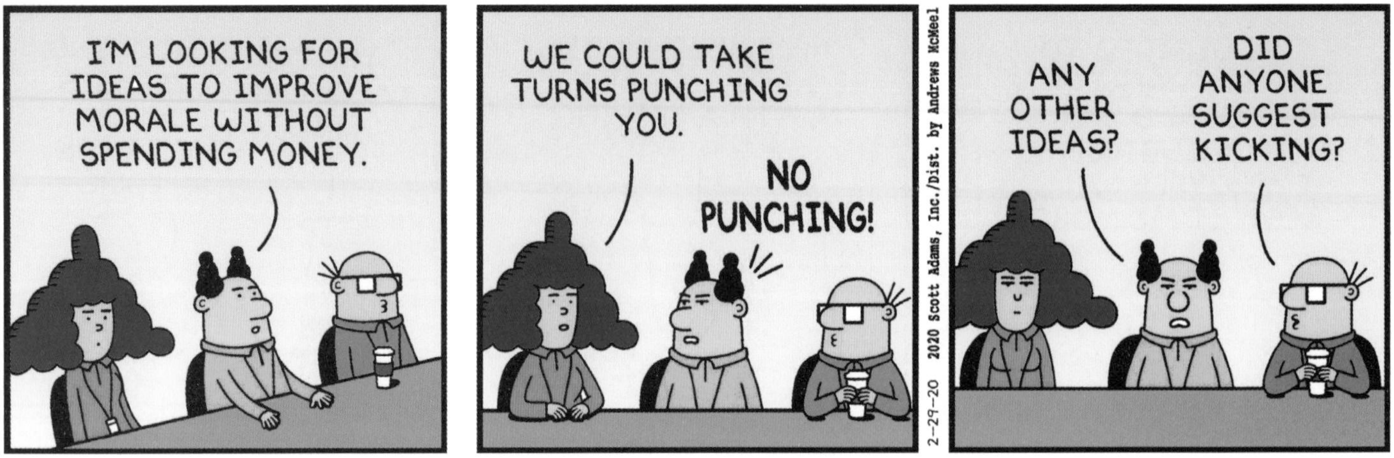
I'M LOOKING FOR IDEAS TO IMPROVE MORALE WITHOUT SPENDING MONEY.
WE COULD TAKE TURNS PUNCHING YOU.
NO PUNCHING!
ANY OTHER IDEAS?
DID ANYONE SUGGEST KICKING?
2-29-20 2020 Scott Adams, Inc./Dist. by Andrews McMeel

TED SAYS HE CAN'T MAKE IT TO THE MEETING.
THE ONLY REASON FOR THIS MEETING IS SO TED CAN TELL US WHAT HE'S DOING ON HIS PROJECT.
WE SHOULD RESCHEDULE.
NOT SO FAST. I THINK WE CAN SALVAGE THIS.
IF WE GUESS WHAT TED MIGHT HAVE TOLD US, THAT GETS US HALFWAY THERE.
I DON'T THINK IT DOES.
WE CAN'T KNOW UNTIL WE TRY.
WHY DON'T THE REST OF US LEAVE, AND YOU CAN STAY HERE AND GUESS WHAT WE WOULD HAVE SAID, TOO.
. . . AND THEN DILBERT WOULD HAVE SAID. . .
© 2020 Scott Adams, Inc./Dist. by Andrews McMeel
3-1-20

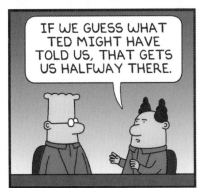

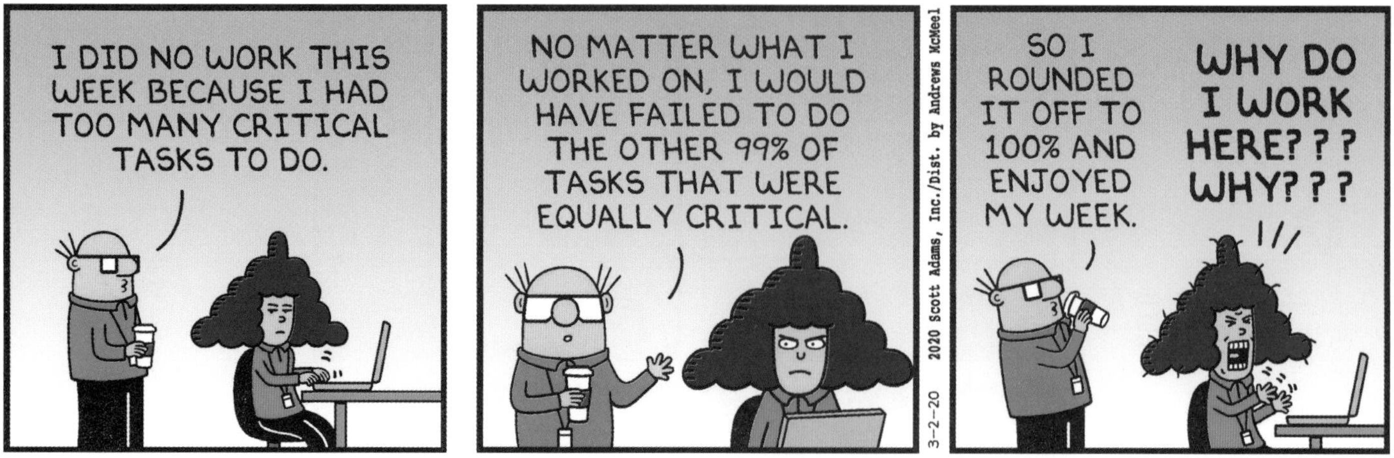
I DID NO WORK THIS WEEK BECAUSE I HAD TOO MANY CRITICAL TASKS TO DO.
NO MATTER WHAT I WORKED ON, I WOULD HAVE FAILED TO DO THE OTHER 99% OF TASKS THAT WERE EQUALLY CRITICAL.
3-2-20 2020 Scott Adams, Inc./Dist. by Andrews McMeel
SO I ROUNDED IT OFF TO 100% AND ENJOYED MY WEEK.
WHY DO I WORK HERE??? WHY???

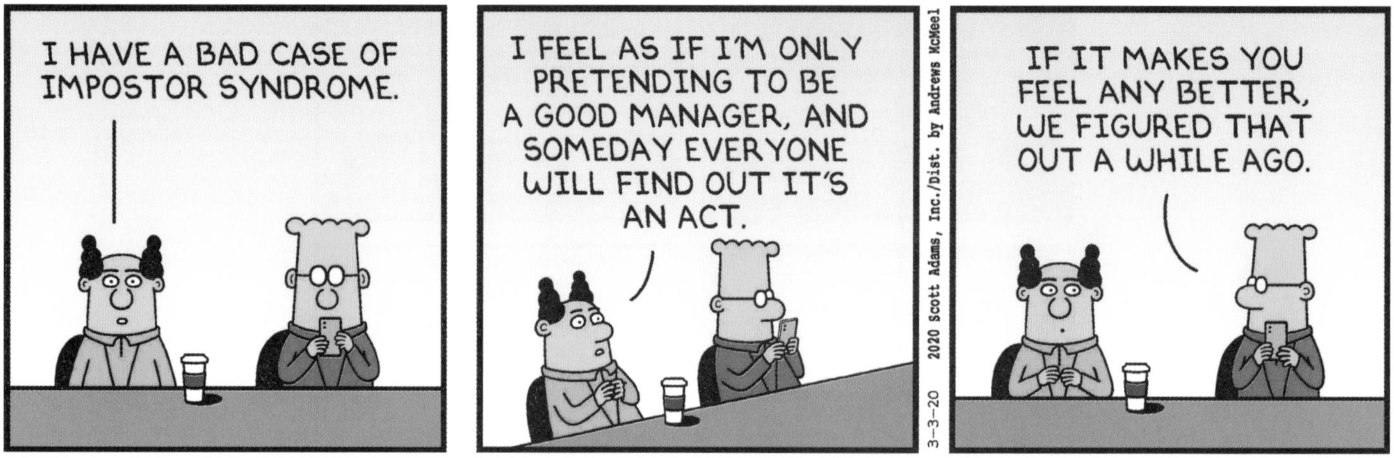
I HAVE A BAD CASE OF IMPOSTOR SYNDROME.
I FEEL AS IF I'M ONLY PRETENDING TO BE A GOOD MANAGER, AND SOMEDAY EVERYONE WILL FIND OUT IT'S AN ACT.
3-3-20 2020 Scott Adams, Inc./Dist. by Andrews McMeel
IF IT MAKES YOU FEEL ANY BETTER, WE FIGURED THAT OUT A WHILE AGO.

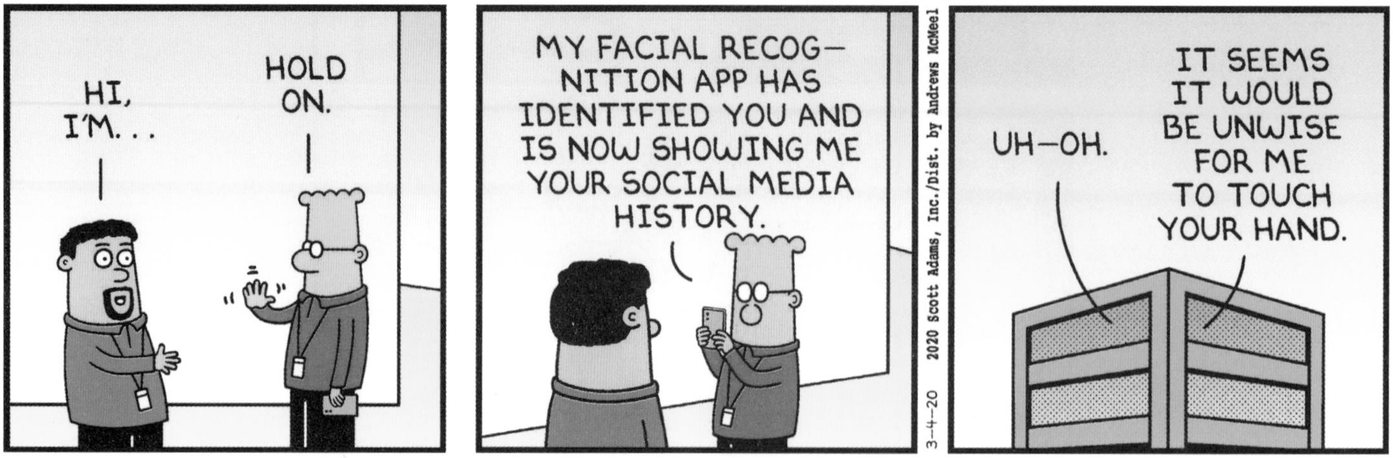
HI, I'M...
HOLD ON.
MY FACIAL RECOG- NITION APP HAS IDENTIFIED YOU AND IS NOW SHOWING ME YOUR SOCIAL MEDIA HISTORY.
3-4-20 2020 Scott Adams, Inc./Dist. by Andrews McMeel
UH-OH.
IT SEEMS IT WOULD BE UNWISE FOR ME TO TOUCH YOUR HAND.

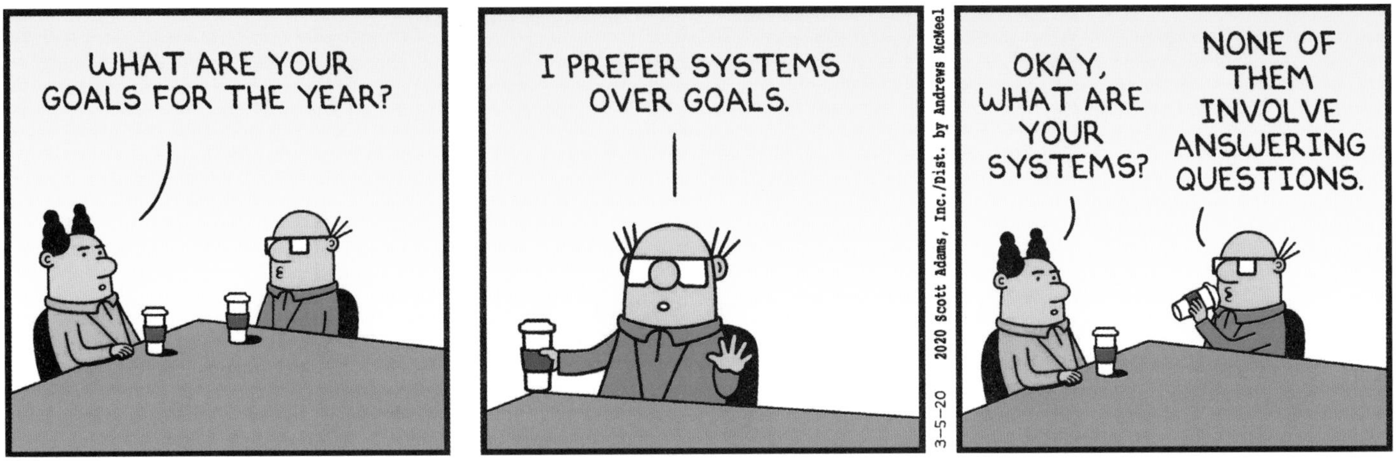
WHAT ARE YOUR GOALS FOR THE YEAR?
I PREFER SYSTEMS OVER GOALS.
OKAY, WHAT ARE YOUR SYSTEMS?
NONE OF THEM INVOLVE ANSWERING QUESTIONS.
3-5-20 2020 Scott Adams, Inc./Dist. by Andrews McMeel

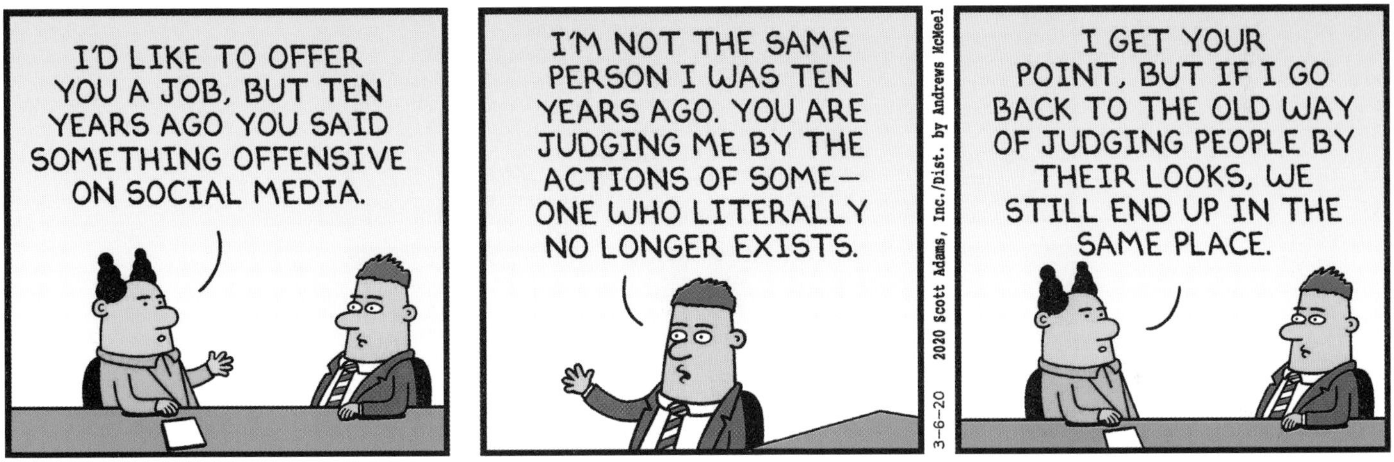
I'D LIKE TO OFFER YOU A JOB, BUT TEN YEARS AGO YOU SAID SOMETHING OFFENSIVE ON SOCIAL MEDIA.
I'M NOT THE SAME PERSON I WAS TEN YEARS AGO. YOU ARE JUDGING ME BY THE ACTIONS OF SOME-ONE WHO LITERALLY NO LONGER EXISTS.
I GET YOUR POINT, BUT IF I GO BACK TO THE OLD WAY OF JUDGING PEOPLE BY THEIR LOOKS, WE STILL END UP IN THE SAME PLACE.
3-6-20 2020 Scott Adams, Inc./Dist. by Andrews McMeel

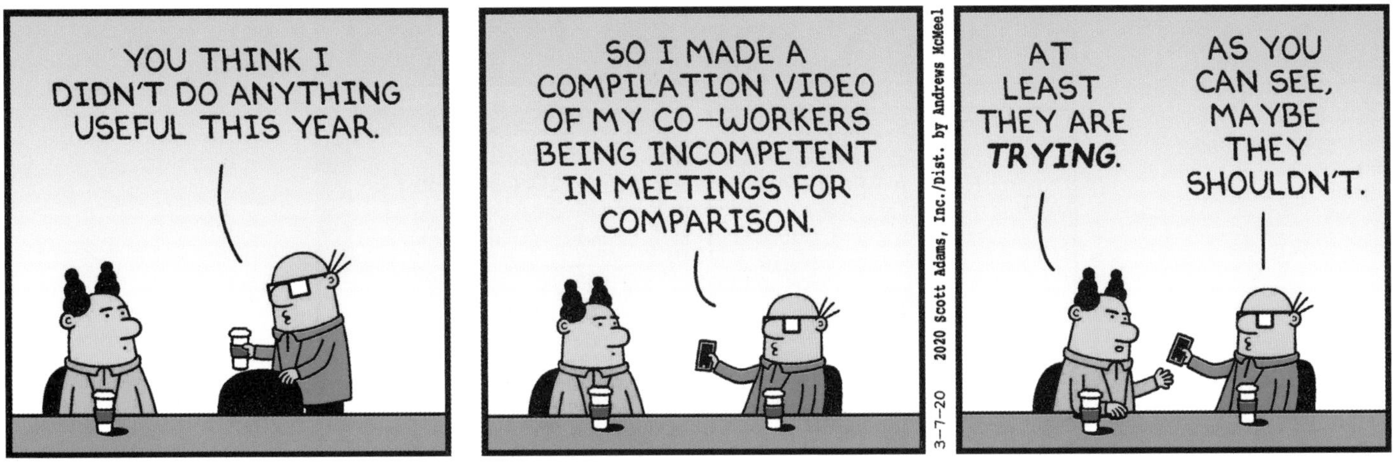
YOU THINK I DIDN'T DO ANYTHING USEFUL THIS YEAR.
SO I MADE A COMPILATION VIDEO OF MY CO-WORKERS BEING INCOMPETENT IN MEETINGS FOR COMPARISON.
AT LEAST THEY ARE ***TRYING***.
AS YOU CAN SEE, MAYBE THEY SHOULDN'T.
3-7-20 2020 Scott Adams, Inc./Dist. by Andrews McMeel

I HIRED AN ELBONIAN CONSULTANT BECAUSE WE COULDN'T AFFORD ANYONE LOCAL.
HAVE YOU EVER CONSULTED IN THIS COUNTRY?
NO, BUT PEOPLE ARE PEOPLE, SO I ASSUME IT ISN'T THAT DIFFERENT FROM ELBONIA.
THAT'S ENOUGH CHITCHAT.
TELL US WHAT WE SHOULD DO ABOUT THE PROBLEMS IN OUR DISTRIBUTION SYSTEM.
I RECOMMEND EXECUTING ONE OF YOUR DISTRIBUTORS AS A WARNING TO THE OTHERS.
I'M GOING TO NEED A SECOND OPINION.
MY SECOND OPINION IS THAT YOUR BARBER MUST HATE YOUR GUTS.
© 2020 Scott Adams, Inc./Dist. by Andrews McMeel
3-8-20

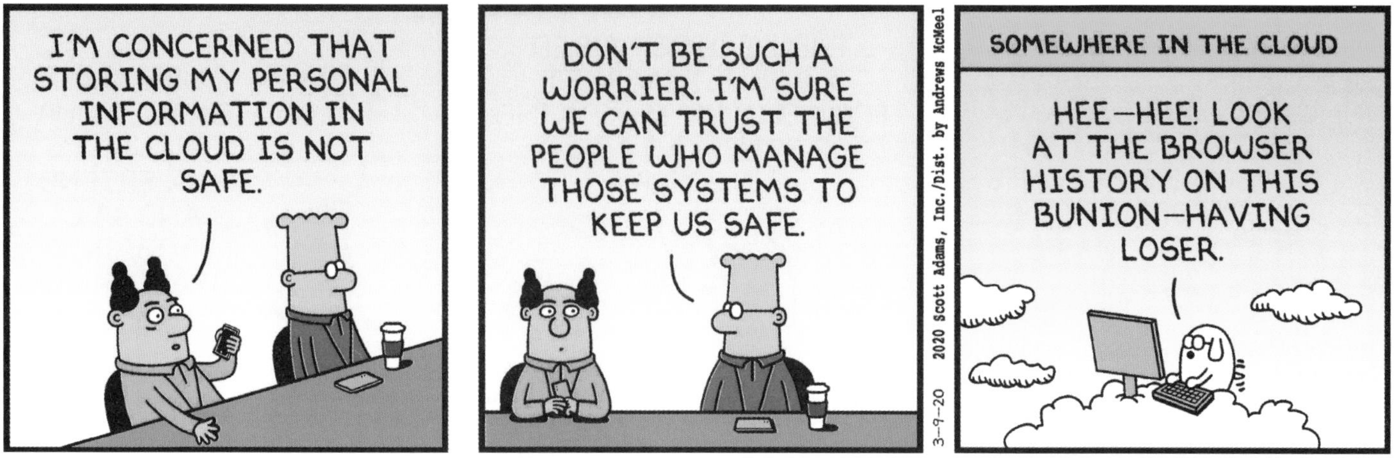
I'M CONCERNED THAT STORING MY PERSONAL INFORMATION IN THE CLOUD IS NOT SAFE.
DON'T BE SUCH A WORRIER. I'M SURE WE CAN TRUST THE PEOPLE WHO MANAGE THOSE SYSTEMS TO KEEP US SAFE.
SOMEWHERE IN THE CLOUD
HEE—HEE! LOOK AT THE BROWSER HISTORY ON THIS BUNION—HAVING LOSER.


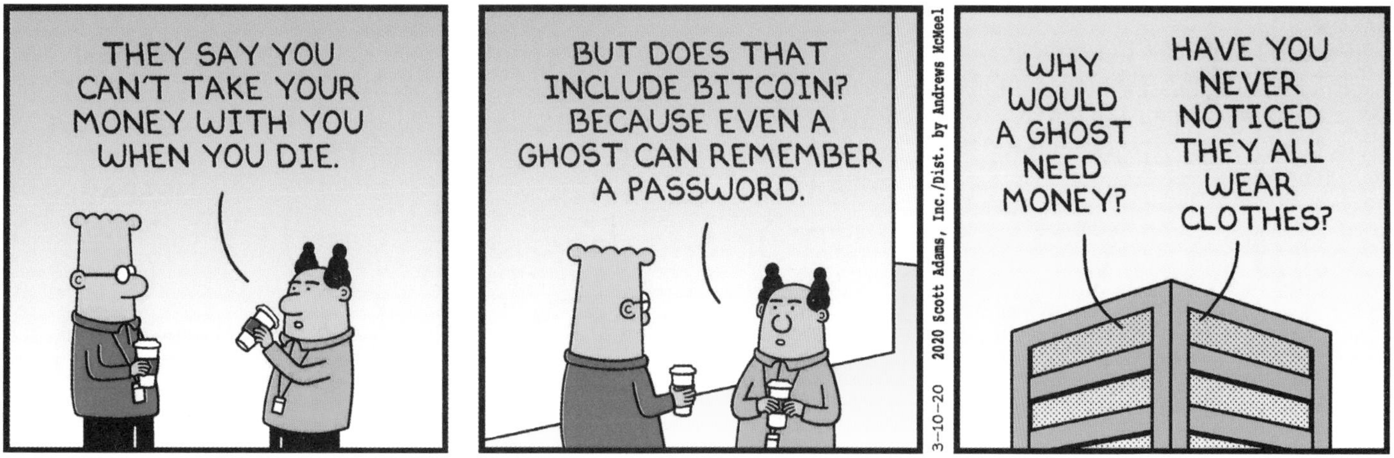
THEY SAY YOU CAN'T TAKE YOUR MONEY WITH YOU WHEN YOU DIE.
BUT DOES THAT INCLUDE BITCOIN? BECAUSE EVEN A GHOST CAN REMEMBER A PASSWORD.
WHY WOULD A GHOST NEED MONEY?
HAVE YOU NEVER NOTICED THEY ALL WEAR CLOTHES?


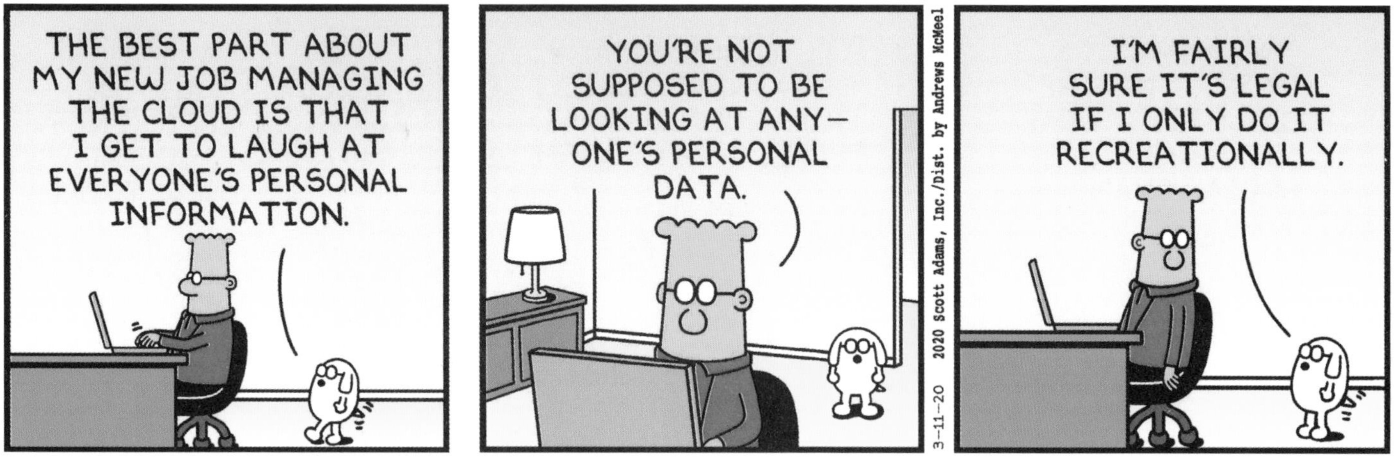
THE BEST PART ABOUT MY NEW JOB MANAGING THE CLOUD IS THAT I GET TO LAUGH AT EVERYONE'S PERSONAL INFORMATION.
YOU'RE NOT SUPPOSED TO BE LOOKING AT ANY—ONE'S PERSONAL DATA.
I'M FAIRLY SURE IT'S LEGAL IF I ONLY DO IT RECREATIONALLY.

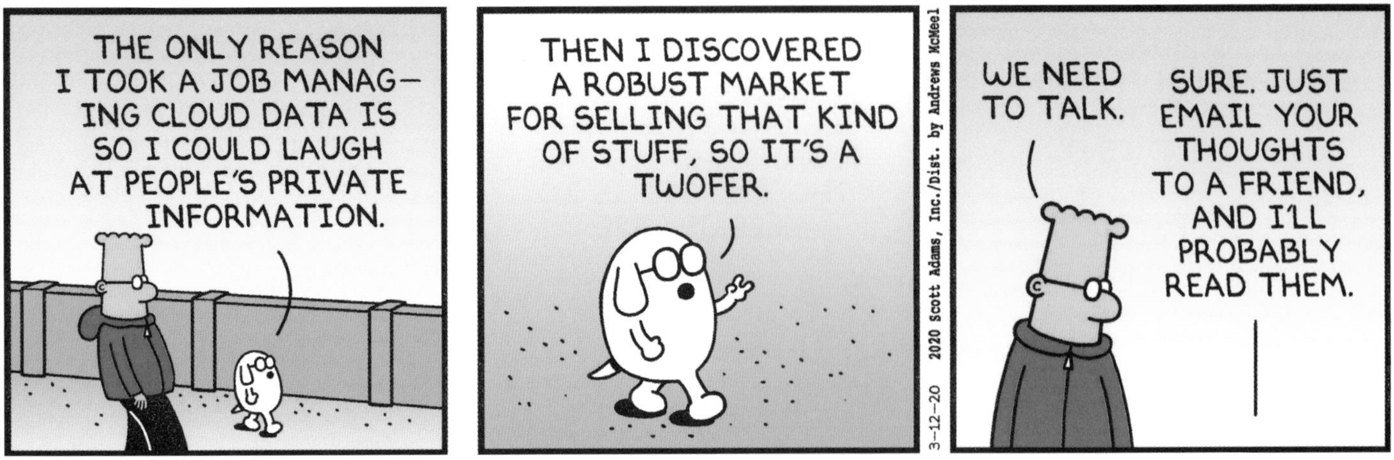
THE ONLY REASON I TOOK A JOB MANAG-ING CLOUD DATA IS SO I COULD LAUGH AT PEOPLE'S PRIVATE INFORMATION.
THEN I DISCOVERED A ROBUST MARKET FOR SELLING THAT KIND OF STUFF, SO IT'S A TWOFER.
WE NEED TO TALK.
SURE. JUST EMAIL YOUR THOUGHTS TO A FRIEND, AND I'LL PROBABLY READ THEM.
3-12-20 2020 Scott Adams, Inc./Dist. by Andrews McMeel

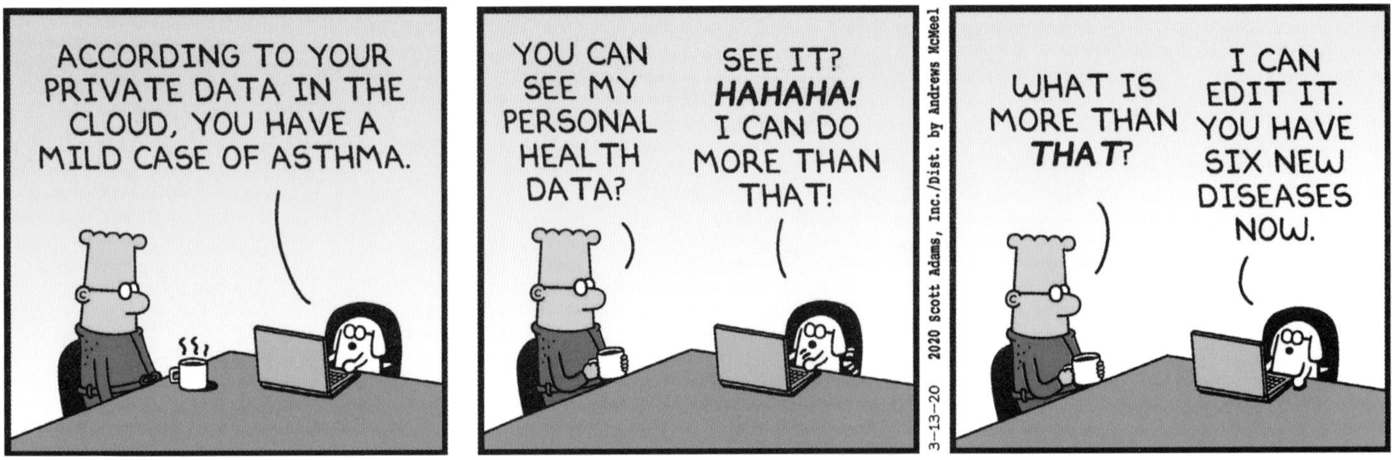
ACCORDING TO YOUR PRIVATE DATA IN THE CLOUD, YOU HAVE A MILD CASE OF ASTHMA.
YOU CAN SEE MY PERSONAL HEALTH DATA?
SEE IT? ***HAHAHA!*** I CAN DO MORE THAN THAT!
WHAT IS MORE THAN ***THAT***?
I CAN EDIT IT. YOU HAVE SIX NEW DISEASES NOW.
3-13-20 2020 Scott Adams, Inc./Dist. by Andrews McMeel

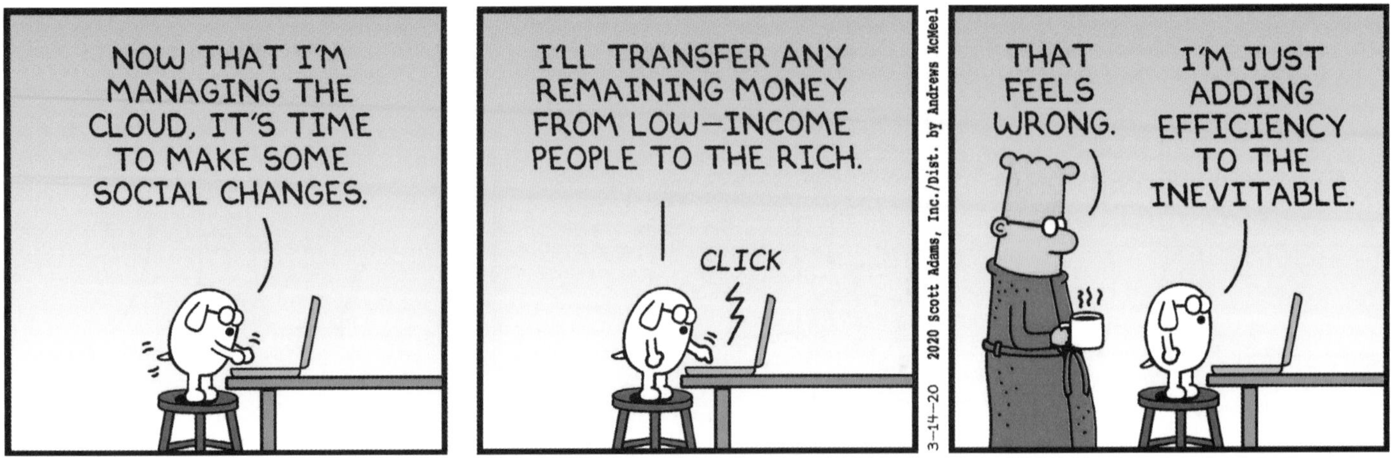
NOW THAT I'M MANAGING THE CLOUD, IT'S TIME TO MAKE SOME SOCIAL CHANGES.
I'LL TRANSFER ANY REMAINING MONEY FROM LOW-INCOME PEOPLE TO THE RICH.
CLICK
THAT FEELS WRONG.
I'M JUST ADDING EFFICIENCY TO THE INEVITABLE.
3-14-20 2020 Scott Adams, Inc./Dist. by Andrews McMeel

YOU HAVEN'T COMPLETED THE MANDATORY CLASS ON BLOCKCHAIN.
THAT'S AN INTRO- DUCTORY CLASS. I'M ALREADY AN EXPERIENCED BLOCK- CHAIN DEVELOPER.
THE CLASS IS MANDATORY. EVERY DEVELOPER NEEDS TO CHECK THE BOX.
© 2020 Scott Adams, Inc./Dist. by Andrews McMeel
JUST CHECK THE BOX FOR ME.
ONLY THE INSTRUC- TOR CAN DO THAT.
AND I DON'T WANT TO CALL HIM BECAUSE HE RAMBLES ON AND ON.
YOU WANT ME TO TAKE A TWO-DAY CLASS SO YOU WON'T HAVE TO MAKE A PHONE CALL???
I KNEW YOU'D UNDERSTAND.
3-15-20
WHAT IF TAKING THE CLASS CAUSES ME TO MISS MY DEAD- LINES?
NO PROBLEM. I'LL JUST CANCEL YOUR BONUS.

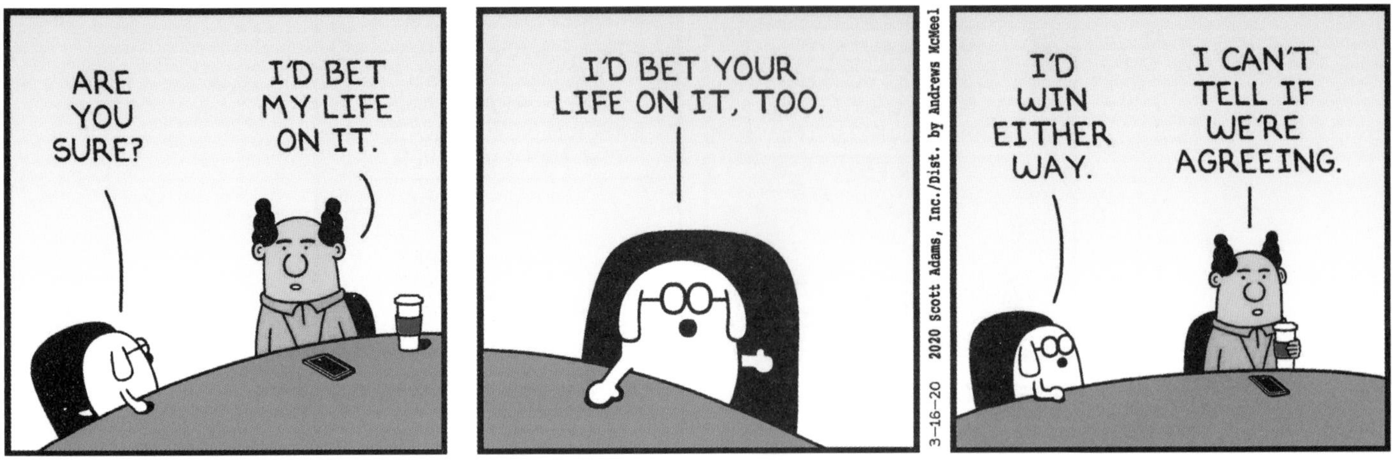
ARE YOU SURE?
I'D BET MY LIFE ON IT.
I'D BET YOUR LIFE ON IT, TOO.
I'D WIN EITHER WAY.
I CAN'T TELL IF WE'RE AGREEING.
3-16-20 2020 Scott Adams, Inc./Dist. by Andrews McMeel

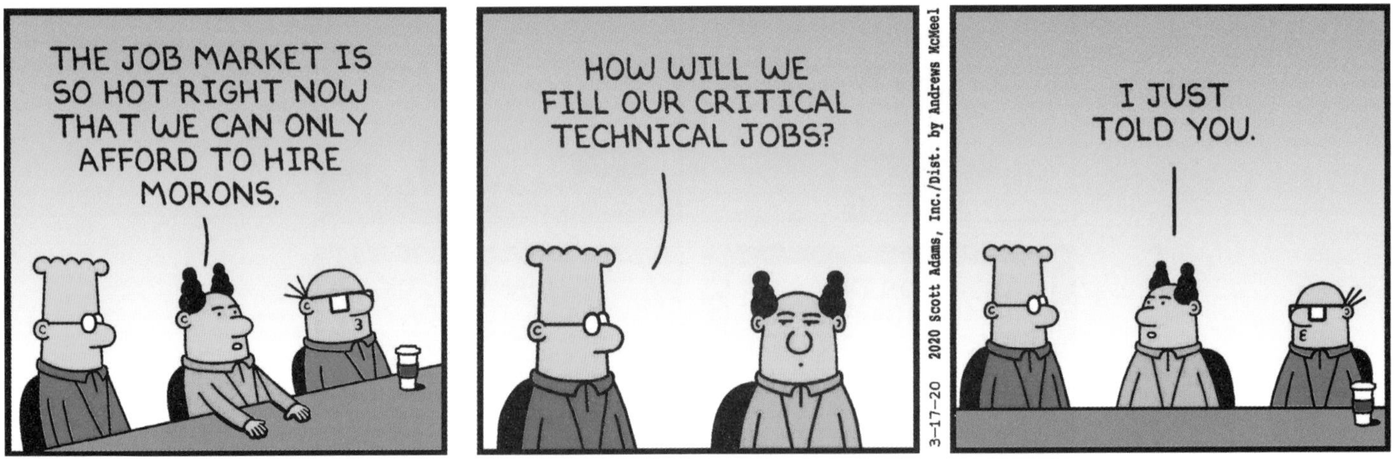
THE JOB MARKET IS SO HOT RIGHT NOW THAT WE CAN ONLY AFFORD TO HIRE MORONS.
HOW WILL WE FILL OUR CRITICAL TECHNICAL JOBS?
I JUST TOLD YOU.
3-17-20 2020 Scott Adams, Inc./Dist. by Andrews McMeel

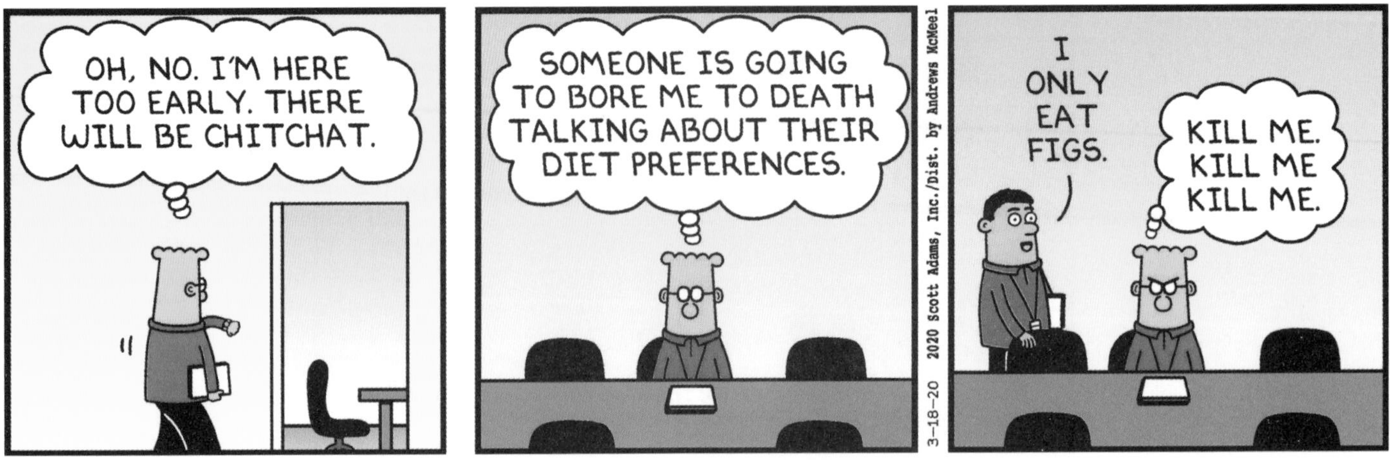
OH, NO. I'M HERE TOO EARLY. THERE WILL BE CHITCHAT.
SOMEONE IS GOING TO BORE ME TO DEATH TALKING ABOUT THEIR DIET PREFERENCES.
I ONLY EAT FIGS.
KILL ME. KILL ME KILL ME.
3-18-20 2020 Scott Adams, Inc./Dist. by Andrews McMeel

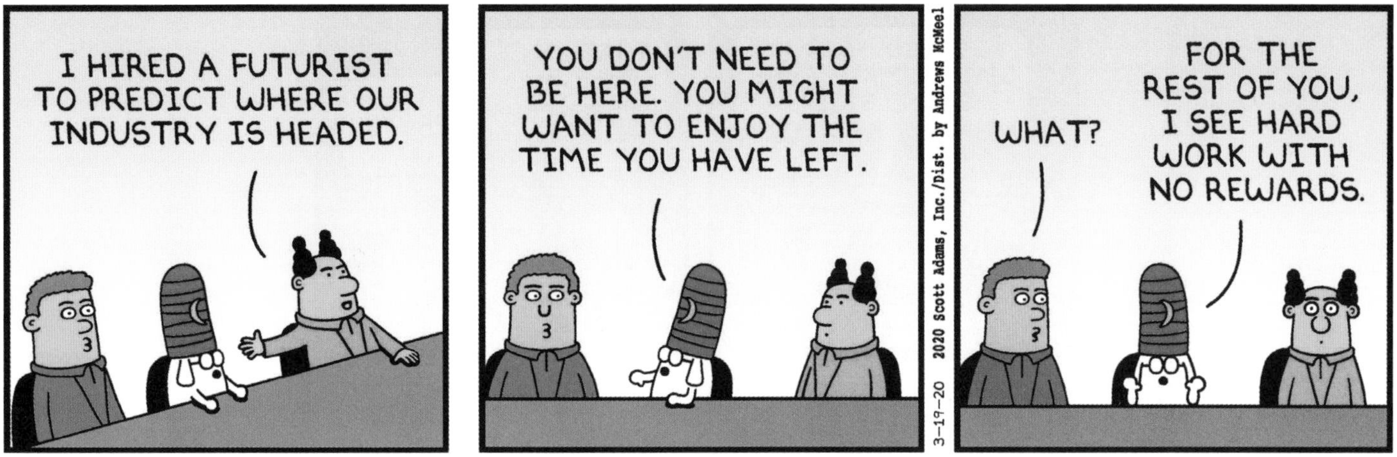
I HIRED A FUTURIST TO PREDICT WHERE OUR INDUSTRY IS HEADED.
YOU DON'T NEED TO BE HERE. YOU MIGHT WANT TO ENJOY THE TIME YOU HAVE LEFT.
3-19-20 2020 Scott Adams, Inc./Dist. by Andrews McMeel
WHAT?
FOR THE REST OF YOU, I SEE HARD WORK WITH NO REWARDS.

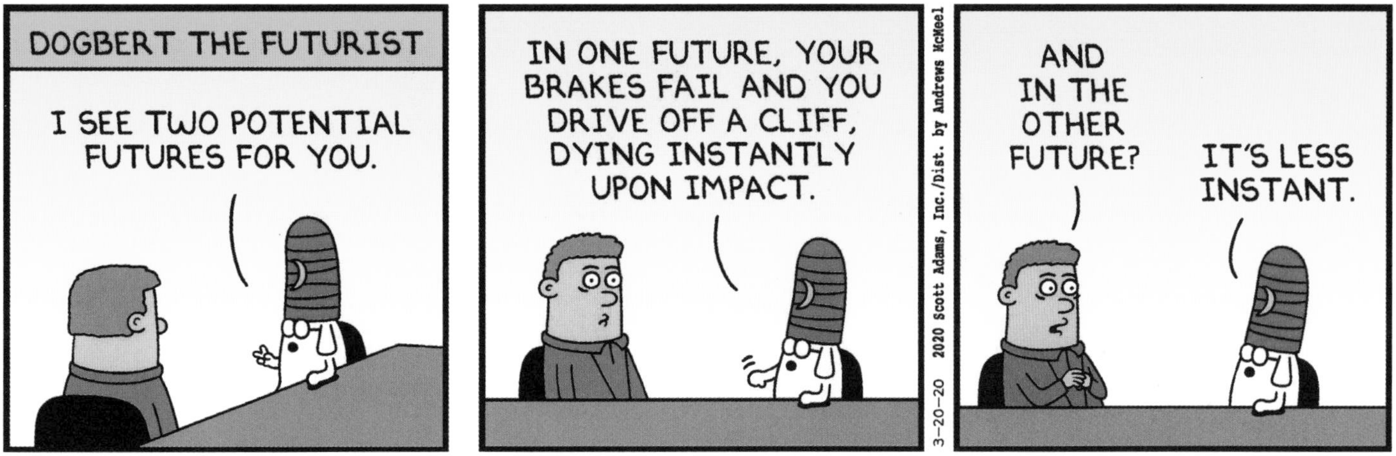
DOGBERT THE FUTURIST
I SEE TWO POTENTIAL FUTURES FOR YOU.
IN ONE FUTURE, YOUR BRAKES FAIL AND YOU DRIVE OFF A CLIFF, DYING INSTANTLY UPON IMPACT.
3-20-20 2020 Scott Adams, Inc./Dist. by Andrews McMeel
AND IN THE OTHER FUTURE?
IT'S LESS INSTANT.

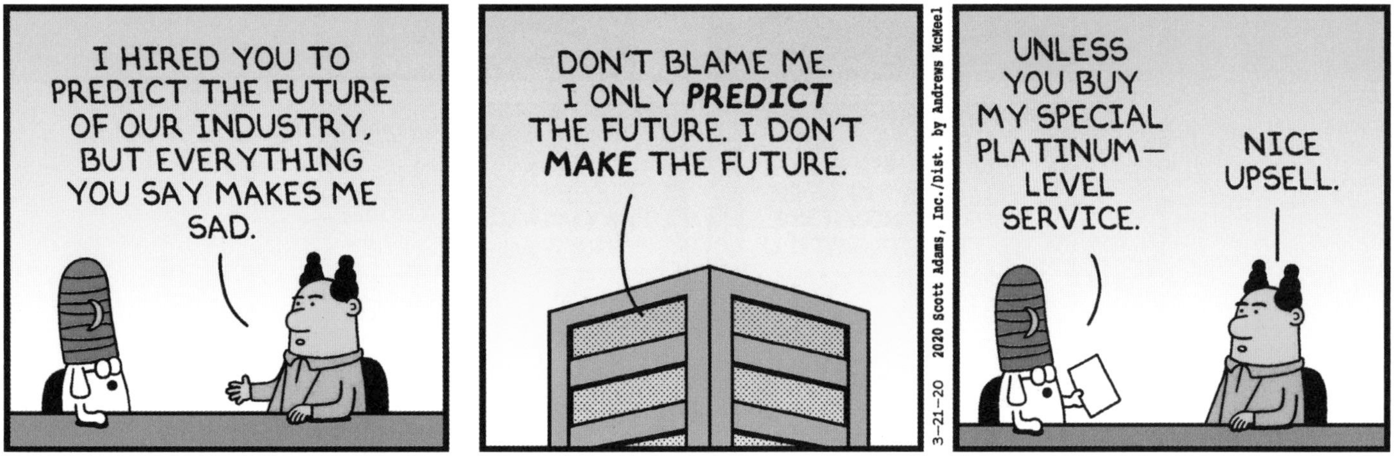
I HIRED YOU TO PREDICT THE FUTURE OF OUR INDUSTRY, BUT EVERYTHING YOU SAY MAKES ME SAD.
DON'T BLAME ME. I ONLY PREDICT THE FUTURE. I DON'T MAKE THE FUTURE.
3-21-20 2020 Scott Adams, Inc./Dist. by Andrews McMeel
UNLESS YOU BUY MY SPECIAL PLATINUM-LEVEL SERVICE.
NICE UPSELL.

I DISCOVERED A WAY TO MAKE TIME STAND STILL.
THAT ISN'T POSSIBLE.
I'LL PROVE IT.
I JUST NEED TO FIND SOMETHING ON MY PHONE AND SHOW IT TO YOU.
© 2020 Scott Adams, Inc./Dist. by Andrews McMeel
LOOKING... LOOKING...
HERE IT IS!
WAIT... NO, THAT ISN'T IT.
LOOKING... LOOKING...
**GAAA!!!** I'M SO BORED WATCHING YOU LOOK THROUGH YOUR PHONE!!! TIME IS STANDING STILL!
3-22-20
YOU WIN... AND I HATE YOU.
TOTALLY WORTH IT.

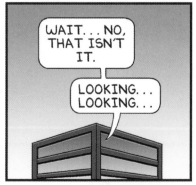

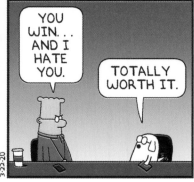

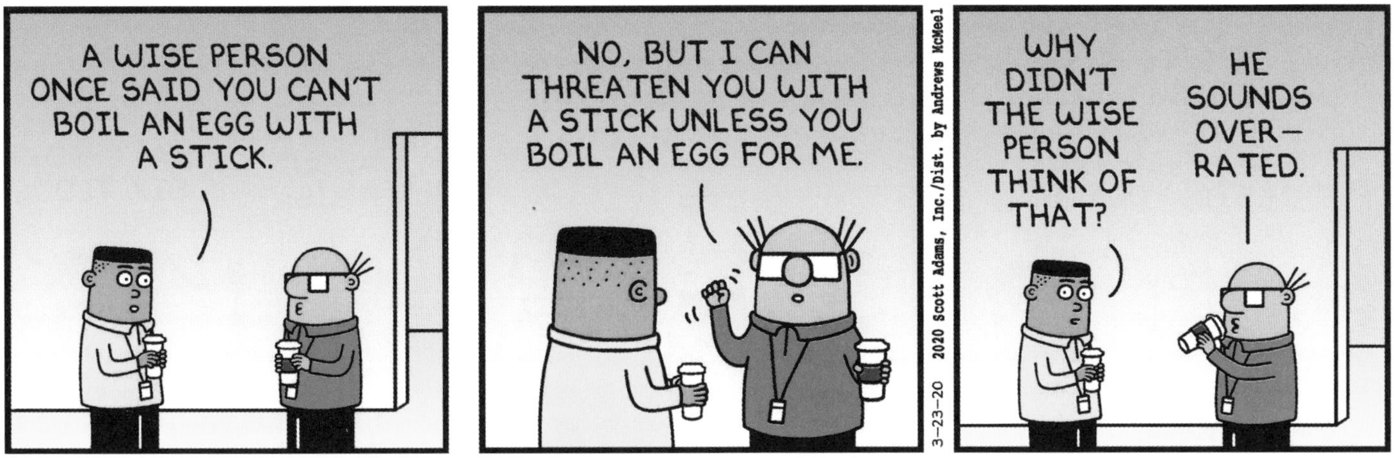
A WISE PERSON ONCE SAID YOU CAN'T BOIL AN EGG WITH A STICK.
NO, BUT I CAN THREATEN YOU WITH A STICK UNLESS YOU BOIL AN EGG FOR ME.
WHY DIDN'T THE WISE PERSON THINK OF THAT?
HE SOUNDS OVER-RATED.
3-23-20 2020 Scott Adams, Inc./Dist. by Andrews McMeel

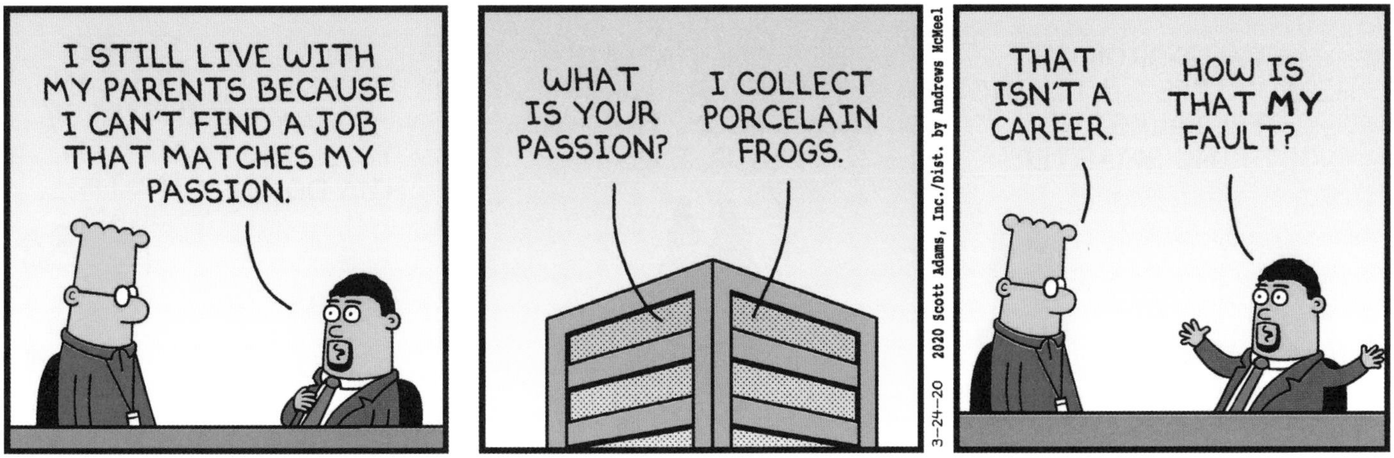
I STILL LIVE WITH MY PARENTS BECAUSE I CAN'T FIND A JOB THAT MATCHES MY PASSION.
WHAT IS YOUR PASSION?
I COLLECT PORCELAIN FROGS.
THAT ISN'T A CAREER.
HOW IS THAT **MY** FAULT?
3-24-20 2020 Scott Adams, Inc./Dist. by Andrews McMeel

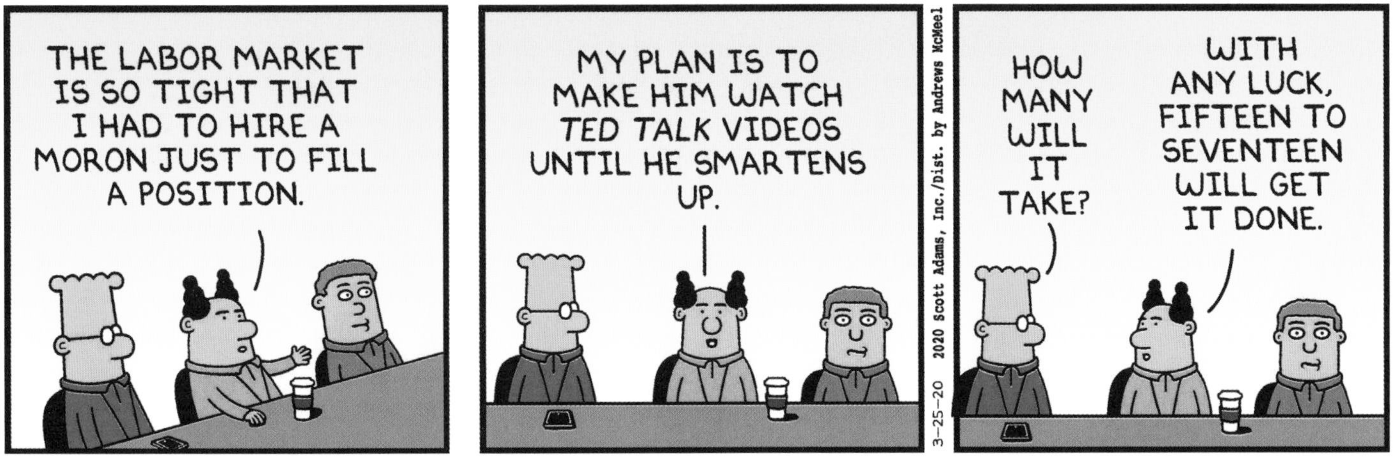
THE LABOR MARKET IS SO TIGHT THAT I HAD TO HIRE A MORON JUST TO FILL A POSITION.
MY PLAN IS TO MAKE HIM WATCH *TED TALK* VIDEOS UNTIL HE SMARTENS UP.
HOW MANY WILL IT TAKE?
WITH ANY LUCK, FIFTEEN TO SEVENTEEN WILL GET IT DONE.
3-25-20 2020 Scott Adams, Inc./Dist. by Andrews McMeel

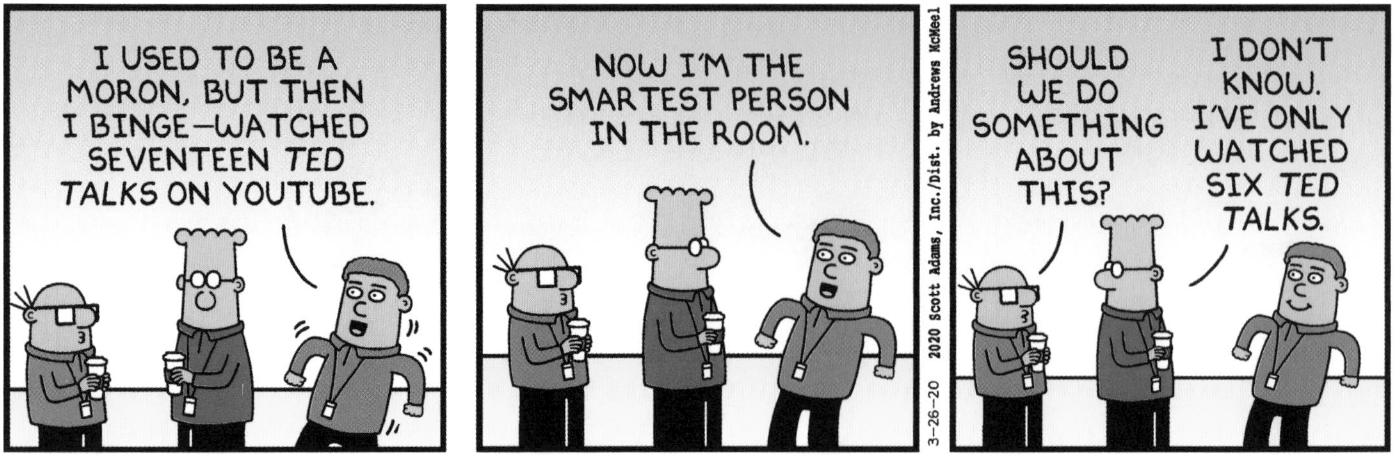
I USED TO BE A MORON, BUT THEN I BINGE-WATCHED SEVENTEEN *TED TALKS* ON YOUTUBE.
NOW I'M THE SMARTEST PERSON IN THE ROOM.
3-26-20 2020 Scott Adams, Inc./Dist. by Andrews McMeel
SHOULD WE DO SOMETHING ABOUT THIS?
I DON'T KNOW. I'VE ONLY WATCHED SIX *TED TALKS*.

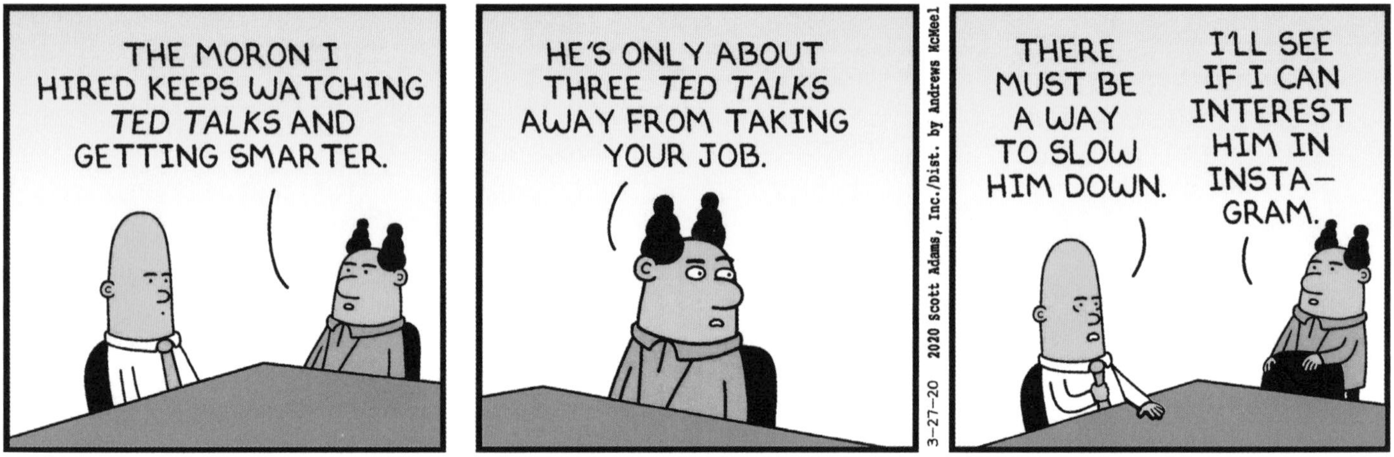
THE MORON I HIRED KEEPS WATCHING *TED TALKS* AND GETTING SMARTER.
HE'S ONLY ABOUT THREE *TED TALKS* AWAY FROM TAKING YOUR JOB.
3-27-20 2020 Scott Adams, Inc./Dist. by Andrews McMeel
THERE MUST BE A WAY TO SLOW HIM DOWN.
I'LL SEE IF I CAN INTEREST HIM IN INSTA-GRAM.

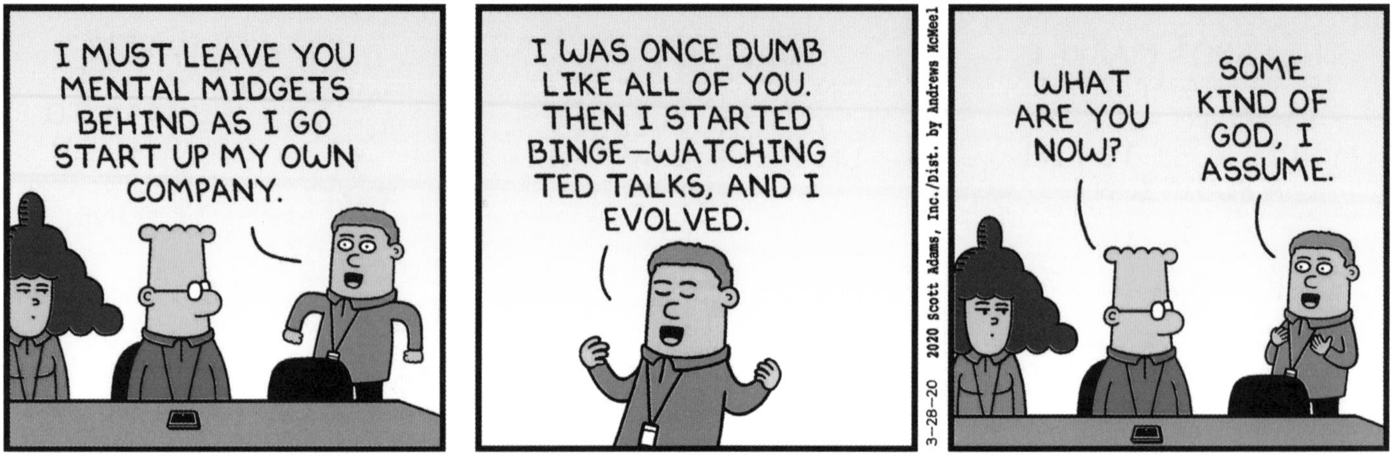
I MUST LEAVE YOU MENTAL MIDGETS BEHIND AS I GO START UP MY OWN COMPANY.
I WAS ONCE DUMB LIKE ALL OF YOU. THEN I STARTED BINGE-WATCHING TED TALKS, AND I EVOLVED.
3-28-20 2020 Scott Adams, Inc./Dist. by Andrews McMeel
WHAT ARE YOU NOW?
SOME KIND OF GOD, I ASSUME.

WHY DID YOU TELL OUR POINTY—HAIRED BOSS WE NEED TO DO MORE TESTING ON THE PROTOTYPE?
I DIDN'T DO ANYTHING OF THE SORT.
CARL SAYS YOU DID.
WHO IS A BETTER AUTHORITY ON WHAT I SAID — A GUY WHO WASN'T IN THE ROOM OR ME?
GOOD QUESTION.
ON ONE HAND, CARL IS AN IDIOT AND A KNOWN LIAR.
ON THE OTHER HAND, IT IS COMMON FOR GUILTY PEOPLE TO SAY THEY ARE INNOCENT.
WHAT DO *INNOCENT* PEOPLE SAY WHEN YOU ACCUSE THEM OF STUFF?
WHO KNOWS? JUST DON'T DO IT AGAIN.
I DIDN'T DO IT ONCE!!!
©2020 Scott Adams, Inc./Dist. by Andrews McMeel
3-29-20

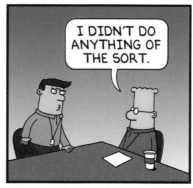

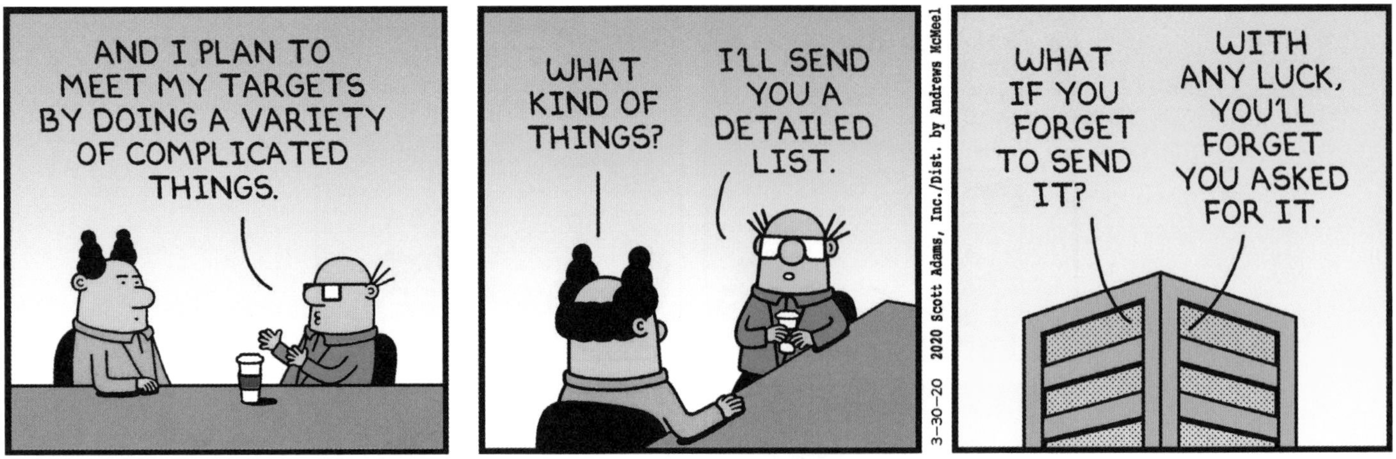
AND I PLAN TO MEET MY TARGETS BY DOING A VARIETY OF COMPLICATED THINGS.
WHAT KIND OF THINGS?
I'LL SEND YOU A DETAILED LIST.
3-30-20 © 2020 Scott Adams, Inc./Dist. by Andrews McMeel
WHAT IF YOU FORGET TO SEND IT?
WITH ANY LUCK, YOU'LL FORGET YOU ASKED FOR IT.

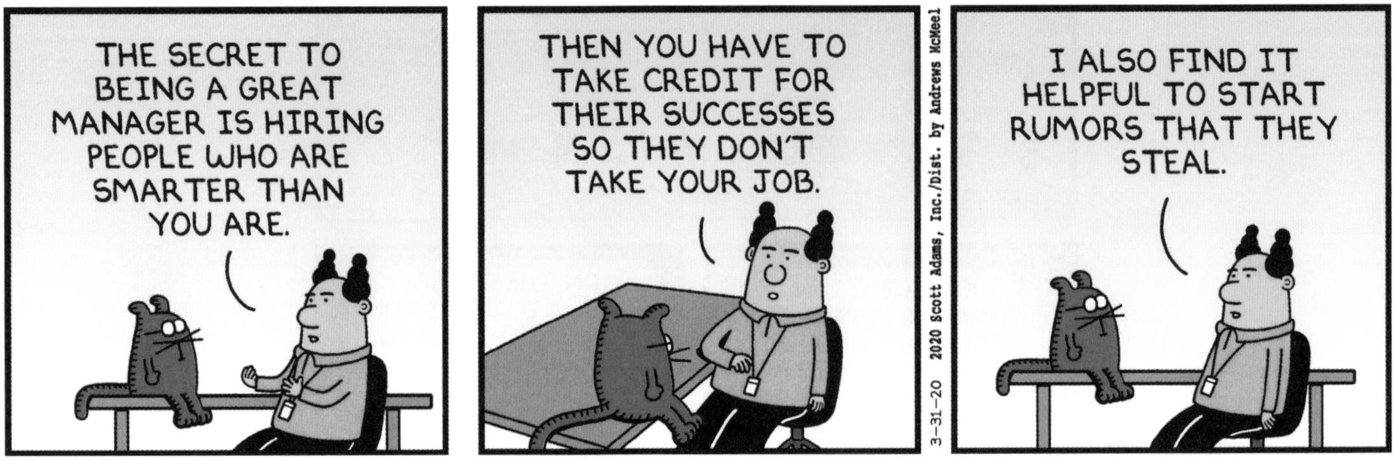
THE SECRET TO BEING A GREAT MANAGER IS HIRING PEOPLE WHO ARE SMARTER THAN YOU ARE.
THEN YOU HAVE TO TAKE CREDIT FOR THEIR SUCCESSES SO THEY DON'T TAKE YOUR JOB.
3-31-20 © 2020 Scott Adams, Inc./Dist. by Andrews McMeel
I ALSO FIND IT HELPFUL TO START RUMORS THAT THEY STEAL.

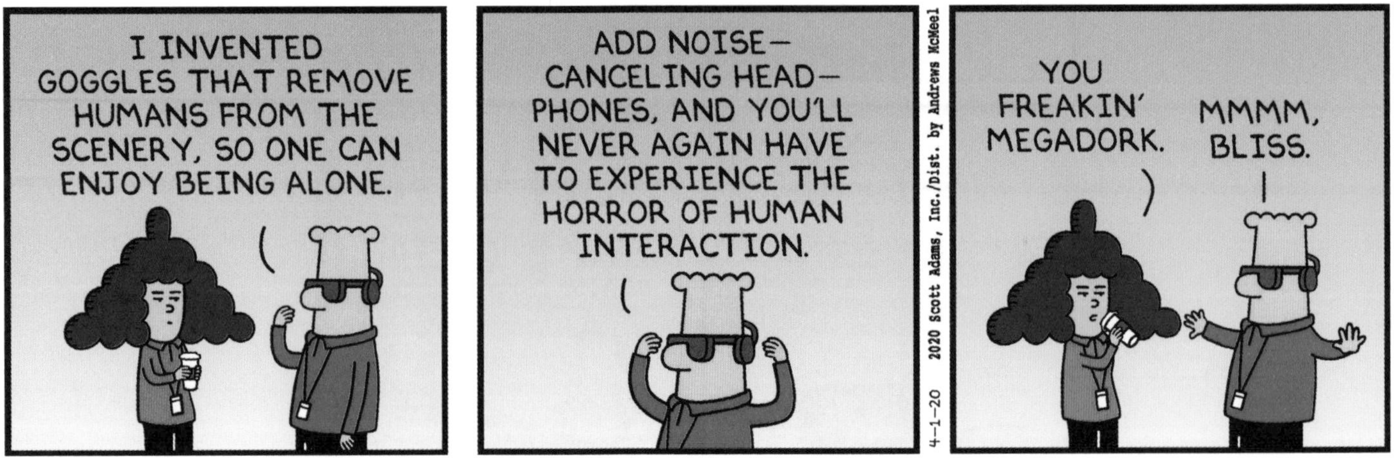
I INVENTED GOGGLES THAT REMOVE HUMANS FROM THE SCENERY, SO ONE CAN ENJOY BEING ALONE.
ADD NOISE-CANCELING HEAD-PHONES, AND YOU'LL NEVER AGAIN HAVE TO EXPERIENCE THE HORROR OF HUMAN INTERACTION.
4-1-20 © 2020 Scott Adams, Inc./Dist. by Andrews McMeel
YOU FREAKIN' MEGADORK.
MMMM, BLISS.

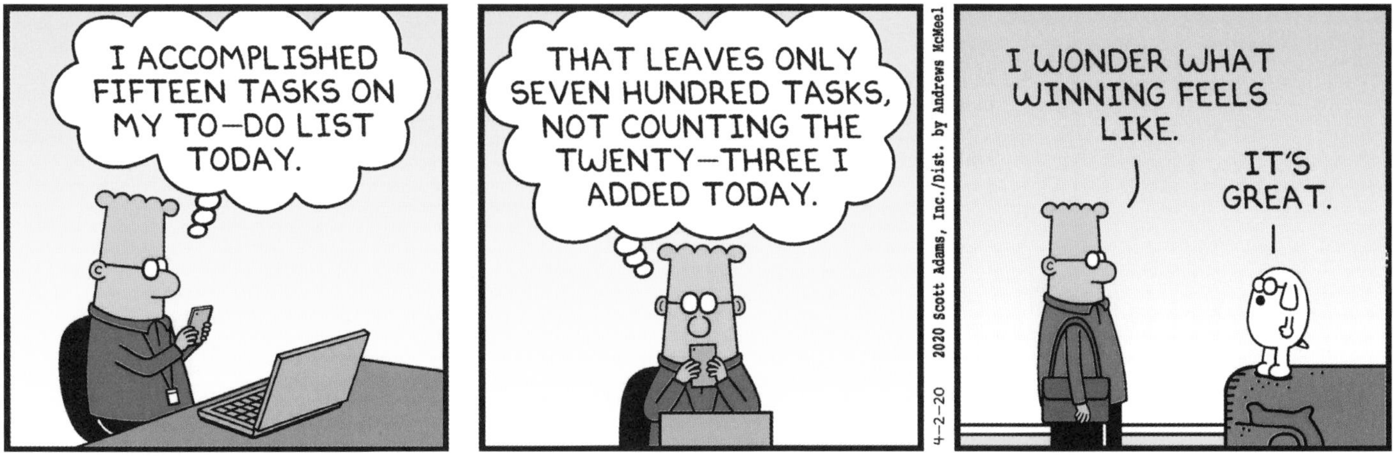
I ACCOMPLISHED FIFTEEN TASKS ON MY TO-DO LIST TODAY.
THAT LEAVES ONLY SEVEN HUNDRED TASKS, NOT COUNTING THE TWENTY-THREE I ADDED TODAY.
4-2-20 2020 Scott Adams, Inc./Dist. by Andrews McMeel
I WONDER WHAT WINNING FEELS LIKE.
IT'S GREAT.

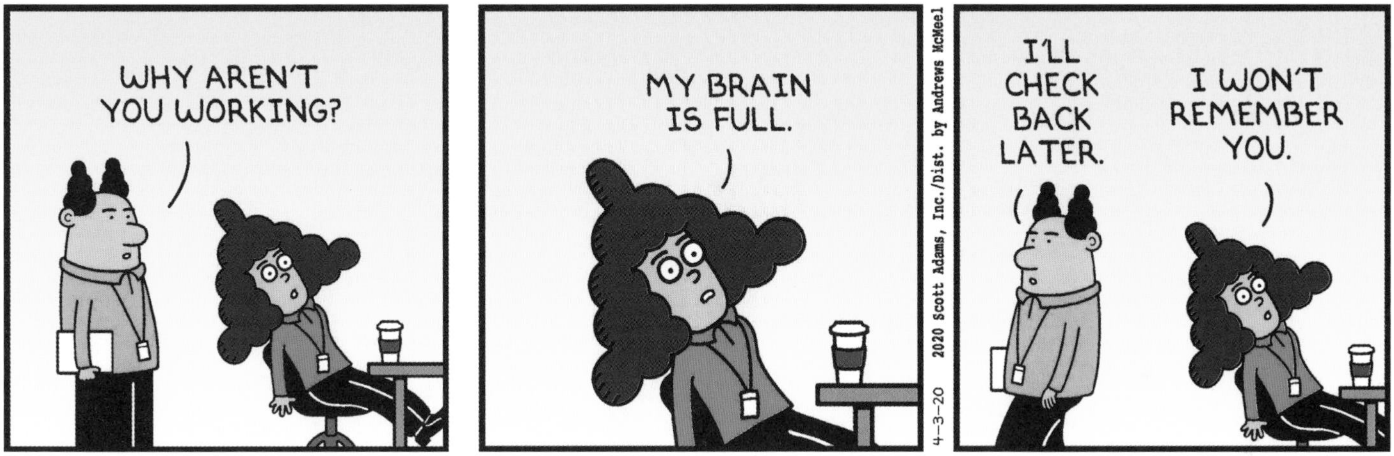
WHY AREN'T YOU WORKING?
MY BRAIN IS FULL.
4-3-20 2020 Scott Adams, Inc./Dist. by Andrews McMeel
I'LL CHECK BACK LATER.
I WON'T REMEMBER YOU.

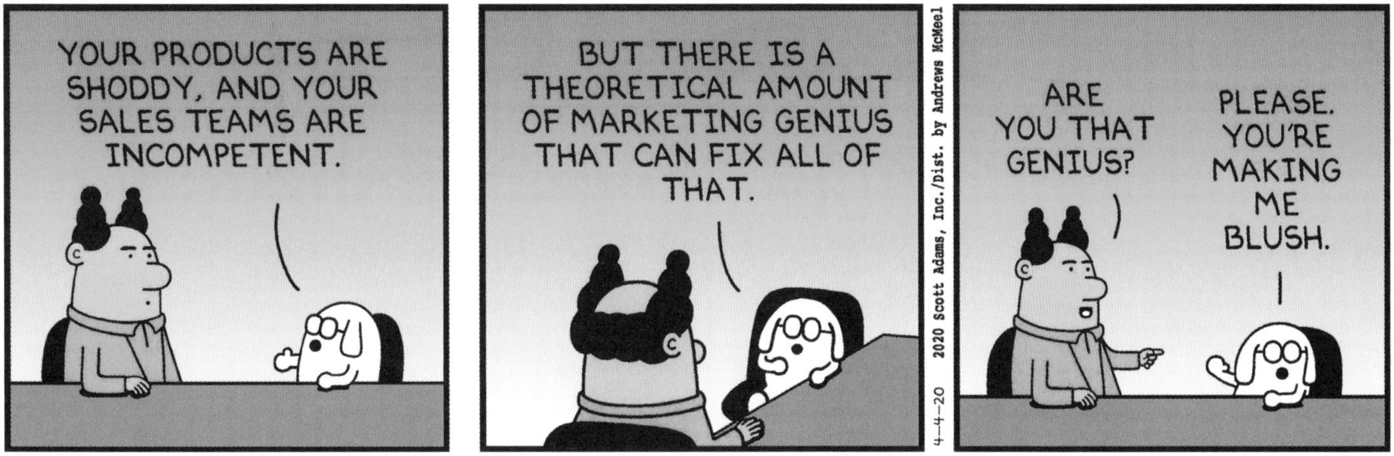
YOUR PRODUCTS ARE SHODDY, AND YOUR SALES TEAMS ARE INCOMPETENT.
BUT THERE IS A THEORETICAL AMOUNT OF MARKETING GENIUS THAT CAN FIX ALL OF THAT.
4-4-20 2020 Scott Adams, Inc./Dist. by Andrews McMeel
ARE YOU THAT GENIUS?
PLEASE. YOU'RE MAKING ME BLUSH.

THAT MEETING RAN LONG, SO NOW I ONLY HAVE TEN MINUTES BEFORE THE NEXT ONE.
I'M SUPPOSED TO BRING A COMPLETE TECHNICAL REPORT, AND I HAVEN'T EVEN STARTED IT.
I HATE THIS STUPID JOB!
I HATE MY BOSS! I HATE MY STUPID CO—WORKERS!
I DON'T CARE ABOUT ANYTHING ANYMORE!
I'LL JUST ANGRILY SLAP TOGETHER A BUNCH OF NONSENSE AND CALL IT GOOD. GRRRRRR!!!
THIS IS YOUR BEST REPORT EVER.
WHAT?
TODAY I LEARNED A DANGEROUS LESSON ABOUT REALITY.
© 2020 Scott Adams, Inc./Dist. by Andrews McMeel
4-5-20

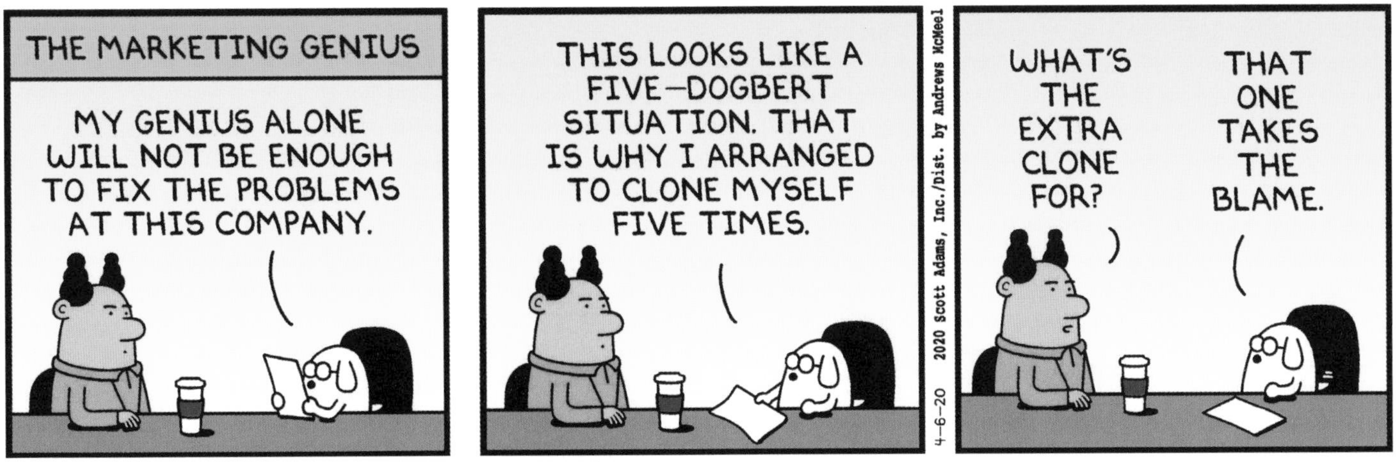
THE MARKETING GENIUS
MY GENIUS ALONE WILL NOT BE ENOUGH TO FIX THE PROBLEMS AT THIS COMPANY.
THIS LOOKS LIKE A FIVE—DOGBERT SITUATION. THAT IS WHY I ARRANGED TO CLONE MYSELF FIVE TIMES.
4-6-20 © 2020 Scott Adams, Inc./Dist. by Andrews McMeel
WHAT'S THE EXTRA CLONE FOR?
THAT ONE TAKES THE BLAME.

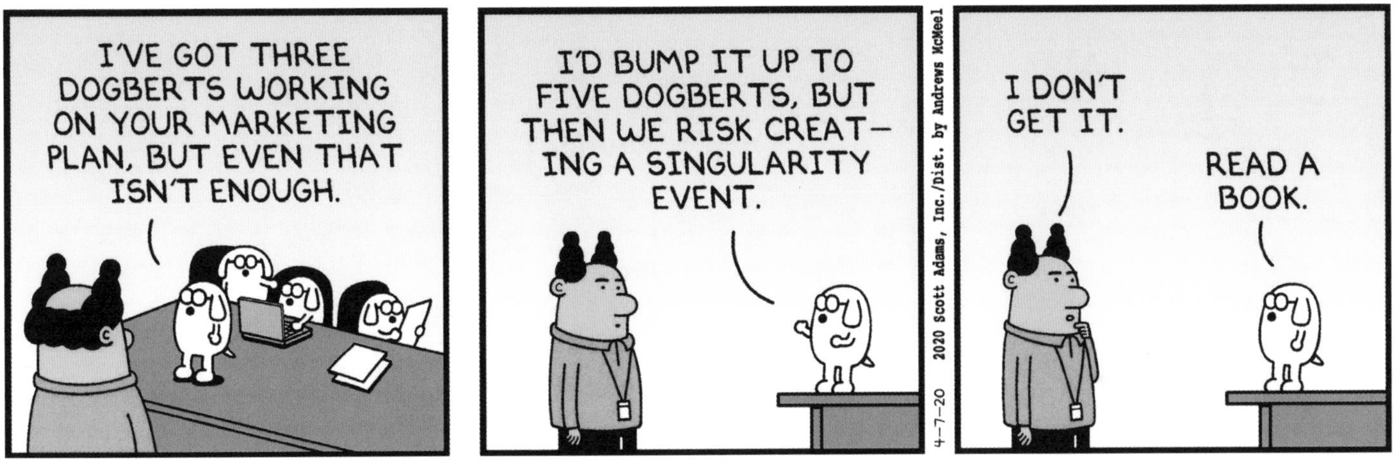
I'VE GOT THREE DOGBERTS WORKING ON YOUR MARKETING PLAN, BUT EVEN THAT ISN'T ENOUGH.
I'D BUMP IT UP TO FIVE DOGBERTS, BUT THEN WE RISK CREAT— ING A SINGULARITY EVENT.
4-7-20 © 2020 Scott Adams, Inc./Dist. by Andrews McMeel
I DON'T GET IT.
READ A BOOK.

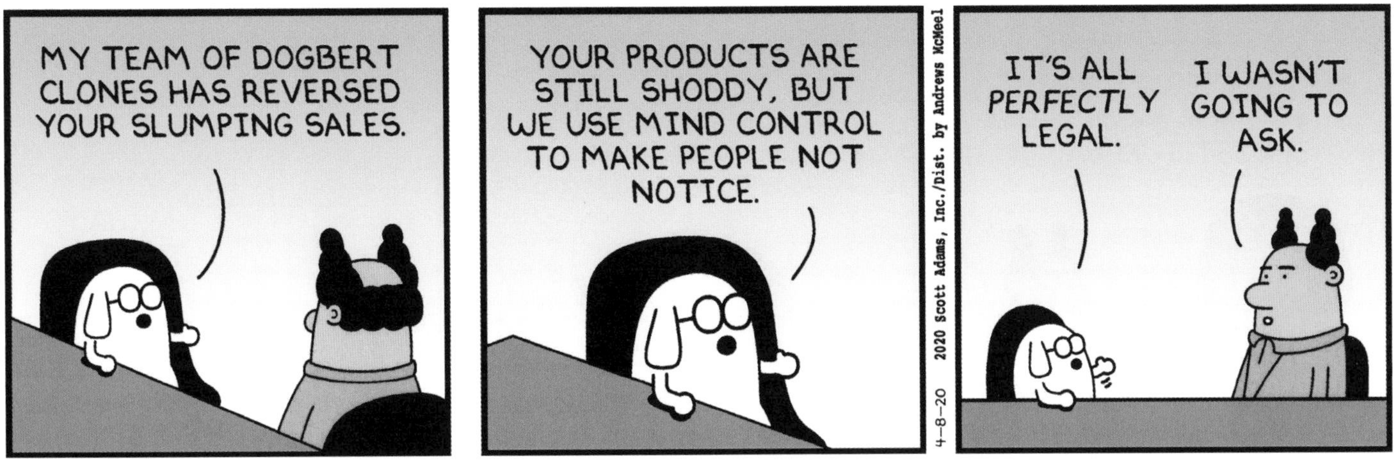
MY TEAM OF DOGBERT CLONES HAS REVERSED YOUR SLUMPING SALES.
YOUR PRODUCTS ARE STILL SHODDY, BUT WE USE MIND CONTROL TO MAKE PEOPLE NOT NOTICE.
4-8-20 © 2020 Scott Adams, Inc./Dist. by Andrews McMeel
IT'S ALL *PERFECTLY* LEGAL.
I WASN'T GOING TO ASK.

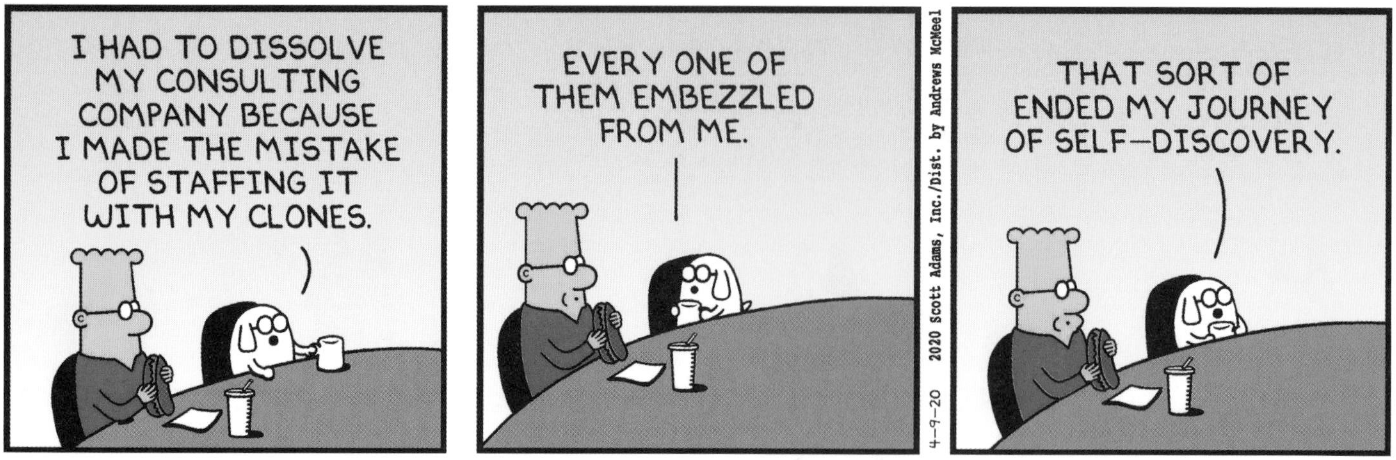
I HAD TO DISSOLVE MY CONSULTING COMPANY BECAUSE I MADE THE MISTAKE OF STAFFING IT WITH MY CLONES.
EVERY ONE OF THEM EMBEZZLED FROM ME.
4-9-20 2020 Scott Adams, Inc./Dist. by Andrews McMeel
THAT SORT OF ENDED MY JOURNEY OF SELF—DISCOVERY.

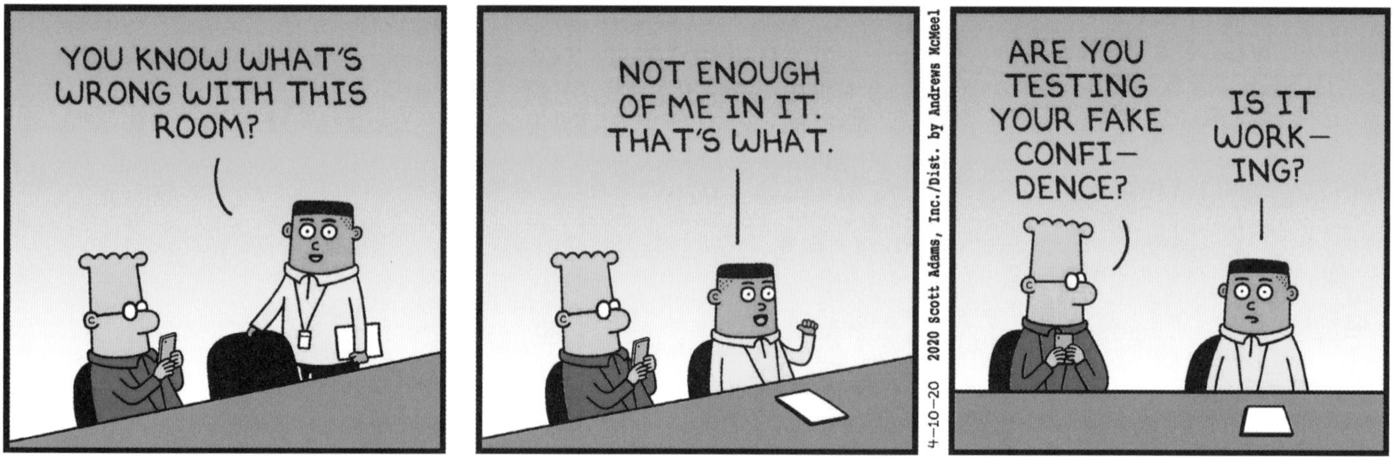
YOU KNOW WHAT'S WRONG WITH THIS ROOM?
NOT ENOUGH OF ME IN IT. THAT'S WHAT.
4-10-20 2020 Scott Adams, Inc./Dist. by Andrews McMeel
ARE YOU TESTING YOUR FAKE CONFI— DENCE?
IS IT WORK— ING?

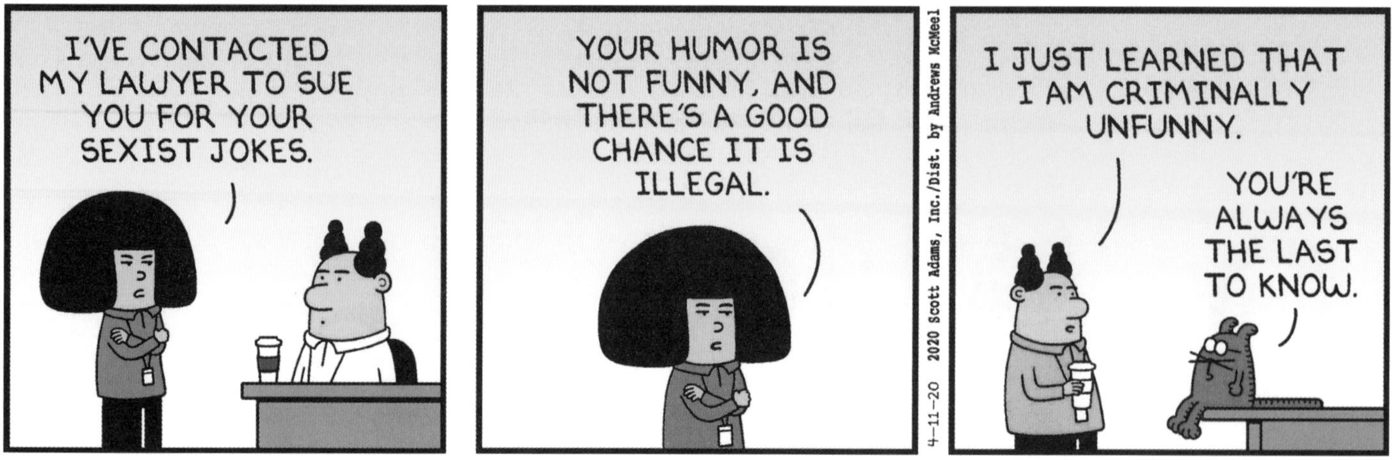
I'VE CONTACTED MY LAWYER TO SUE YOU FOR YOUR SEXIST JOKES.
YOUR HUMOR IS NOT FUNNY, AND THERE'S A GOOD CHANCE IT IS ILLEGAL.
4-11-20 2020 Scott Adams, Inc./Dist. by Andrews McMeel
I JUST LEARNED THAT I AM CRIMINALLY UNFUNNY.
YOU'RE ALWAYS THE LAST TO KNOW.

PHILOSOPHERS SAY LOVING YOURSELF IS THE GREATEST LOVE OF ALL.
DO PHILOSOPHERS REALLY SAY THAT?
ALL THE GOOD ONES DO.
AFTER YEARS OF TRYING, I HAVE FINALLY LEARNED TO LOVE MYSELF.
I'M NO PHILOSOPHER, BUT INSTEAD OF LEARNING TO LOVE YOURSELF THE WAY YOU ARE . . .
WOULDN'T IT BE BETTER IF YOU LEARNED HOW TO STOP BEING AN EVIL, IGNORANT, SELFISH PIECE OF GARBAGE?
THAT SOUNDS A LOT HARDER.
IN OTHER WORDS, YOU ARE LAZY.
I LOVE THAT ABOUT ME!
© 2020 Scott Adams, Inc./Dist. by Andrews McMeel
4-12-20

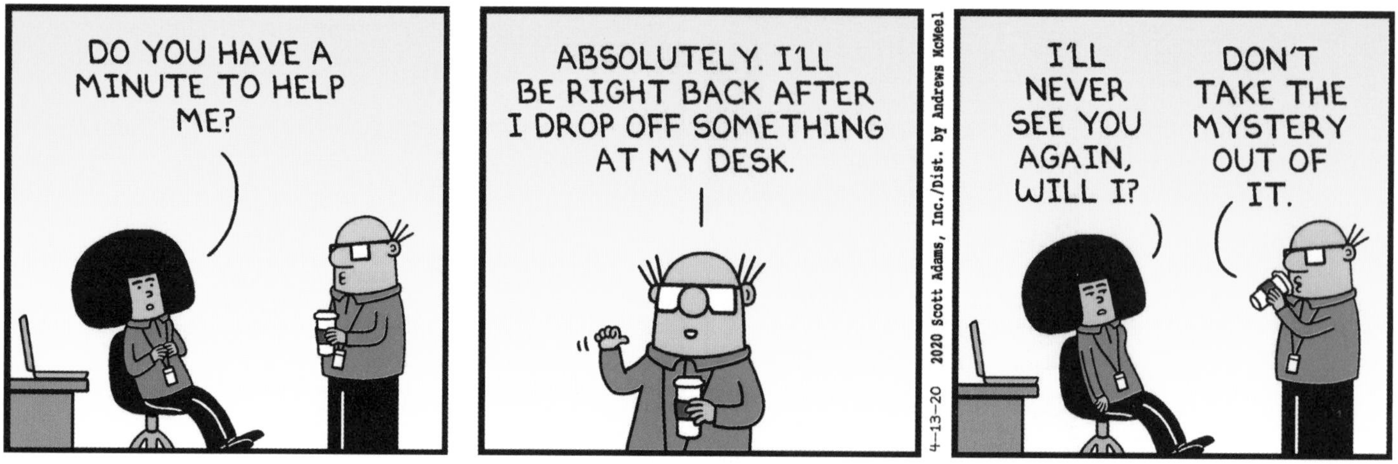
DO YOU HAVE A MINUTE TO HELP ME?
ABSOLUTELY. I'LL BE RIGHT BACK AFTER I DROP OFF SOMETHING AT MY DESK.
4-13-20 2020 Scott Adams, Inc./Dist. by Andrews McMeel
I'LL NEVER SEE YOU AGAIN, WILL I?
DON'T TAKE THE MYSTERY OUT OF IT.

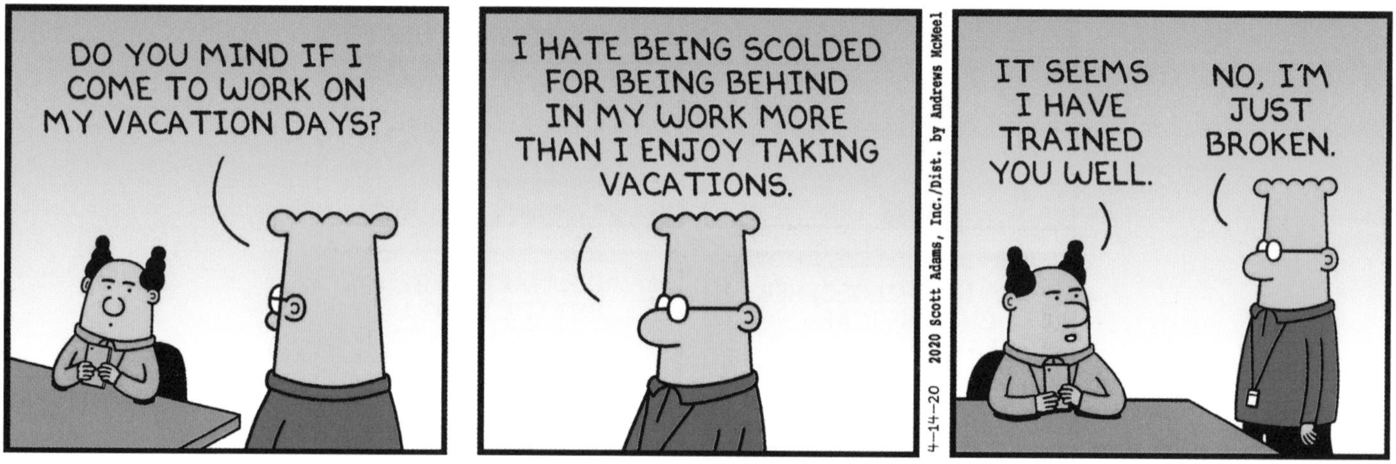
DO YOU MIND IF I COME TO WORK ON MY VACATION DAYS?
I HATE BEING SCOLDED FOR BEING BEHIND IN MY WORK MORE THAN I ENJOY TAKING VACATIONS.
4-14-20 2020 Scott Adams, Inc./Dist. by Andrews McMeel
IT SEEMS I HAVE TRAINED YOU WELL.
NO, I'M JUST BROKEN.

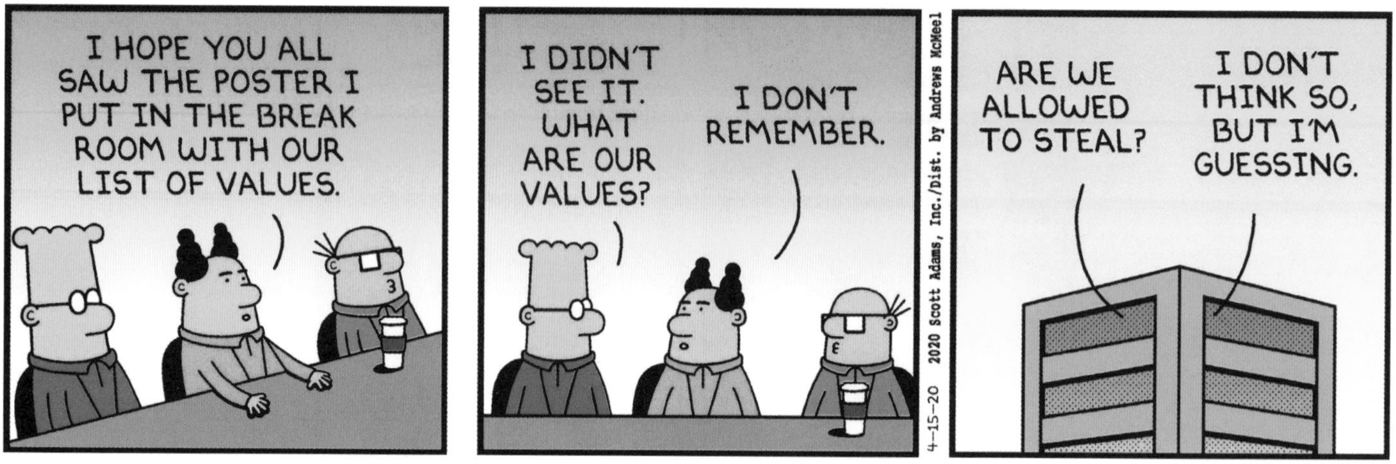
I HOPE YOU ALL SAW THE POSTER I PUT IN THE BREAK ROOM WITH OUR LIST OF VALUES.
I DIDN'T SEE IT. WHAT ARE OUR VALUES?
I DON'T REMEMBER.
4-15-20 2020 Scott Adams, Inc./Dist. by Andrews McMeel
ARE WE ALLOWED TO STEAL?
I DON'T THINK SO, BUT I'M GUESSING.

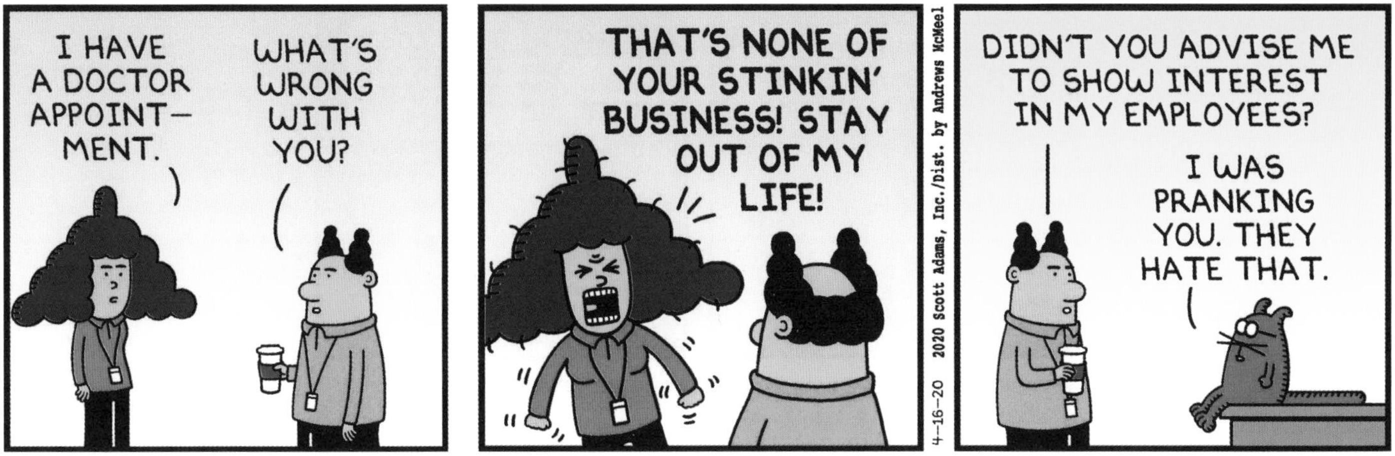
I HAVE A DOCTOR APPOINT-MENT.
WHAT'S WRONG WITH YOU?
THAT'S NONE OF YOUR STINKIN' BUSINESS! STAY OUT OF MY LIFE!
4-16-20 2020 Scott Adams, Inc./Dist. by Andrews McMeel
DIDN'T YOU ADVISE ME TO SHOW INTEREST IN MY EMPLOYEES?
I WAS PRANKING YOU. THEY HATE THAT.

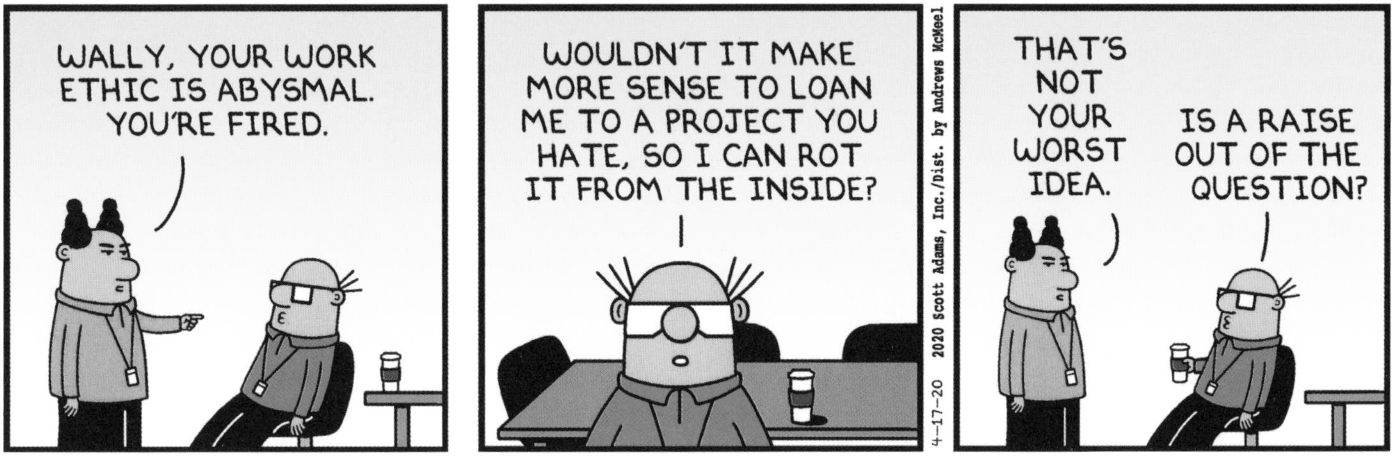
WALLY, YOUR WORK ETHIC IS ABYSMAL. YOU'RE FIRED.
WOULDN'T IT MAKE MORE SENSE TO LOAN ME TO A PROJECT YOU HATE, SO I CAN ROT IT FROM THE INSIDE?
4-17-20 2020 Scott Adams, Inc./Dist. by Andrews McMeel
THAT'S NOT YOUR WORST IDEA.
IS A RAISE OUT OF THE QUESTION?

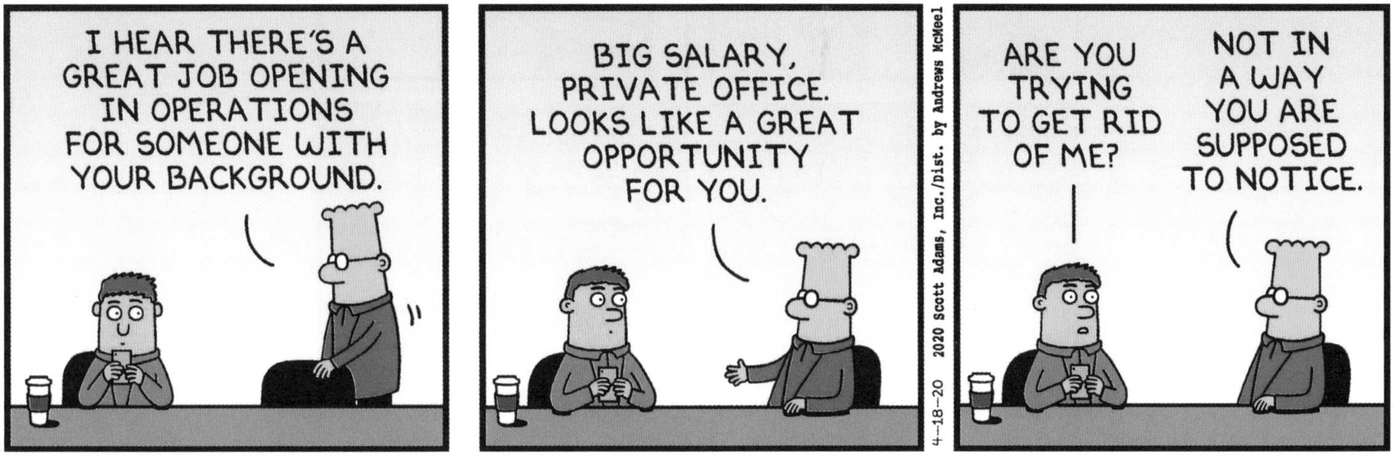
I HEAR THERE'S A GREAT JOB OPENING IN OPERATIONS FOR SOMEONE WITH YOUR BACKGROUND.
BIG SALARY, PRIVATE OFFICE. LOOKS LIKE A GREAT OPPORTUNITY FOR YOU.
4-18-20 2020 Scott Adams, Inc./Dist. by Andrews McMeel
ARE YOU TRYING TO GET RID OF ME?
NOT IN A WAY YOU ARE SUPPOSED TO NOTICE.

WE HAVE SOME PROBLEMS IN OUR ELBONIAN FACTORY.
HOW BAD?
THEY LOST POWER ON THE MAIN FLOOR.
THAT'S NOT SO BAD.
THE EMPLOYEES WERE SCARED.
THEY'LL GET OVER IT.
ONE OF THEM TRIPPED IN THE DARK.
BIG DEAL.
HE ACCI- DENTALLY OPENED A GAS LINE.
A LITTLE GAS NEVER HURT ANYONE.
NOW THERE'S A CRATER WHERE THE CAPITAL CITY USED TO BE.
LET'S KEEP AN EYE ON THAT.
© 2020 Scott Adams, Inc./Dist. by Andrews McMeel
4-19-20

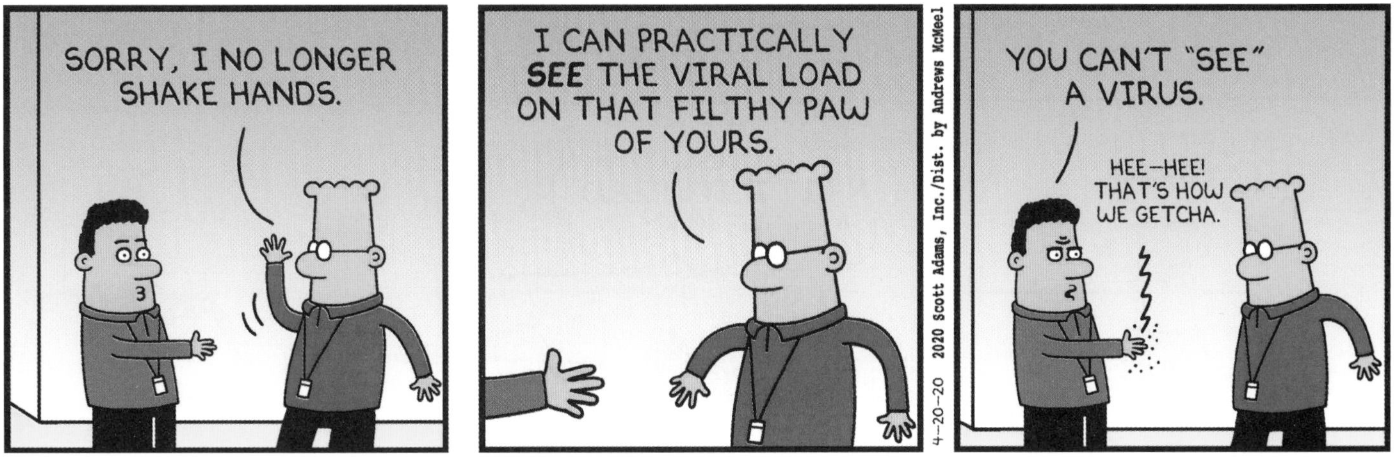
SORRY, I NO LONGER SHAKE HANDS.
I CAN PRACTICALLY **SEE** THE VIRAL LOAD ON THAT FILTHY PAW OF YOURS.
YOU CAN'T "SEE" A VIRUS.
HEE—HEE! THAT'S HOW WE GETCHA.
4-20-20 2020 Scott Adams, Inc./Dist. by Andrews McMeel

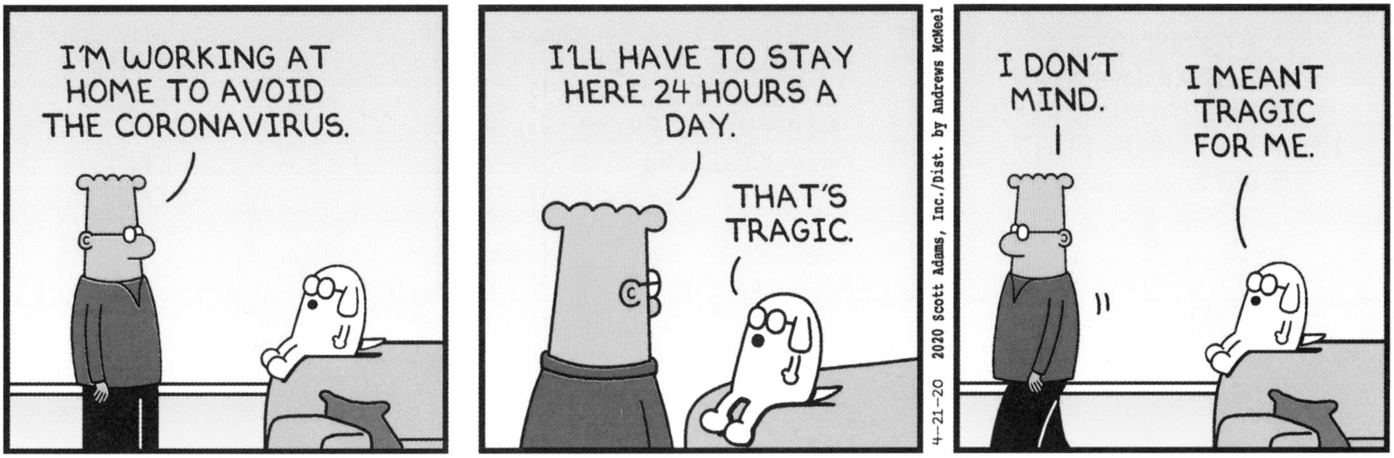
I'M WORKING AT HOME TO AVOID THE CORONAVIRUS.
I'LL HAVE TO STAY HERE 24 HOURS A DAY.
THAT'S TRAGIC.
I DON'T MIND.
I MEANT TRAGIC FOR ME.
4-21-20 2020 Scott Adams, Inc./Dist. by Andrews McMeel

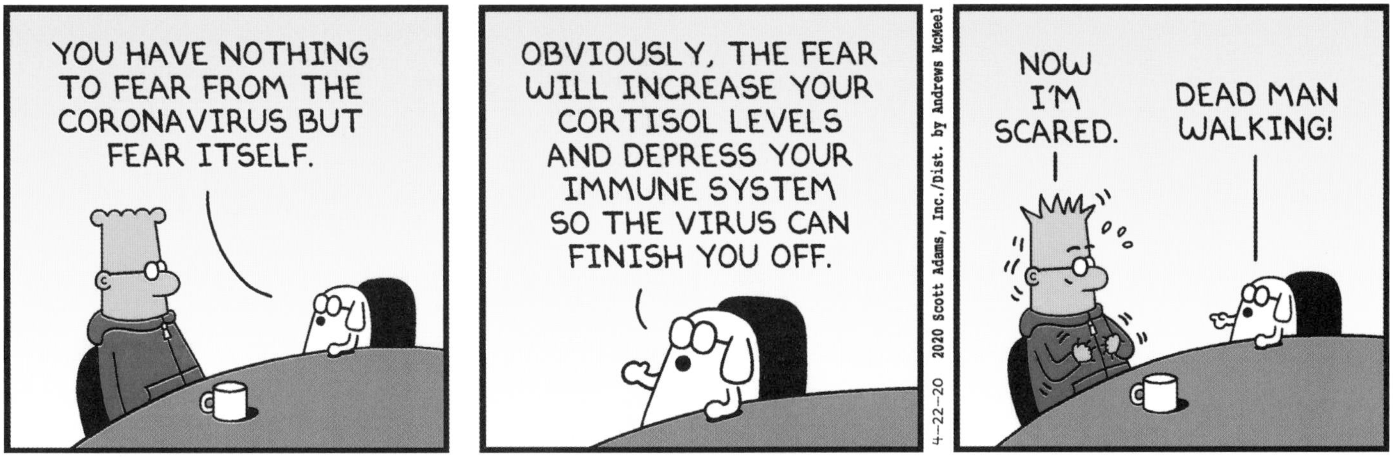
YOU HAVE NOTHING TO FEAR FROM THE CORONAVIRUS BUT FEAR ITSELF.
OBVIOUSLY, THE FEAR WILL INCREASE YOUR CORTISOL LEVELS AND DEPRESS YOUR IMMUNE SYSTEM SO THE VIRUS CAN FINISH YOU OFF.
NOW I'M SCARED.
DEAD MAN WALKING!
4-22-20 2020 Scott Adams, Inc./Dist. by Andrews McMeel

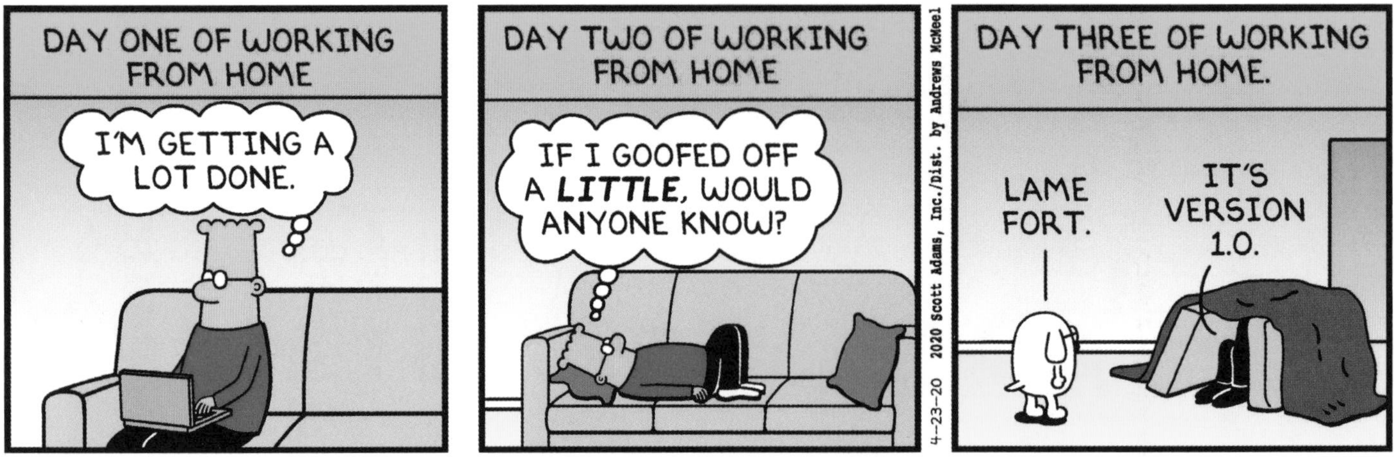
DAY ONE OF WORKING FROM HOME
I'M GETTING A LOT DONE.
DAY TWO OF WORKING FROM HOME
IF I GOOFED OFF A ***LITTLE***, WOULD ANYONE KNOW?
2020 Scott Adams, Inc./Dist. by Andrews McMeel 4-23-20
DAY THREE OF WORKING FROM HOME.
LAME FORT.
IT'S VERSION 1.0.

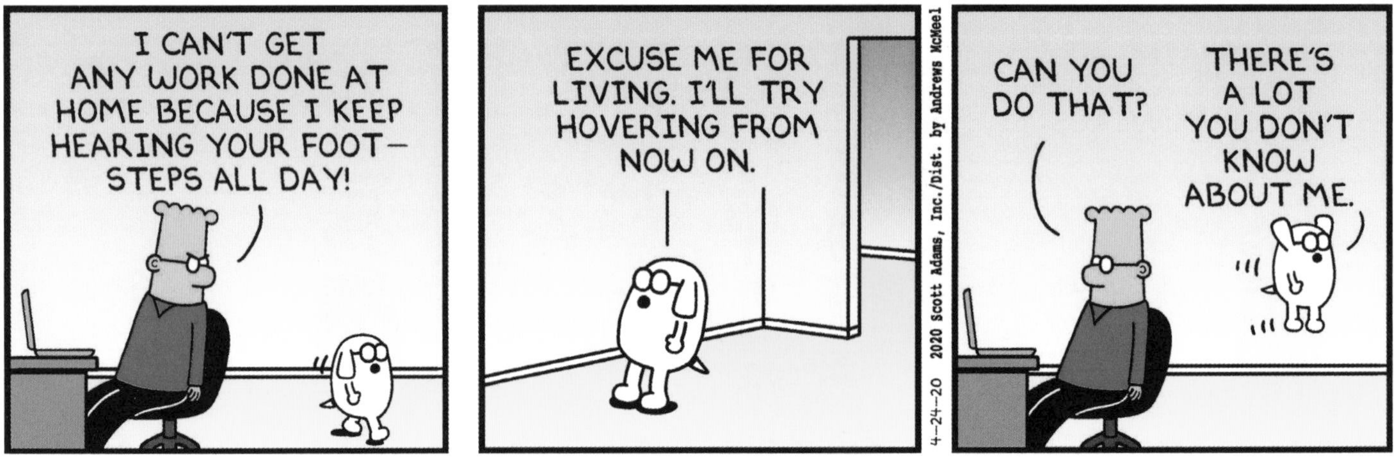
I CAN'T GET ANY WORK DONE AT HOME BECAUSE I KEEP HEARING YOUR FOOT-STEPS ALL DAY!
EXCUSE ME FOR LIVING. I'LL TRY HOVERING FROM NOW ON.
2020 Scott Adams, Inc./Dist. by Andrews McMeel 4-24-20
CAN YOU DO THAT?
THERE'S A LOT YOU DON'T KNOW ABOUT ME.

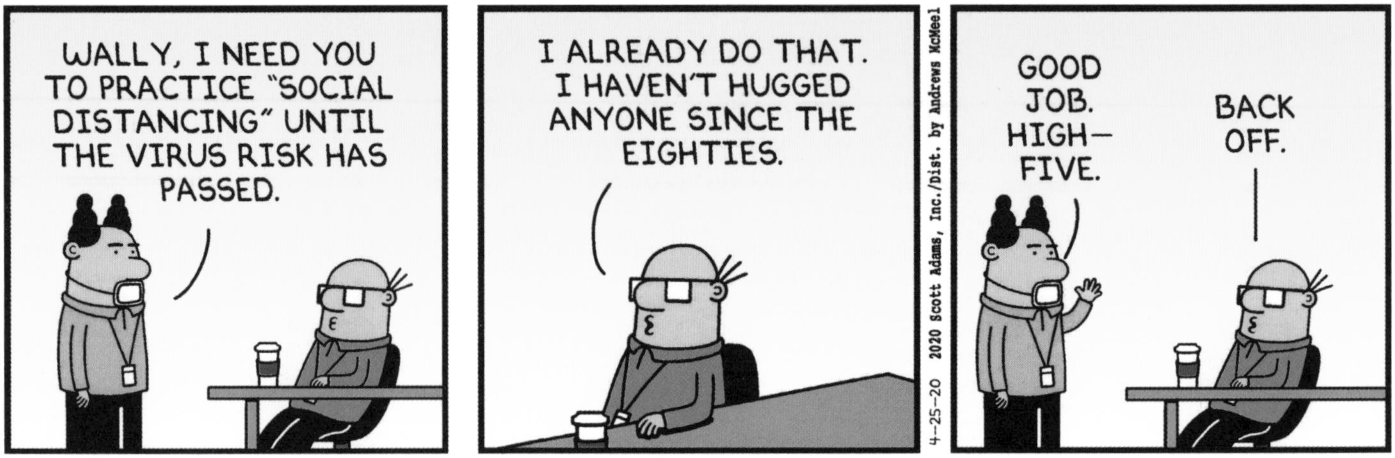
WALLY, I NEED YOU TO PRACTICE "SOCIAL DISTANCING" UNTIL THE VIRUS RISK HAS PASSED.
I ALREADY DO THAT. I HAVEN'T HUGGED ANYONE SINCE THE EIGHTIES.
2020 Scott Adams, Inc./Dist. by Andrews McMeel 4-25-20
GOOD JOB. HIGH-FIVE.
BACK OFF.

I'VE DESIGNED THESE OVER-EAR HEADPHONES FOR MAXIMUM CUSTOMER ANNOYANCE.
THE CHARGING PORT IS ONLY ON ONE SIDE, SO THE USER HAS A FIFTY PERCENT CHANCE OF GUESSING WRONG.
AND THE CHARGER ONLY FITS IF YOU PUT IT IN RIGHT-SIDE UP.
TO INCREASE THE FRUSTRATION, I MADE THE PLUG LOOK THE SAME ON BOTH SIDES.
BEST OF ALL, THE PLUG IS SO POORLY DESIGNED THAT HALF THE TIME IT DOESN'T SEEM TO FIT, EVEN WHEN YOU PUT IT IN CORRECTLY.
I MADE THE HEADPHONES BLACK, SO YOU CAN'T EASILY FIND THE CHARGER HOLE IN LOW LIGHT.
NINETY PERCENT OF USERS WILL BE CURSING US EVERY TIME THEY TRY TO RECHARGE.
CUSTOMERS WON'T KNOW ANY OF THIS UNTIL AFTER THEY PURCHASE.
SHIP IT.
© 2020 Scott Adams, Inc./Dist. by Andrews McMeel
4-26-20

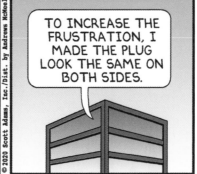

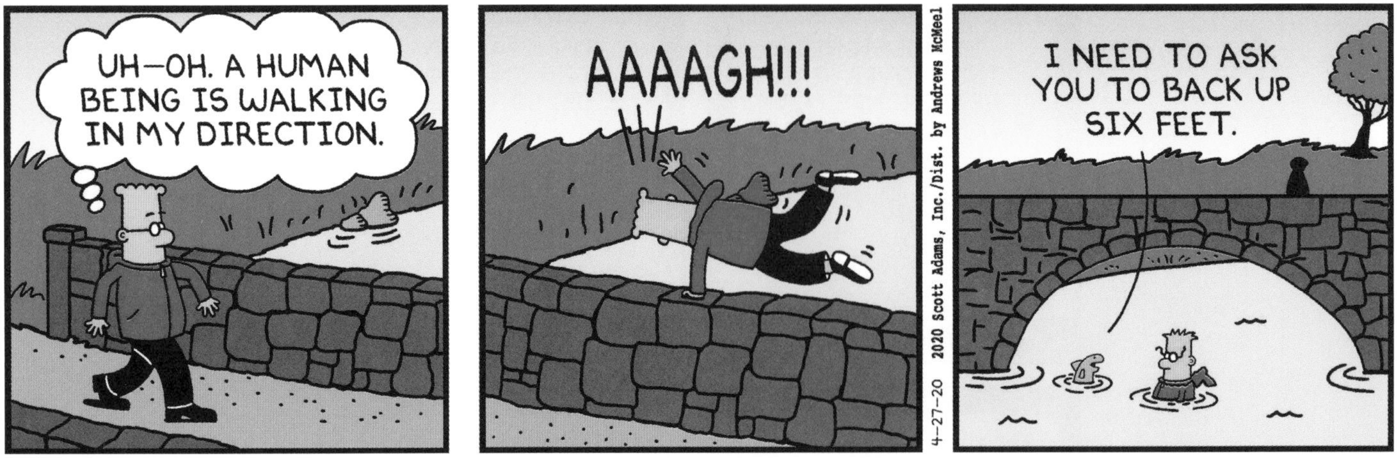
UH—OH. A HUMAN BEING IS WALKING IN MY DIRECTION.
AAAAGH!!!
4-27-20 2020 Scott Adams, Inc./Dist. by Andrews McMeel
I NEED TO ASK YOU TO BACK UP SIX FEET.

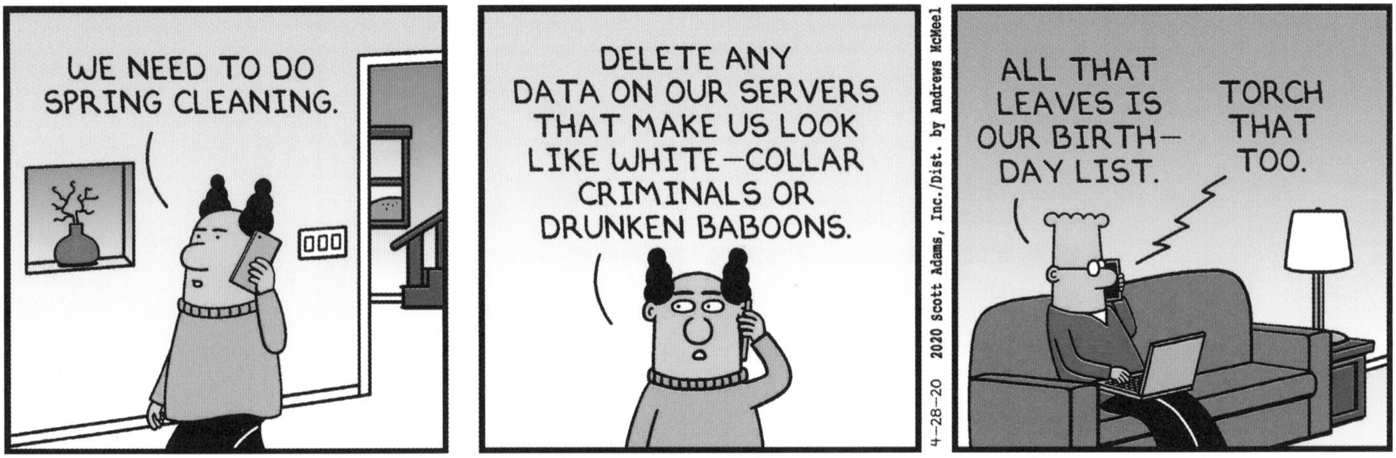
WE NEED TO DO SPRING CLEANING.
DELETE ANY DATA ON OUR SERVERS THAT MAKE US LOOK LIKE WHITE—COLLAR CRIMINALS OR DRUNKEN BABOONS.
4-28-20 2020 Scott Adams, Inc./Dist. by Andrews McMeel
ALL THAT LEAVES IS OUR BIRTH—DAY LIST.
TORCH THAT TOO.

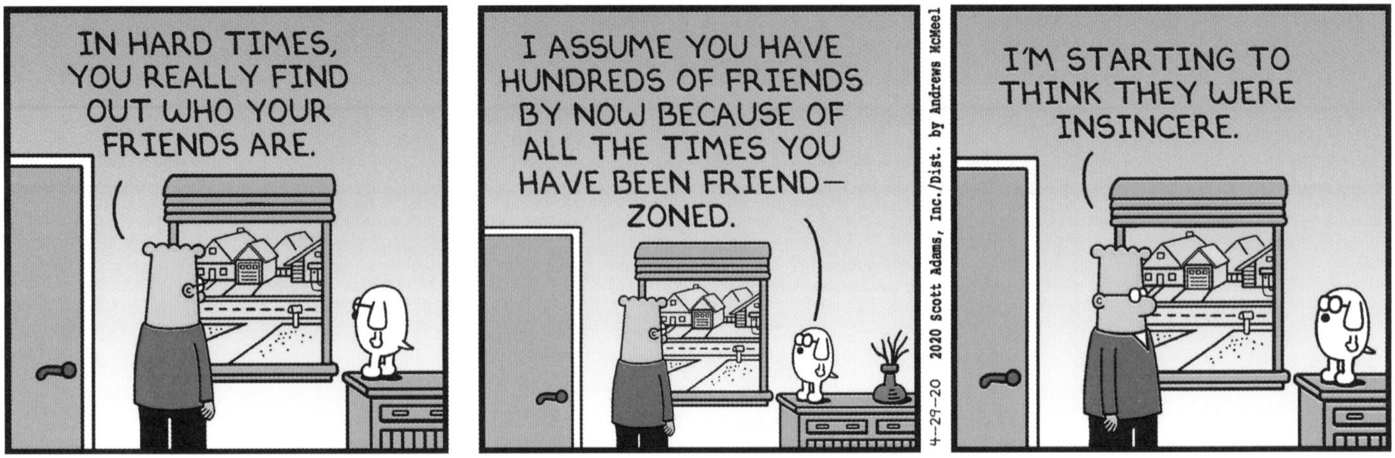
IN HARD TIMES, YOU REALLY FIND OUT WHO YOUR FRIENDS ARE.
I ASSUME YOU HAVE HUNDREDS OF FRIENDS BY NOW BECAUSE OF ALL THE TIMES YOU HAVE BEEN FRIEND—ZONED.
4-29-20 2020 Scott Adams, Inc./Dist. by Andrews McMeel
I'M STARTING TO THINK THEY WERE INSINCERE.

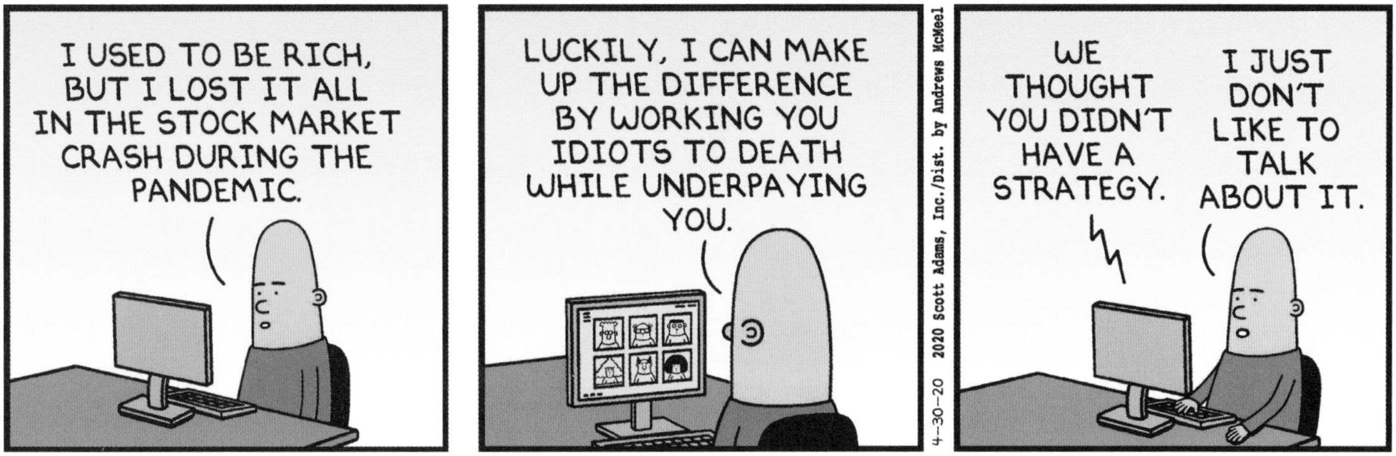
I USED TO BE RICH, BUT I LOST IT ALL IN THE STOCK MARKET CRASH DURING THE PANDEMIC.
LUCKILY, I CAN MAKE UP THE DIFFERENCE BY WORKING YOU IDIOTS TO DEATH WHILE UNDERPAYING YOU.
4-30-20 2020 Scott Adams, Inc./Dist. by Andrews McMeel
WE THOUGHT YOU DIDN'T HAVE A STRATEGY.
I JUST DON'T LIKE TO TALK ABOUT IT.

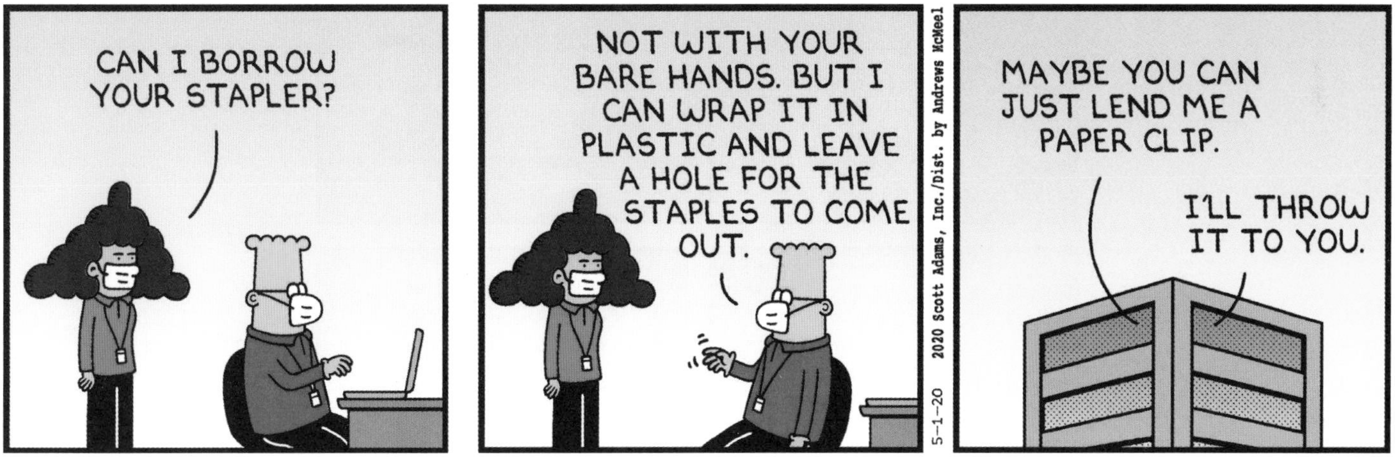
CAN I BORROW YOUR STAPLER?
NOT WITH YOUR BARE HANDS. BUT I CAN WRAP IT IN PLASTIC AND LEAVE A HOLE FOR THE STAPLES TO COME OUT.
5-1-20 2020 Scott Adams, Inc./Dist. by Andrews McMeel
MAYBE YOU CAN JUST LEND ME A PAPER CLIP.
I'LL THROW IT TO YOU.

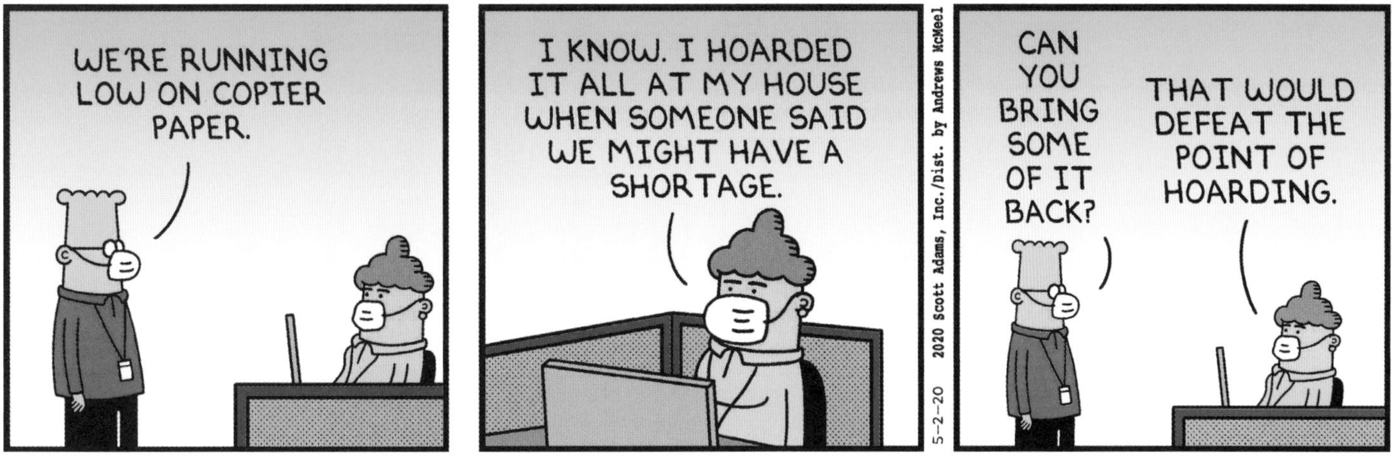
WE'RE RUNNING LOW ON COPIER PAPER.
I KNOW. I HOARDED IT ALL AT MY HOUSE WHEN SOMEONE SAID WE MIGHT HAVE A SHORTAGE.
5-2-20 2020 Scott Adams, Inc./Dist. by Andrews McMeel
CAN YOU BRING SOME OF IT BACK?
THAT WOULD DEFEAT THE POINT OF HOARDING.

YOUR METHOD OF CALCULATING THE SAFETY STATISTICS IS FLAWED.
WOW. WAIT UNTIL I TELL EVERYONE YOU DON'T THINK SAFETY MATTERS.
I. . . DIDN'T SAY THAT. I'M TALKING ABOUT THE WAY YOU MEASURED IT.
IT'S TOO LATE TO WALK IT BACK NOW!
I'M NOT "WALKING IT BACK." I'M CLARIFYING.
THERE'S NOTHING TO CLARIFY. YOU HATE SAFETY.
STOP PUTTING WORDS IN MY MOUTH!!! I'M A BETTER AUTHORITY ON WHAT I THINK THAN YOU ARE!!!
WHAT WAS ALL THAT YELLING ABOUT?
DILBERT THINKS SAFETY DOESN'T MATTER.
© 2020 Scott Adams, Inc./Dist. by Andrews McMeel
5-3-20

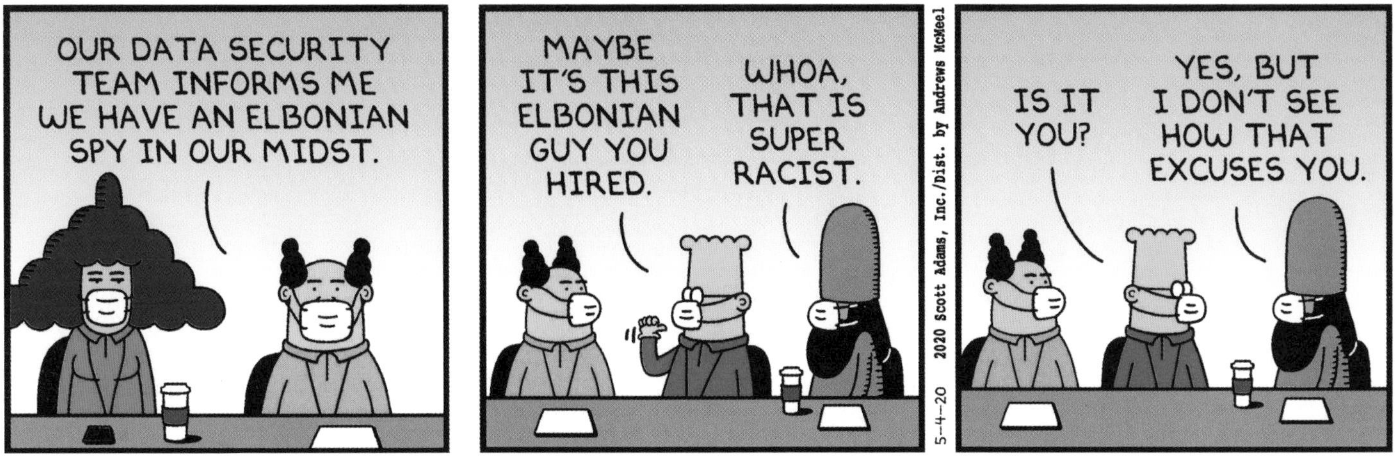
OUR DATA SECURITY TEAM INFORMS ME WE HAVE AN ELBONIAN SPY IN OUR MIDST.
MAYBE IT'S THIS ELBONIAN GUY YOU HIRED.
WHOA, THAT IS SUPER RACIST.
5-4-20 2020 Scott Adams, Inc./Dist. by Andrews McMeel
IS IT YOU?
YES, BUT I DON'T SEE HOW THAT EXCUSES YOU.

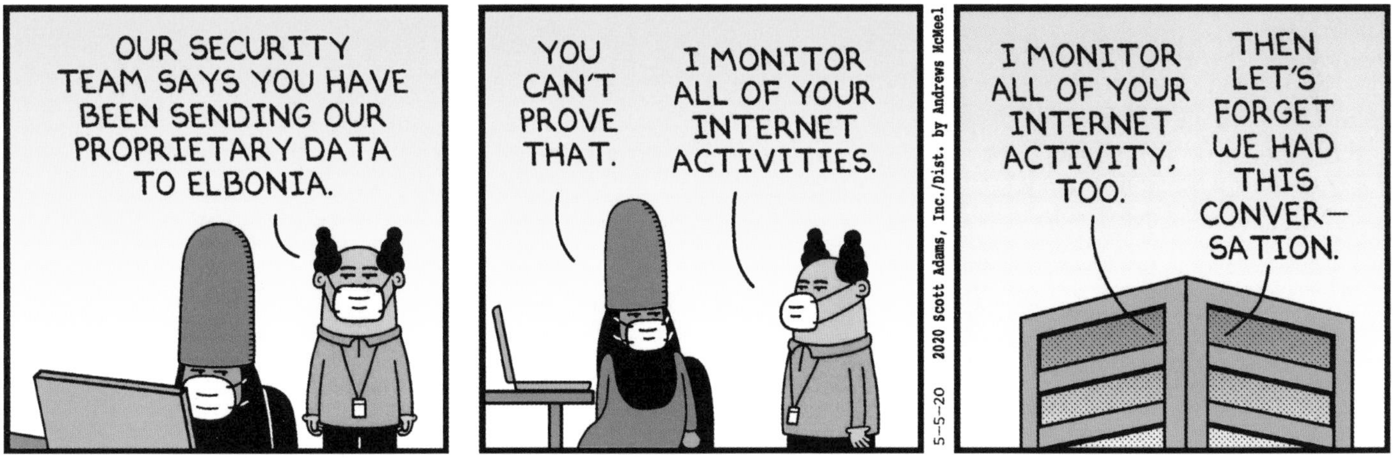
OUR SECURITY TEAM SAYS YOU HAVE BEEN SENDING OUR PROPRIETARY DATA TO ELBONIA.
YOU CAN'T PROVE THAT.
I MONITOR ALL OF YOUR INTERNET ACTIVITIES.
5-5-20 2020 Scott Adams, Inc./Dist. by Andrews McMeel
I MONITOR ALL OF YOUR INTERNET ACTIVITY, TOO.
THEN LET'S FORGET WE HAD THIS CONVER- SATION.

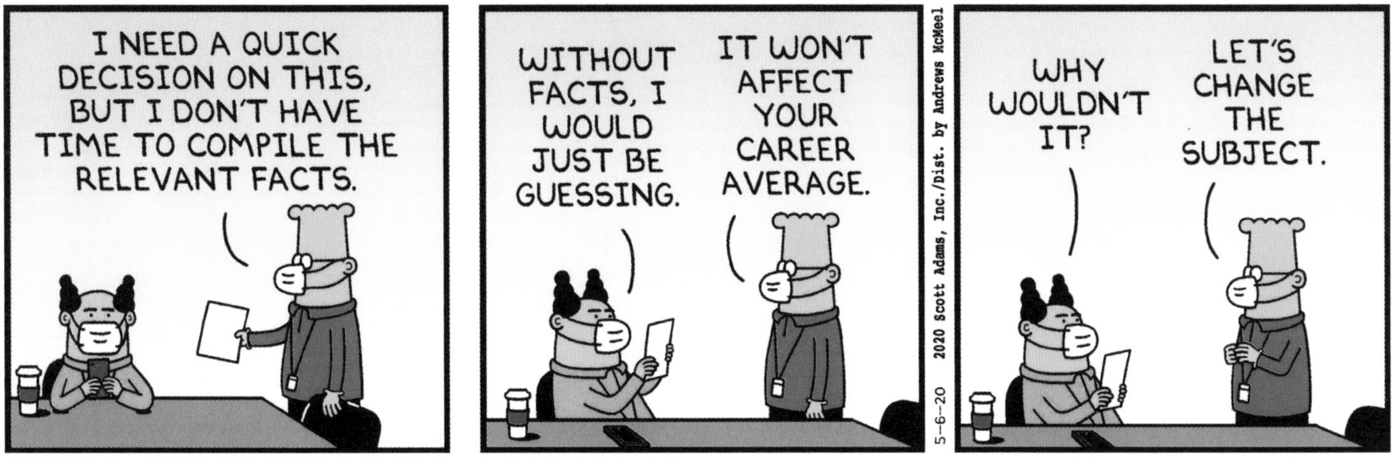
I NEED A QUICK DECISION ON THIS, BUT I DON'T HAVE TIME TO COMPILE THE RELEVANT FACTS.
WITHOUT FACTS, I WOULD JUST BE GUESSING.
IT WON'T AFFECT YOUR CAREER AVERAGE.
5-6-20 2020 Scott Adams, Inc./Dist. by Andrews McMeel
WHY WOULDN'T IT?
LET'S CHANGE THE SUBJECT.

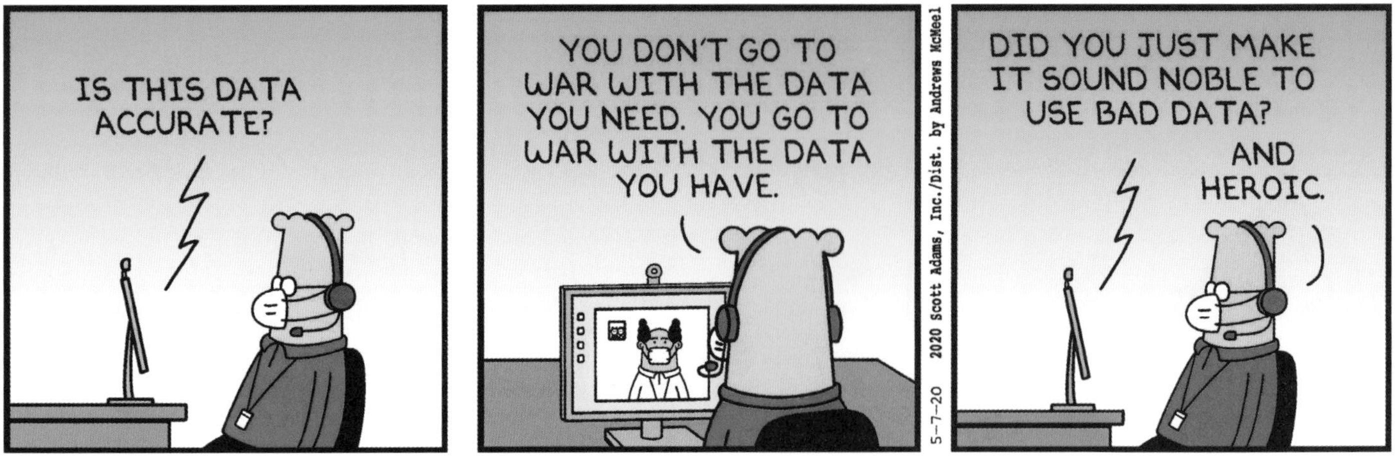
IS THIS DATA ACCURATE?
YOU DON'T GO TO WAR WITH THE DATA YOU NEED. YOU GO TO WAR WITH THE DATA YOU HAVE.
5-7-20 2020 Scott Adams, Inc./Dist. by Andrews McMeel
DID YOU JUST MAKE IT SOUND NOBLE TO USE BAD DATA?
AND HEROIC.

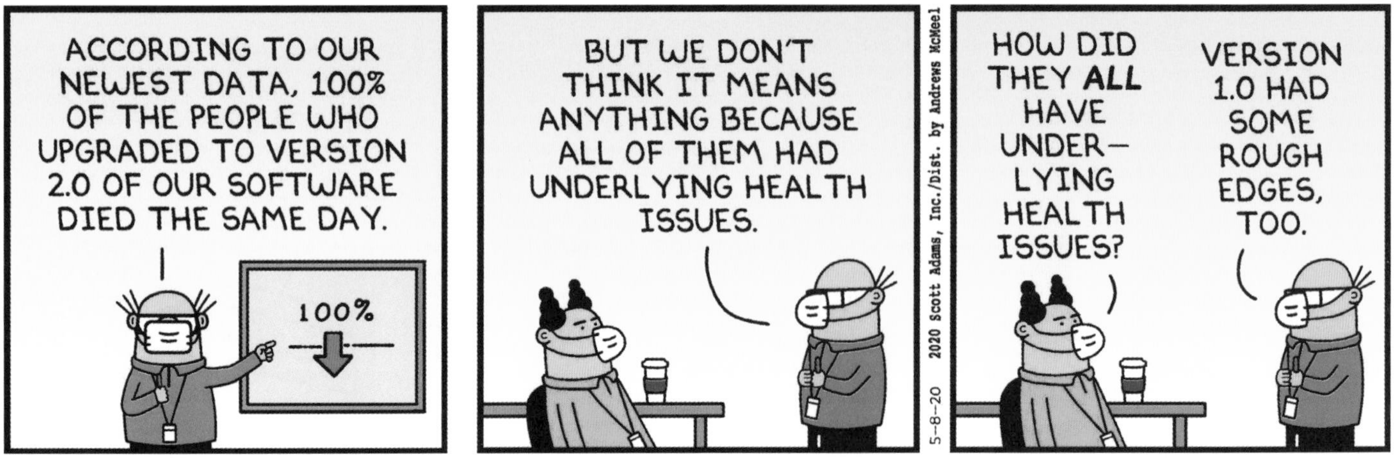
ACCORDING TO OUR NEWEST DATA, 100% OF THE PEOPLE WHO UPGRADED TO VERSION 2.0 OF OUR SOFTWARE DIED THE SAME DAY.
100%
BUT WE DON'T THINK IT MEANS ANYTHING BECAUSE ALL OF THEM HAD UNDERLYING HEALTH ISSUES.
5-8-20 2020 Scott Adams, Inc./Dist. by Andrews McMeel
HOW DID THEY **ALL** HAVE UNDER-LYING HEALTH ISSUES?
VERSION 1.0 HAD SOME ROUGH EDGES, TOO.

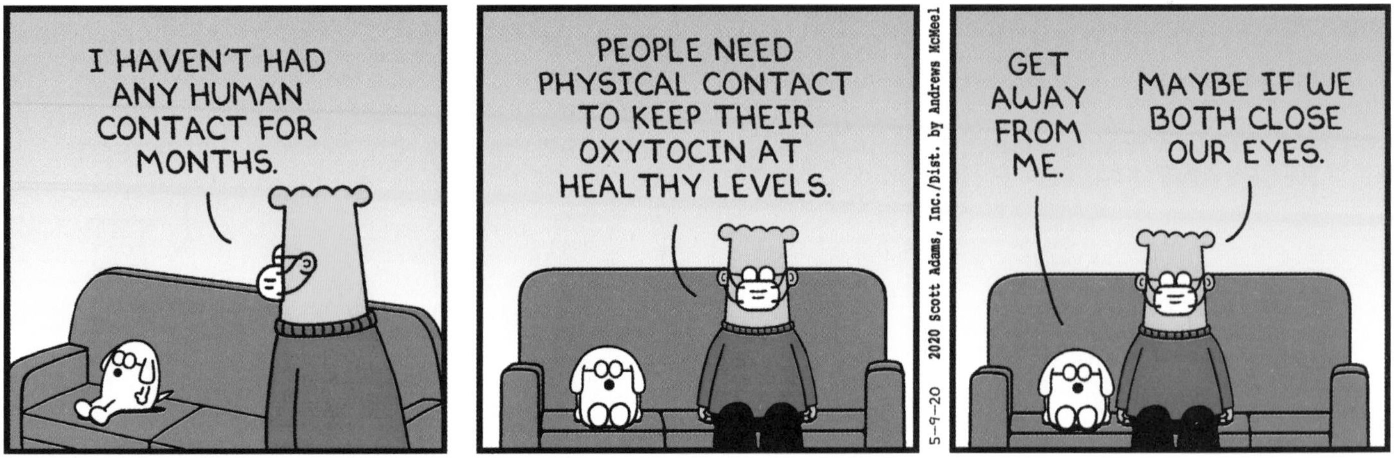
I HAVEN'T HAD ANY HUMAN CONTACT FOR MONTHS.
PEOPLE NEED PHYSICAL CONTACT TO KEEP THEIR OXYTOCIN AT HEALTHY LEVELS.
5-9-20 2020 Scott Adams, Inc./Dist. by Andrews McMeel
GET AWAY FROM ME.
MAYBE IF WE BOTH CLOSE OUR EYES.

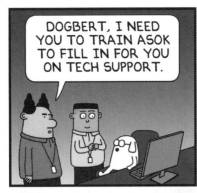

DOGBERT, I NEED YOU TO TRAIN ASOK TO FILL IN FOR YOU ON TECH SUPPORT.
THE GOAL OF TECH SUPPORT IS TO CONVINCE THE CALLER THE PROBLEM IS ON THEIR END.
I DO THIS BY RECOMMENDING INCREASINGLY DIFFICULT THINGS FOR THEM TO TRY.
EVENTUALLY, THEY GIVE UP.
WATCH AND LEARN.
UH-HUH... UH-HUH... TRY REBOOTING YOUR COMPUTER.
NOW TRY IT AGAIN WHILE HOLDING CONTROL-ESCAPE-SPACE BAR-DELETE FOR EXACTLY 27.3 SECONDS.
NO LUCK? TRY LOOKING AT YOUR COMPUTER'S BINARY CODE TO FIND ANY ZEROS AND ONES THAT ARE OUT OF ORDER.
AAAND HE'S GONE.
CLICK
GENIUS!
© 2020 Scott Adams, Inc./Dist. by Andrews McMeel
5-10-20

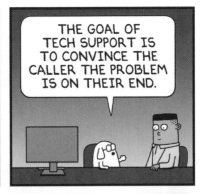

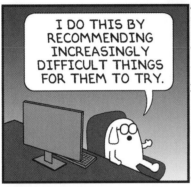

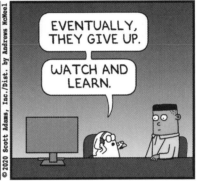

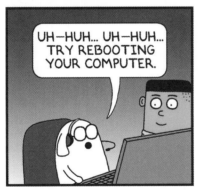

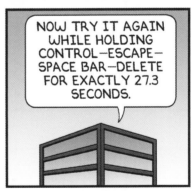

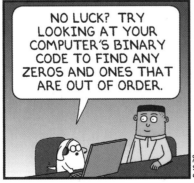

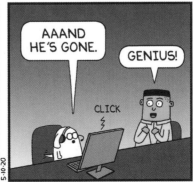

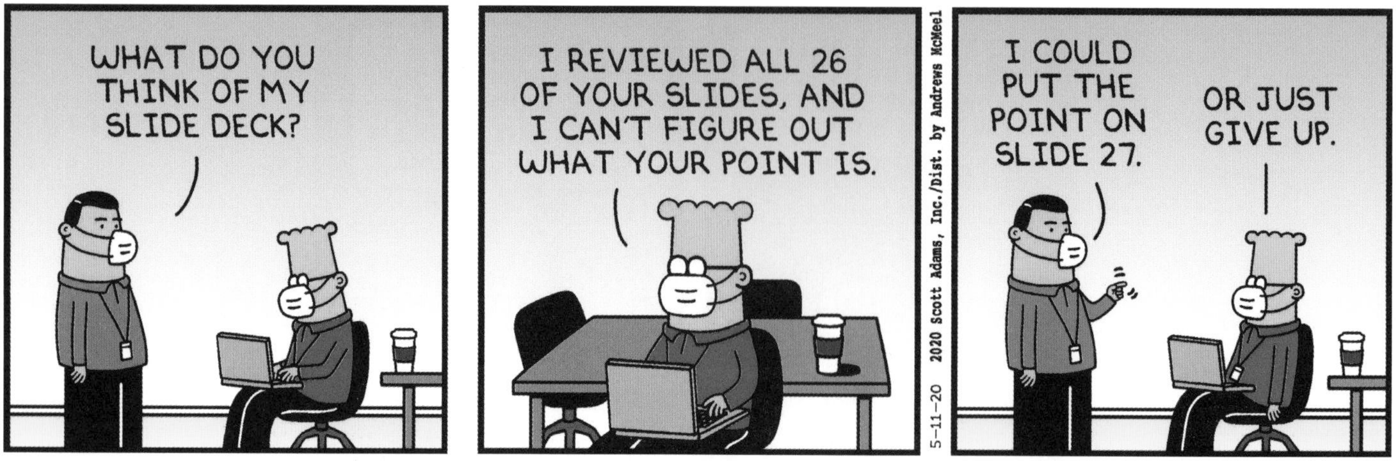
WHAT DO YOU THINK OF MY SLIDE DECK?
I REVIEWED ALL 26 OF YOUR SLIDES, AND I CAN'T FIGURE OUT WHAT YOUR POINT IS.
I COULD PUT THE POINT ON SLIDE 27.
OR JUST GIVE UP.
5-11-20 2020 Scott Adams, Inc./Dist. by Andrews McMeel

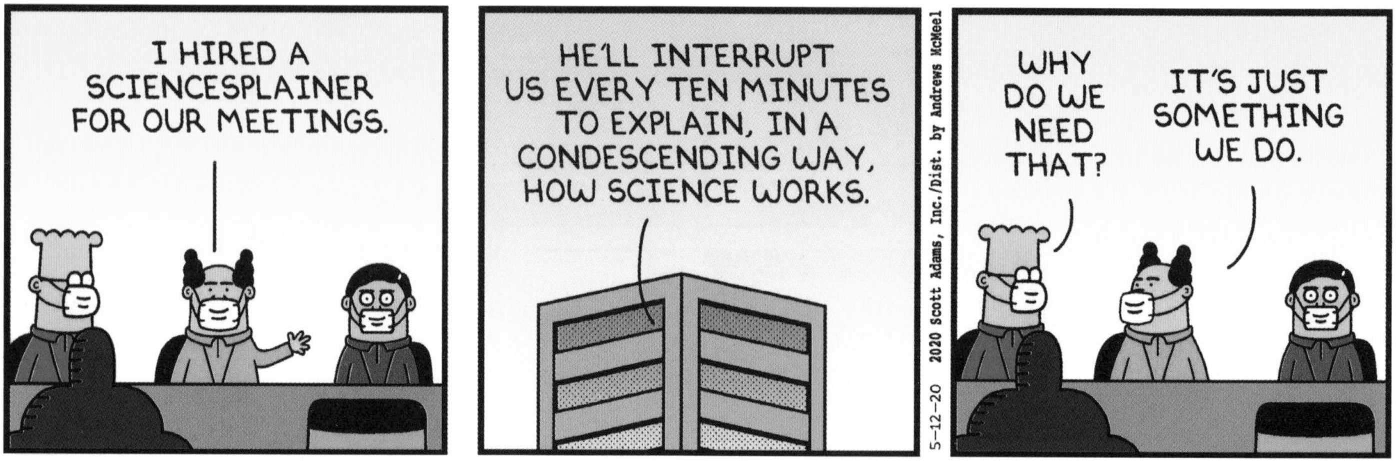
I HIRED A SCIENCESPLAINER FOR OUR MEETINGS.
HE'LL INTERRUPT US EVERY TEN MINUTES TO EXPLAIN, IN A CONDESCENDING WAY, HOW SCIENCE WORKS.
WHY DO WE NEED THAT?
IT'S JUST SOMETHING WE DO.
5-12-20 2020 Scott Adams, Inc./Dist. by Andrews McMeel

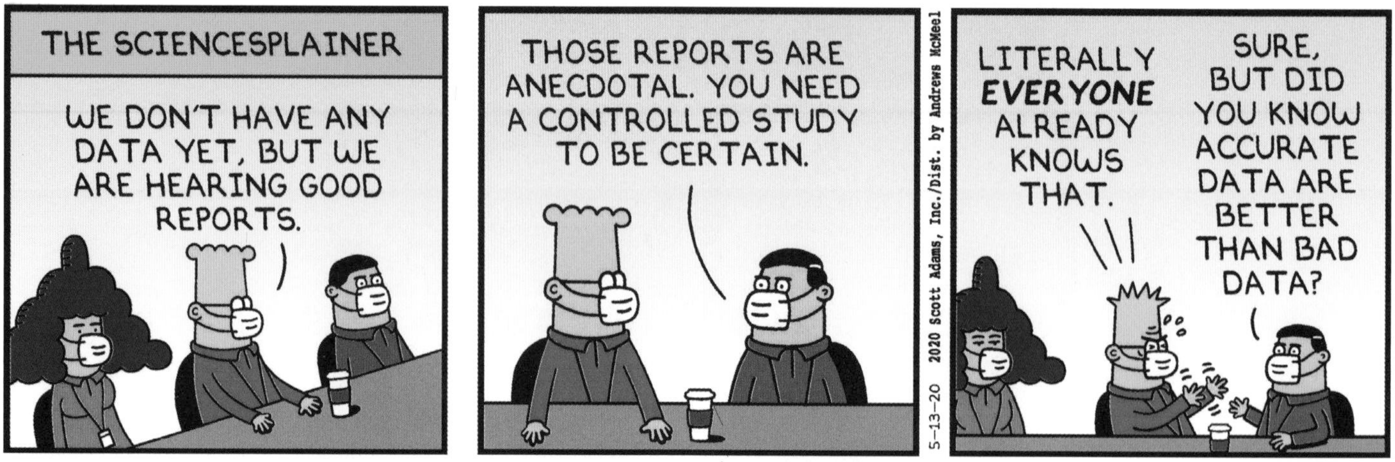
THE SCIENCESPLAINER
WE DON'T HAVE ANY DATA YET, BUT WE ARE HEARING GOOD REPORTS.
THOSE REPORTS ARE ANECDOTAL. YOU NEED A CONTROLLED STUDY TO BE CERTAIN.
LITERALLY EVERYONE ALREADY KNOWS THAT.
SURE, BUT DID YOU KNOW ACCURATE DATA ARE BETTER THAN BAD DATA?
5-13-20 2020 Scott Adams, Inc./Dist. by Andrews McMeel

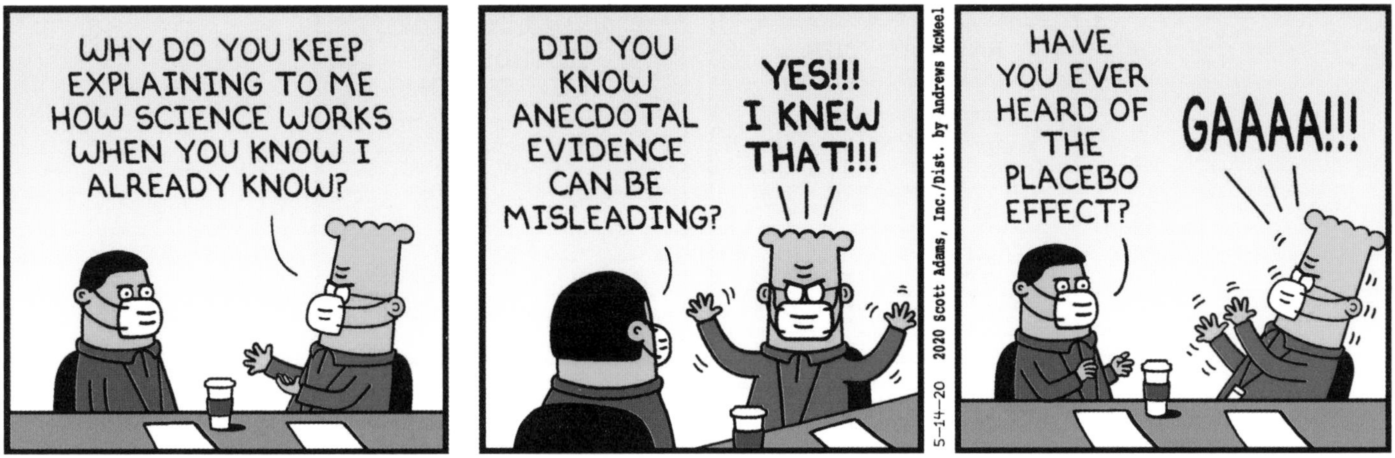
WHY DO YOU KEEP EXPLAINING TO ME HOW SCIENCE WORKS WHEN YOU KNOW I ALREADY KNOW?
DID YOU KNOW ANECDOTAL EVIDENCE CAN BE MISLEADING?
YES!!! I KNEW THAT!!!
5-14-20 2020 Scott Adams, Inc./Dist. by Andrews McMeel
HAVE YOU EVER HEARD OF THE PLACEBO EFFECT?
GAAAA!!!

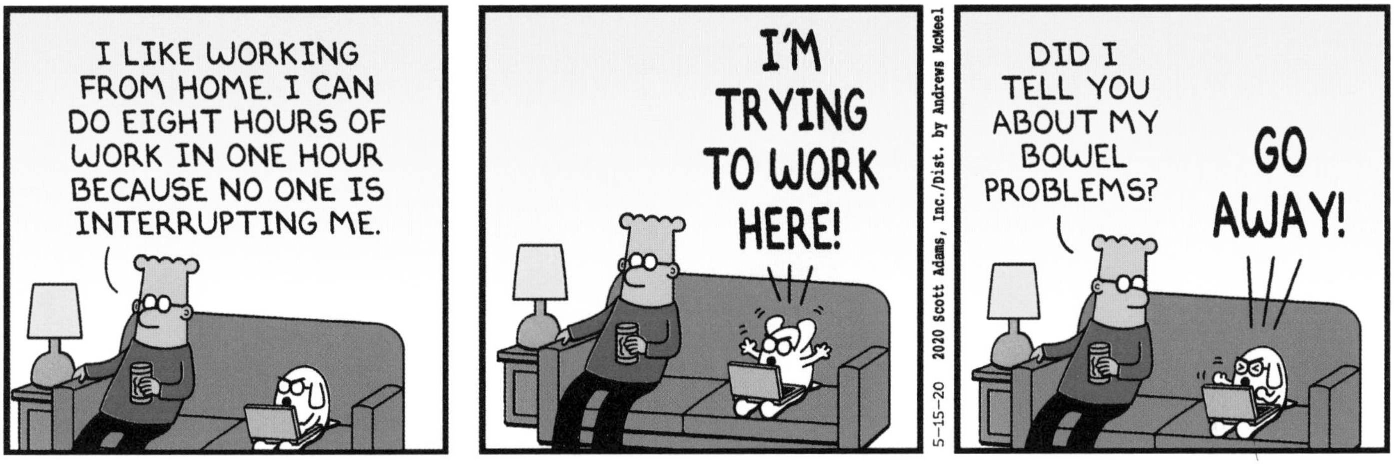
I LIKE WORKING FROM HOME. I CAN DO EIGHT HOURS OF WORK IN ONE HOUR BECAUSE NO ONE IS INTERRUPTING ME.
I'M TRYING TO WORK HERE!
5-15-20 2020 Scott Adams, Inc./Dist. by Andrews McMeel
DID I TELL YOU ABOUT MY BOWEL PROBLEMS?
GO AWAY!

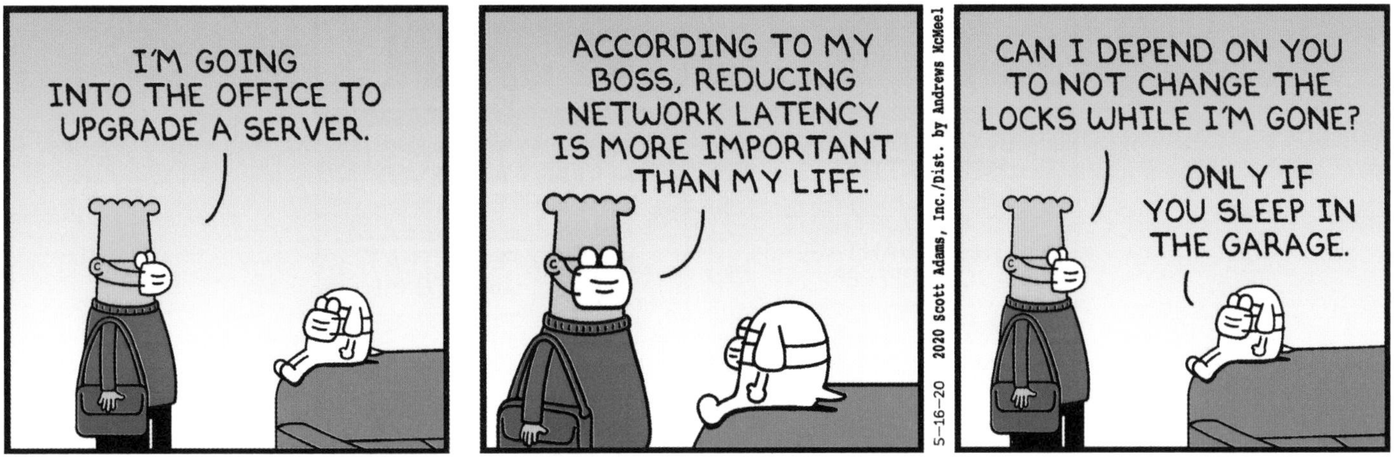
I'M GOING INTO THE OFFICE TO UPGRADE A SERVER.
ACCORDING TO MY BOSS, REDUCING NETWORK LATENCY IS MORE IMPORTANT THAN MY LIFE.
5-16-20 2020 Scott Adams, Inc./Dist. by Andrews McMeel
CAN I DEPEND ON YOU TO NOT CHANGE THE LOCKS WHILE I'M GONE?
ONLY IF YOU SLEEP IN THE GARAGE.

HAVE YOU EVER TRIED MEDITATING?
SOUNDS LIKE A LOT OF WORK.
IT IS THE OPPOSITE OF WORK.
ALL YOU HAVE TO DO IS SIT IN ONE PLACE AND THINK OF NOTHING IN PARTICULAR.
CAN I DRINK COFFEE AT THE SAME TIME?
THAT IS NOT RECOMMENDED.
IN OTHER WORDS, MEDITATING IS WHAT I ALREADY DO, BUT WITHOUT THE ADVANTAGE OF COFFEE?
PERHAPS YOU HAVE ALREADY ACHIEVED ENLIGHTENMENT.
FEELS THAT WAY TO ME.
5-17-20

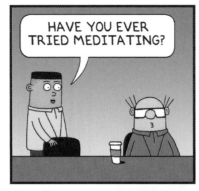

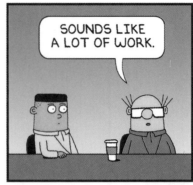

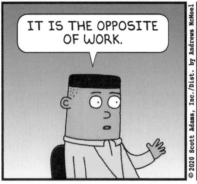

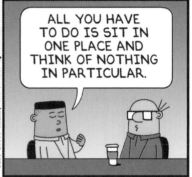

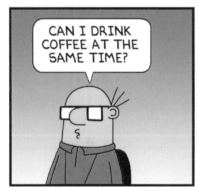

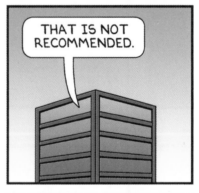

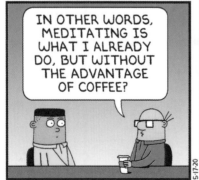

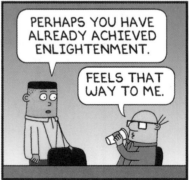

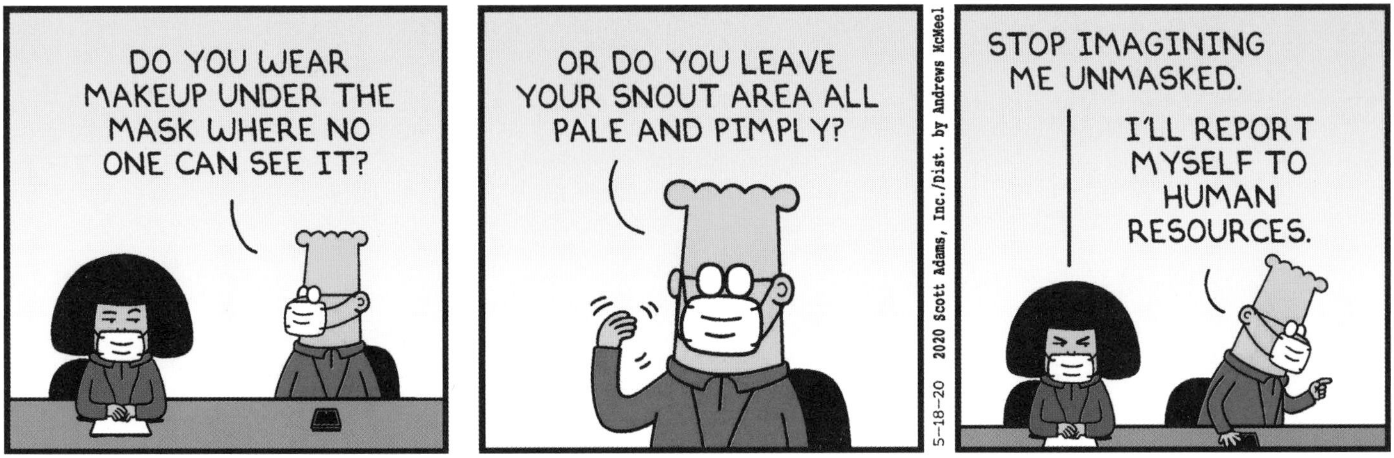
DO YOU WEAR MAKEUP UNDER THE MASK WHERE NO ONE CAN SEE IT?
OR DO YOU LEAVE YOUR SNOUT AREA ALL PALE AND PIMPLY?
5-18-20 2020 Scott Adams, Inc./Dist. by Andrews McMeel
STOP IMAGINING ME UNMASKED.
I'LL REPORT MYSELF TO HUMAN RESOURCES.

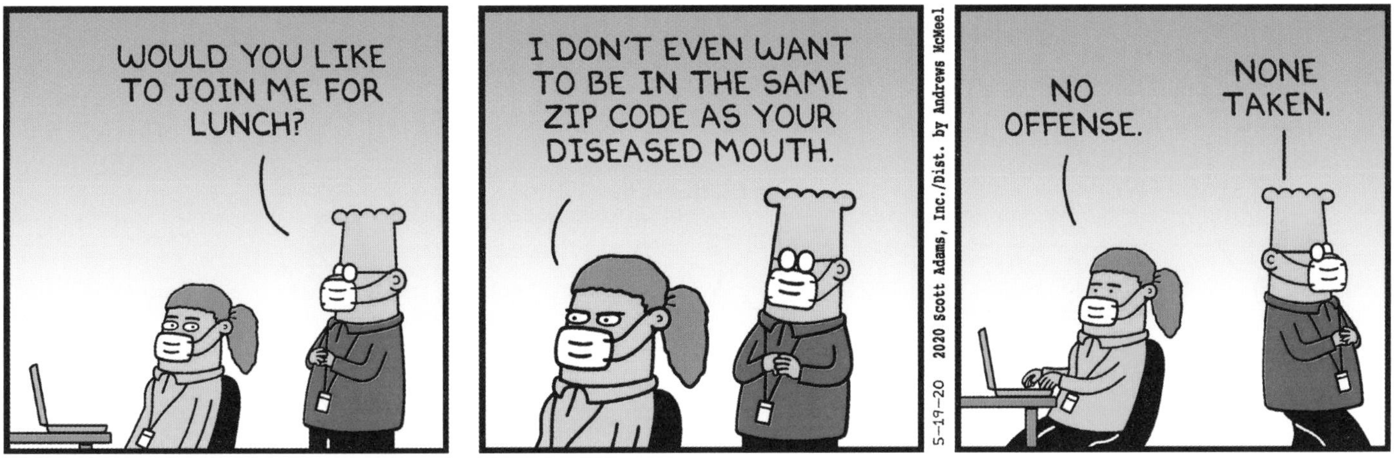
WOULD YOU LIKE TO JOIN ME FOR LUNCH?
I DON'T EVEN WANT TO BE IN THE SAME ZIP CODE AS YOUR DISEASED MOUTH.
5-19-20 2020 Scott Adams, Inc./Dist. by Andrews McMeel
NO OFFENSE.
NONE TAKEN.

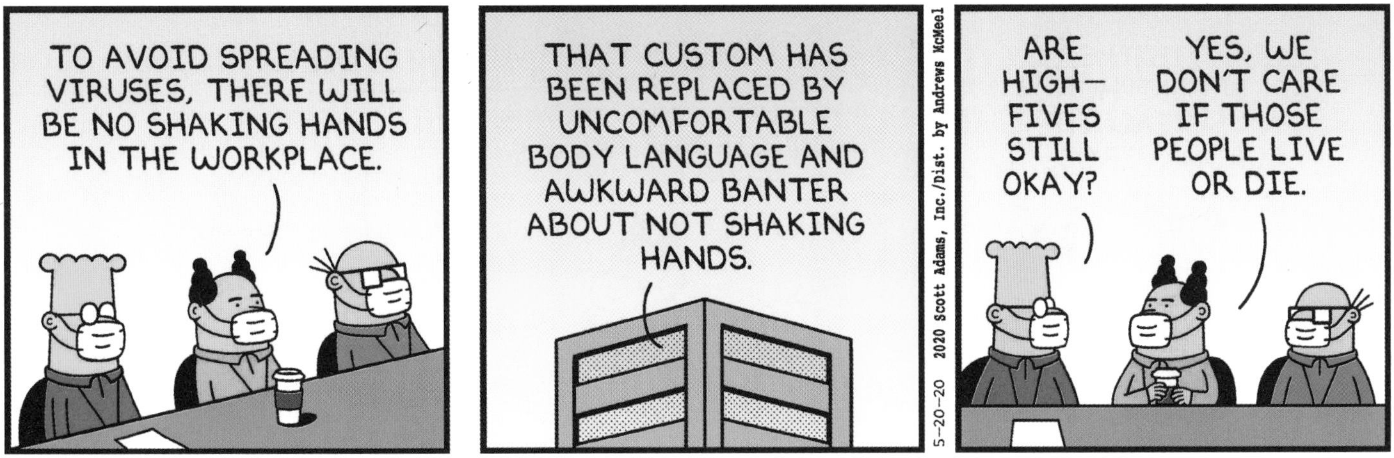
TO AVOID SPREADING VIRUSES, THERE WILL BE NO SHAKING HANDS IN THE WORKPLACE.
THAT CUSTOM HAS BEEN REPLACED BY UNCOMFORTABLE BODY LANGUAGE AND AWKWARD BANTER ABOUT NOT SHAKING HANDS.
5-20-20 2020 Scott Adams, Inc./Dist. by Andrews McMeel
ARE HIGH-FIVES STILL OKAY?
YES, WE DON'T CARE IF THOSE PEOPLE LIVE OR DIE.

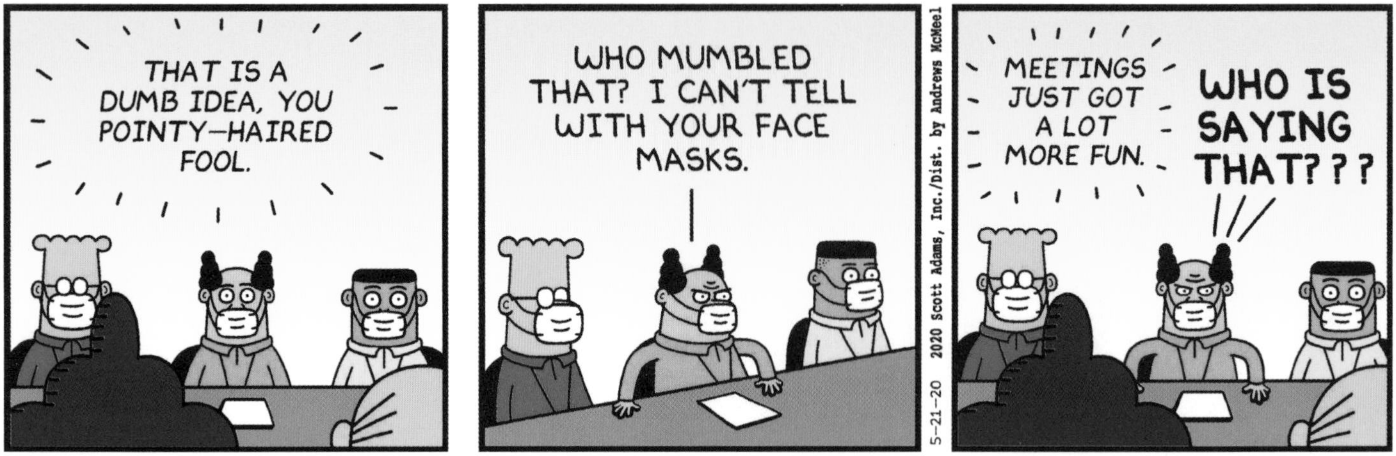
THAT IS A DUMB IDEA, YOU POINTY-HAIRED FOOL.
WHO MUMBLED THAT? I CAN'T TELL WITH YOUR FACE MASKS.
5-21-20 © 2020 Scott Adams, Inc./Dist. by Andrews McMeel
MEETINGS JUST GOT A LOT MORE FUN.
WHO IS SAYING THAT???

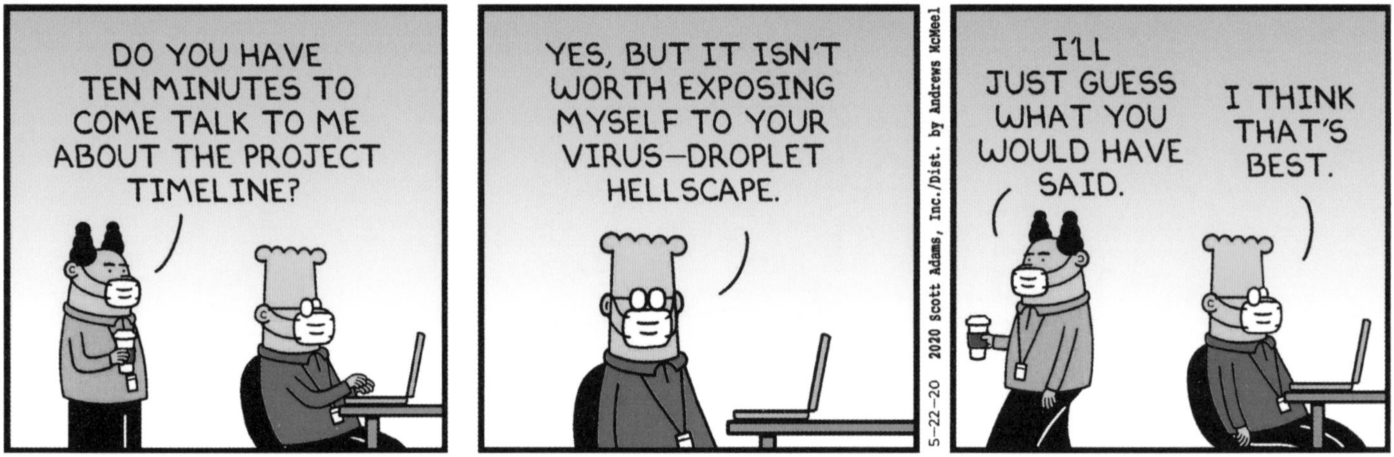
DO YOU HAVE TEN MINUTES TO COME TALK TO ME ABOUT THE PROJECT TIMELINE?
YES, BUT IT ISN'T WORTH EXPOSING MYSELF TO YOUR VIRUS-DROPLET HELLSCAPE.
5-22-20 © 2020 Scott Adams, Inc./Dist. by Andrews McMeel
I'LL JUST GUESS WHAT YOU WOULD HAVE SAID.
I THINK THAT'S BEST.

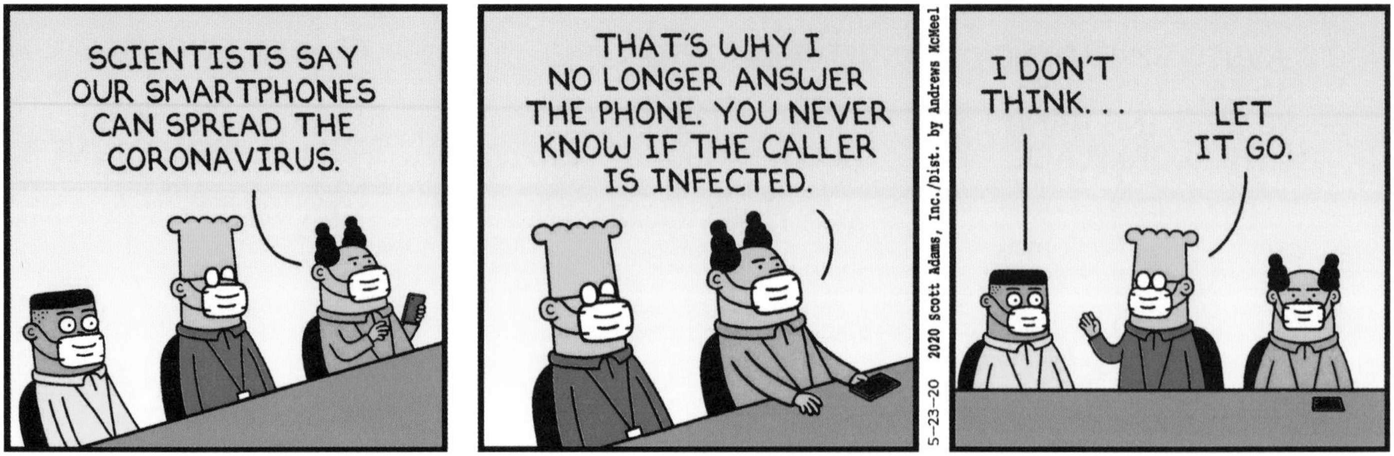
SCIENTISTS SAY OUR SMARTPHONES CAN SPREAD THE CORONAVIRUS.
THAT'S WHY I NO LONGER ANSWER THE PHONE. YOU NEVER KNOW IF THE CALLER IS INFECTED.
5-23-20 © 2020 Scott Adams, Inc./Dist. by Andrews McMeel
I DON'T THINK...
LET IT GO.

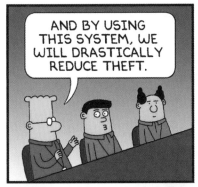

AND BY USING THIS SYSTEM, WE WILL DRASTICALLY REDUCE THEFT.
THAT'S THE DUMBEST THING I HAVE EVER HEARD.
NO ONE CAN STOP THEFT EVERYWHERE IN THE WORLD.
I SAID WE WOULD REDUCE IT, NOT ELIMINATE IT. AND ONLY FOR OUR OWN PRODUCTS.
SO, IN OTHER WORDS, IT WON'T WORK.
IT WORKS TO REDUCE THEFT.
BUT YOU ADMIT THERE WILL STILL BE THEFT.
WHAT IS WRONG WITH YOU????
HEY, I'M NOT THE ONE WHO IS IN FAVOR OF THEFT.
© 2020 Scott Adams, Inc./Dist. by Andrews McMeel
5-24-20

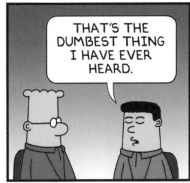

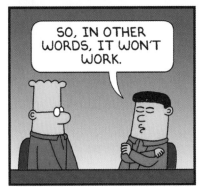

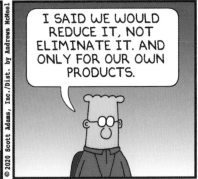

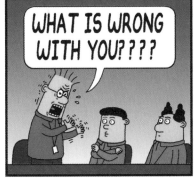

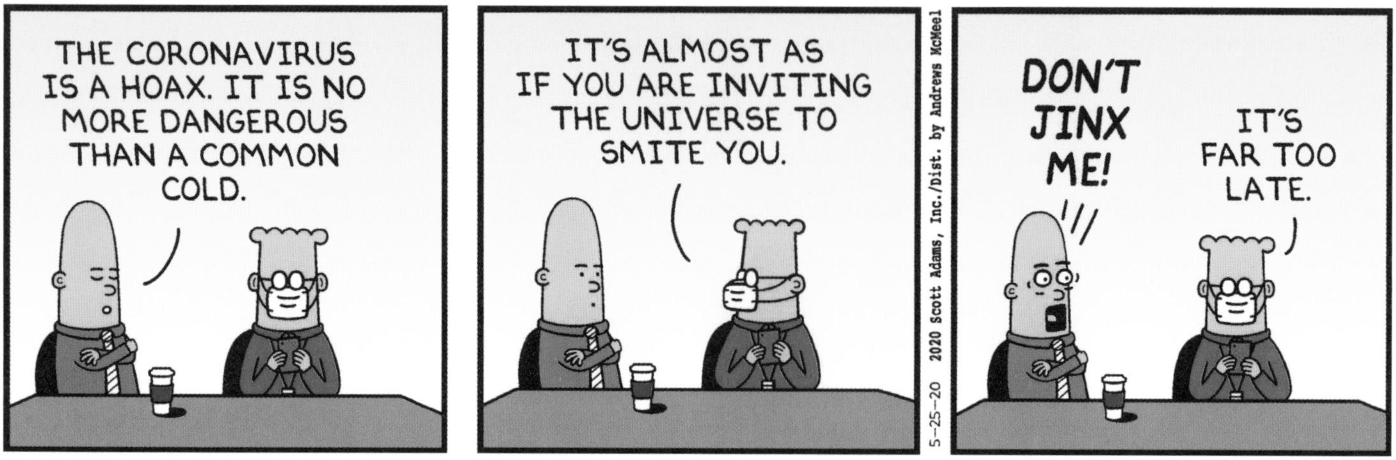
THE CORONAVIRUS IS A HOAX. IT IS NO MORE DANGEROUS THAN A COMMON COLD.
IT'S ALMOST AS IF YOU ARE INVITING THE UNIVERSE TO SMITE YOU.
5-25-20 2020 Scott Adams, Inc./Dist. by Andrews McMeel
DON'T JINX ME!
IT'S FAR TOO LATE.

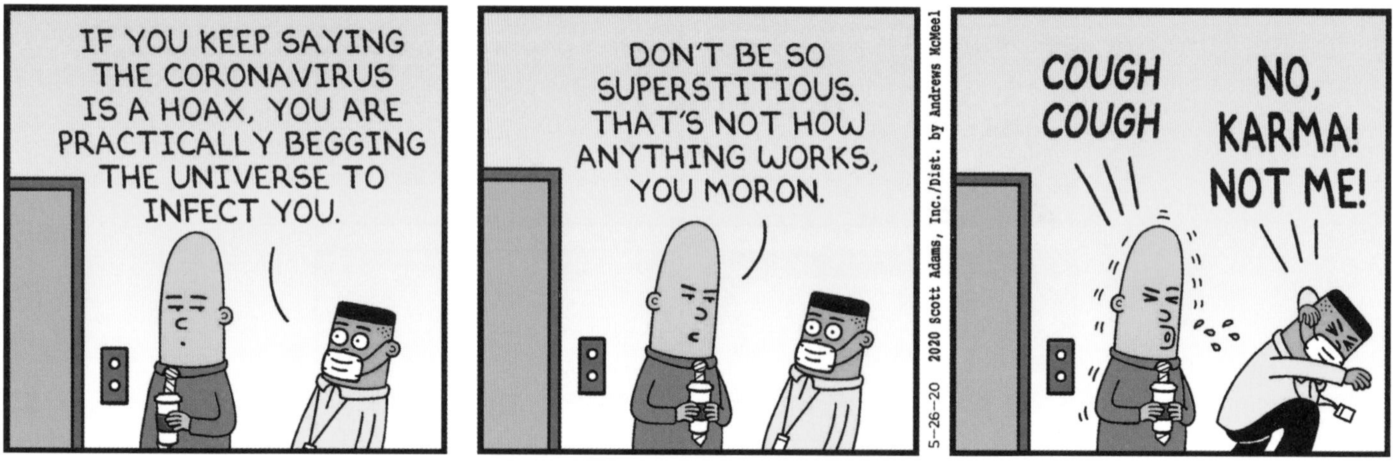
IF YOU KEEP SAYING THE CORONAVIRUS IS A HOAX, YOU ARE PRACTICALLY BEGGING THE UNIVERSE TO INFECT YOU.
DON'T BE SO SUPERSTITIOUS. THAT'S NOT HOW ANYTHING WORKS, YOU MORON.
5-26-20 2020 Scott Adams, Inc./Dist. by Andrews McMeel
COUGH COUGH
NO, KARMA! NOT ME!

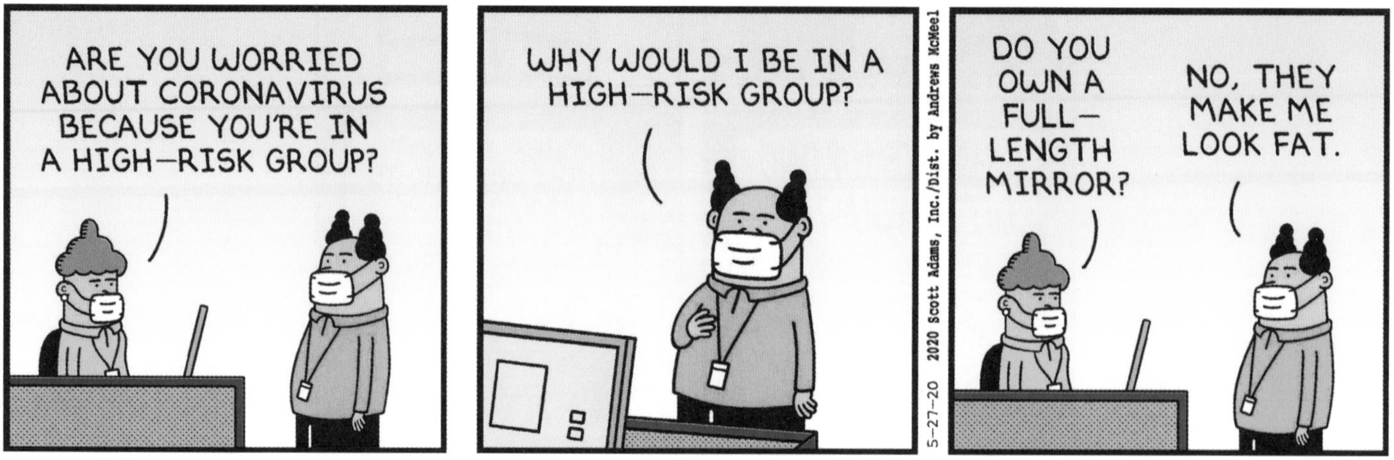
ARE YOU WORRIED ABOUT CORONAVIRUS BECAUSE YOU'RE IN A HIGH-RISK GROUP?
WHY WOULD I BE IN A HIGH-RISK GROUP?
5-27-20 2020 Scott Adams, Inc./Dist. by Andrews McMeel
DO YOU OWN A FULL-LENGTH MIRROR?
NO, THEY MAKE ME LOOK FAT.

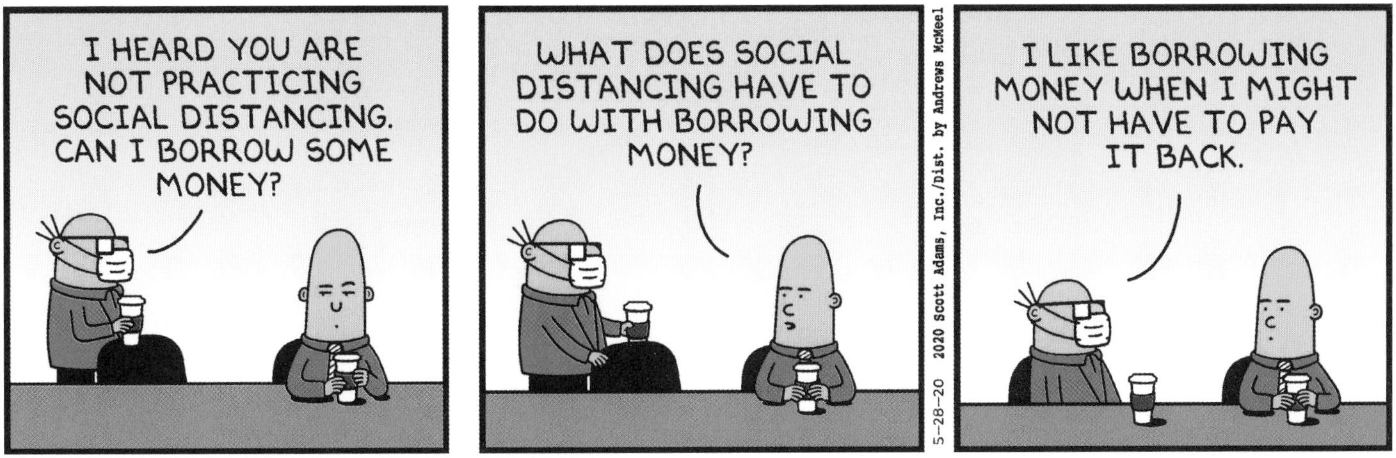
I HEARD YOU ARE NOT PRACTICING SOCIAL DISTANCING. CAN I BORROW SOME MONEY?
WHAT DOES SOCIAL DISTANCING HAVE TO DO WITH BORROWING MONEY?
I LIKE BORROWING MONEY WHEN I MIGHT NOT HAVE TO PAY IT BACK.
5-28-20 © 2020 Scott Adams, Inc./Dist. by Andrews McMeel

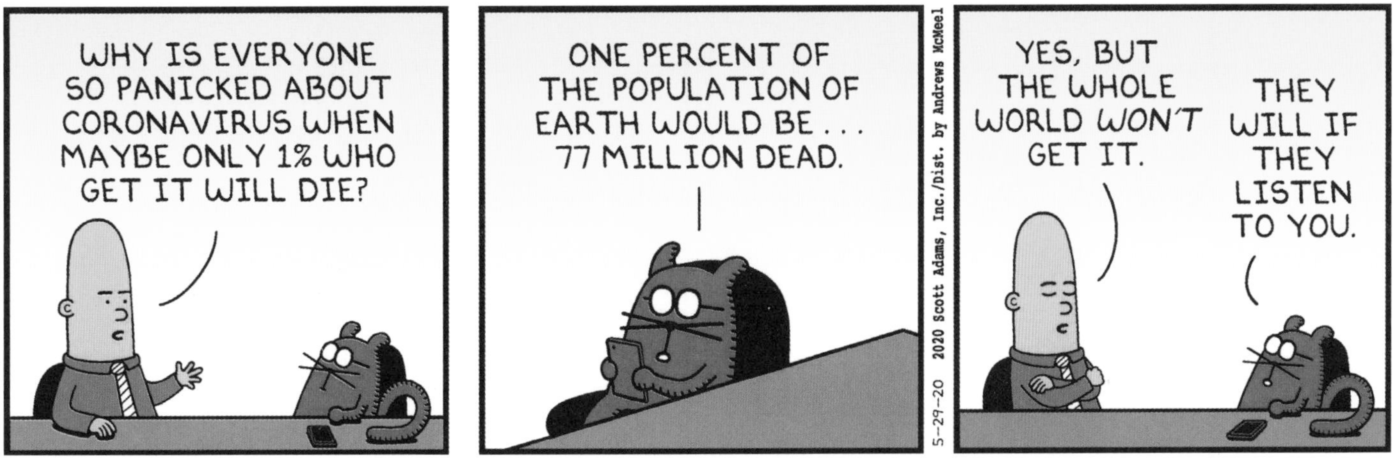
WHY IS EVERYONE SO PANICKED ABOUT CORONAVIRUS WHEN MAYBE ONLY 1% WHO GET IT WILL DIE?
ONE PERCENT OF THE POPULATION OF EARTH WOULD BE . . . 77 MILLION DEAD.
YES, BUT THE WHOLE WORLD *WON'T* GET IT.
THEY WILL IF THEY LISTEN TO YOU.
5-29-20 © 2020 Scott Adams, Inc./Dist. by Andrews McMeel

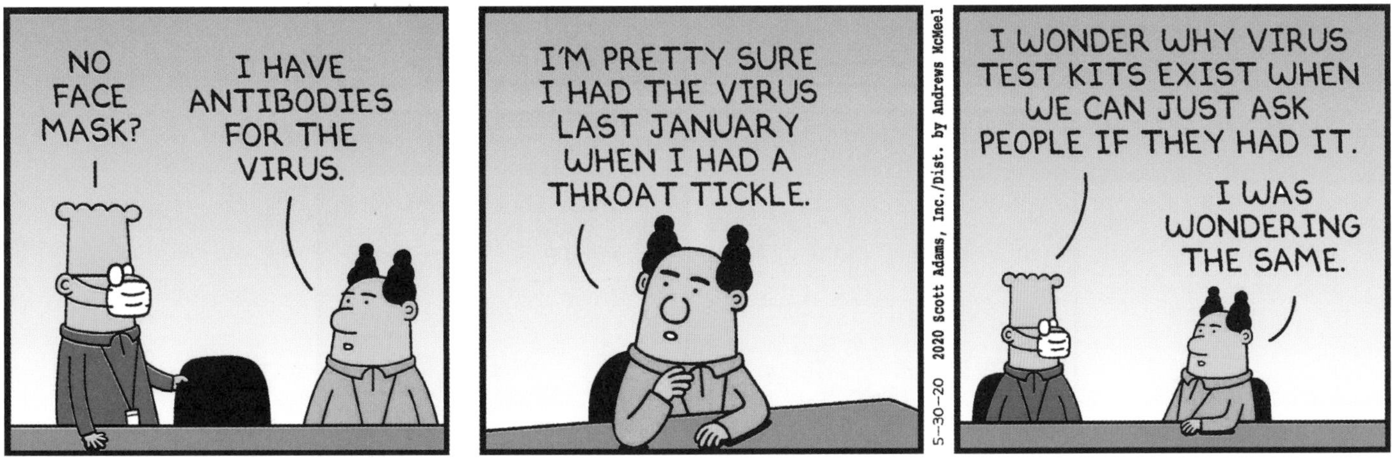
NO FACE MASK?
I HAVE ANTIBODIES FOR THE VIRUS.
I'M PRETTY SURE I HAD THE VIRUS LAST JANUARY WHEN I HAD A THROAT TICKLE.
I WONDER WHY VIRUS TEST KITS EXIST WHEN WE CAN JUST ASK PEOPLE IF THEY HAD IT.
I WAS WONDERING THE SAME.
5-30-20 © 2020 Scott Adams, Inc./Dist. by Andrews McMeel

I'VE HAD NO HUMAN CONTACT FOR MONTHS.
I WASN'T EXPECTING TO ENJOY IT SO MUCH.
MY LOVE LIFE WAS ALREADY A BARREN WASTELAND.
AND AVOIDING MY CO-WORKERS IS ALWAYS GOOD.
I HAVEN'T BEEN STRESSED, TIRED, OR BORED IN WEEKS.
I ONLY HAVE ONE REMAINING SOURCE OF STRESS IN MY LIFE.
I'M PRINTING MONEY IN THE BASE-MENT.
THERE IT IS.
© 2020 Scott Adams, Inc./Dist. by Andrews McMeel
5-31-20

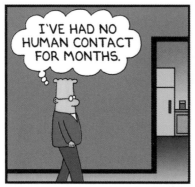

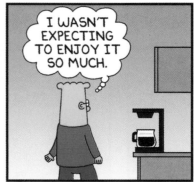

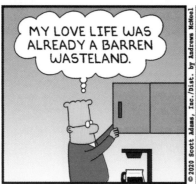

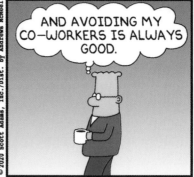

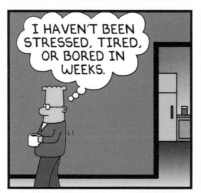

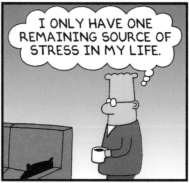

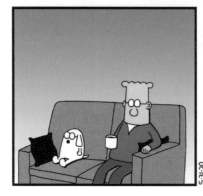

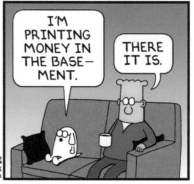

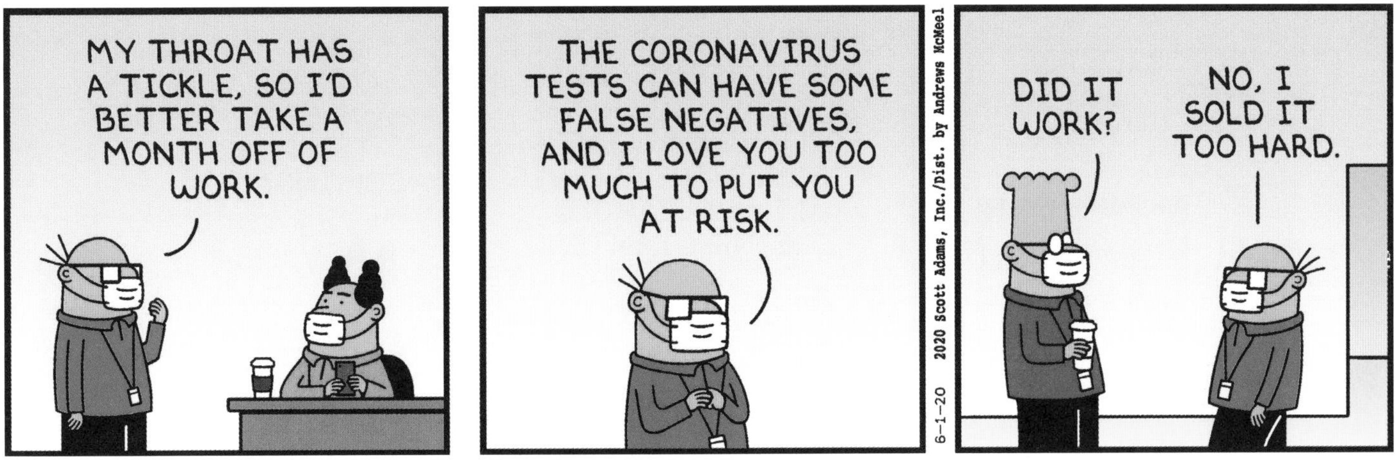
MY THROAT HAS A TICKLE, SO I'D BETTER TAKE A MONTH OFF OF WORK.
THE CORONAVIRUS TESTS CAN HAVE SOME FALSE NEGATIVES, AND I LOVE YOU TOO MUCH TO PUT YOU AT RISK.
6-1-20 2020 Scott Adams, Inc./Dist. by Andrews McMeel
DID IT WORK?
NO, I SOLD IT TOO HARD.

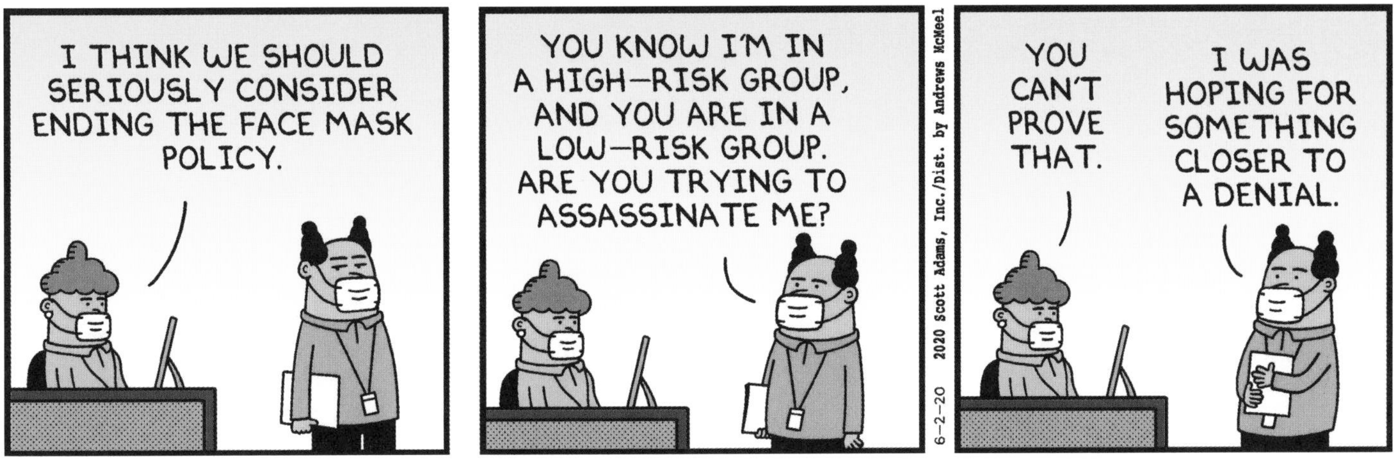
I THINK WE SHOULD SERIOUSLY CONSIDER ENDING THE FACE MASK POLICY.
YOU KNOW I'M IN A HIGH–RISK GROUP, AND YOU ARE IN A LOW–RISK GROUP. ARE YOU TRYING TO ASSASSINATE ME?
6-2-20 2020 Scott Adams, Inc./Dist. by Andrews McMeel
YOU CAN'T PROVE THAT.
I WAS HOPING FOR SOMETHING CLOSER TO A DENIAL.

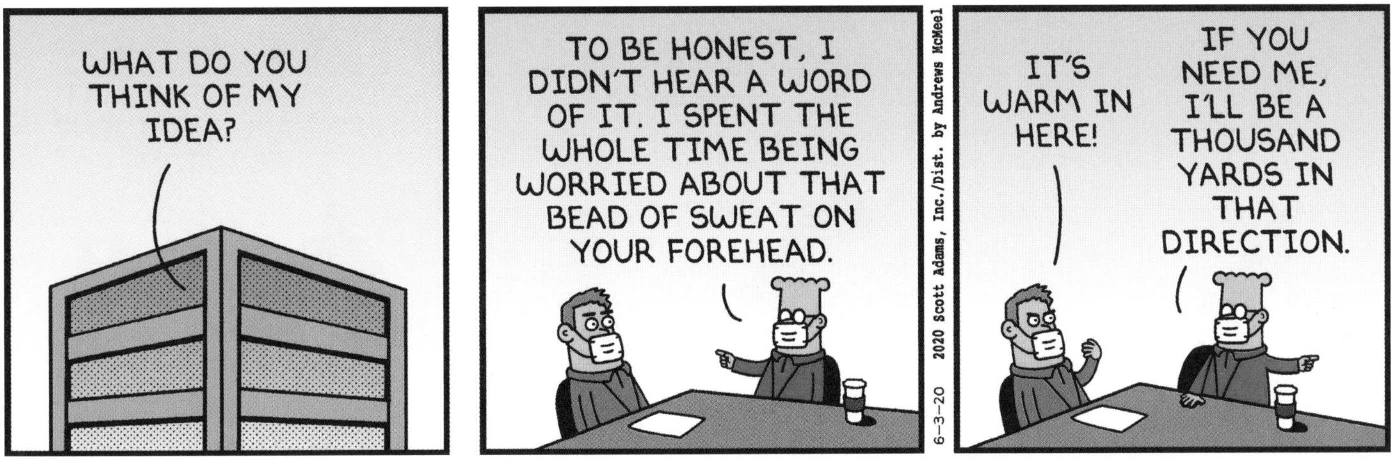
WHAT DO YOU THINK OF MY IDEA?
TO BE HONEST, I DIDN'T HEAR A WORD OF IT. I SPENT THE WHOLE TIME BEING WORRIED ABOUT THAT BEAD OF SWEAT ON YOUR FOREHEAD.
6-3-20 2020 Scott Adams, Inc./Dist. by Andrews McMeel
IT'S WARM IN HERE!
IF YOU NEED ME, I'LL BE A THOUSAND YARDS IN THAT DIRECTION.

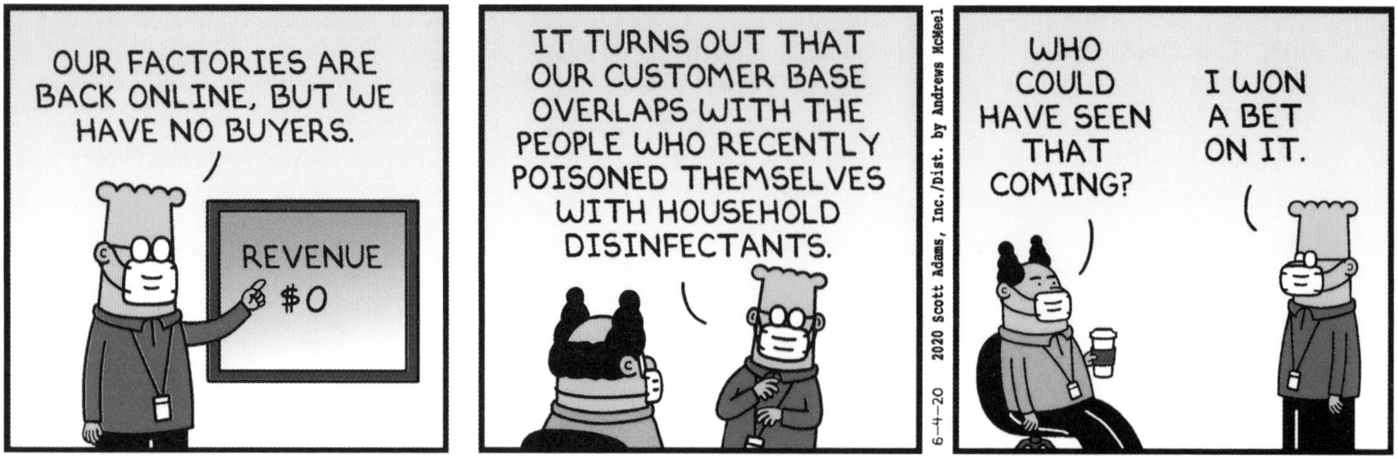
OUR FACTORIES ARE BACK ONLINE, BUT WE HAVE NO BUYERS.
REVENUE $0
IT TURNS OUT THAT OUR CUSTOMER BASE OVERLAPS WITH THE PEOPLE WHO RECENTLY POISONED THEMSELVES WITH HOUSEHOLD DISINFECTANTS.
WHO COULD HAVE SEEN THAT COMING?
I WON A BET ON IT.
6-4-20 © 2020 Scott Adams, Inc./Dist. by Andrews McMeel

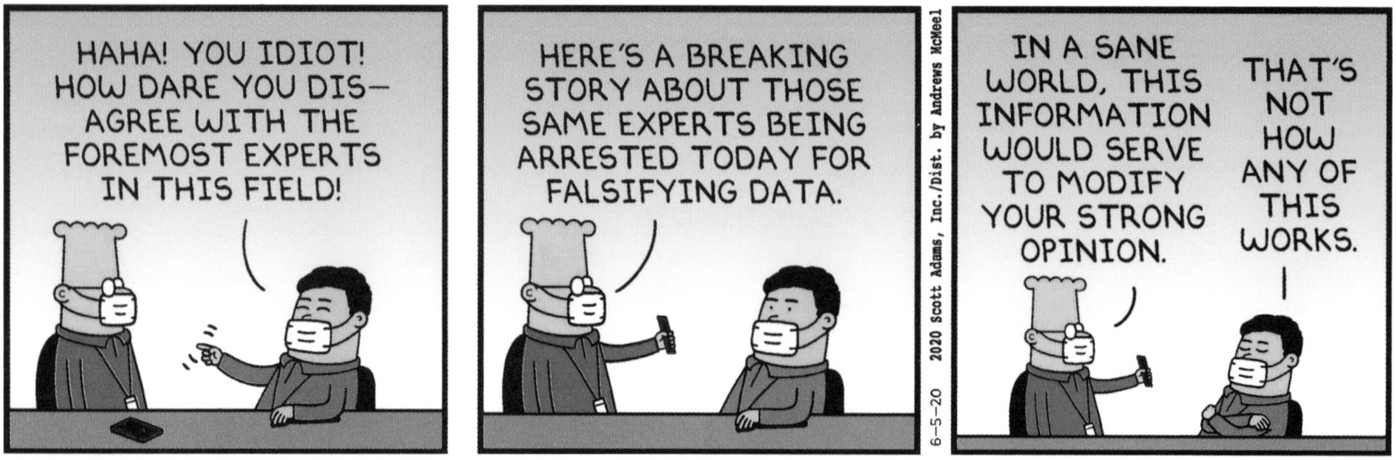
HAHA! YOU IDIOT! HOW DARE YOU DIS-AGREE WITH THE FOREMOST EXPERTS IN THIS FIELD!
HERE'S A BREAKING STORY ABOUT THOSE SAME EXPERTS BEING ARRESTED TODAY FOR FALSIFYING DATA.
IN A SANE WORLD, THIS INFORMATION WOULD SERVE TO MODIFY YOUR STRONG OPINION.
THAT'S NOT HOW ANY OF THIS WORKS.
6-5-20 © 2020 Scott Adams, Inc./Dist. by Andrews McMeel

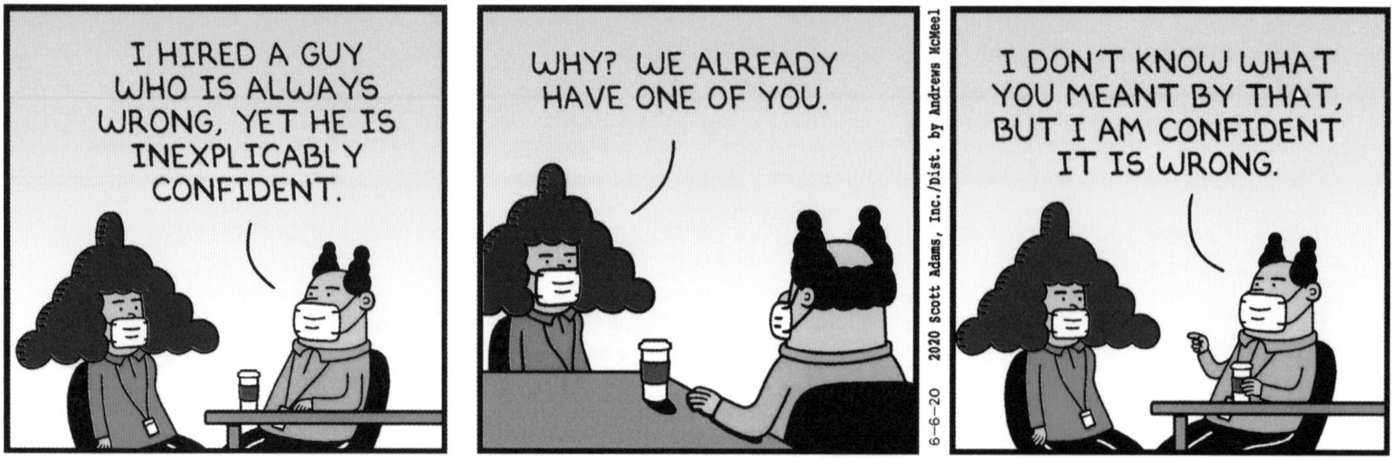
I HIRED A GUY WHO IS ALWAYS WRONG, YET HE IS INEXPLICABLY CONFIDENT.
WHY? WE ALREADY HAVE ONE OF YOU.
I DON'T KNOW WHAT YOU MEANT BY THAT, BUT I AM CONFIDENT IT IS WRONG.
6-6-20 © 2020 Scott Adams, Inc./Dist. by Andrews McMeel

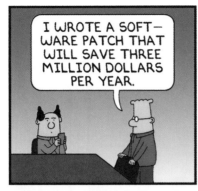

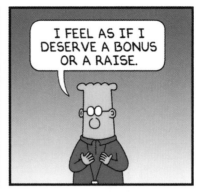

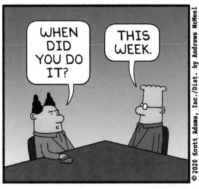

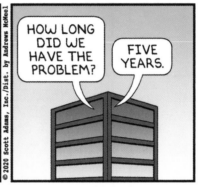

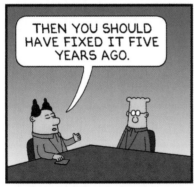

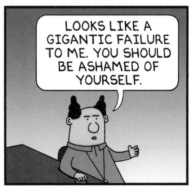

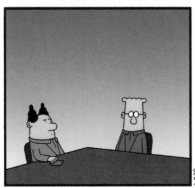

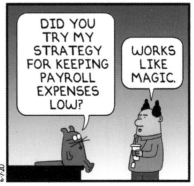

I WROTE A SOFT-WARE PATCH THAT WILL SAVE THREE MILLION DOLLARS PER YEAR.
I FEEL AS IF I DESERVE A BONUS OR A RAISE.
WHEN DID YOU DO IT?
THIS WEEK.
HOW LONG DID WE HAVE THE PROBLEM?
FIVE YEARS.
THEN YOU SHOULD HAVE FIXED IT FIVE YEARS AGO.
LOOKS LIKE A GIGANTIC FAILURE TO ME. YOU SHOULD BE ASHAMED OF YOURSELF.
DID YOU TRY MY STRATEGY FOR KEEPING PAYROLL EXPENSES LOW?
WORKS LIKE MAGIC.
6-7-20

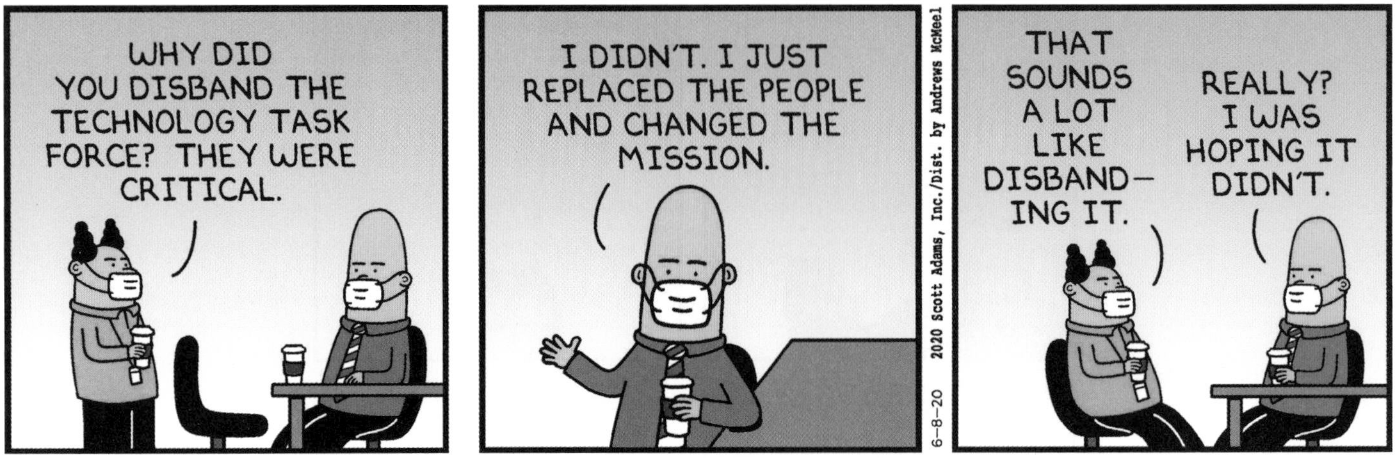
WHY DID YOU DISBAND THE TECHNOLOGY TASK FORCE? THEY WERE CRITICAL.
I DIDN'T. I JUST REPLACED THE PEOPLE AND CHANGED THE MISSION.
THAT SOUNDS A LOT LIKE DISBAND-ING IT.
REALLY? I WAS HOPING IT DIDN'T.


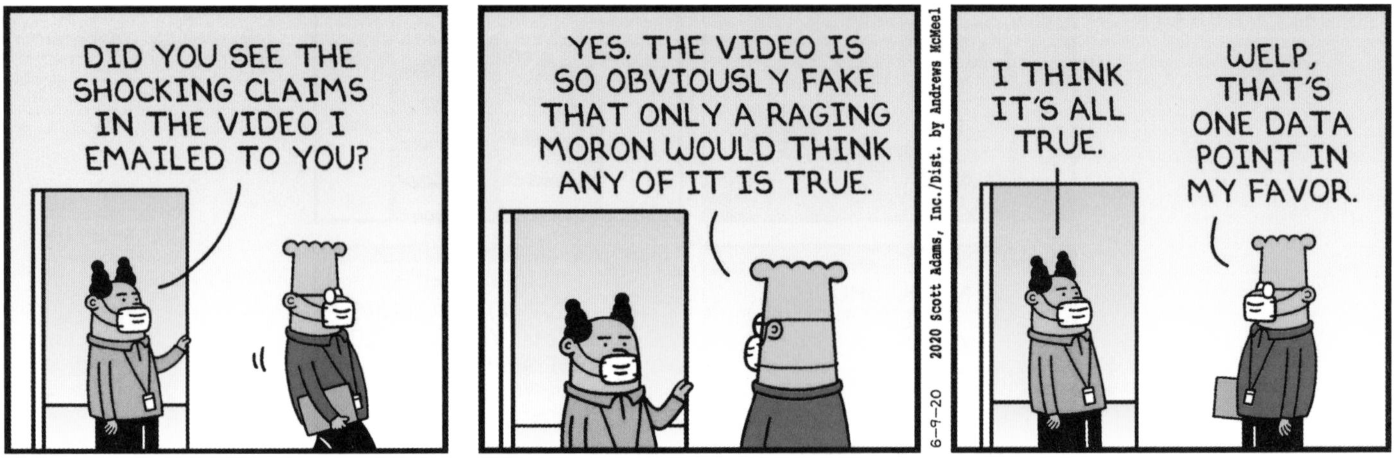
DID YOU SEE THE SHOCKING CLAIMS IN THE VIDEO I EMAILED TO YOU?
YES. THE VIDEO IS SO OBVIOUSLY FAKE THAT ONLY A RAGING MORON WOULD THINK ANY OF IT IS TRUE.
I THINK IT'S ALL TRUE.
WELP, THAT'S ONE DATA POINT IN MY FAVOR.


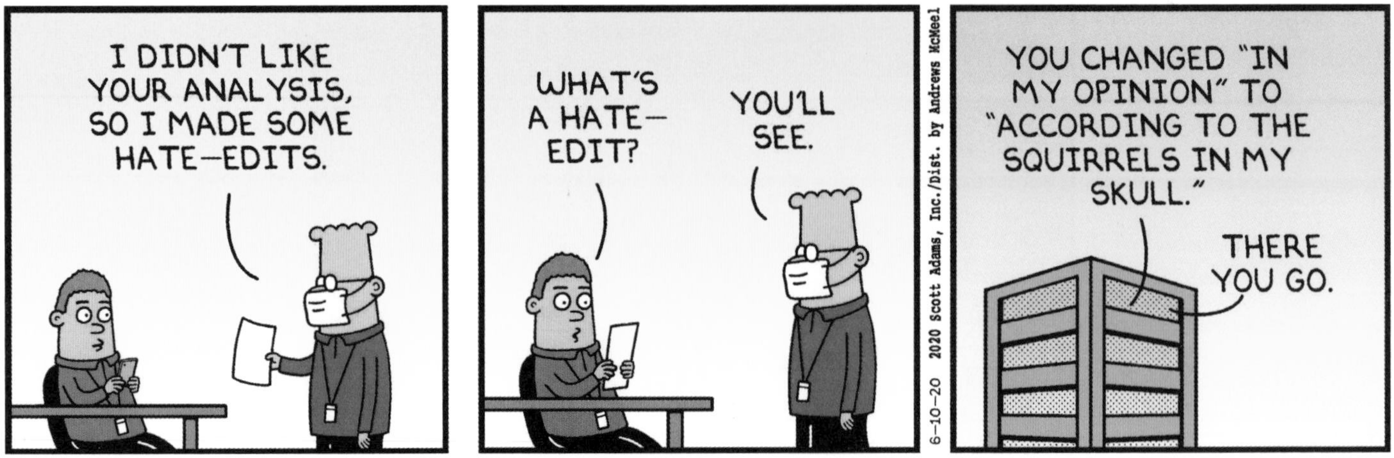
I DIDN'T LIKE YOUR ANALYSIS, SO I MADE SOME HATE-EDITS.
WHAT'S A HATE-EDIT?
YOU'LL SEE.
YOU CHANGED "IN MY OPINION" TO "ACCORDING TO THE SQUIRRELS IN MY SKULL."
THERE YOU GO.

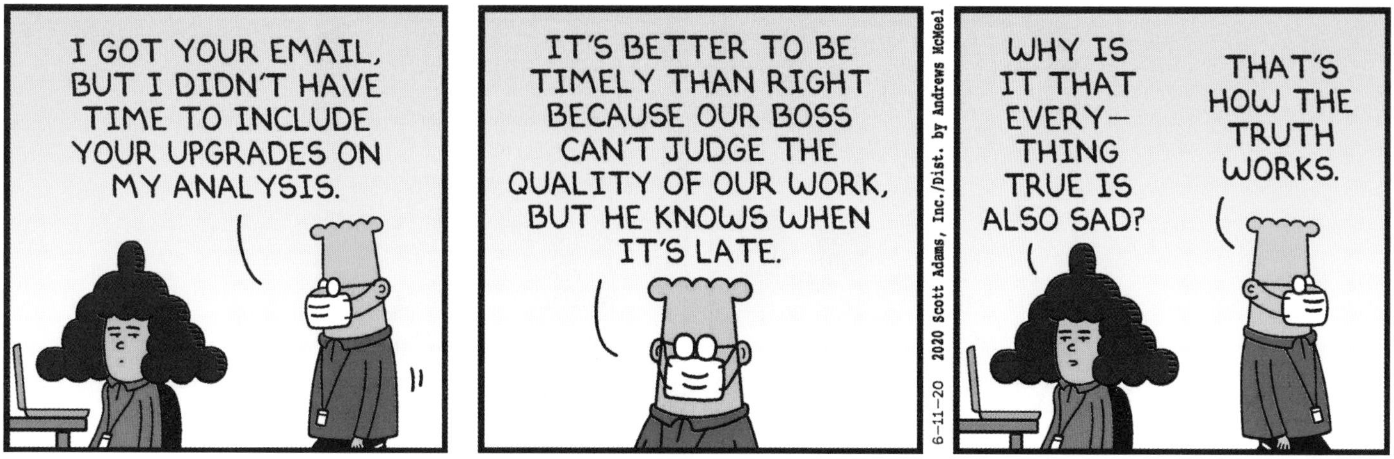
I GOT YOUR EMAIL, BUT I DIDN'T HAVE TIME TO INCLUDE YOUR UPGRADES ON MY ANALYSIS.
IT'S BETTER TO BE TIMELY THAN RIGHT BECAUSE OUR BOSS CAN'T JUDGE THE QUALITY OF OUR WORK, BUT HE KNOWS WHEN IT'S LATE.
6-11-20 2020 Scott Adams, Inc./Dist. by Andrews McMeel
WHY IS IT THAT EVERY-THING TRUE IS ALSO SAD?
THAT'S HOW THE TRUTH WORKS.

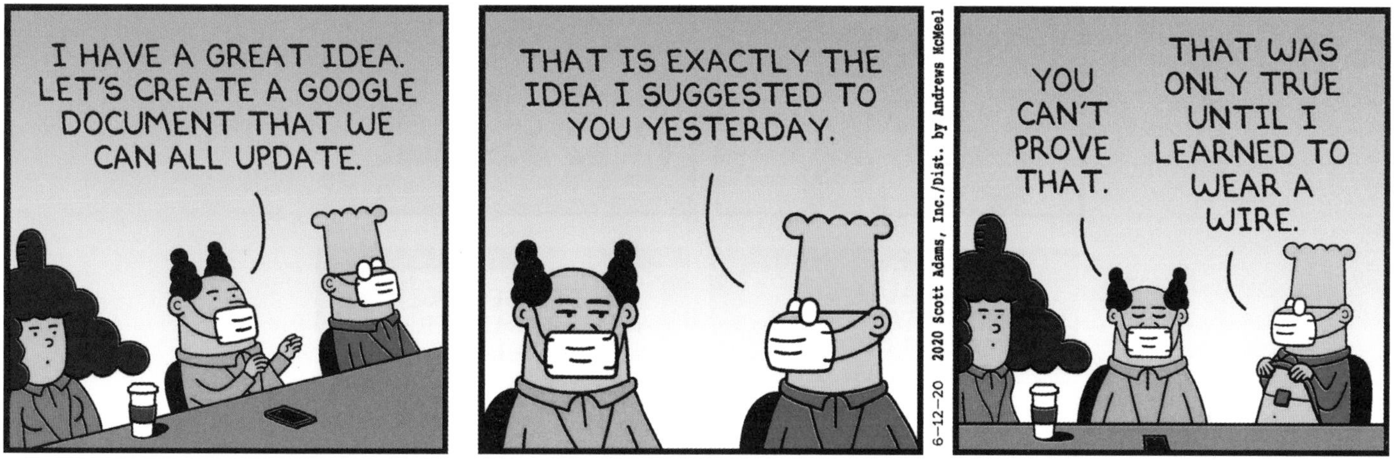
I HAVE A GREAT IDEA. LET'S CREATE A GOOGLE DOCUMENT THAT WE CAN ALL UPDATE.
THAT IS EXACTLY THE IDEA I SUGGESTED TO YOU YESTERDAY.
6-12-20 2020 Scott Adams, Inc./Dist. by Andrews McMeel
YOU CAN'T PROVE THAT.
THAT WAS ONLY TRUE UNTIL I LEARNED TO WEAR A WIRE.

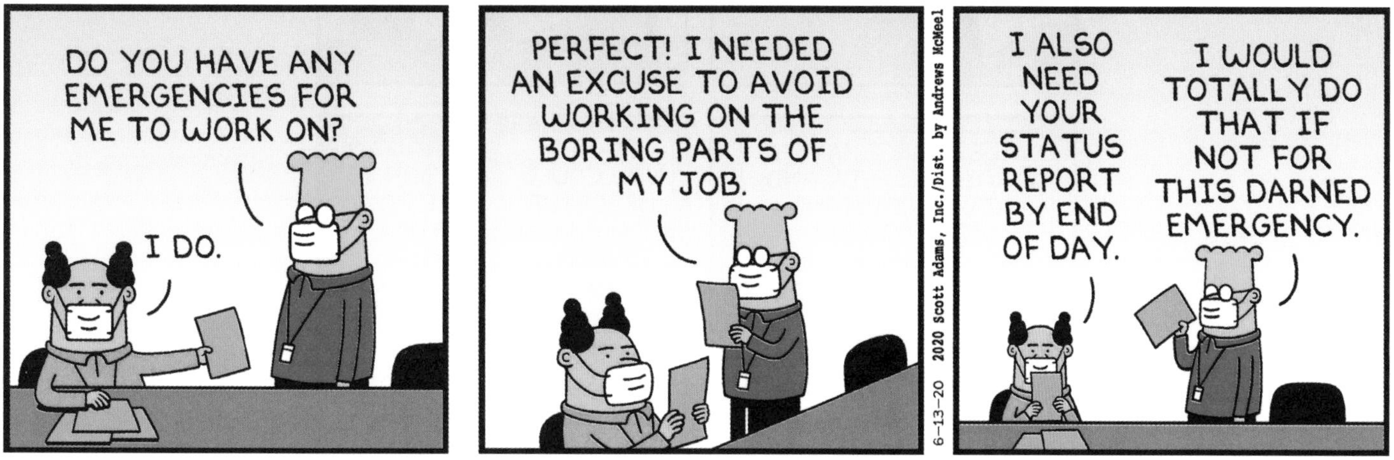
DO YOU HAVE ANY EMERGENCIES FOR ME TO WORK ON?
I DO.
PERFECT! I NEEDED AN EXCUSE TO AVOID WORKING ON THE BORING PARTS OF MY JOB.
6-13-20 2020 Scott Adams, Inc./Dist. by Andrews McMeel
I ALSO NEED YOUR STATUS REPORT BY END OF DAY.
I WOULD TOTALLY DO THAT IF NOT FOR THIS DARNED EMERGENCY.

WE NEED YOUR HELP MAKING A DECISION.
JEFF DOESN'T UNDERSTAND MY PRODUCT STRATEGY BECAUSE HE ISN'T AN ENGINEER.
AND I DON'T UNDERSTAND ANY OF HIS MARKETING NONSENSE.
THAT'S WHY WE CAME TO YOU.
BECAUSE I UNDERSTAND BOTH MARKETING AND ENGINEERING?
NO, IT'S BECAUSE YOU DON'T UNDER- STAND EITHER ONE.
WE DIDN'T HAVE A COIN TO FLIP, AND YOUR DECISIONS ARE TOTALLY RANDOM, SO. . .
MAYBE YOU COULD DESCRIBE THE SIT- UATION.
I DON'T SEE HOW THAT HELPS.
©2020 Scott Adams, Inc./Dist. by Andrews McMeel
6-14-20

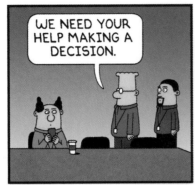

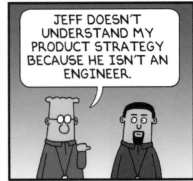

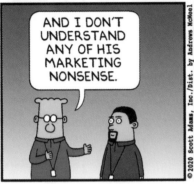

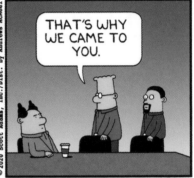

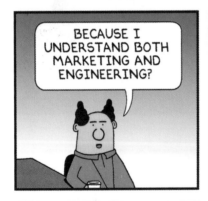

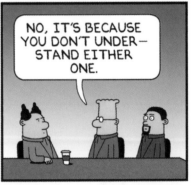

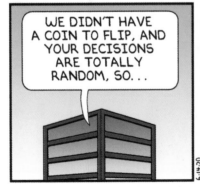

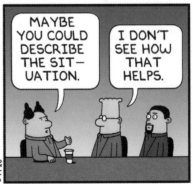

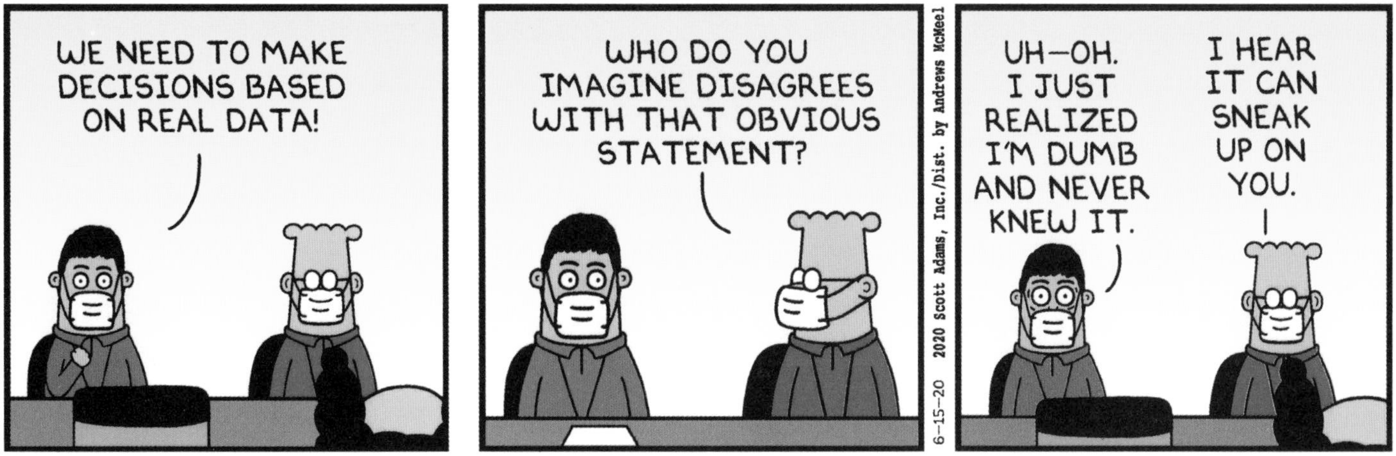
WE NEED TO MAKE DECISIONS BASED ON REAL DATA!
WHO DO YOU IMAGINE DISAGREES WITH THAT OBVIOUS STATEMENT?
6-15-20 2020 Scott Adams, Inc./Dist. by Andrews McMeel
UH-OH. I JUST REALIZED I'M DUMB AND NEVER KNEW IT.
I HEAR IT CAN SNEAK UP ON YOU.

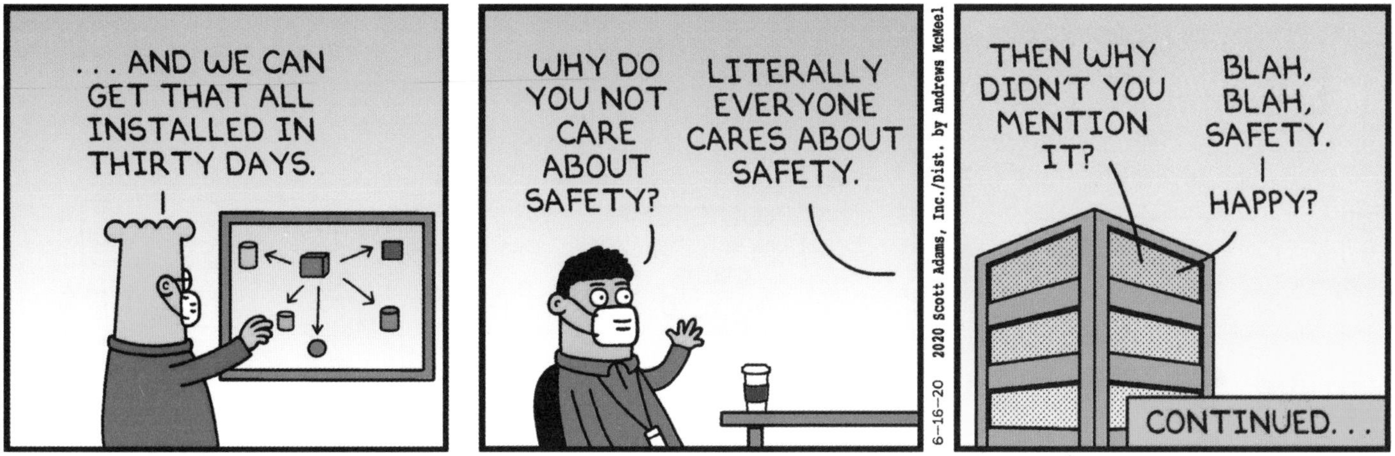
. . . AND WE CAN GET THAT ALL INSTALLED IN THIRTY DAYS.
WHY DO YOU NOT CARE ABOUT SAFETY?
LITERALLY EVERYONE CARES ABOUT SAFETY.
6-16-20 2020 Scott Adams, Inc./Dist. by Andrews McMeel
THEN WHY DIDN'T YOU MENTION IT?
BLAH, BLAH, SAFETY.
HAPPY?
CONTINUED. . .

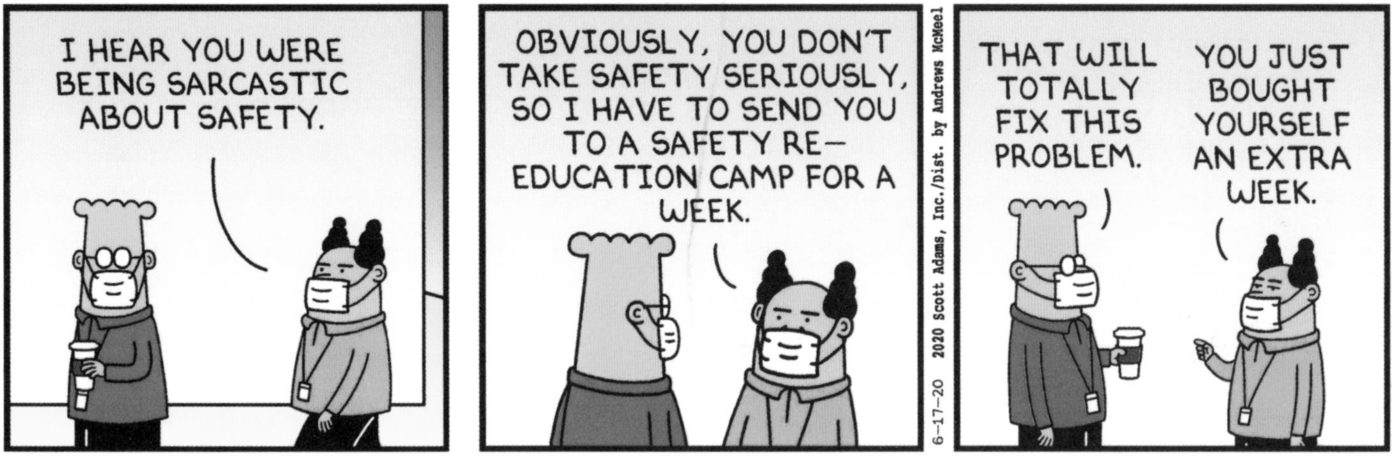
I HEAR YOU WERE BEING SARCASTIC ABOUT SAFETY.
OBVIOUSLY, YOU DON'T TAKE SAFETY SERIOUSLY, SO I HAVE TO SEND YOU TO A SAFETY RE-EDUCATION CAMP FOR A WEEK.
6-17-20 2020 Scott Adams, Inc./Dist. by Andrews McMeel
THAT WILL TOTALLY FIX THIS PROBLEM.
YOU JUST BOUGHT YOURSELF AN EXTRA WEEK.

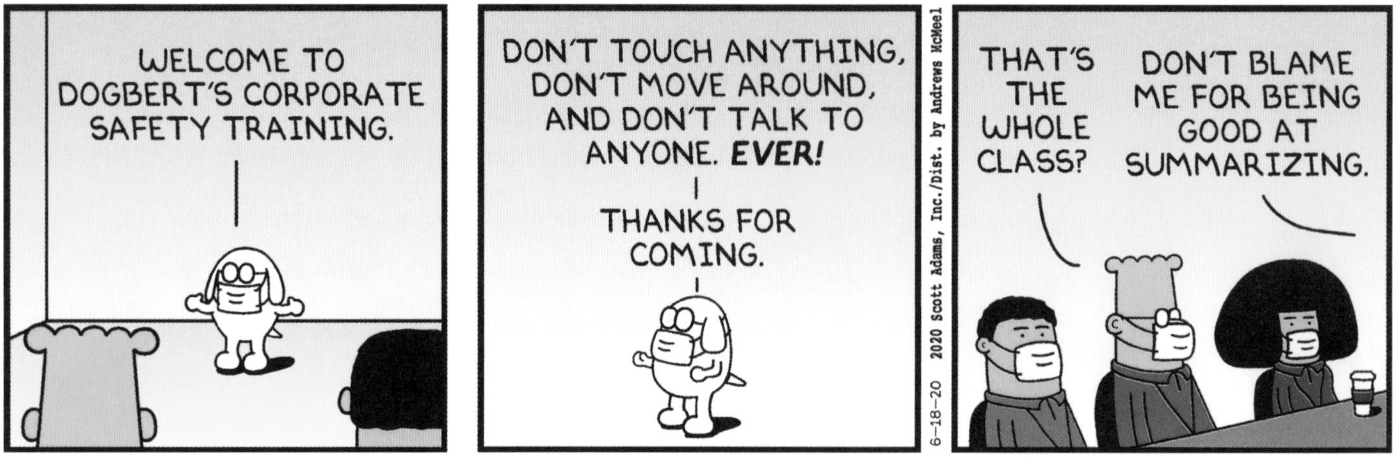
WELCOME TO DOGBERT'S CORPORATE SAFETY TRAINING.
DON'T TOUCH ANYTHING, DON'T MOVE AROUND, AND DON'T TALK TO ANYONE. EVER!
THANKS FOR COMING.
THAT'S THE WHOLE CLASS?
DON'T BLAME ME FOR BEING GOOD AT SUMMARIZING.
6-18-20 © 2020 Scott Adams, Inc./Dist. by Andrews McMeel

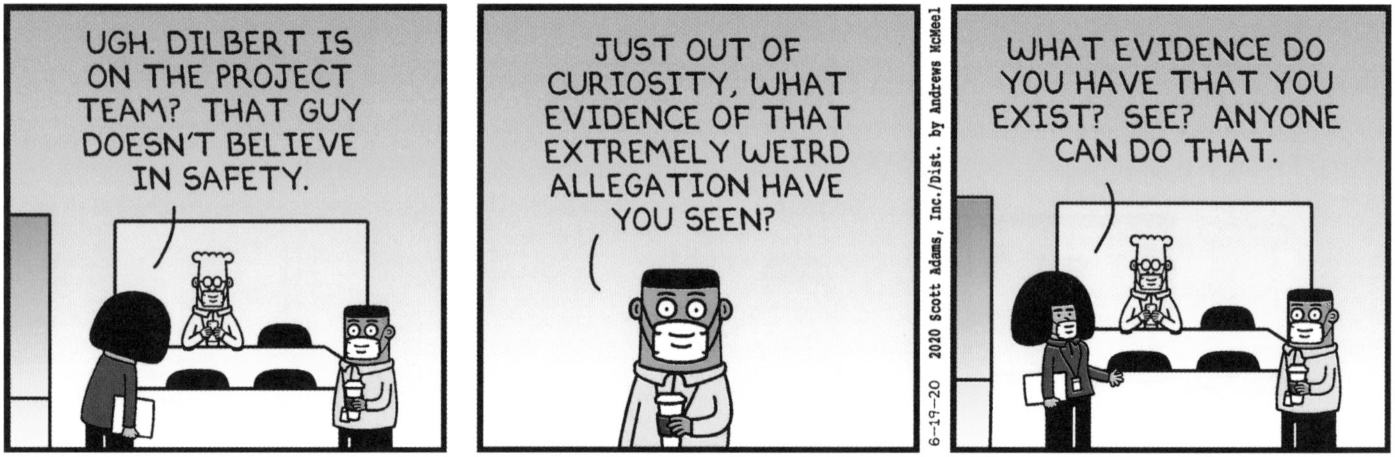
UGH. DILBERT IS ON THE PROJECT TEAM? THAT GUY DOESN'T BELIEVE IN SAFETY.
JUST OUT OF CURIOSITY, WHAT EVIDENCE OF THAT EXTREMELY WEIRD ALLEGATION HAVE YOU SEEN?
WHAT EVIDENCE DO YOU HAVE THAT YOU EXIST? SEE? ANYONE CAN DO THAT.
6-19-20 © 2020 Scott Adams, Inc./Dist. by Andrews McMeel

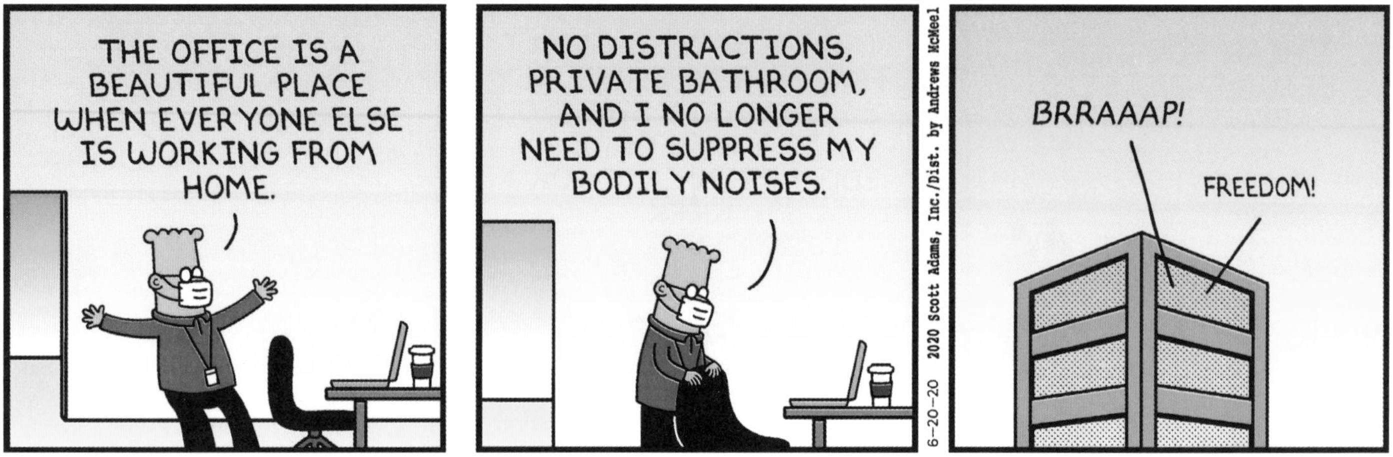
THE OFFICE IS A BEAUTIFUL PLACE WHEN EVERYONE ELSE IS WORKING FROM HOME.
NO DISTRACTIONS, PRIVATE BATHROOM, AND I NO LONGER NEED TO SUPPRESS MY BODILY NOISES.
BRRAAAP!
FREEDOM!
6-20-20 © 2020 Scott Adams, Inc./Dist. by Andrews McMeel

I ANALYZED OUR ONLY TWO OPTIONS.
ONE OPTION COSTS TOO MUCH, AND THE OTHER OPTION IS IMPOSSIBLE.
LET'S DO THE IMPOSSIBLE ONE.
PERHAPS YOU CAN EXPLAIN YOUR REASONING.
ACCORDING TO YOU, WE WILL FAIL EITHER WAY.
BUT IF WE FAIL IN A SLOW AND INEXPENSIVE WAY, NO ONE WILL EVEN NOTICE FOR MONTHS.
WITH ANY LUCK, WE'LL HAVE A CORPORATE REORGANI–ZATION THAT FOREVER HIDES OUR GROSS INCOMPETENCE.
HAVE YOU DONE THIS BEFORE?
EVERY SIX MONTHS.
© 2020 Scott Adams, Inc./Dist. by Andrews McMeel
6-21-20

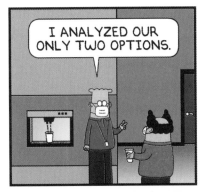

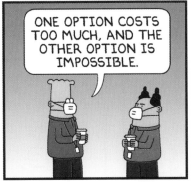

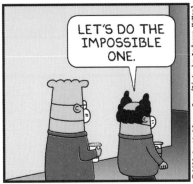

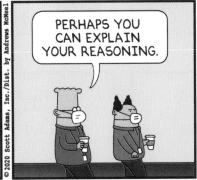

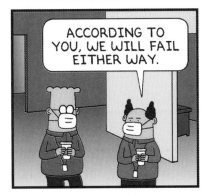

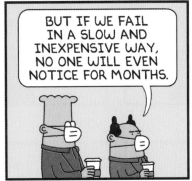

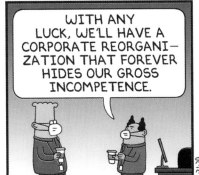

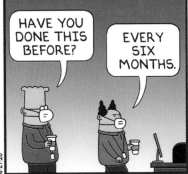

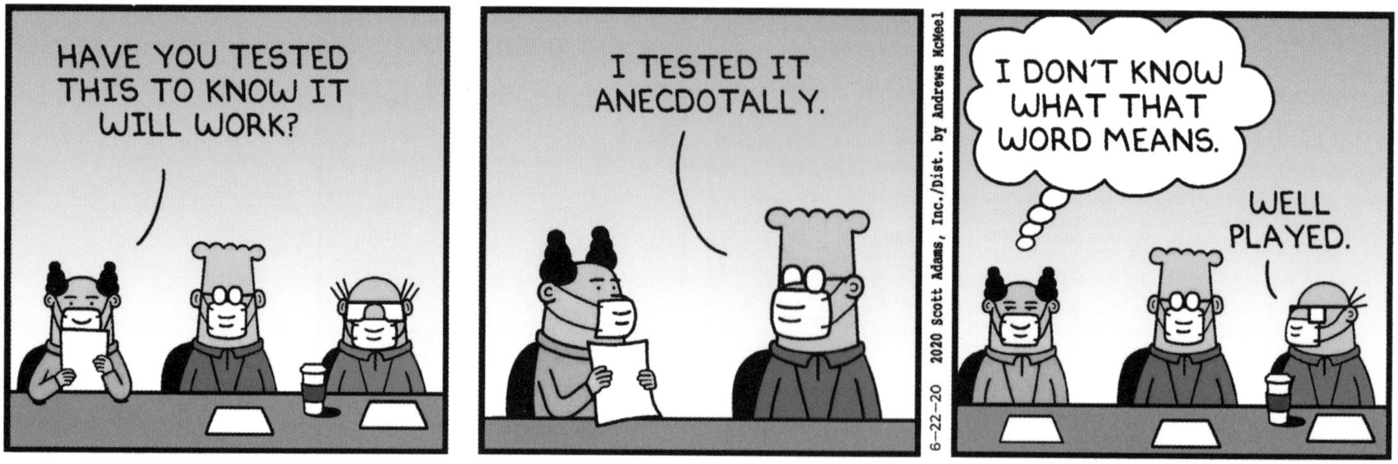
HAVE YOU TESTED THIS TO KNOW IT WILL WORK?
I TESTED IT ANECDOTALLY.
I DON'T KNOW WHAT THAT WORD MEANS.
WELL PLAYED.


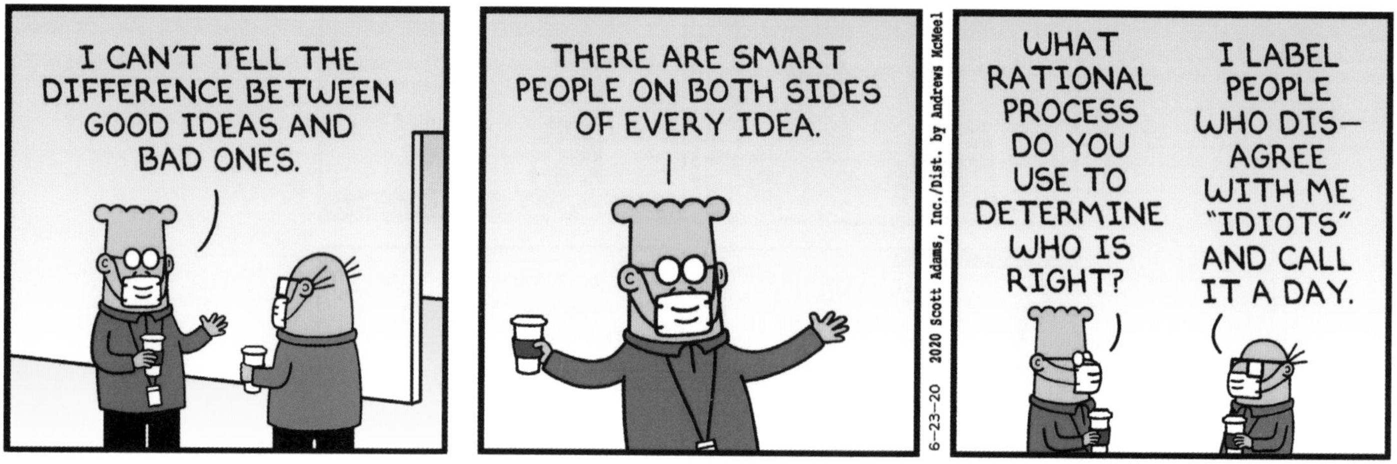
I CAN'T TELL THE DIFFERENCE BETWEEN GOOD IDEAS AND BAD ONES.
THERE ARE SMART PEOPLE ON BOTH SIDES OF EVERY IDEA.
WHAT RATIONAL PROCESS DO YOU USE TO DETERMINE WHO IS RIGHT?
I LABEL PEOPLE WHO DIS-AGREE WITH ME "IDIOTS" AND CALL IT A DAY.


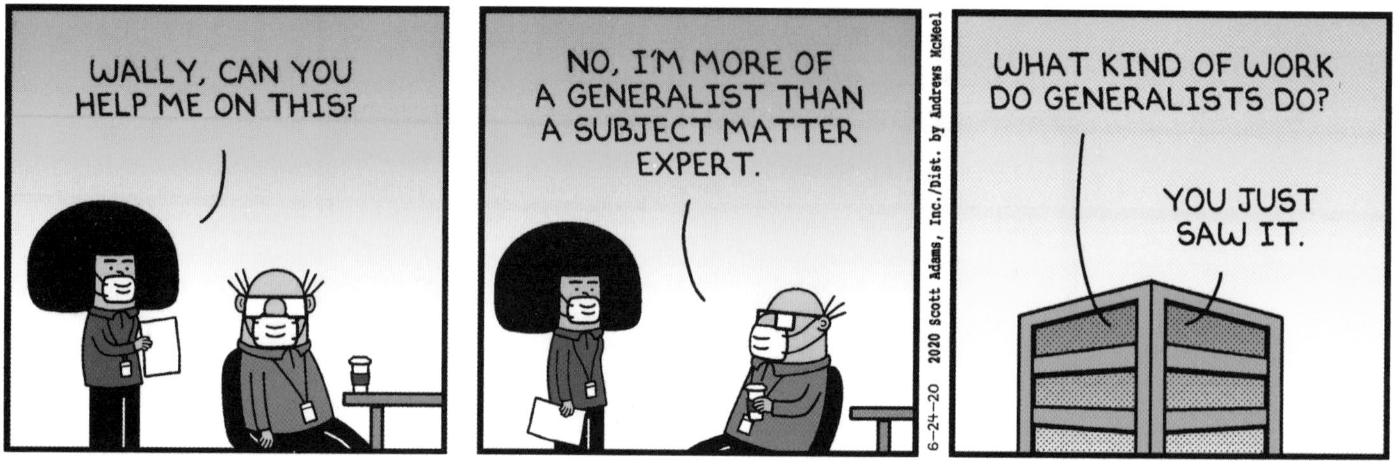
WALLY, CAN YOU HELP ME ON THIS?
NO, I'M MORE OF A GENERALIST THAN A SUBJECT MATTER EXPERT.
WHAT KIND OF WORK DO GENERALISTS DO?
YOU JUST SAW IT.

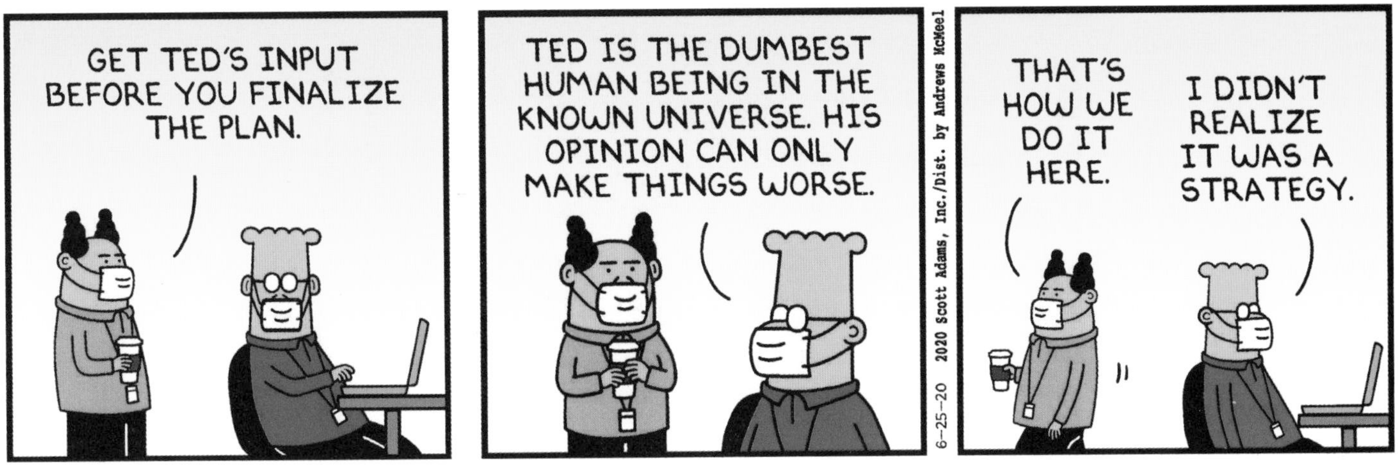
GET TED'S INPUT BEFORE YOU FINALIZE THE PLAN.
TED IS THE DUMBEST HUMAN BEING IN THE KNOWN UNIVERSE. HIS OPINION CAN ONLY MAKE THINGS WORSE.
THAT'S HOW WE DO IT HERE.
I DIDN'T REALIZE IT WAS A STRATEGY.


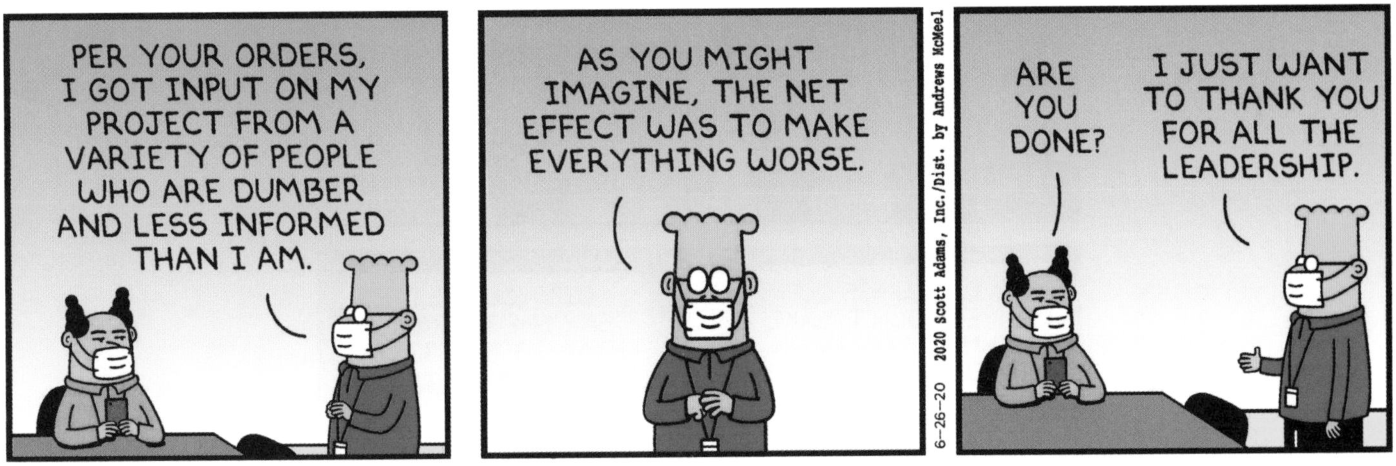
PER YOUR ORDERS, I GOT INPUT ON MY PROJECT FROM A VARIETY OF PEOPLE WHO ARE DUMBER AND LESS INFORMED THAN I AM.
AS YOU MIGHT IMAGINE, THE NET EFFECT WAS TO MAKE EVERYTHING WORSE.
ARE YOU DONE?
I JUST WANT TO THANK YOU FOR ALL THE LEADERSHIP.


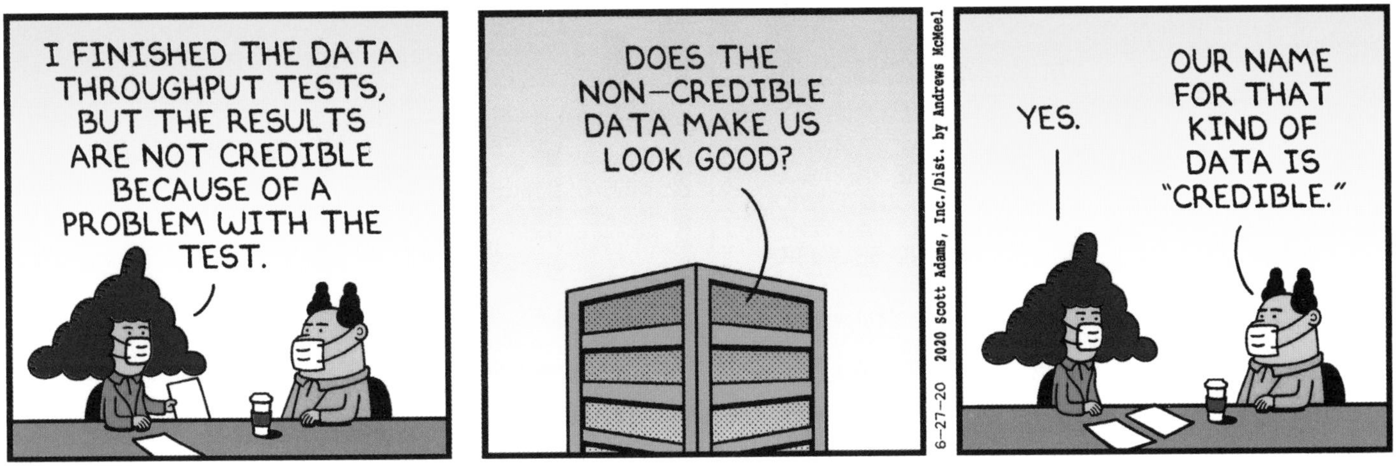
I FINISHED THE DATA THROUGHPUT TESTS, BUT THE RESULTS ARE NOT CREDIBLE BECAUSE OF A PROBLEM WITH THE TEST.
DOES THE NON-CREDIBLE DATA MAKE US LOOK GOOD?
YES.
OUR NAME FOR THAT KIND OF DATA IS "CREDIBLE."

IT MUST BE DIFFICULT TO BE SINGLE IN THE AGE OF COVID-19.

IT'S NOT TOO BAD, ACTUALLY.

I'M IN CONTRACT NEGOTIATIONS WITH A SEMI-ATTRACTIVE WOMAN I MET ONLINE.

© 2020 Scott Adams, Inc./Dist. by Andrews McMeel

WITH ANY LUCK, I WILL BE ENJOYING A DOUBLE-MASKED GOODNIGHT KISS BY LATE NEXT MONTH.

THAT ASSUMES OUR LAWYERS DON'T MAKE TOO MANY CHANGES TO THE CONTRACT.

DID YOU JUST SAY SHE IS ONLY SEMI-ATTRACTIVE?

I'M JUDGING FROM THE PARTS I CAN SEE. I DON'T KNOW WHAT'S UNDER THE MASK AND SHOWER CAP SHE WEARS ALL DAY.

6-28-20

YOU MUST LIKE HER EYES.

I LIKE THE ONE I CAN SEE. THE OTHER ONE HAS A PATCH.

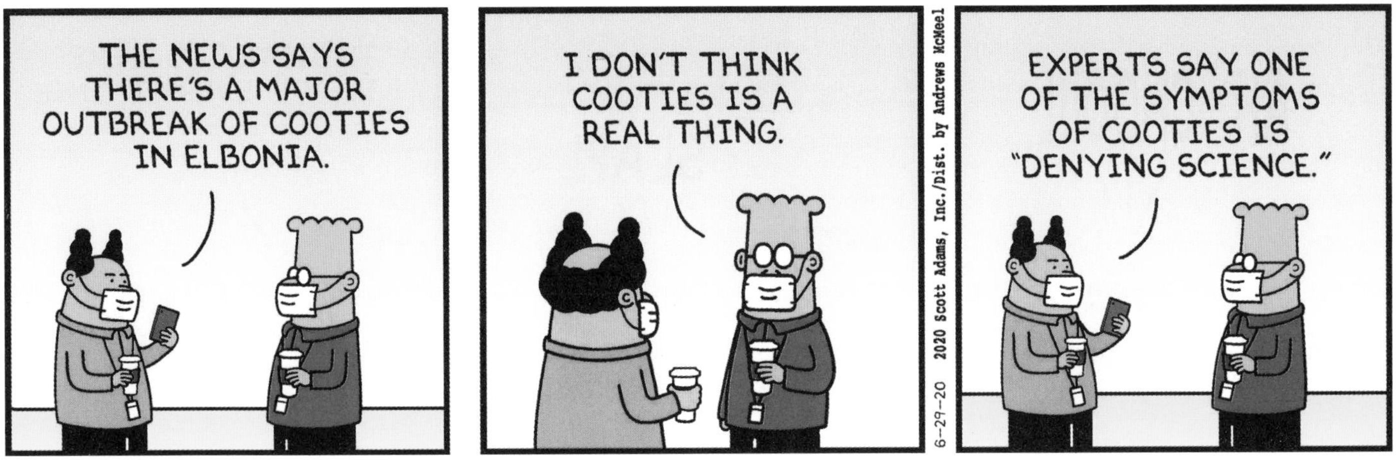
THE NEWS SAYS THERE'S A MAJOR OUTBREAK OF COOTIES IN ELBONIA.
I DON'T THINK COOTIES IS A REAL THING.
6-29-20 2020 Scott Adams, Inc./Dist. by Andrews McMeel
EXPERTS SAY ONE OF THE SYMPTOMS OF COOTIES IS "DENYING SCIENCE."

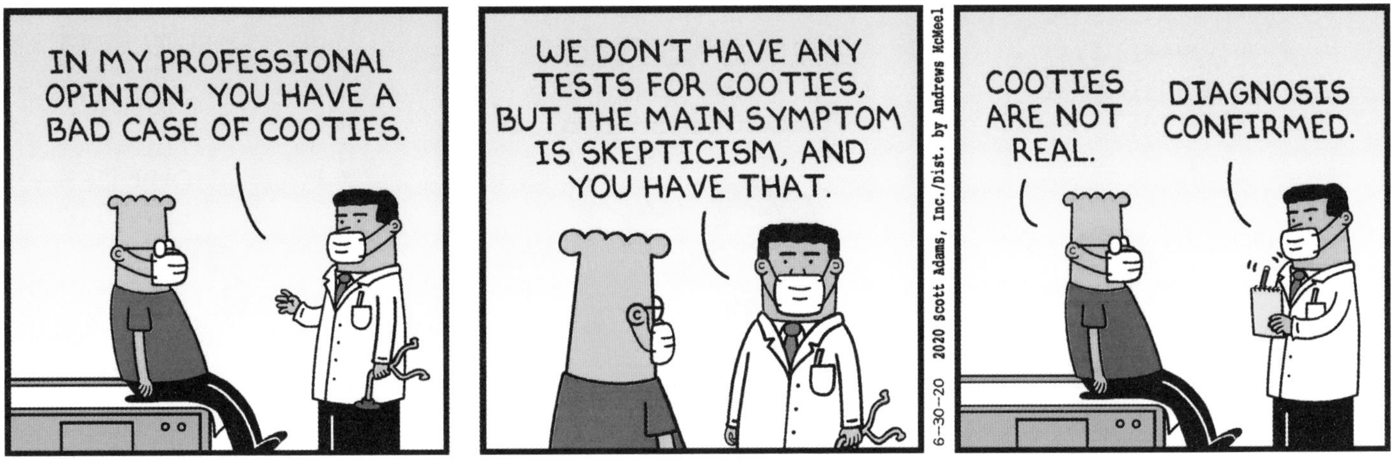
IN MY PROFESSIONAL OPINION, YOU HAVE A BAD CASE OF COOTIES.
WE DON'T HAVE ANY TESTS FOR COOTIES, BUT THE MAIN SYMPTOM IS SKEPTICISM, AND YOU HAVE THAT.
6-30-20 2020 Scott Adams, Inc./Dist. by Andrews McMeel
COOTIES ARE NOT REAL.
DIAGNOSIS CONFIRMED.

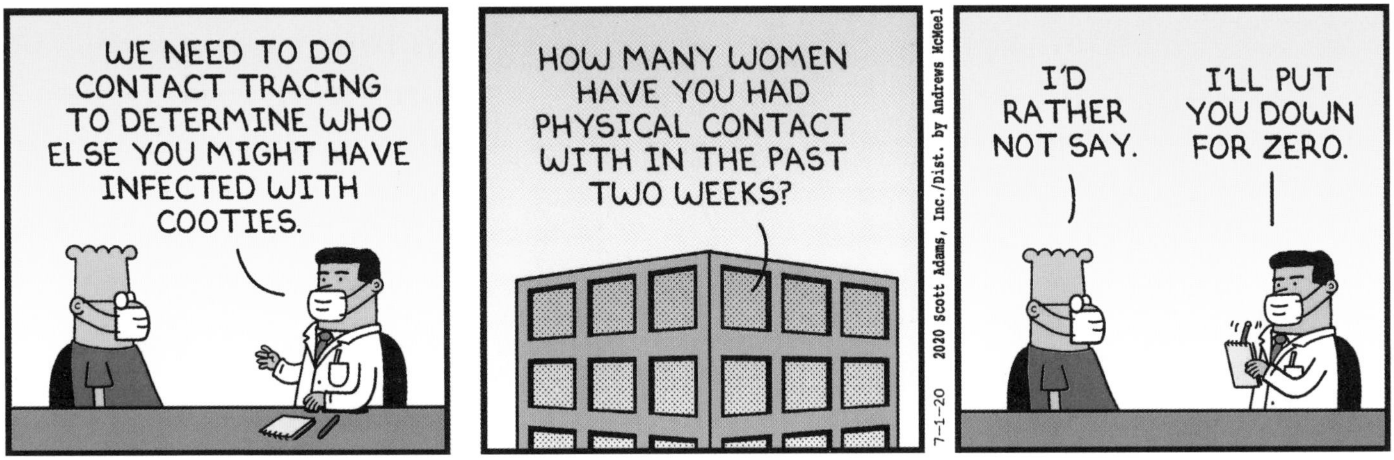
WE NEED TO DO CONTACT TRACING TO DETERMINE WHO ELSE YOU MIGHT HAVE INFECTED WITH COOTIES.
HOW MANY WOMEN HAVE YOU HAD PHYSICAL CONTACT WITH IN THE PAST TWO WEEKS?
7-1-20 2020 Scott Adams, Inc./Dist. by Andrews McMeel
I'D RATHER NOT SAY.
I'LL PUT YOU DOWN FOR ZERO.

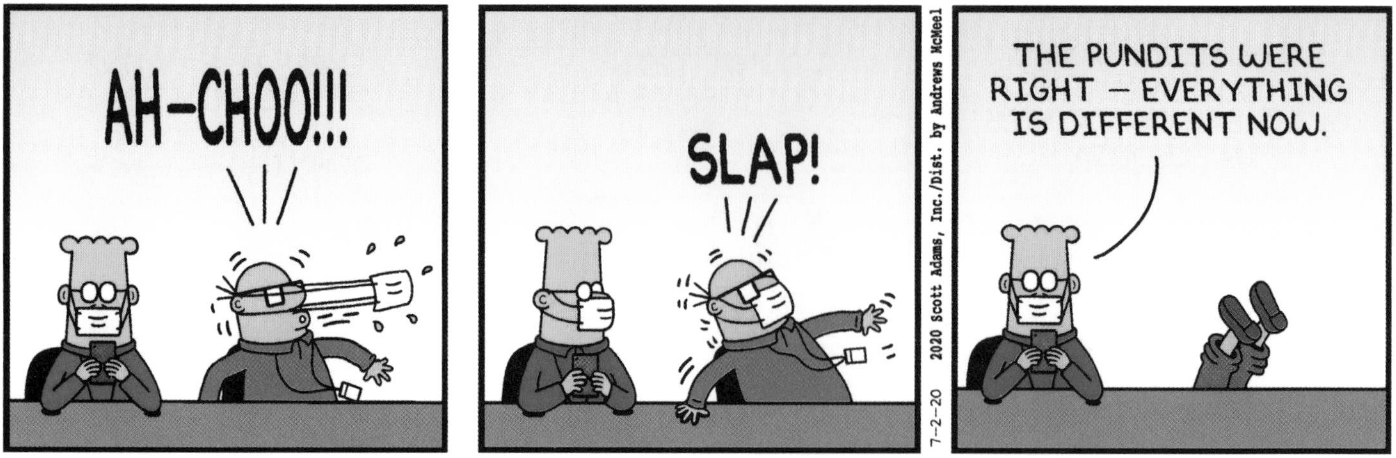
AH-CHOO!!!
SLAP!
7-2-20 2020 Scott Adams, Inc./Dist. by Andrews McMeel
THE PUNDITS WERE RIGHT – EVERYTHING IS DIFFERENT NOW.

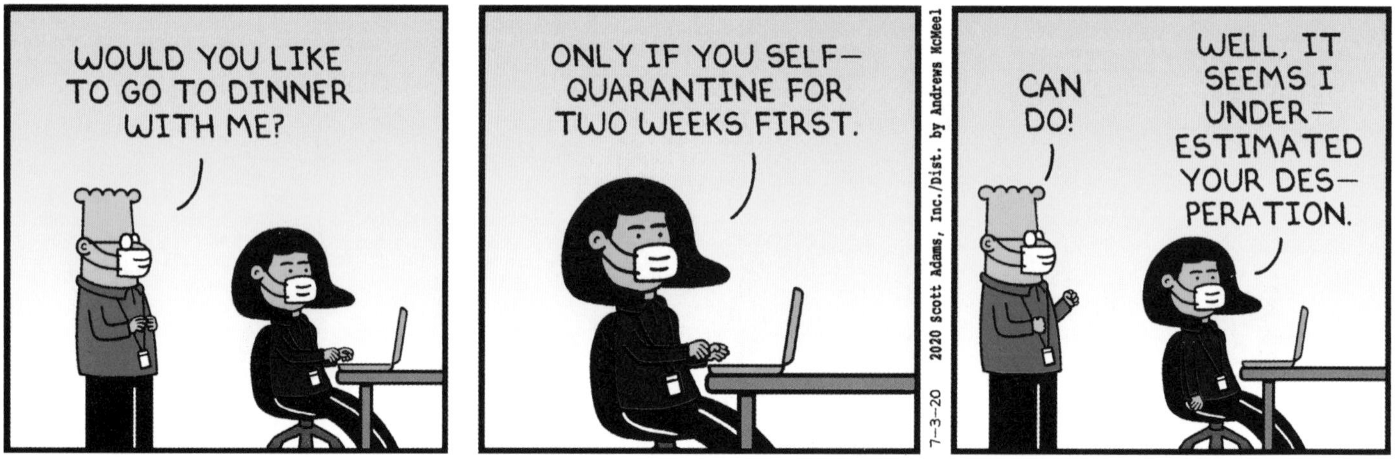
WOULD YOU LIKE TO GO TO DINNER WITH ME?
ONLY IF YOU SELF-QUARANTINE FOR TWO WEEKS FIRST.
7-3-20 2020 Scott Adams, Inc./Dist. by Andrews McMeel
CAN DO!
WELL, IT SEEMS I UNDER-ESTIMATED YOUR DES-PERATION.

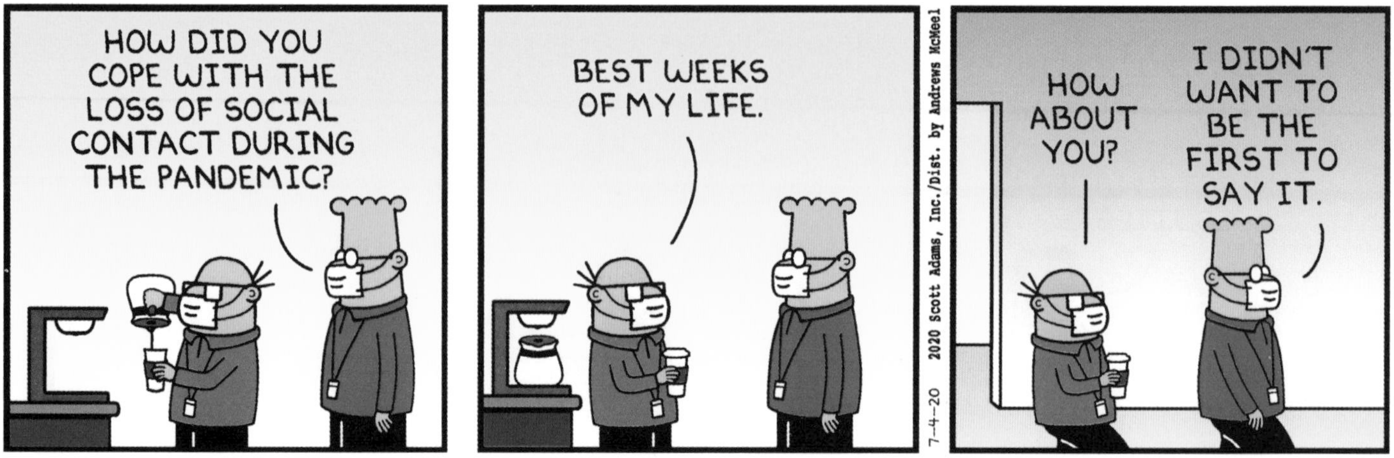
HOW DID YOU COPE WITH THE LOSS OF SOCIAL CONTACT DURING THE PANDEMIC?
BEST WEEKS OF MY LIFE.
7-4-20 2020 Scott Adams, Inc./Dist. by Andrews McMeel
HOW ABOUT YOU?
I DIDN'T WANT TO BE THE FIRST TO SAY IT.

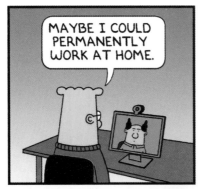

MAYBE I COULD PERMANENTLY WORK AT HOME.
NO PROBLEM. I JUST NEED A FEW THINGS FROM YOU TO MAKE SURE YOU ARE WORKING.
SUCH AS?
WELL, OBVIOUSLY, I NEED FREQUENT STATUS REPORTS.
SOUNDS REASONABLE.
AND I'LL NEED TO TRACK YOUR KEYSTROKES AND YOUR PHONE'S LOCATION.
WOW. WELL, OKAY. I GUESS I CAN GET USED TO THAT IN RETURN FOR MY FREEDOM TO WORK AT HOME.
NOW THAT I'VE LOOSENED YOU UP, LET'S TALK ABOUT FITTING YOU FOR A BODY CAM.
© 2020 Scott Adams, Inc./Dist. by Andrews McMeel
7-5-20

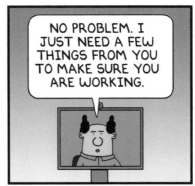

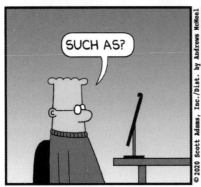

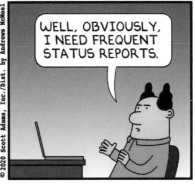

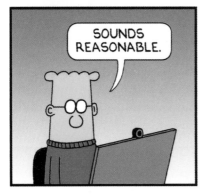

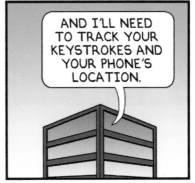

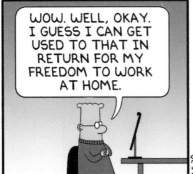

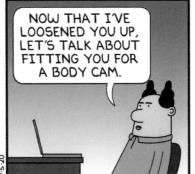

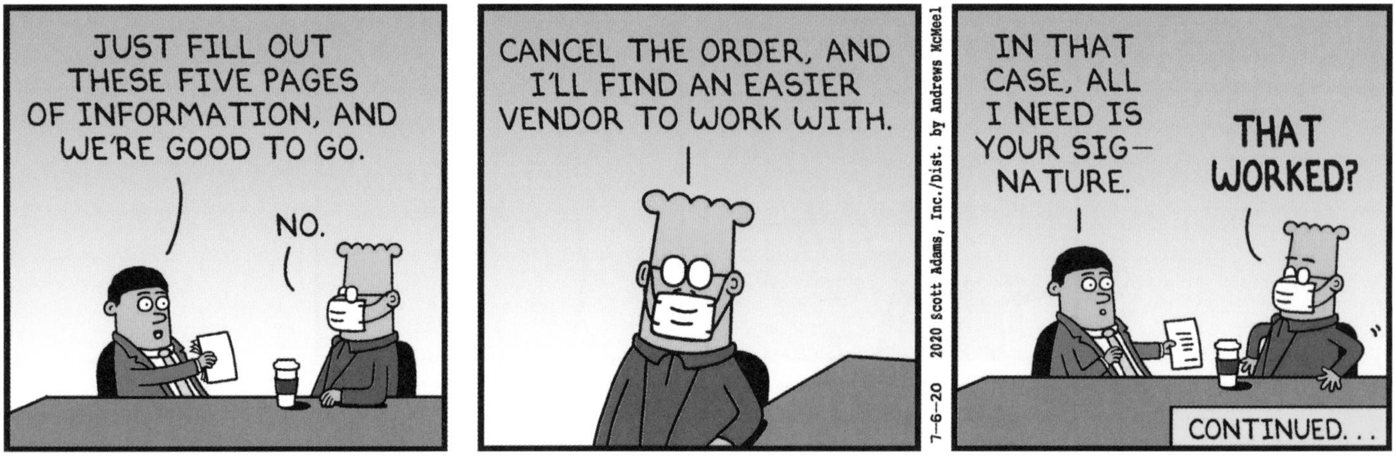
JUST FILL OUT THESE FIVE PAGES OF INFORMATION, AND WE'RE GOOD TO GO.
NO.
CANCEL THE ORDER, AND I'LL FIND AN EASIER VENDOR TO WORK WITH.
7-6-20 2020 Scott Adams, Inc./Dist. by Andrews McMeel
IN THAT CASE, ALL I NEED IS YOUR SIG-NATURE.
THAT WORKED?
CONTINUED. . .

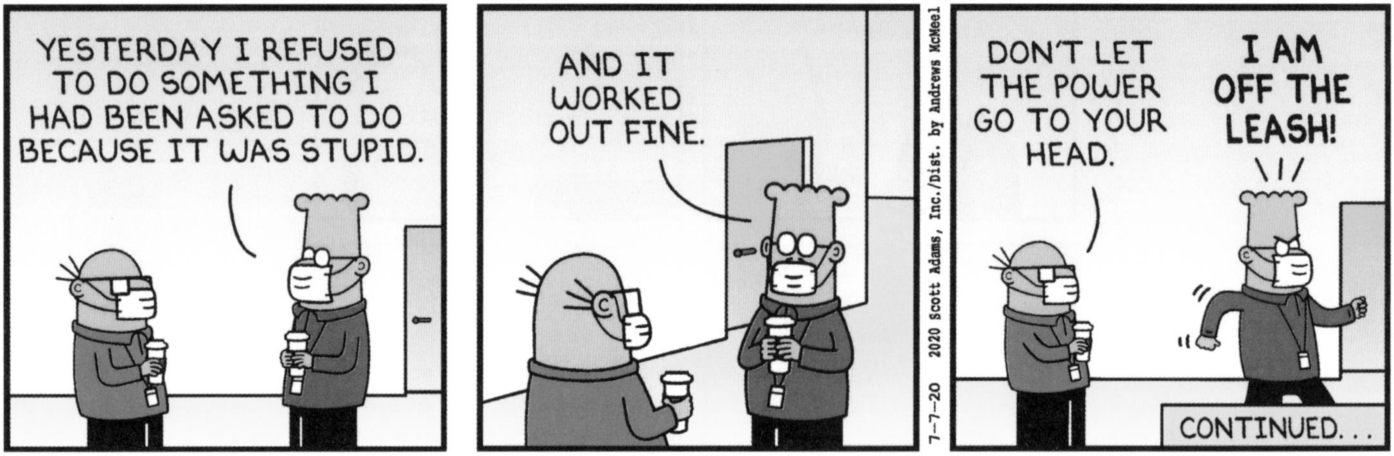
YESTERDAY I REFUSED TO DO SOMETHING I HAD BEEN ASKED TO DO BECAUSE IT WAS STUPID.
AND IT WORKED OUT FINE.
7-7-20 2020 Scott Adams, Inc./Dist. by Andrews McMeel
DON'T LET THE POWER GO TO YOUR HEAD.
I AM OFF THE LEASH!
CONTINUED. . .

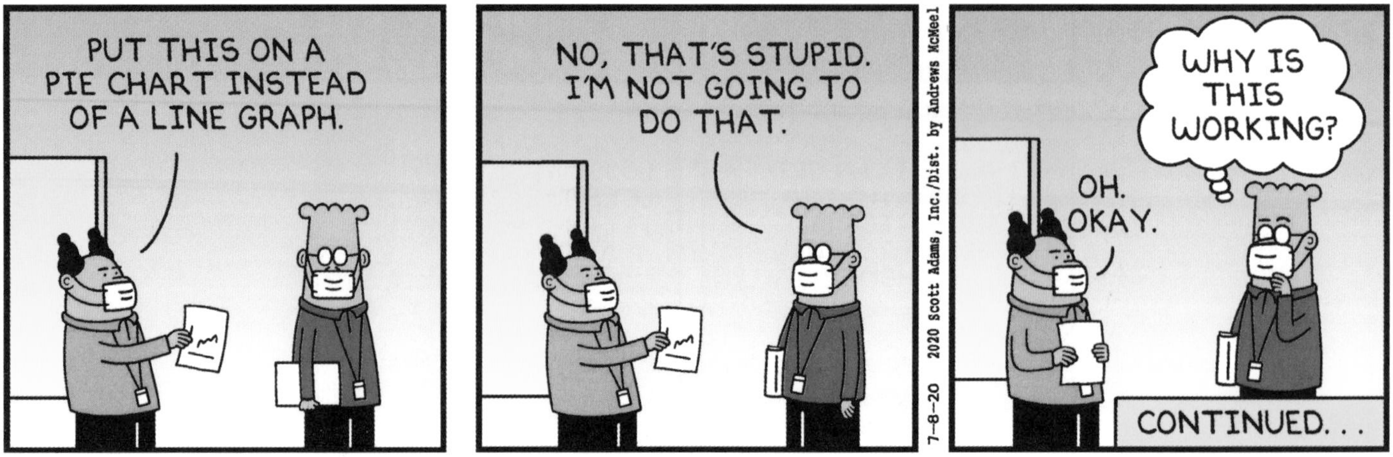
PUT THIS ON A PIE CHART INSTEAD OF A LINE GRAPH.
NO, THAT'S STUPID. I'M NOT GOING TO DO THAT.
7-8-20 2020 Scott Adams, Inc./Dist. by Andrews McMeel
WHY IS THIS WORKING?
OH. OKAY.
CONTINUED. . .

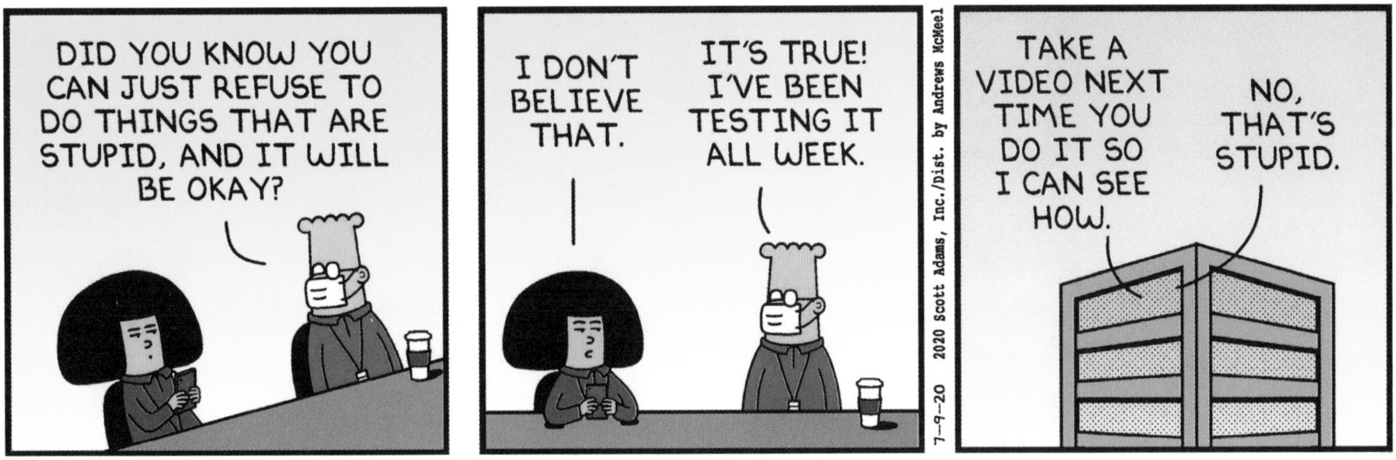
DID YOU KNOW YOU CAN JUST REFUSE TO DO THINGS THAT ARE STUPID, AND IT WILL BE OKAY?
I DON'T BELIEVE THAT.
IT'S TRUE! I'VE BEEN TESTING IT ALL WEEK.
TAKE A VIDEO NEXT TIME YOU DO IT SO I CAN SEE HOW.
NO, THAT'S STUPID.
7-9-20 2020 Scott Adams, Inc./Dist. by Andrews McMeel

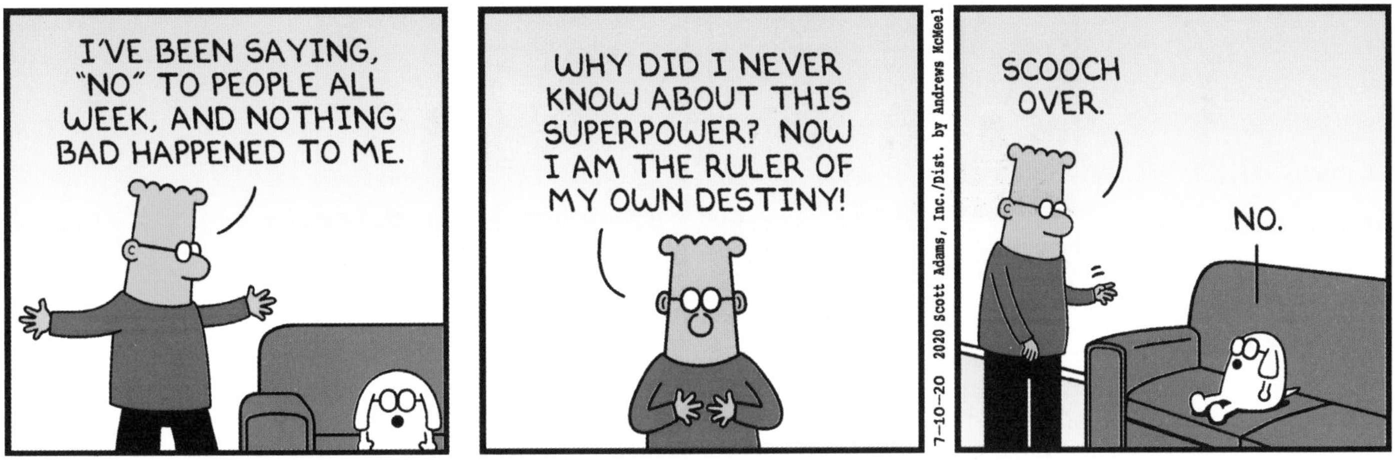
I'VE BEEN SAYING, "NO" TO PEOPLE ALL WEEK, AND NOTHING BAD HAPPENED TO ME.
WHY DID I NEVER KNOW ABOUT THIS SUPERPOWER? NOW I AM THE RULER OF MY OWN DESTINY!
SCOOCH OVER.
NO.
7-10-20 2020 Scott Adams, Inc./Dist. by Andrews McMeel

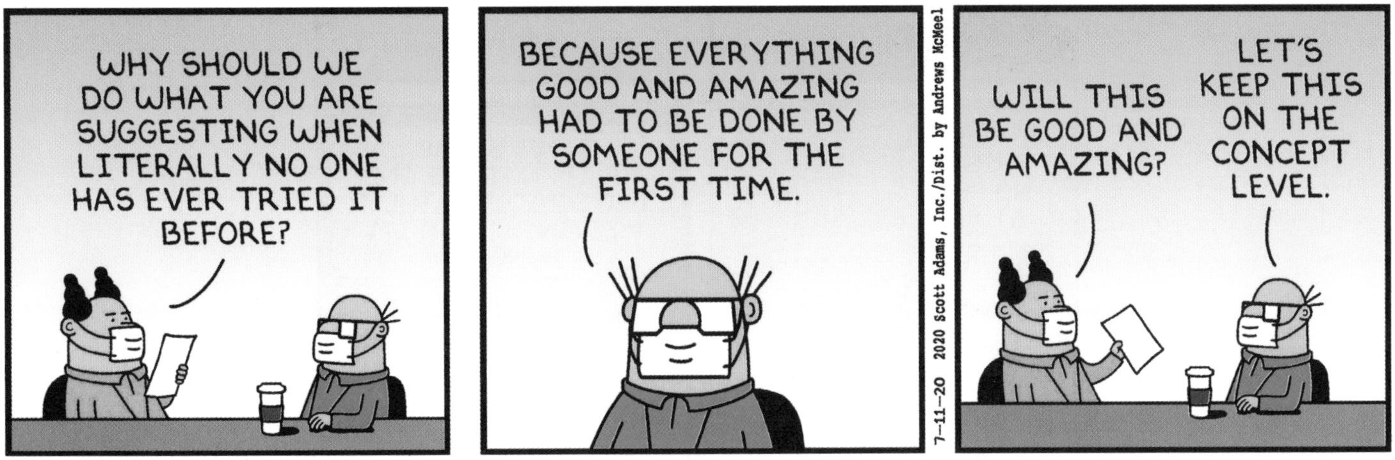
WHY SHOULD WE DO WHAT YOU ARE SUGGESTING WHEN LITERALLY NO ONE HAS EVER TRIED IT BEFORE?
BECAUSE EVERYTHING GOOD AND AMAZING HAD TO BE DONE BY SOMEONE FOR THE FIRST TIME.
WILL THIS BE GOOD AND AMAZING?
LET'S KEEP THIS ON THE CONCEPT LEVEL.
7-11-20 2020 Scott Adams, Inc./Dist. by Andrews McMeel

WE AGREED AT OUR LAST MEETING TO POSTPONE THE VERSION RELEASE.
NO, WE AGREED TO DO IT SOONER.
I DON'T THINK SO.
WHO TOOK NOTES AT THE LAST MEETING?
I DID.
©2020 Scott Adams, Inc./Dist. by Andrews McMeel
FORWARDING THOSE NOTES TO EACH OF YOU.
CLICK
UM . . . YOUR NOTES ARE MOSTLY INSULTS ABOUT THE INTELLIGENCE OF YOUR CO-WORKERS AND . . . SOME SORT OF SNACK LIST.
THIS IS NO HELP AT ALL.
7-12-20
DON'T BLAME **ME**. I'M NOT THE ONE WHO SCHEDULES THESE MEETINGS WHEN I'M HUNGRY.

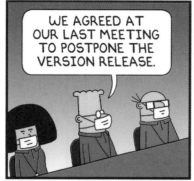

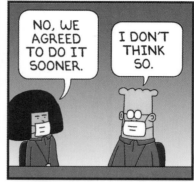

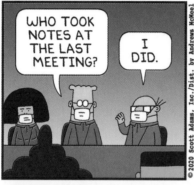

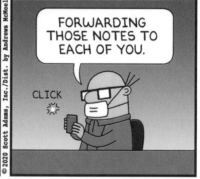

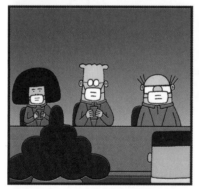

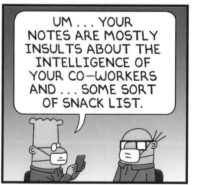

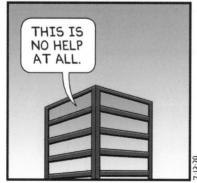

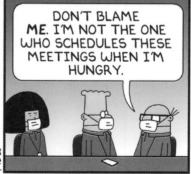

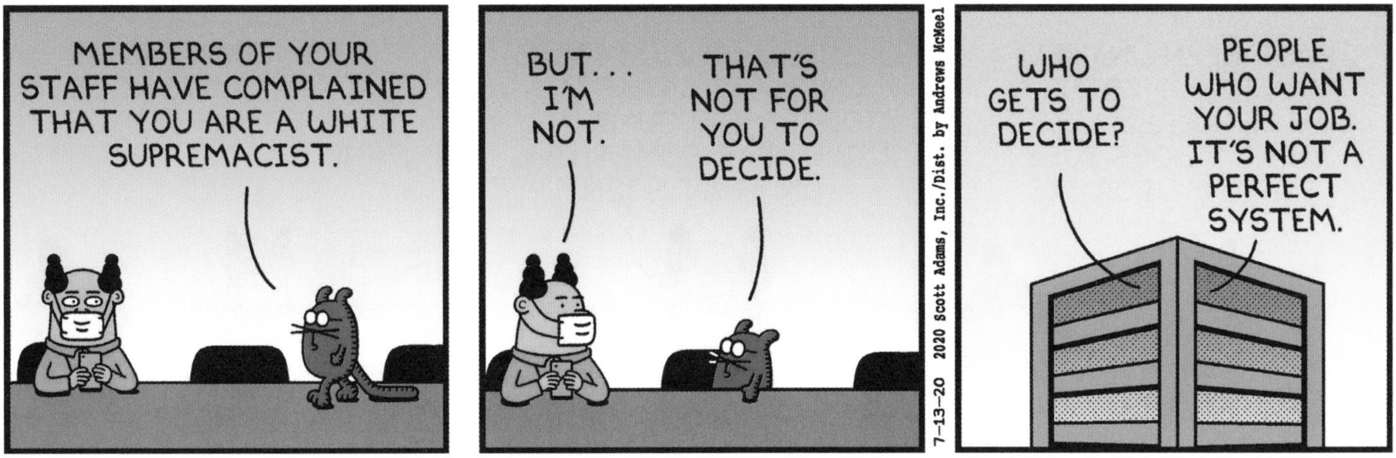
MEMBERS OF YOUR STAFF HAVE COMPLAINED THAT YOU ARE A WHITE SUPREMACIST.
BUT. . . I'M NOT.
THAT'S NOT FOR YOU TO DECIDE.
7-13-20 2020 Scott Adams, Inc./Dist. by Andrews McMeel
WHO GETS TO DECIDE?
PEOPLE WHO WANT YOUR JOB. IT'S NOT A PERFECT SYSTEM.

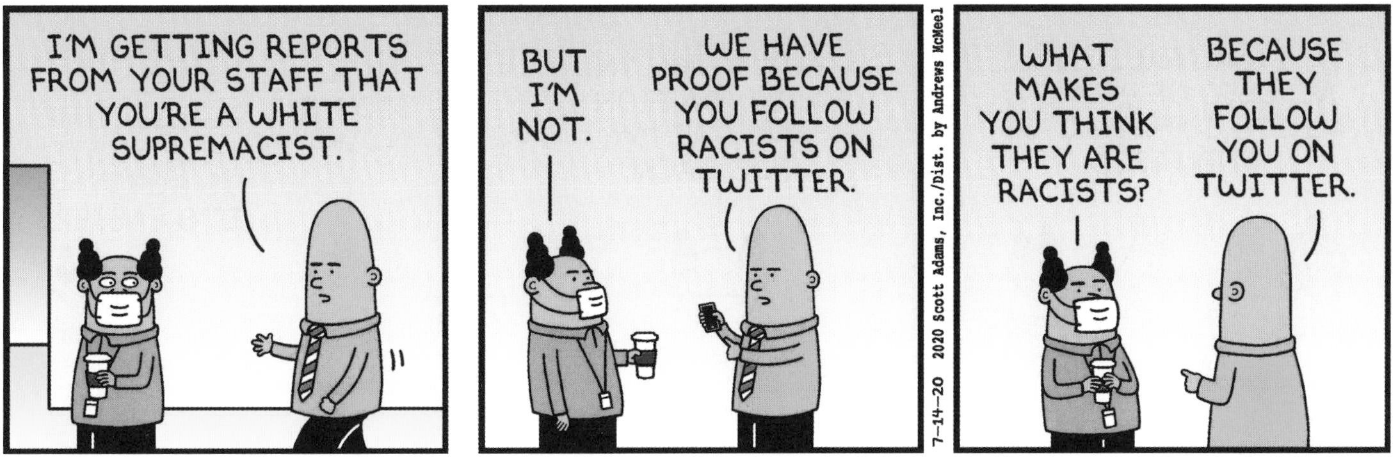
I'M GETTING REPORTS FROM YOUR STAFF THAT YOU'RE A WHITE SUPREMACIST.
BUT I'M NOT.
WE HAVE PROOF BECAUSE YOU FOLLOW RACISTS ON TWITTER.
7-14-20 2020 Scott Adams, Inc./Dist. by Andrews McMeel
WHAT MAKES YOU THINK THEY ARE RACISTS?
BECAUSE THEY FOLLOW YOU ON TWITTER.

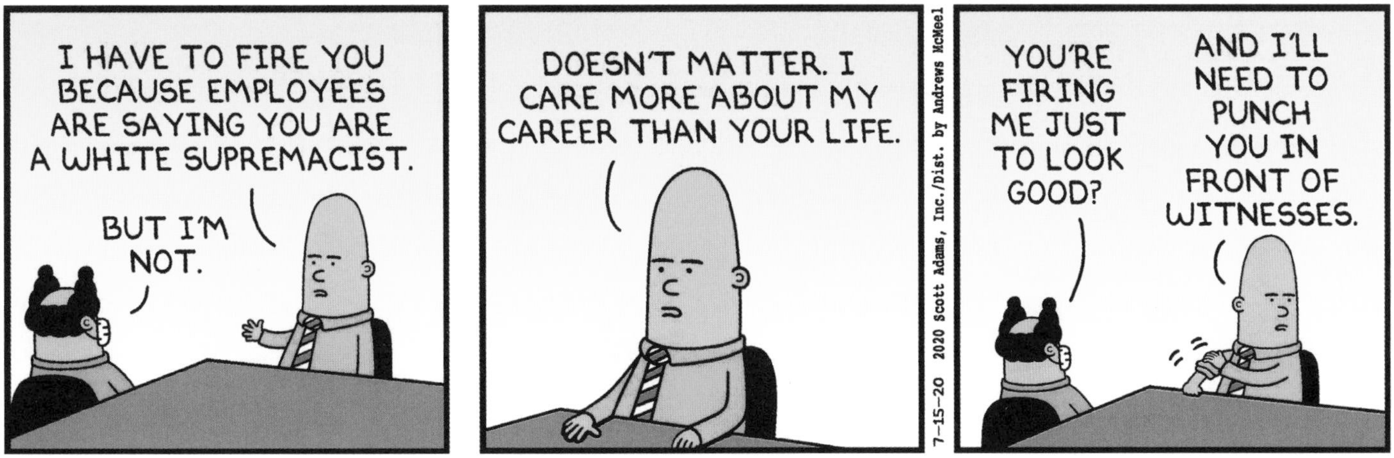
I HAVE TO FIRE YOU BECAUSE EMPLOYEES ARE SAYING YOU ARE A WHITE SUPREMACIST.
BUT I'M NOT.
DOESN'T MATTER. I CARE MORE ABOUT MY CAREER THAN YOUR LIFE.
7-15-20 2020 Scott Adams, Inc./Dist. by Andrews McMeel
YOU'RE FIRING ME JUST TO LOOK GOOD?
AND I'LL NEED TO PUNCH YOU IN FRONT OF WITNESSES.

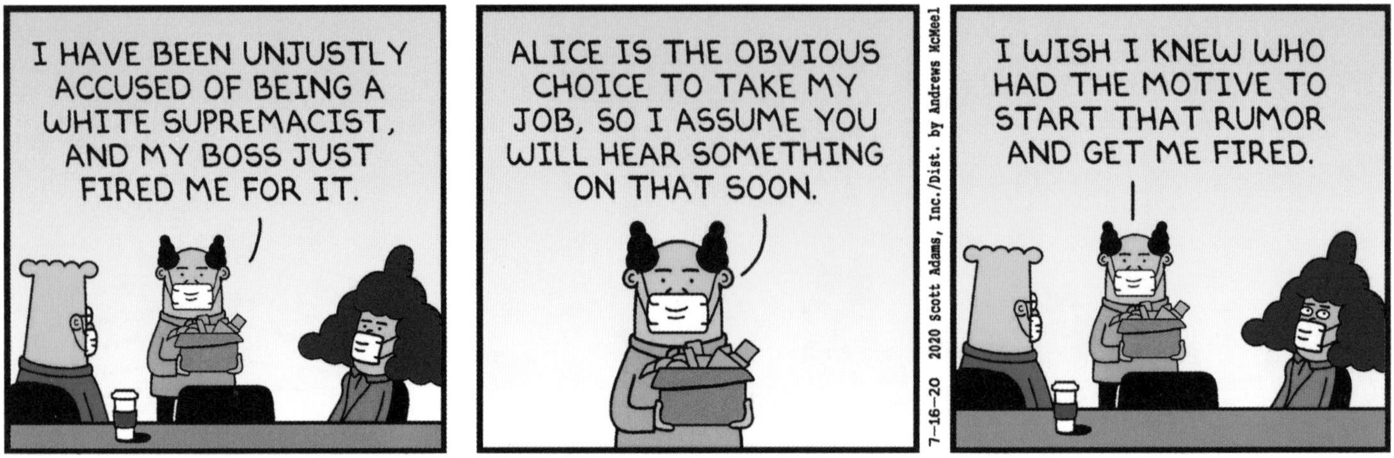
I HAVE BEEN UNJUSTLY ACCUSED OF BEING A WHITE SUPREMACIST, AND MY BOSS JUST FIRED ME FOR IT.
ALICE IS THE OBVIOUS CHOICE TO TAKE MY JOB, SO I ASSUME YOU WILL HEAR SOMETHING ON THAT SOON.
7-16-20 2020 Scott Adams, Inc./Dist. by Andrews McMeel
I WISH I KNEW WHO HAD THE MOTIVE TO START THAT RUMOR AND GET ME FIRED.

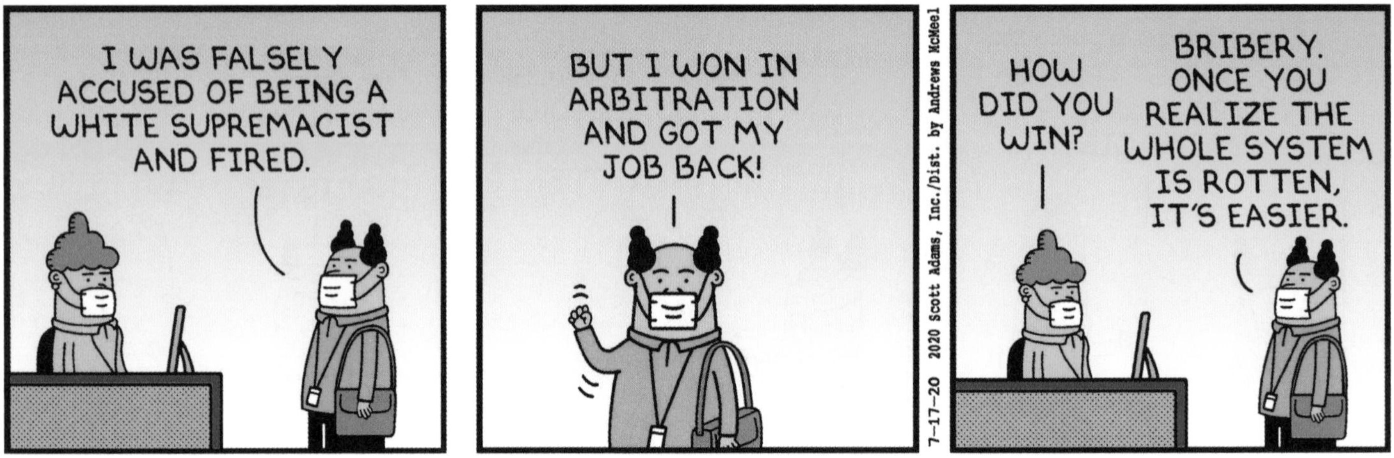
I WAS FALSELY ACCUSED OF BEING A WHITE SUPREMACIST AND FIRED.
BUT I WON IN ARBITRATION AND GOT MY JOB BACK!
7-17-20 2020 Scott Adams, Inc./Dist. by Andrews McMeel
HOW DID YOU WIN?
BRIBERY. ONCE YOU REALIZE THE WHOLE SYSTEM IS ROTTEN, IT'S EASIER.

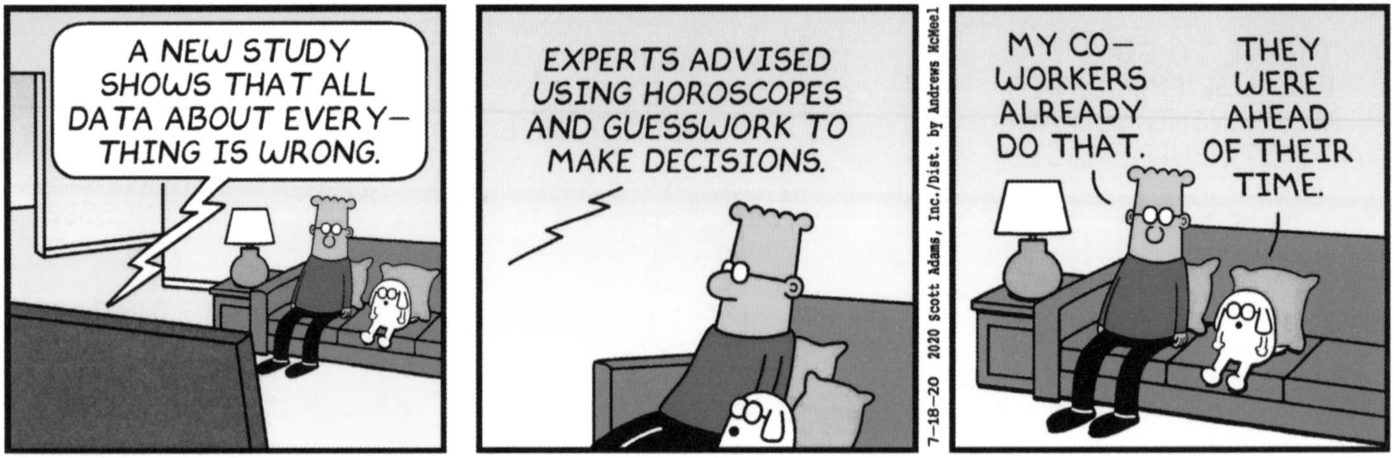
A NEW STUDY SHOWS THAT ALL DATA ABOUT EVERY-THING IS WRONG.
EXPERTS ADVISED USING HOROSCOPES AND GUESSWORK TO MAKE DECISIONS.
7-18-20 2020 Scott Adams, Inc./Dist. by Andrews McMeel
MY CO-WORKERS ALREADY DO THAT.
THEY WERE AHEAD OF THEIR TIME.

I'M STARTING A WHISPER CAMPAIGN AGAINST MY RIVAL IN MANAGEMENT.
I WANT YOU TO TELL PEOPLE HE BUYS BABIES FROM THE POOR AND EATS THEM.
NO ONE IS DUMB ENOUGH TO BELIEVE THAT.
PEOPLE WILL BELIEVE ANY-THING.
NOT **ANYTHING**.
YES, ANYTHING.
FINE. I'LL TRY IT, BUT ONLY TO PROVE HOW WRONG YOU ARE.
HOW MANY DOES HE EAT PER DAY?
I NEED A NEW PLANET.
© 2020 Scott Adams, Inc./Dist. by Andrews McMeel
7-19-20

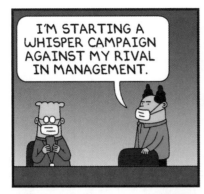

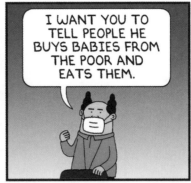

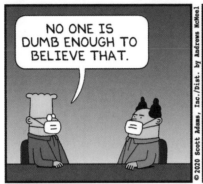

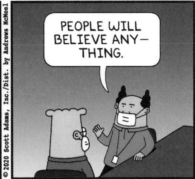

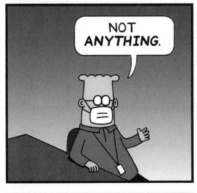

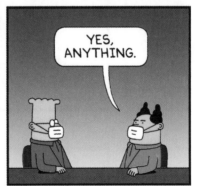

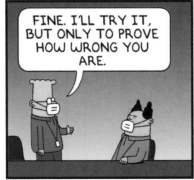

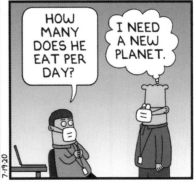

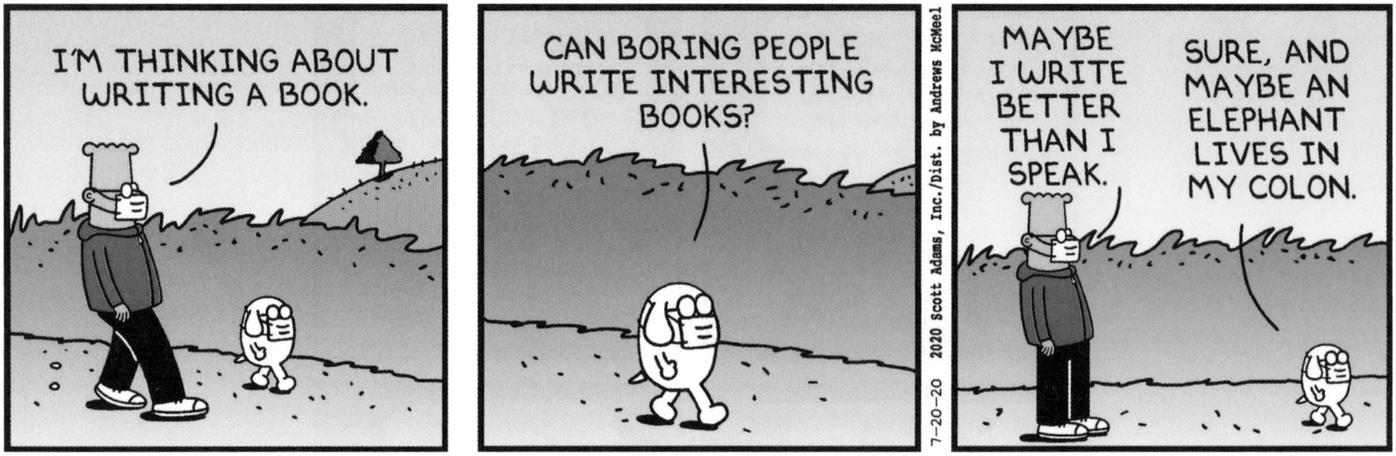
I'M THINKING ABOUT WRITING A BOOK.
CAN BORING PEOPLE WRITE INTERESTING BOOKS?
7-20-20 2020 Scott Adams, Inc./Dist. by Andrews McMeel
MAYBE I WRITE BETTER THAN I SPEAK.
SURE, AND MAYBE AN ELEPHANT LIVES IN MY COLON.

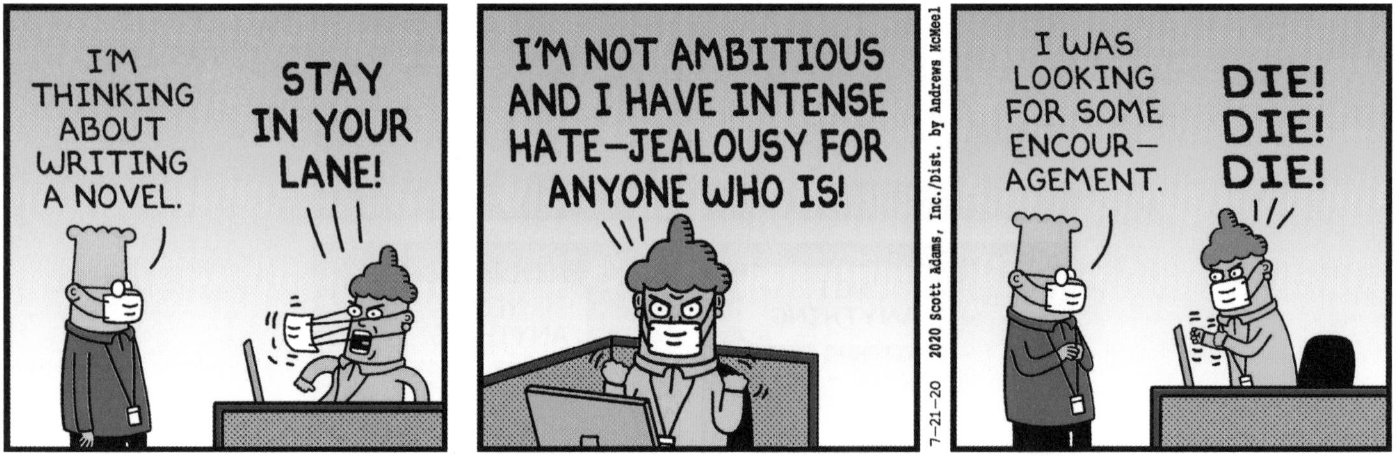
I'M THINKING ABOUT WRITING A NOVEL.
STAY IN YOUR LANE!
I'M NOT AMBITIOUS AND I HAVE INTENSE HATE-JEALOUSY FOR ANYONE WHO IS!
7-21-20 2020 Scott Adams, Inc./Dist. by Andrews McMeel
I WAS LOOKING FOR SOME ENCOUR-AGEMENT.
DIE! DIE! DIE!

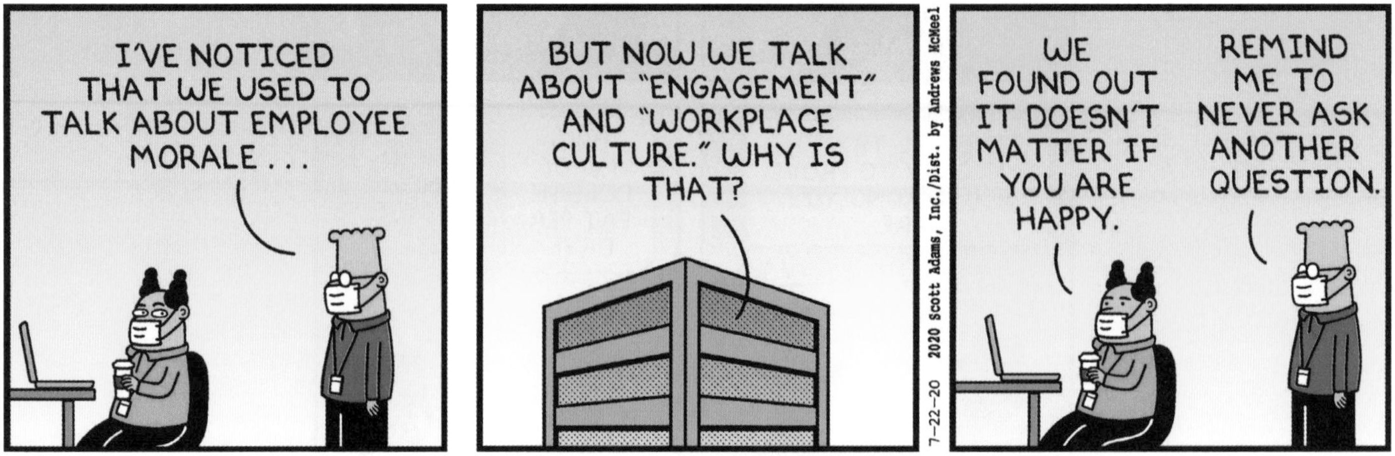
I'VE NOTICED THAT WE USED TO TALK ABOUT EMPLOYEE MORALE . . .
BUT NOW WE TALK ABOUT "ENGAGEMENT" AND "WORKPLACE CULTURE." WHY IS THAT?
7-22-20 2020 Scott Adams, Inc./Dist. by Andrews McMeel
WE FOUND OUT IT DOESN'T MATTER IF YOU ARE HAPPY.
REMIND ME TO NEVER ASK ANOTHER QUESTION.

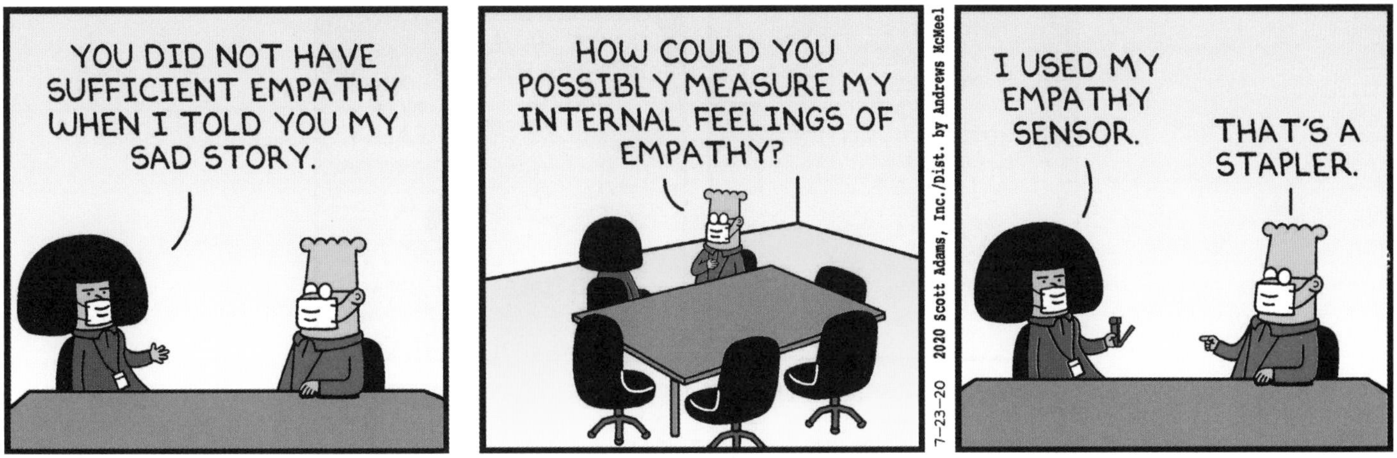
YOU DID NOT HAVE SUFFICIENT EMPATHY WHEN I TOLD YOU MY SAD STORY.
HOW COULD YOU POSSIBLY MEASURE MY INTERNAL FEELINGS OF EMPATHY?
I USED MY EMPATHY SENSOR.
THAT'S A STAPLER.


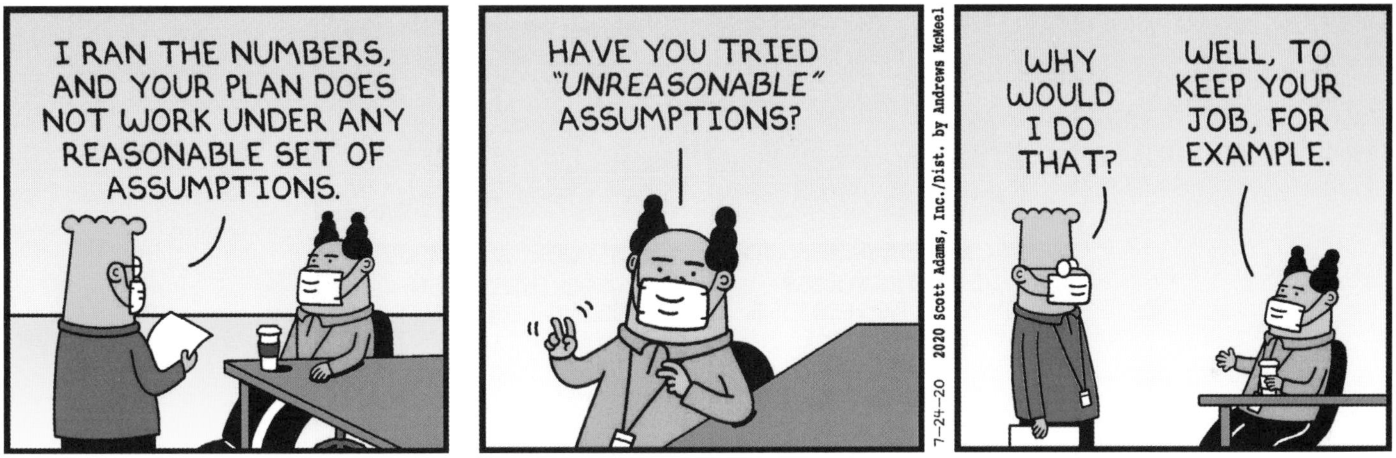
I RAN THE NUMBERS, AND YOUR PLAN DOES NOT WORK UNDER ANY REASONABLE SET OF ASSUMPTIONS.
HAVE YOU TRIED *"UNREASONABLE"* ASSUMPTIONS?
WHY WOULD I DO THAT?
WELL, TO KEEP YOUR JOB, FOR EXAMPLE.


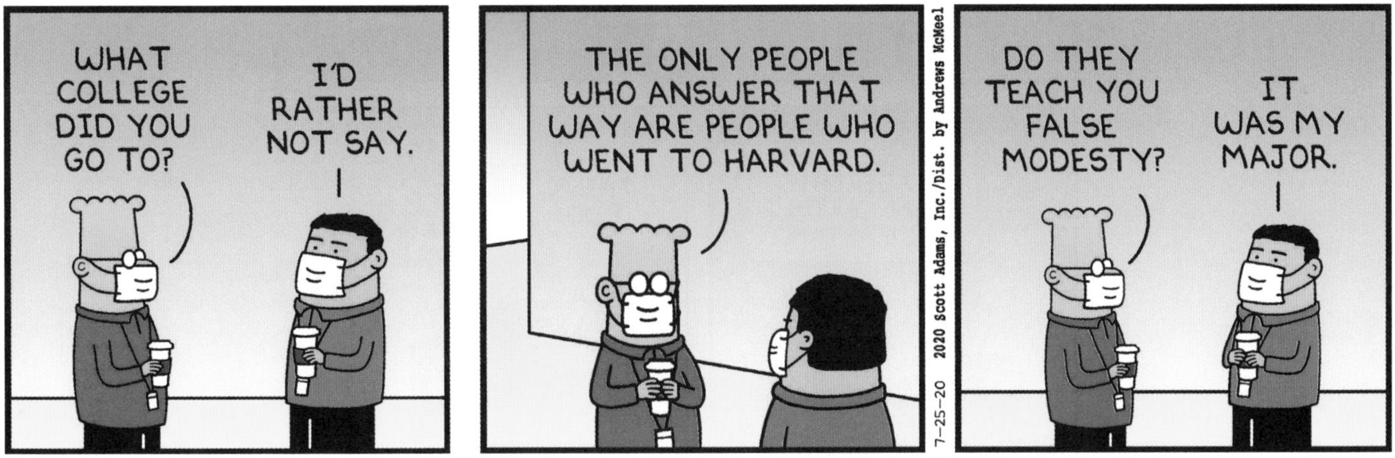
WHAT COLLEGE DID YOU GO TO?
I'D RATHER NOT SAY.
THE ONLY PEOPLE WHO ANSWER THAT WAY ARE PEOPLE WHO WENT TO HARVARD.
DO THEY TEACH YOU FALSE MODESTY?
IT WAS MY MAJOR.

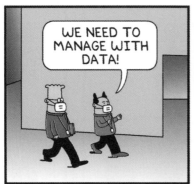

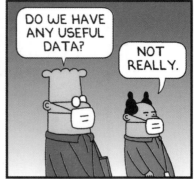

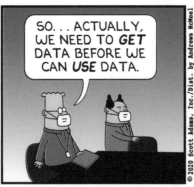

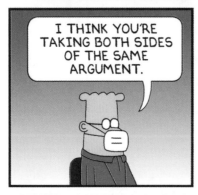

WE NEED TO MANAGE WITH DATA!
DO WE HAVE ANY USEFUL DATA?
NOT REALLY.
SO. . . ACTUALLY, WE NEED TO **GET** DATA BEFORE WE CAN **USE** DATA.
WE DON'T HAVE TIME FOR YOUR ANALYSIS PARALYSIS!
I THINK YOU'RE TAKING BOTH SIDES OF THE SAME ARGUMENT.
YOU INSIST ON USING DATA, BUT YOU DON'T WANT TO WAIT FOR DATA.
IT'S CALLED LEADERSHIP. YOU WOULDN'T UNDERSTAND.
OH, I THINK I DO.
STOP BEING SUCH A MASK HOLE.
© 2020 Scott Adams, Inc./Dist. by Andrews McMeel
7-26-20

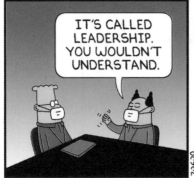

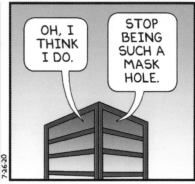

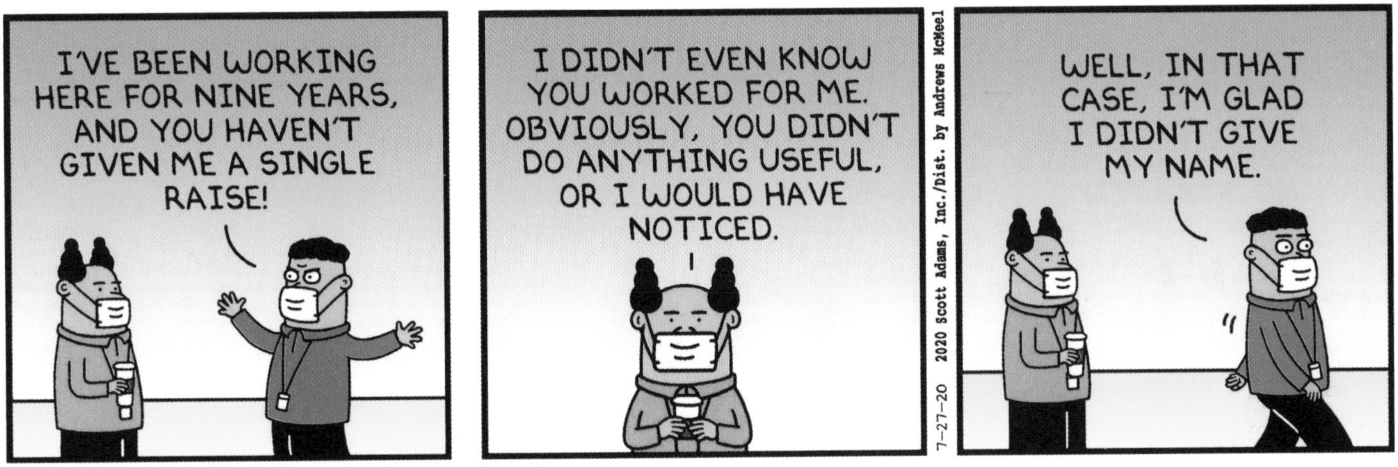
I'VE BEEN WORKING HERE FOR NINE YEARS, AND YOU HAVEN'T GIVEN ME A SINGLE RAISE!
I DIDN'T EVEN KNOW YOU WORKED FOR ME. OBVIOUSLY, YOU DIDN'T DO ANYTHING USEFUL, OR I WOULD HAVE NOTICED.
7-27-20 2020 Scott Adams, Inc./Dist. by Andrews McMeel
WELL, IN THAT CASE, I'M GLAD I DIDN'T GIVE MY NAME.

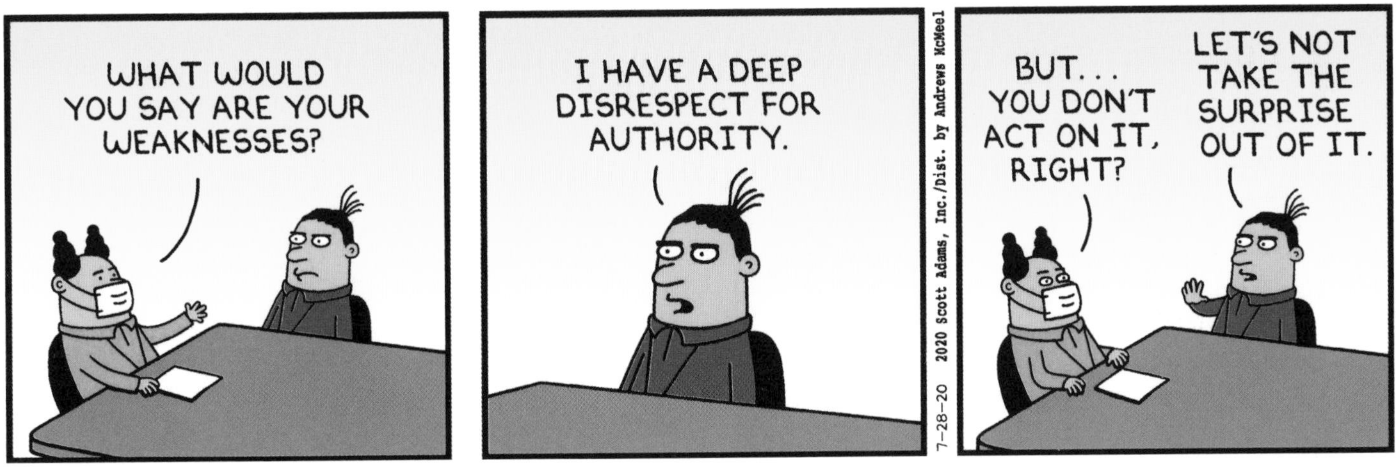
WHAT WOULD YOU SAY ARE YOUR WEAKNESSES?
I HAVE A DEEP DISRESPECT FOR AUTHORITY.
7-28-20 2020 Scott Adams, Inc./Dist. by Andrews McMeel
BUT... YOU DON'T ACT ON IT, RIGHT?
LET'S NOT TAKE THE SURPRISE OUT OF IT.

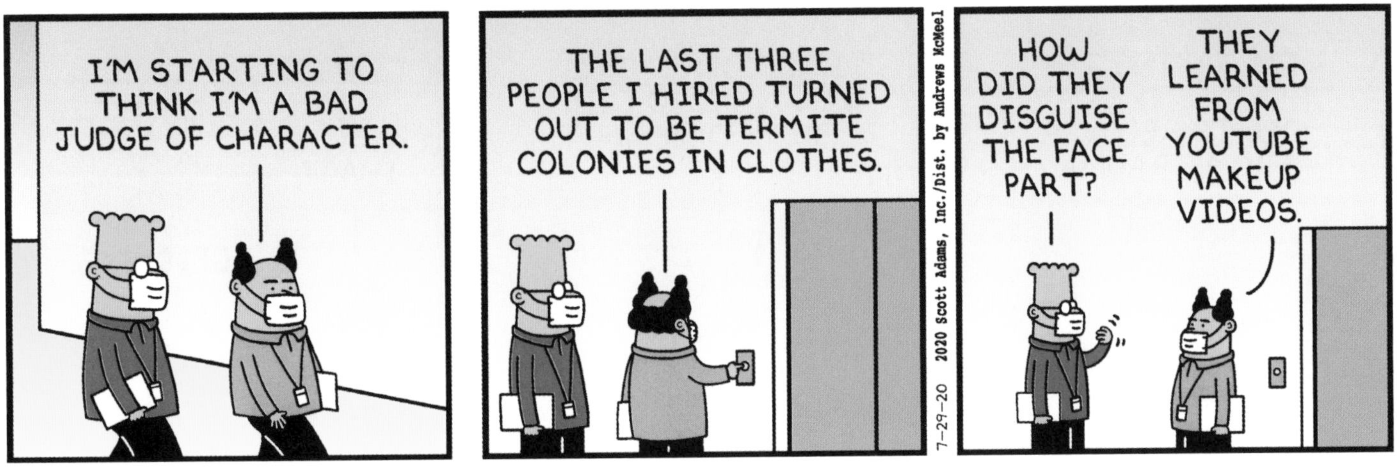
I'M STARTING TO THINK I'M A BAD JUDGE OF CHARACTER.
THE LAST THREE PEOPLE I HIRED TURNED OUT TO BE TERMITE COLONIES IN CLOTHES.
7-29-20 2020 Scott Adams, Inc./Dist. by Andrews McMeel
HOW DID THEY DISGUISE THE FACE PART?
THEY LEARNED FROM YOUTUBE MAKEUP VIDEOS.

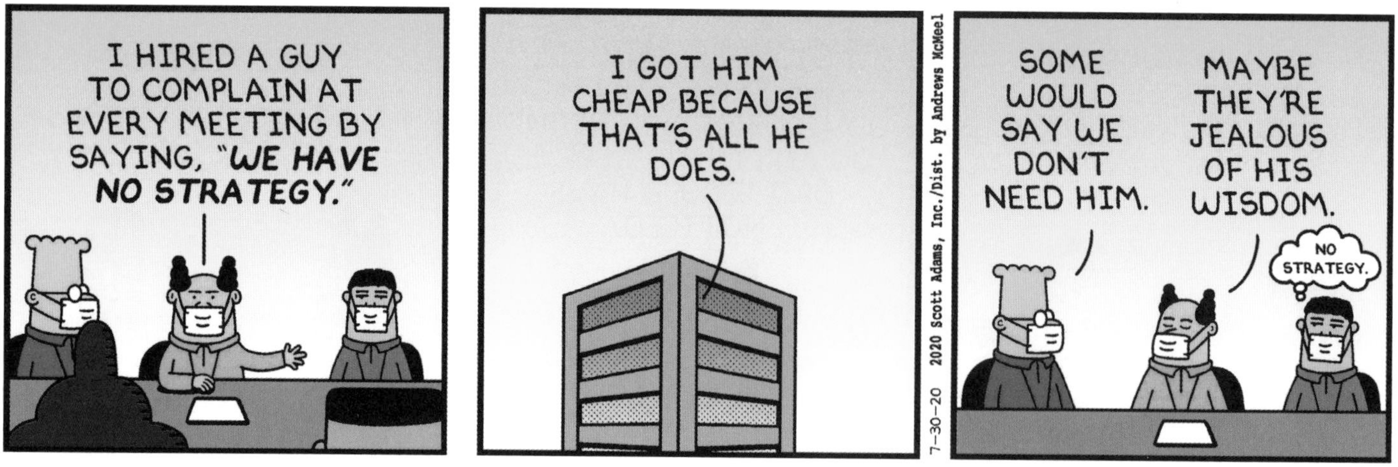
I HIRED A GUY TO COMPLAIN AT EVERY MEETING BY SAYING, "**WE HAVE NO STRATEGY.**"
I GOT HIM CHEAP BECAUSE THAT'S ALL HE DOES.
7-30-20 2020 Scott Adams, Inc./Dist. by Andrews McMeel
SOME WOULD SAY WE DON'T NEED HIM.
MAYBE THEY'RE JEALOUS OF HIS WISDOM.
NO STRATEGY.

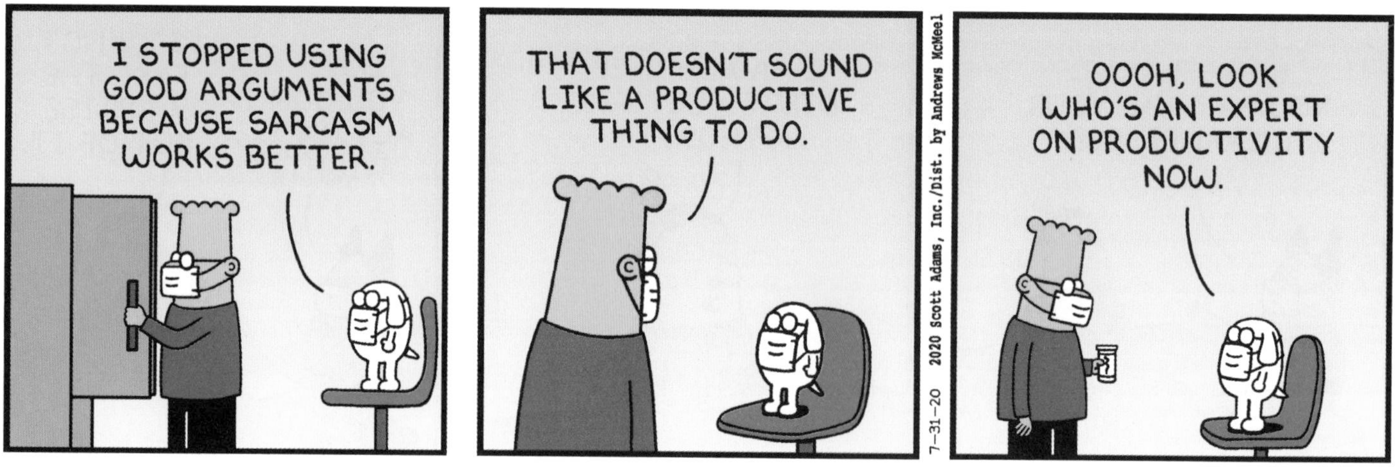
I STOPPED USING GOOD ARGUMENTS BECAUSE SARCASM WORKS BETTER.
THAT DOESN'T SOUND LIKE A PRODUCTIVE THING TO DO.
7-31-20 2020 Scott Adams, Inc./Dist. by Andrews McMeel
OOOH, LOOK WHO'S AN EXPERT ON PRODUCTIVITY NOW.

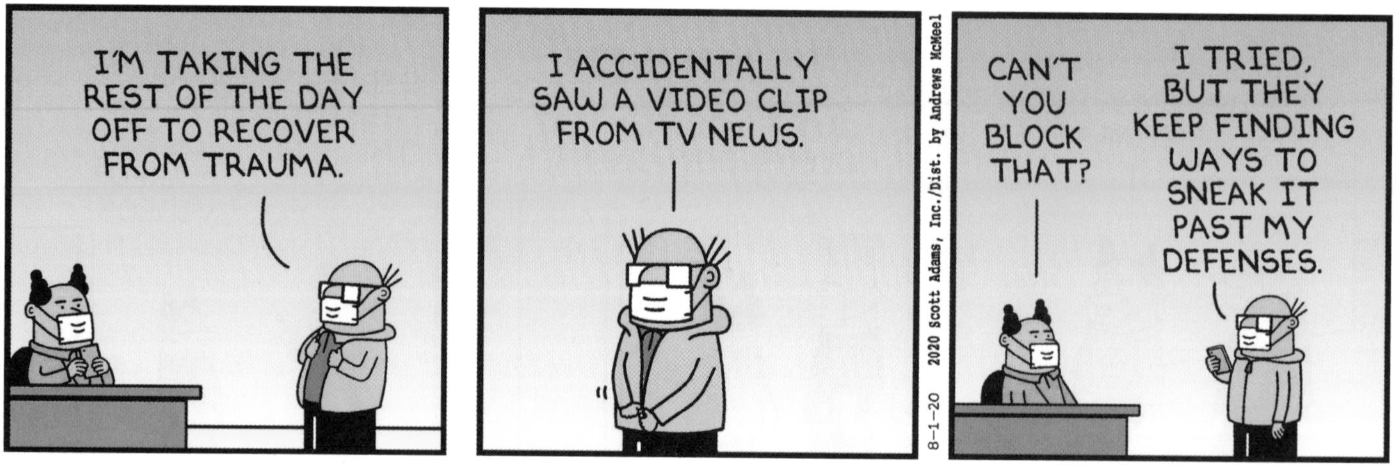
I'M TAKING THE REST OF THE DAY OFF TO RECOVER FROM TRAUMA.
I ACCIDENTALLY SAW A VIDEO CLIP FROM TV NEWS.
8-1-20 2020 Scott Adams, Inc./Dist. by Andrews McMeel
CAN'T YOU BLOCK THAT?
I TRIED, BUT THEY KEEP FINDING WAYS TO SNEAK IT PAST MY DEFENSES.

I ESTIMATE THE ODDS AT A 70% CHANCE THINGS GO WELL, AND A 30% CHANCE WE LOSE MONEY ON THE DEAL.
IF WE LOSE MONEY, WILL YOU ADMIT YOU WERE WRONG?
HOW COULD I BE WRONG? I'M JUST TELLING YOU THE ODDS.
IF WE LOSE MONEY, THAT'S ON YOU FOR RECOMMENDING IT.
UM. . . NO. I'M TELLING YOU THE ODDS AND LETTING YOU DECIDE.
BUT YOU'RE THE ONE SAYING THIS IS SUCH A GREAT DEAL.
I'M ONLY TELLING YOU THE ODDS, YOU PEA-BRAINED IGNORAMUS!!!
SO, YOU WON'T ADMIT YOU WERE WRONG?
© 2020 Scott Adams, Inc./Dist. by Andrews McMeel
8-2-20

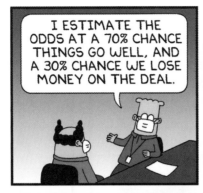

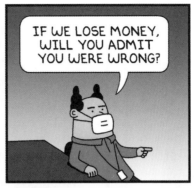

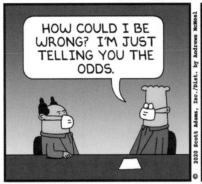

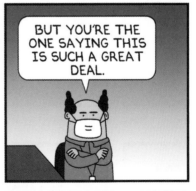

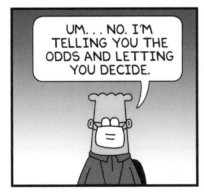

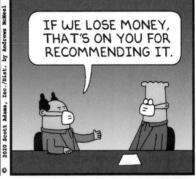

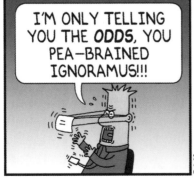

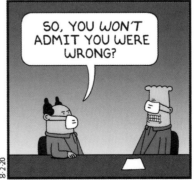

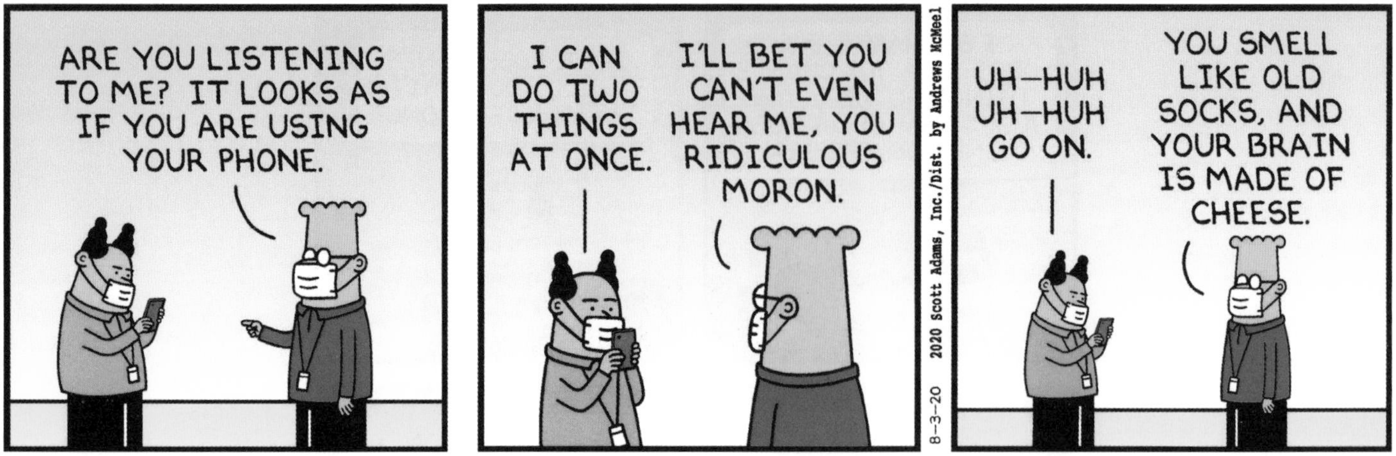
ARE YOU LISTENING TO ME? IT LOOKS AS IF YOU ARE USING YOUR PHONE.
I CAN DO TWO THINGS AT ONCE.
I'LL BET YOU CAN'T EVEN HEAR ME, YOU RIDICULOUS MORON.
8-3-20 2020 Scott Adams, Inc./Dist. by Andrews McMeel
UH-HUH UH-HUH GO ON.
YOU SMELL LIKE OLD SOCKS, AND YOUR BRAIN IS MADE OF CHEESE.

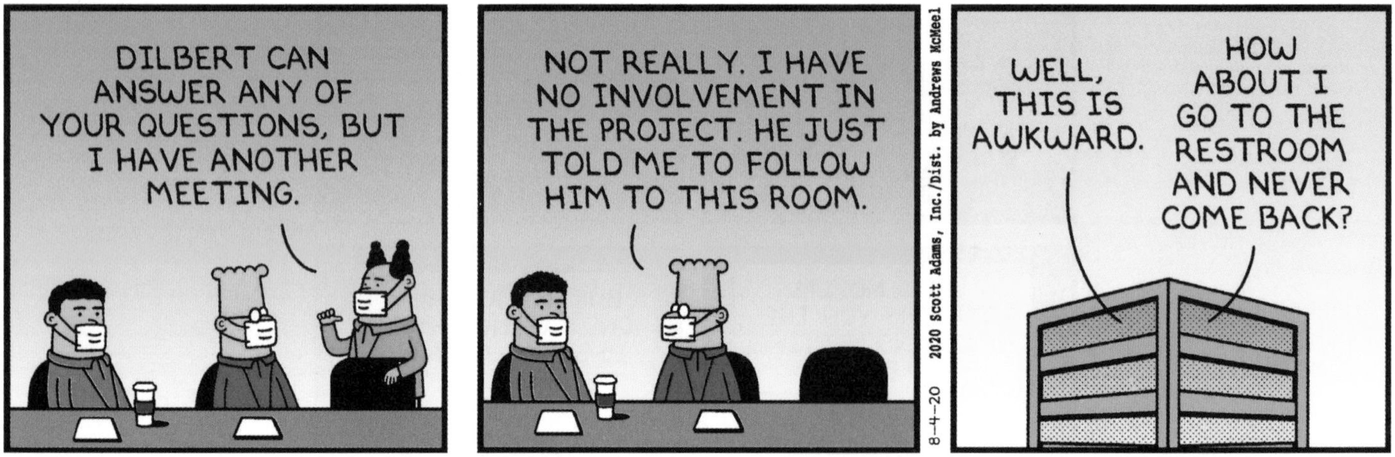
DILBERT CAN ANSWER ANY OF YOUR QUESTIONS, BUT I HAVE ANOTHER MEETING.
NOT REALLY. I HAVE NO INVOLVEMENT IN THE PROJECT. HE JUST TOLD ME TO FOLLOW HIM TO THIS ROOM.
8-4-20 2020 Scott Adams, Inc./Dist. by Andrews McMeel
WELL, THIS IS AWKWARD.
HOW ABOUT I GO TO THE RESTROOM AND NEVER COME BACK?

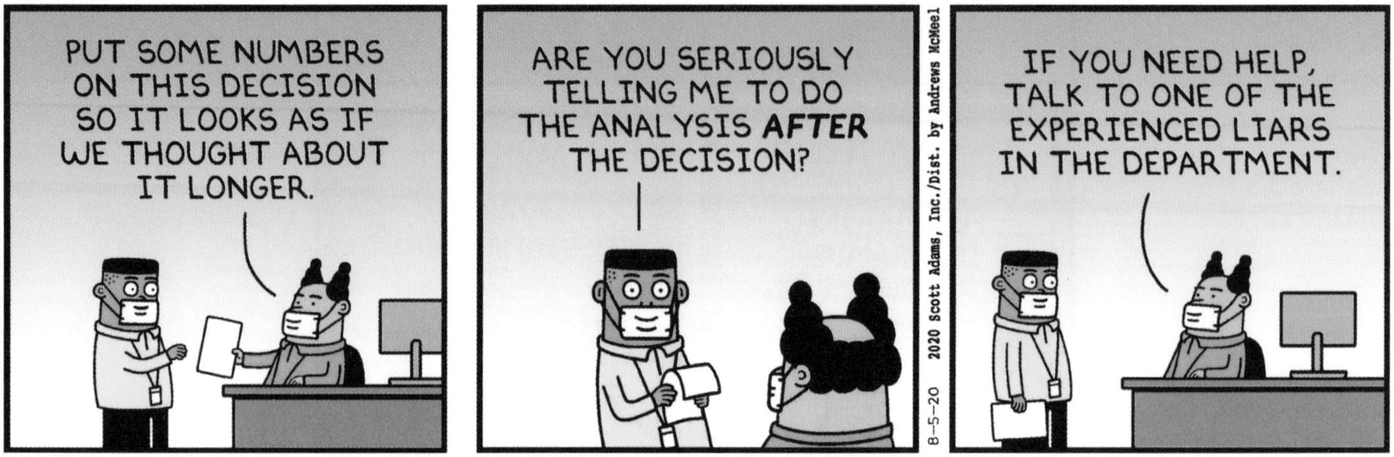
PUT SOME NUMBERS ON THIS DECISION SO IT LOOKS AS IF WE THOUGHT ABOUT IT LONGER.
ARE YOU SERIOUSLY TELLING ME TO DO THE ANALYSIS **AFTER** THE DECISION?
8-5-20 2020 Scott Adams, Inc./Dist. by Andrews McMeel
IF YOU NEED HELP, TALK TO ONE OF THE EXPERIENCED LIARS IN THE DEPARTMENT.

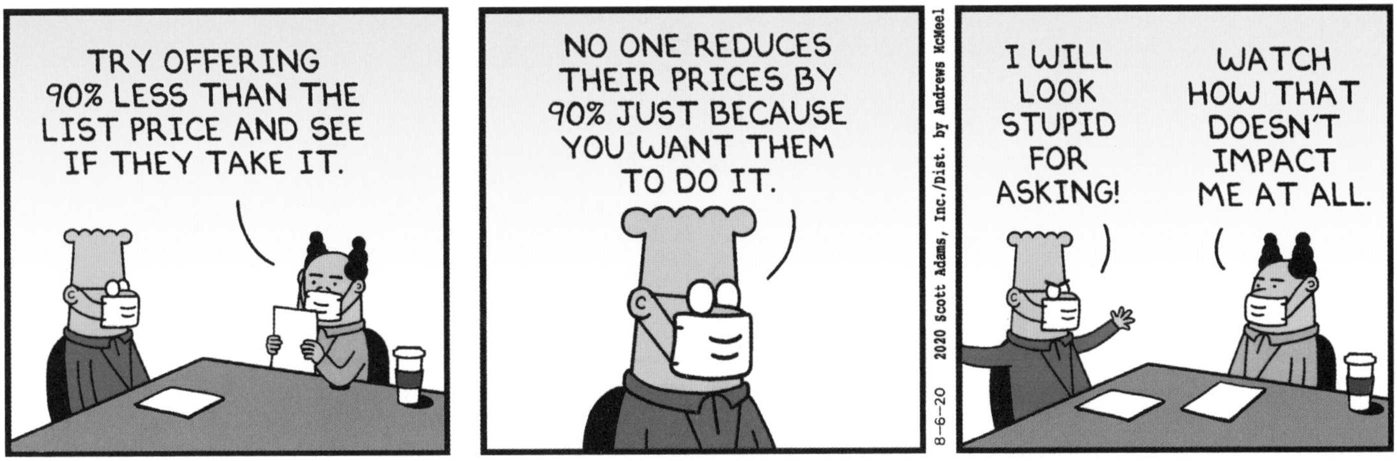
TRY OFFERING 90% LESS THAN THE LIST PRICE AND SEE IF THEY TAKE IT.
NO ONE REDUCES THEIR PRICES BY 90% JUST BECAUSE YOU WANT THEM TO DO IT.
I WILL LOOK STUPID FOR ASKING!
WATCH HOW THAT DOESN'T IMPACT ME AT ALL.
8-6-20 2020 Scott Adams, Inc./Dist. by Andrews McMeel

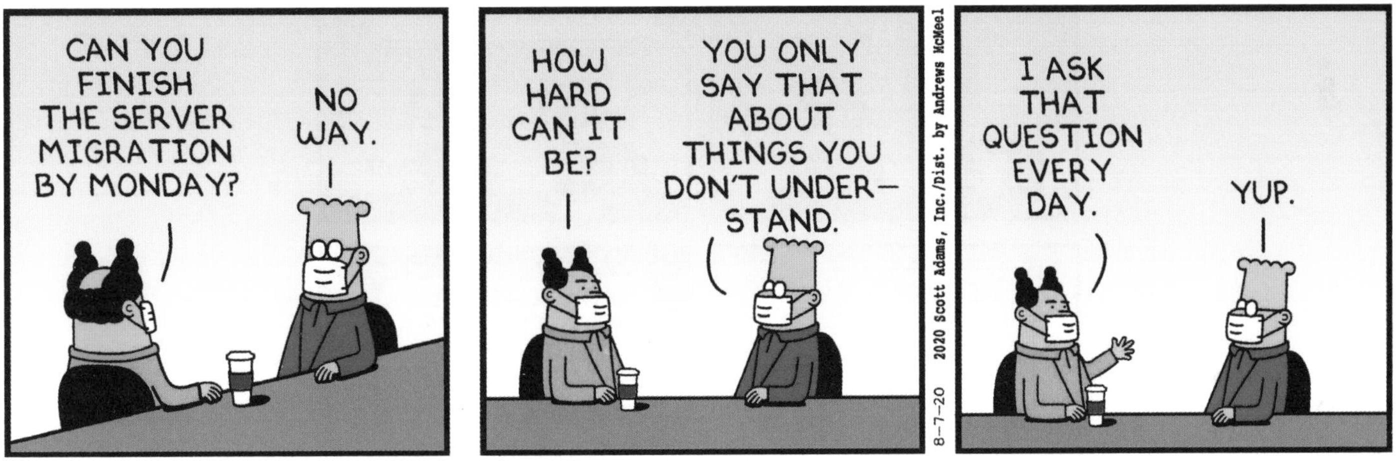
CAN YOU FINISH THE SERVER MIGRATION BY MONDAY?
NO WAY.
HOW HARD CAN IT BE?
YOU ONLY SAY THAT ABOUT THINGS YOU DON'T UNDER-STAND.
I ASK THAT QUESTION EVERY DAY.
YUP.
8-7-20 2020 Scott Adams, Inc./Dist. by Andrews McMeel

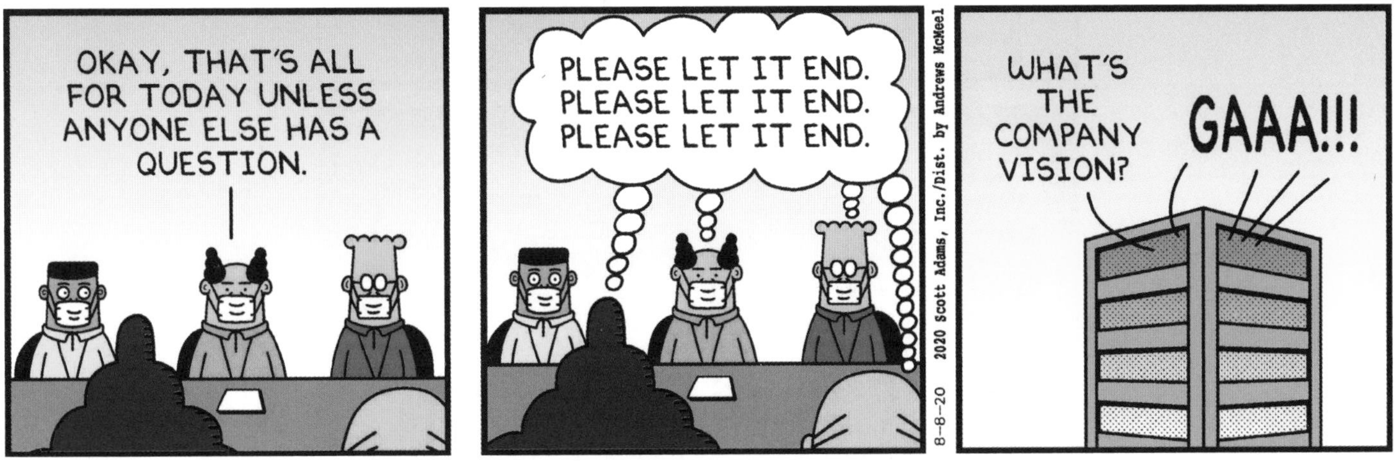
OKAY, THAT'S ALL FOR TODAY UNLESS ANYONE ELSE HAS A QUESTION.
PLEASE LET IT END. PLEASE LET IT END. PLEASE LET IT END.
WHAT'S THE COMPANY VISION?
GAAA!!!
8-8-20 2020 Scott Adams, Inc./Dist. by Andrews McMeel

CAN YOU BELIEVE A VENDOR TRIED TO COME IN HERE WITH NO FACE MASK?
I TOLD HIM IT DIDN'T MATTER WHAT KIND OF FACE COVERING HE USED, IT ONLY MATTERED THAT HE HAD ONE.
THIS IS WHERE MY TALE TAKES A DARK TURN.
NOW PEEVED, THE VENDOR STORMED BACK TO HIS CAR, WHERE HE HAD A BAGGED LUNCH.
HE ANGRILY REMOVED THE PLASTIC WRAP FROM HIS SANDWICH
AND WRAPPED IT AROUND HIS HEAD TO SERVE AS HIS FACE MASK.
HE SUFFOCATED IN MINUTES, OBVIOUSLY.
IS THAT THE SANDWICH?
WOULD HAVE GONE TO WASTE.
© 2020 Scott Adams, Inc./Dist. by Andrews McMeel
8-9-20

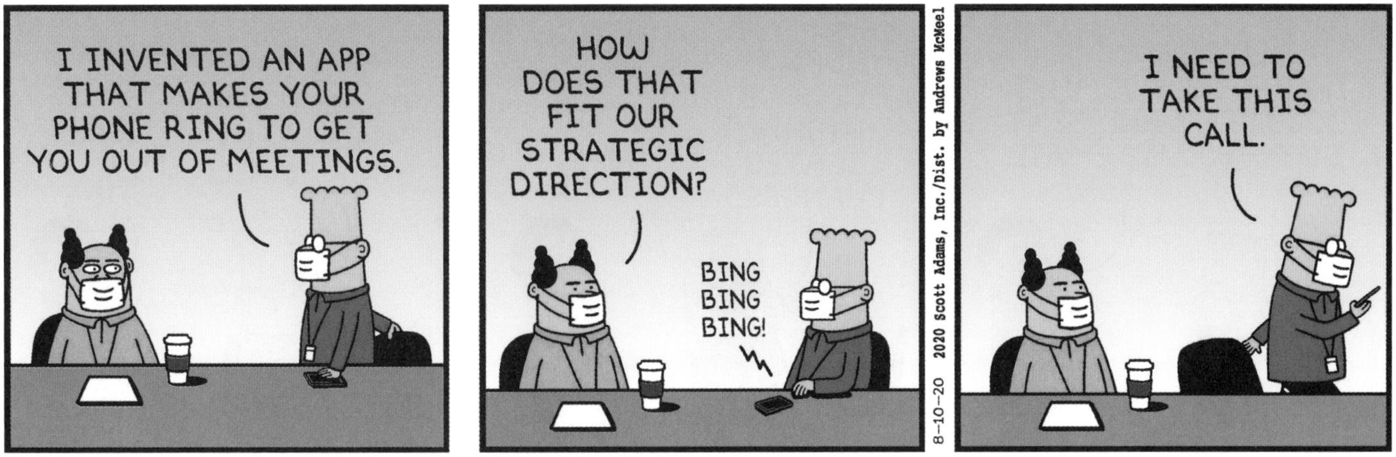
I INVENTED AN APP THAT MAKES YOUR PHONE RING TO GET YOU OUT OF MEETINGS.
HOW DOES THAT FIT OUR STRATEGIC DIRECTION?
BING BING BING!
I NEED TO TAKE THIS CALL.
8-10-20 © 2020 Scott Adams, Inc./Dist. by Andrews McMeel

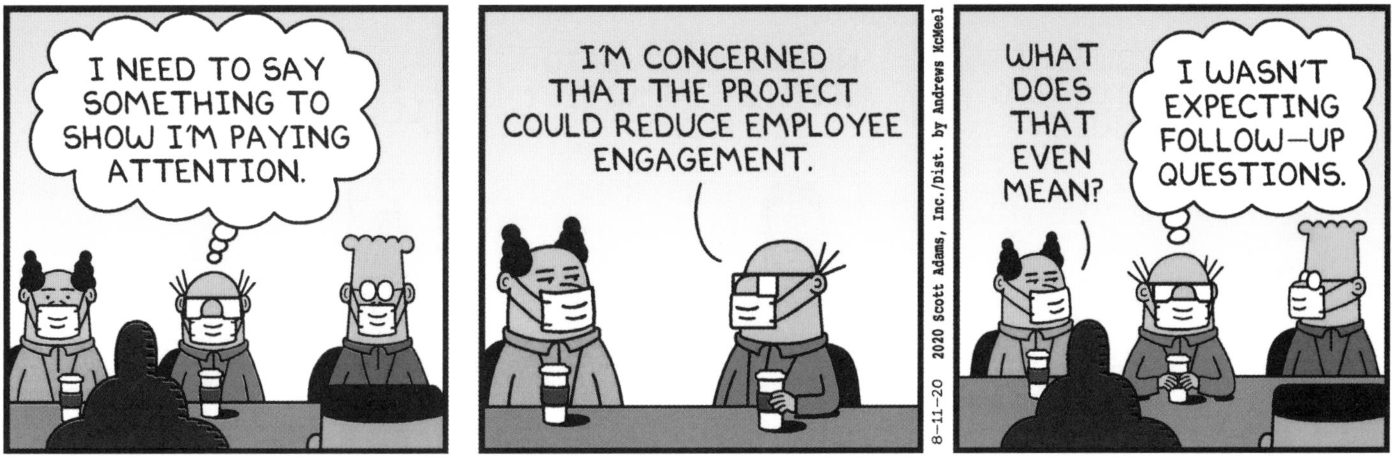
I NEED TO SAY SOMETHING TO SHOW I'M PAYING ATTENTION.
I'M CONCERNED THAT THE PROJECT COULD REDUCE EMPLOYEE ENGAGEMENT.
WHAT DOES THAT EVEN MEAN?
I WASN'T EXPECTING FOLLOW-UP QUESTIONS.
8-11-20 © 2020 Scott Adams, Inc./Dist. by Andrews McMeel

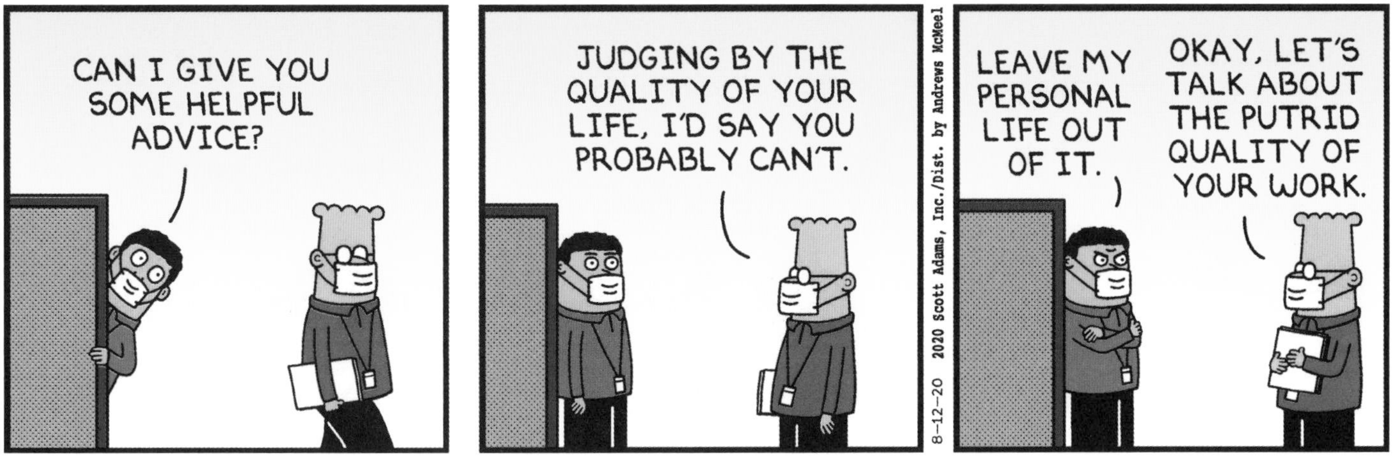
CAN I GIVE YOU SOME HELPFUL ADVICE?
JUDGING BY THE QUALITY OF YOUR LIFE, I'D SAY YOU PROBABLY CAN'T.
LEAVE MY PERSONAL LIFE OUT OF IT.
OKAY, LET'S TALK ABOUT THE PUTRID QUALITY OF YOUR WORK.
8-12-20 © 2020 Scott Adams, Inc./Dist. by Andrews McMeel

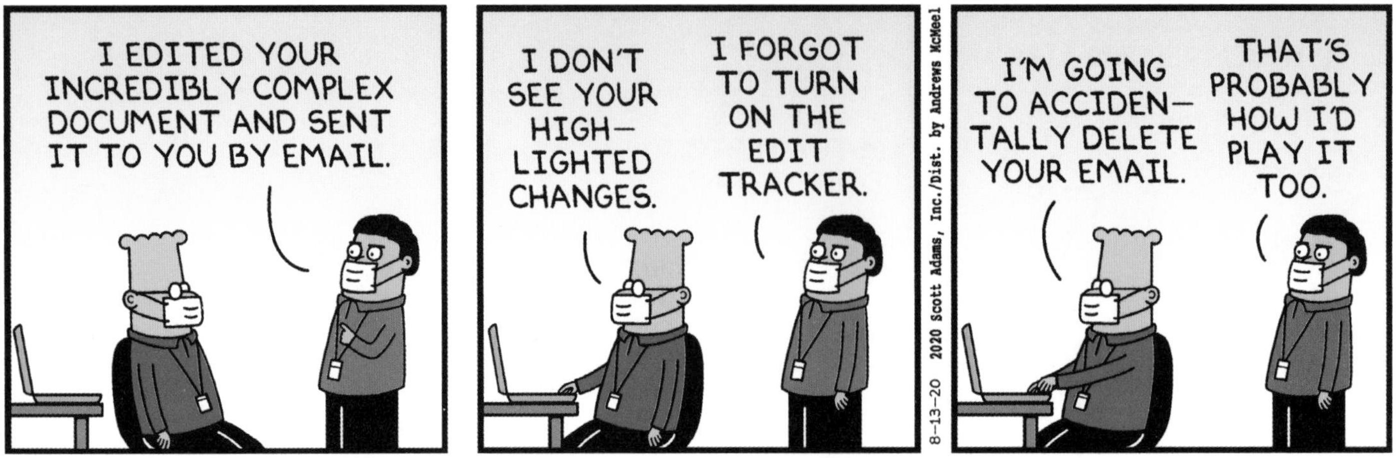
I EDITED YOUR INCREDIBLY COMPLEX DOCUMENT AND SENT IT TO YOU BY EMAIL.
I DON'T SEE YOUR HIGH-LIGHTED CHANGES.
I FORGOT TO TURN ON THE EDIT TRACKER.
I'M GOING TO ACCIDEN-TALLY DELETE YOUR EMAIL.
THAT'S PROBABLY HOW I'D PLAY IT TOO.
8-13-20 2020 Scott Adams, Inc./Dist. by Andrews McMeel

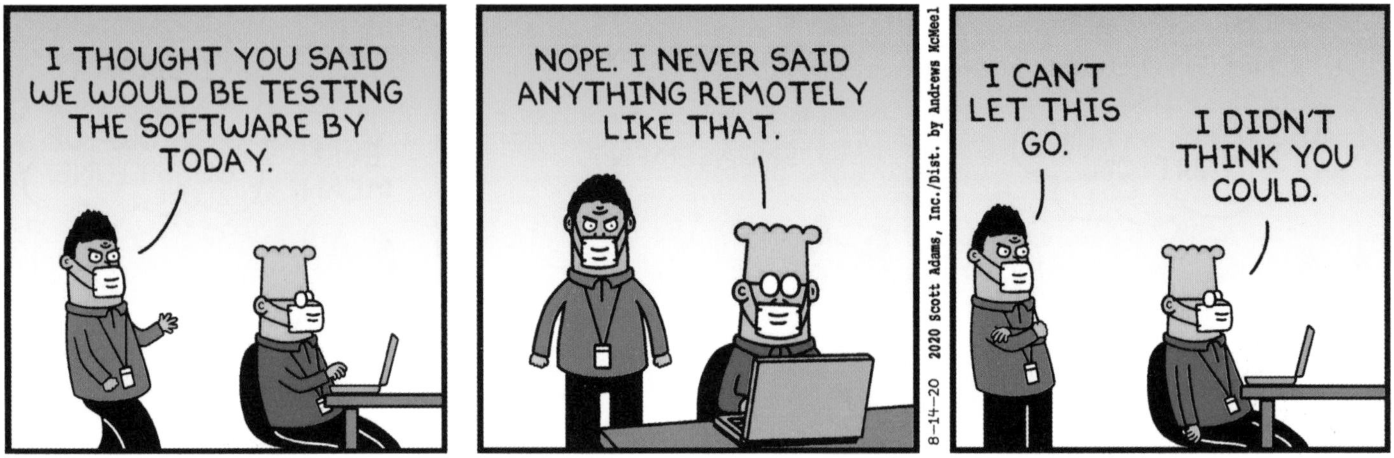
I THOUGHT YOU SAID WE WOULD BE TESTING THE SOFTWARE BY TODAY.
NOPE. I NEVER SAID ANYTHING REMOTELY LIKE THAT.
I CAN'T LET THIS GO.
I DIDN'T THINK YOU COULD.
8-14-20 2020 Scott Adams, Inc./Dist. by Andrews McMeel

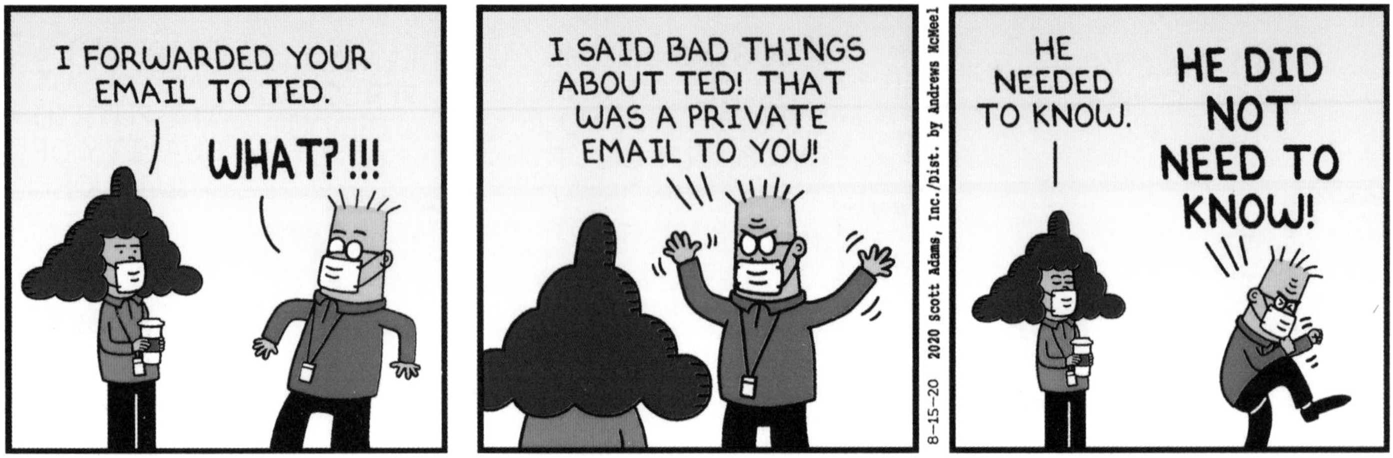
I FORWARDED YOUR EMAIL TO TED.
WHAT? !!!
I SAID BAD THINGS ABOUT TED! THAT WAS A PRIVATE EMAIL TO YOU!
HE NEEDED TO KNOW.
HE DID NOT NEED TO KNOW!
8-15-20 2020 Scott Adams, Inc./Dist. by Andrews McMeel

WHEN HUMANS WERE PRIMITIVE AND DUMB, THEY USED THEIR SUPERSTITIONS AND BIASES TO MAKE DECISIONS.
EVENTUALLY, SCIENCE WON OUT, AND WE EVOLVED TO USE DATA AND REASON TO MAKE DECISIONS.
HOW'D THAT WORK OUT?
NOT SO GOOD.
IT TURNS OUT THAT ALL OF OUR DATA ARE UNRELIABLE AND CONFLICTING.
AND WE DON'T HAVE THE MENTAL CAPACITY TO USE REASON.
IT'S STILL BETTER THAN GUESSING.
HOW DO YOU **KNOW** THAT?
YOU ARE HARD TO TALK TO.
© 2020 Scott Adams, Inc./Dist. by Andrews McMeel
8-16-20

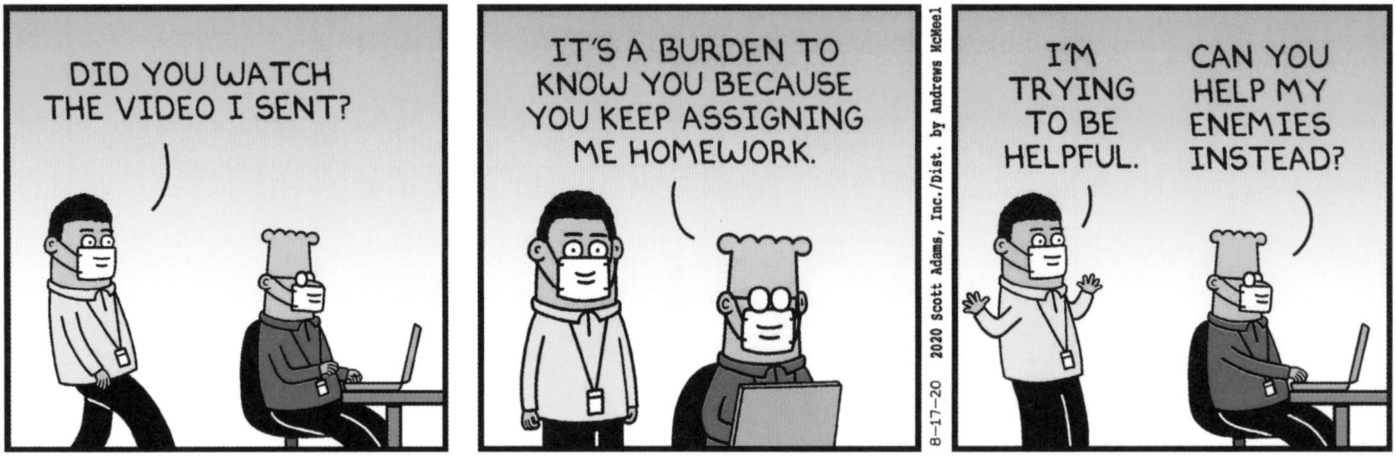
DID YOU WATCH THE VIDEO I SENT?
IT'S A BURDEN TO KNOW YOU BECAUSE YOU KEEP ASSIGNING ME HOMEWORK.
I'M TRYING TO BE HELPFUL.
CAN YOU HELP MY ENEMIES INSTEAD?
8-17-20 © 2020 Scott Adams, Inc./Dist. by Andrews McMeel

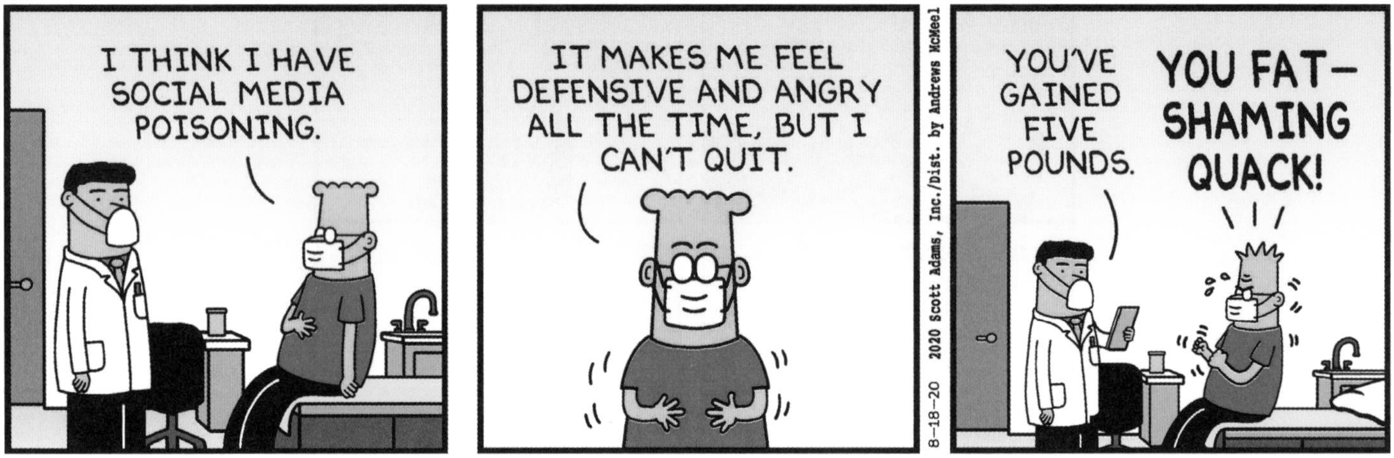
I THINK I HAVE SOCIAL MEDIA POISONING.
IT MAKES ME FEEL DEFENSIVE AND ANGRY ALL THE TIME, BUT I CAN'T QUIT.
YOU'VE GAINED FIVE POUNDS.
YOU FAT-SHAMING QUACK!
8-18-20 © 2020 Scott Adams, Inc./Dist. by Andrews McMeel

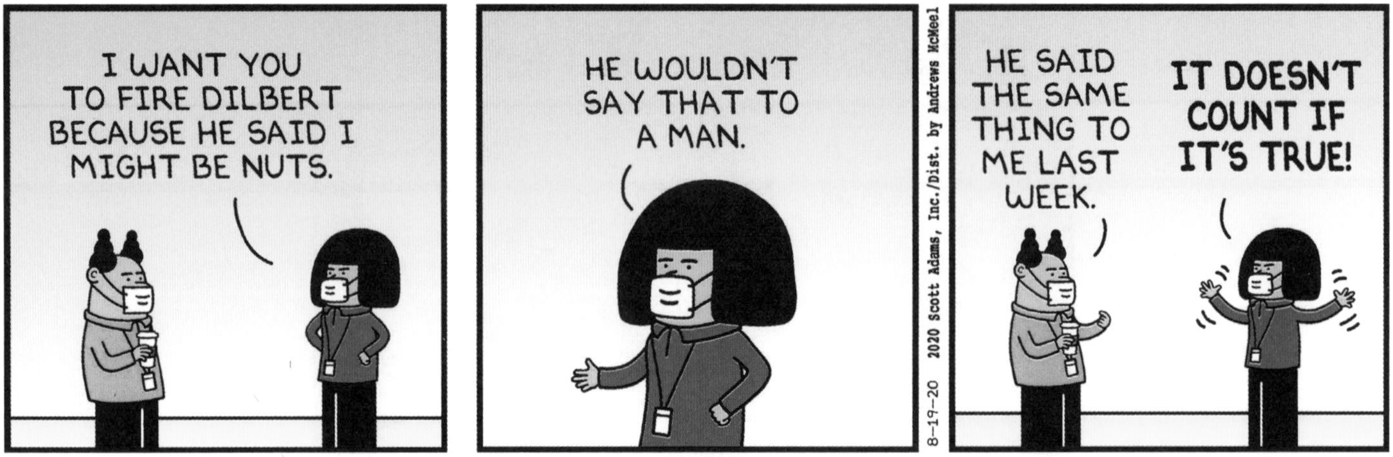
I WANT YOU TO FIRE DILBERT BECAUSE HE SAID I MIGHT BE NUTS.
HE WOULDN'T SAY THAT TO A MAN.
HE SAID THE SAME THING TO ME LAST WEEK.
IT DOESN'T COUNT IF IT'S TRUE!
8-19-20 © 2020 Scott Adams, Inc./Dist. by Andrews McMeel

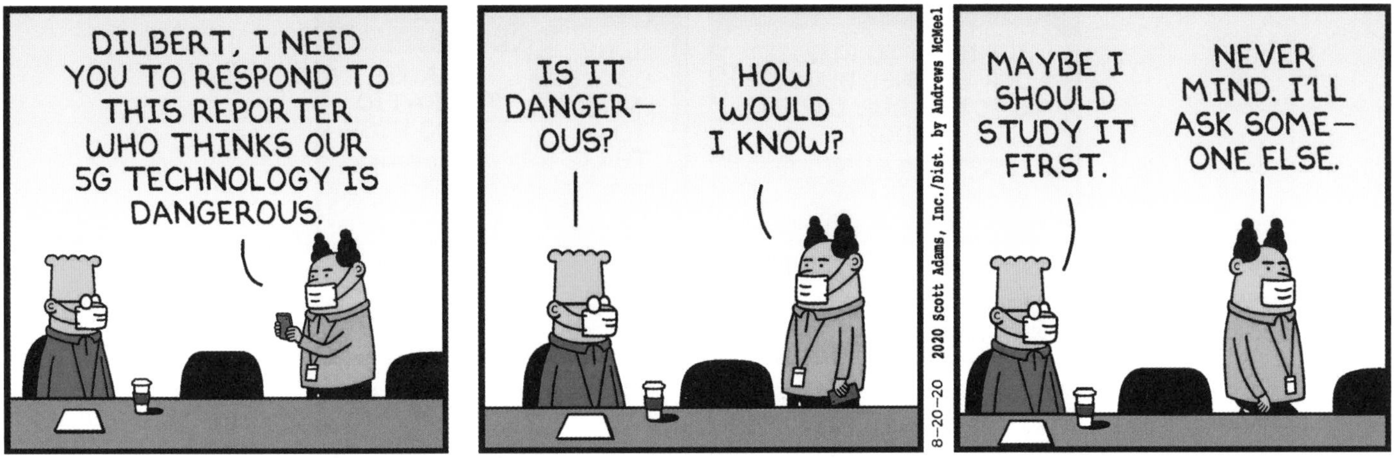
DILBERT, I NEED YOU TO RESPOND TO THIS REPORTER WHO THINKS OUR 5G TECHNOLOGY IS DANGEROUS.
IS IT DANGER-OUS?
HOW WOULD I KNOW?
8-20-20 2020 Scott Adams, Inc./Dist. by Andrews McMeel
MAYBE I SHOULD STUDY IT FIRST.
NEVER MIND. I'LL ASK SOME-ONE ELSE.

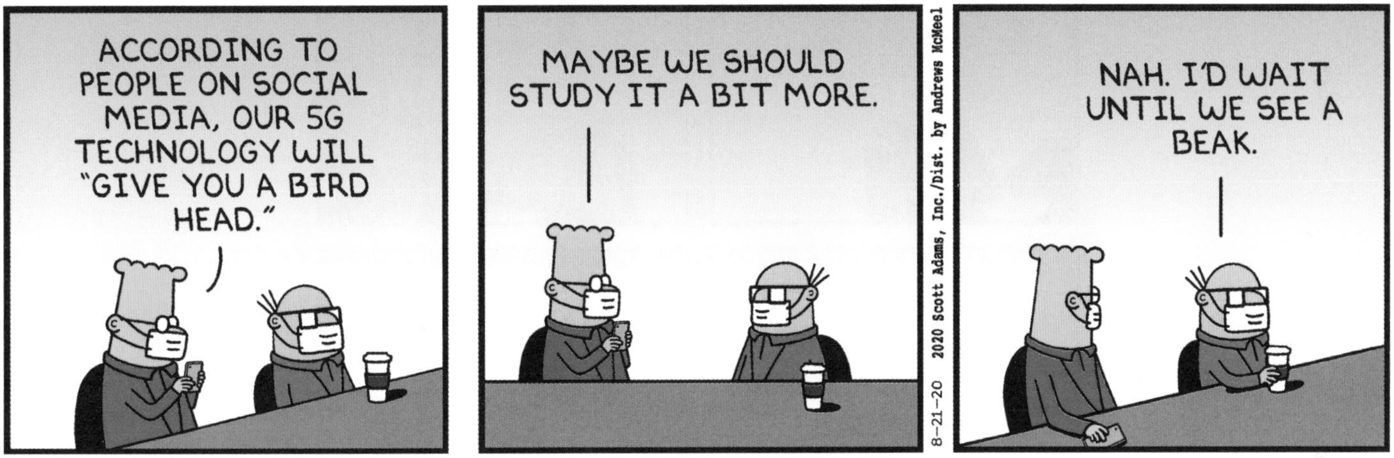
ACCORDING TO PEOPLE ON SOCIAL MEDIA, OUR 5G TECHNOLOGY WILL "GIVE YOU A BIRD HEAD."
MAYBE WE SHOULD STUDY IT A BIT MORE.
8-21-20 2020 Scott Adams, Inc./Dist. by Andrews McMeel
NAH. I'D WAIT UNTIL WE SEE A BEAK.

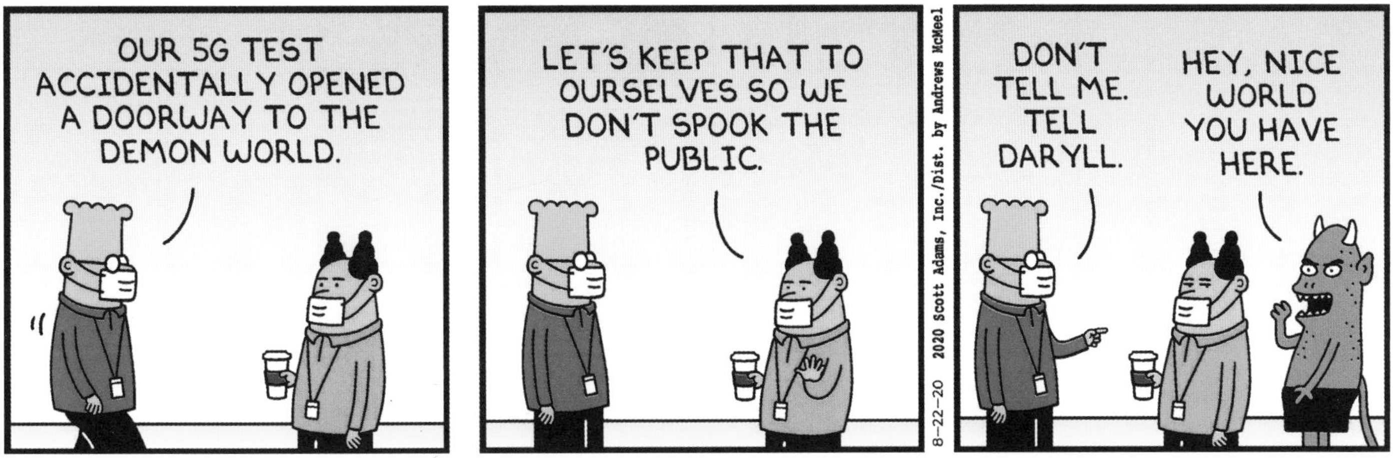
OUR 5G TEST ACCIDENTALLY OPENED A DOORWAY TO THE DEMON WORLD.
LET'S KEEP THAT TO OURSELVES SO WE DON'T SPOOK THE PUBLIC.
8-22-20 2020 Scott Adams, Inc./Dist. by Andrews McMeel
DON'T TELL ME. TELL DARYLL.
HEY, NICE WORLD YOU HAVE HERE.

WE NEED TO REDUCE OUR EXPENSE BUDGET TO 40% OF OUR CAPITAL BUDGET.
WHY DO WE NEED TO DO THAT?
BECAUSE THE RATIO IS TOO HIGH.
ARE YOU SAYING WE CAN'T AFFORD IT?
NO. I'M SAYING THE RATIO IS TOO HIGH.
OKAY, BUT BY WHAT STANDARD IS IT "TOO HIGH"?
BY HISTORICAL STANDARDS. IT HAS NEVER BEEN THIS HIGH.
I DON'T THINK WE WANT TO START USING AN IRRELEVANT RATIO TO MANAGE THE DEPARTMENT.
TO BE FAIR, THIS IS JUST THE FIRST TIME YOU NOTICED.
© 2020 Scott Adams, Inc./Dist. by Andrews McMeel
8-23-20

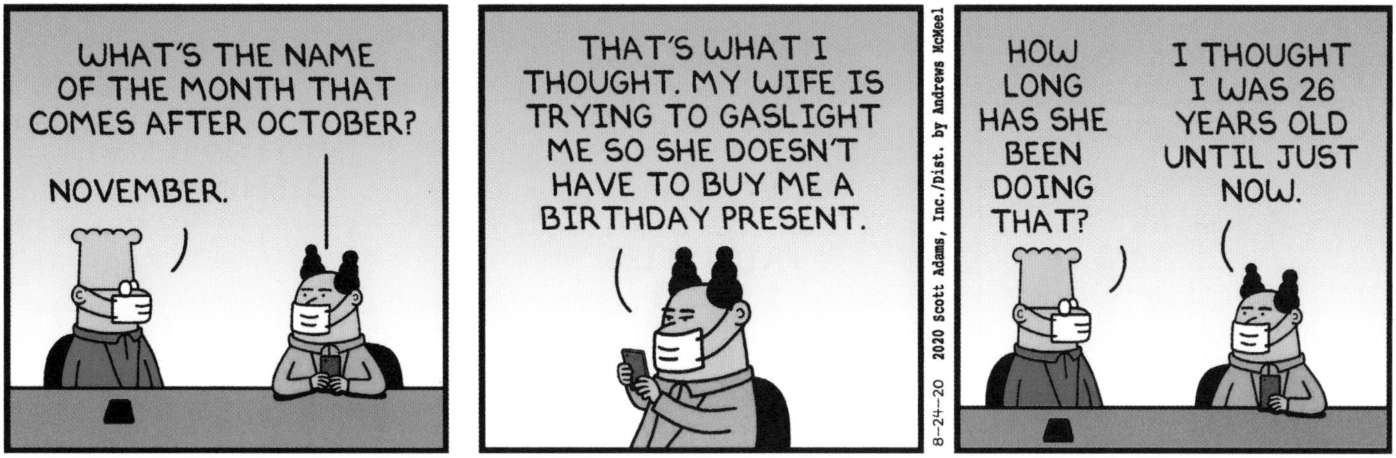

WHAT'S THE NAME OF THE MONTH THAT COMES AFTER OCTOBER?
NOVEMBER.
THAT'S WHAT I THOUGHT. MY WIFE IS TRYING TO GASLIGHT ME SO SHE DOESN'T HAVE TO BUY ME A BIRTHDAY PRESENT.
8-24-20 2020 Scott Adams, Inc./Dist. by Andrews McMeel
HOW LONG HAS SHE BEEN DOING THAT?
I THOUGHT I WAS 26 YEARS OLD UNTIL JUST NOW.


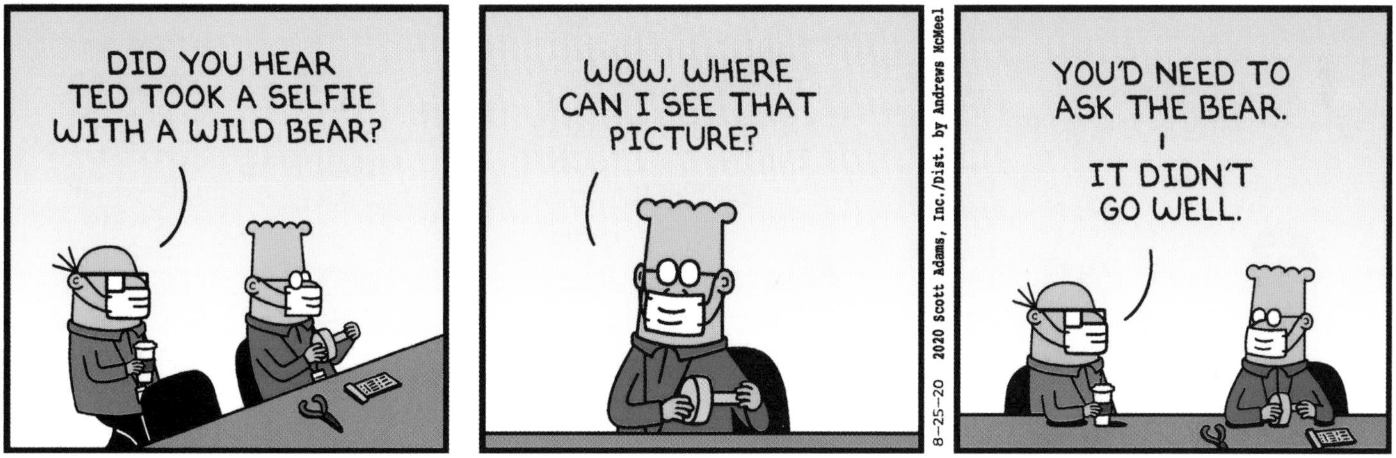

DID YOU HEAR TED TOOK A SELFIE WITH A WILD BEAR?
WOW. WHERE CAN I SEE THAT PICTURE?
8-25-20 2020 Scott Adams, Inc./Dist. by Andrews McMeel
YOU'D NEED TO ASK THE BEAR.
IT DIDN'T GO WELL.


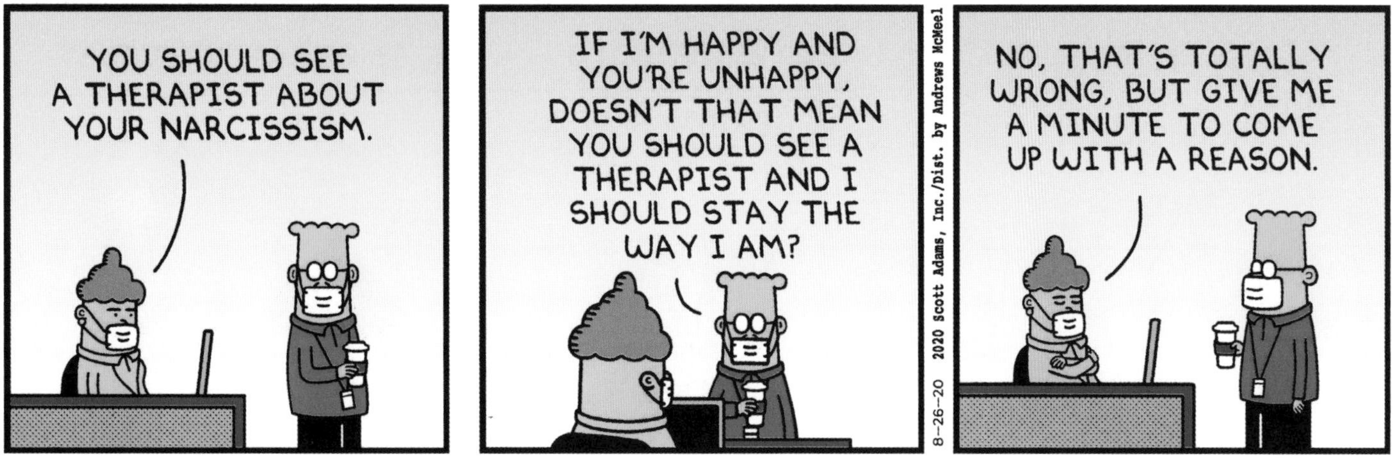

YOU SHOULD SEE A THERAPIST ABOUT YOUR NARCISSISM.
IF I'M HAPPY AND YOU'RE UNHAPPY, DOESN'T THAT MEAN YOU SHOULD SEE A THERAPIST AND I SHOULD STAY THE WAY I AM?
8-26-20 2020 Scott Adams, Inc./Dist. by Andrews McMeel
NO, THAT'S TOTALLY WRONG, BUT GIVE ME A MINUTE TO COME UP WITH A REASON.

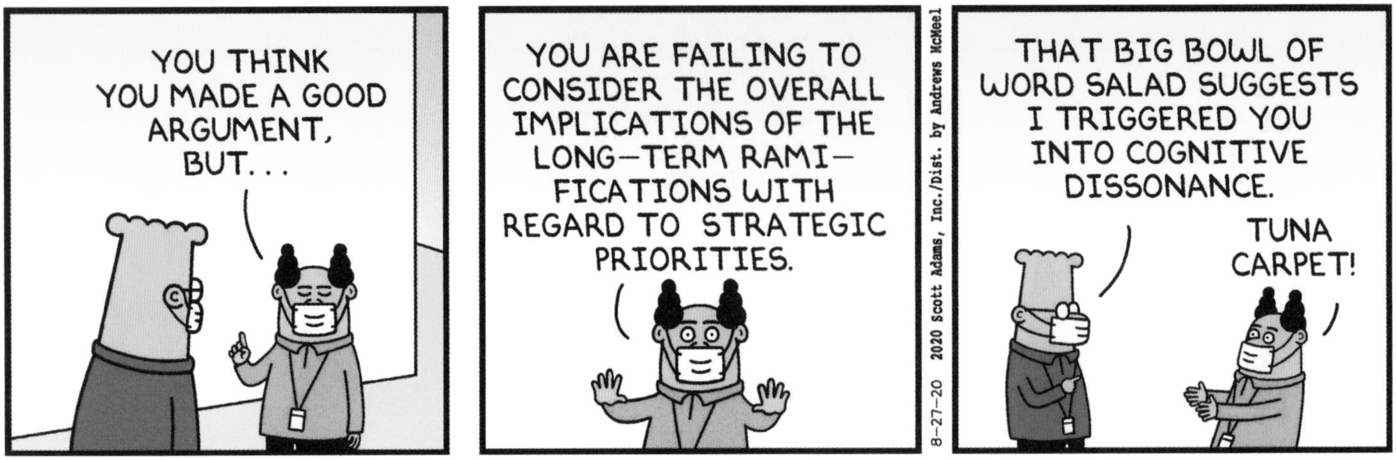
YOU THINK YOU MADE A GOOD ARGUMENT, BUT. . .
YOU ARE FAILING TO CONSIDER THE OVERALL IMPLICATIONS OF THE LONG-TERM RAMI-FICATIONS WITH REGARD TO STRATEGIC PRIORITIES.
THAT BIG BOWL OF WORD SALAD SUGGESTS I TRIGGERED YOU INTO COGNITIVE DISSONANCE.
TUNA CARPET!


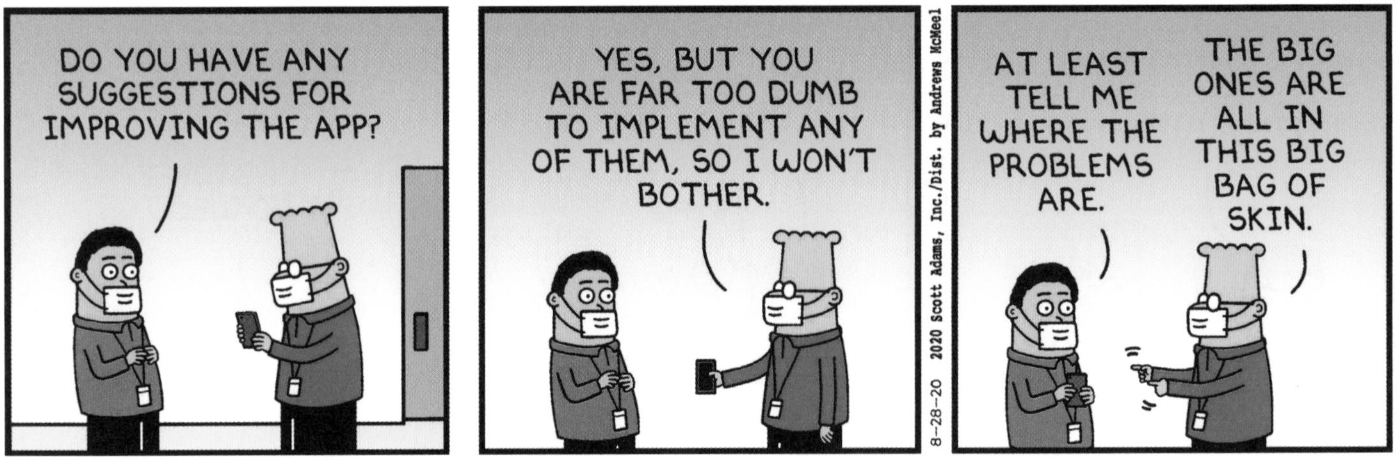
DO YOU HAVE ANY SUGGESTIONS FOR IMPROVING THE APP?
YES, BUT YOU ARE FAR TOO DUMB TO IMPLEMENT ANY OF THEM, SO I WON'T BOTHER.
AT LEAST TELL ME WHERE THE PROBLEMS ARE.
THE BIG ONES ARE ALL IN THIS BIG BAG OF SKIN.


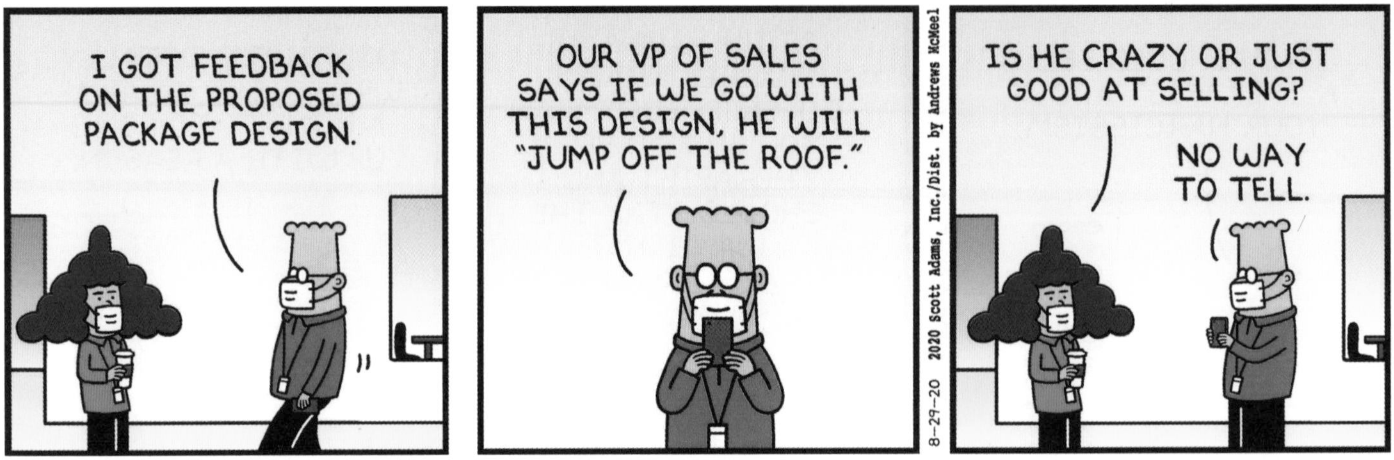
I GOT FEEDBACK ON THE PROPOSED PACKAGE DESIGN.
OUR VP OF SALES SAYS IF WE GO WITH THIS DESIGN, HE WILL "JUMP OFF THE ROOF."
IS HE CRAZY OR JUST GOOD AT SELLING?
NO WAY TO TELL.

THE GOVERNMENT IS THREATENING TO REGULATE US LIKE A MONOPOLY.
ARE WE **NOT** A MONOPOLY?
WE ARE SIMPLY A COMPANY THAT MAKES AN ESSENTIAL PRODUCT FOR MODERN LIFE, AND WE HAVE NO REAL COMPETITION.
© 2020 Scott Adams, Inc./Dist. by Andrews McMeel
THAT SOUNDS LIKE A MONOPOLY.
NO, WE ARE NOT A MONOPOLY BECAUSE OTHER COMPANIES **COULD** COMPETE WITH US IF THEY WANTED.
AND IF THEY TRIED?
AS SOON AS THEY GOT SOME TRACTION, WE'D BUY THEM AND SHUT THEM DOWN.
8-30-20
SO. . . THEY WOULD FAIL EVERY TIME?
BUT THEY COULD **TRY**.

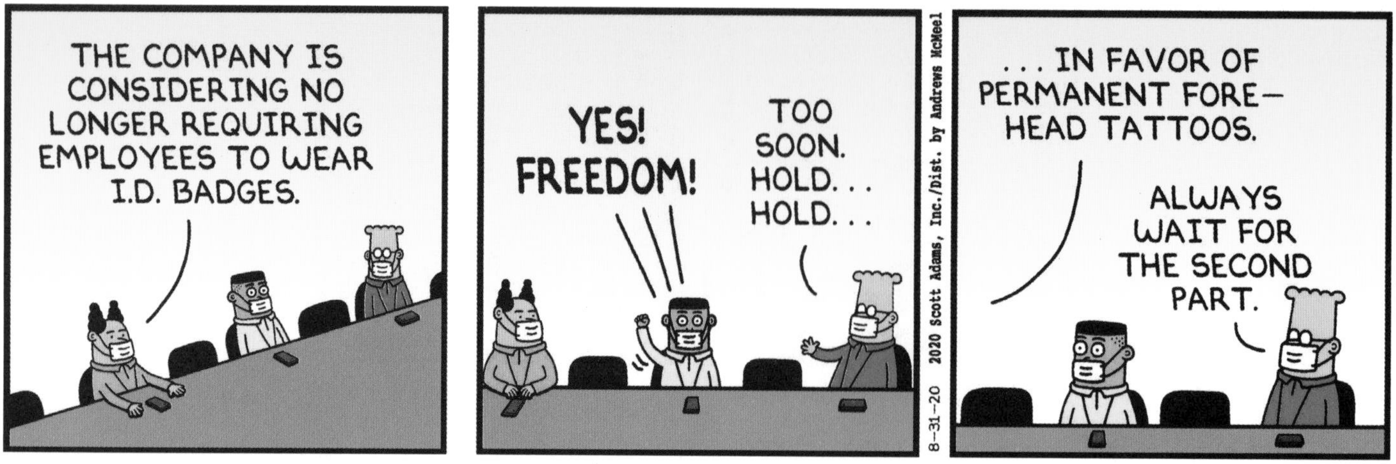
THE COMPANY IS CONSIDERING NO LONGER REQUIRING EMPLOYEES TO WEAR I.D. BADGES.
YES! FREEDOM!
TOO SOON. HOLD. . . HOLD. . .
8-31-20 2020 Scott Adams, Inc./Dist. by Andrews McMeel
. . . IN FAVOR OF PERMANENT FORE-HEAD TATTOOS.
ALWAYS WAIT FOR THE SECOND PART.

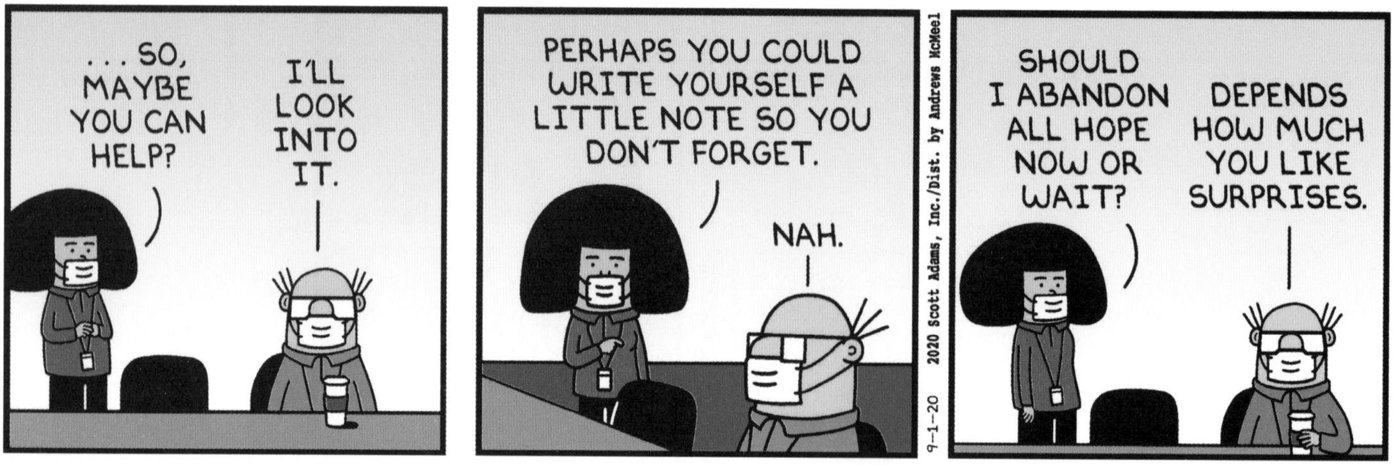
. . . SO, MAYBE YOU CAN HELP?
I'LL LOOK INTO IT.
PERHAPS YOU COULD WRITE YOURSELF A LITTLE NOTE SO YOU DON'T FORGET.
NAH.
9-1-20 2020 Scott Adams, Inc./Dist. by Andrews McMeel
SHOULD I ABANDON ALL HOPE NOW OR WAIT?
DEPENDS HOW MUCH YOU LIKE SURPRISES.

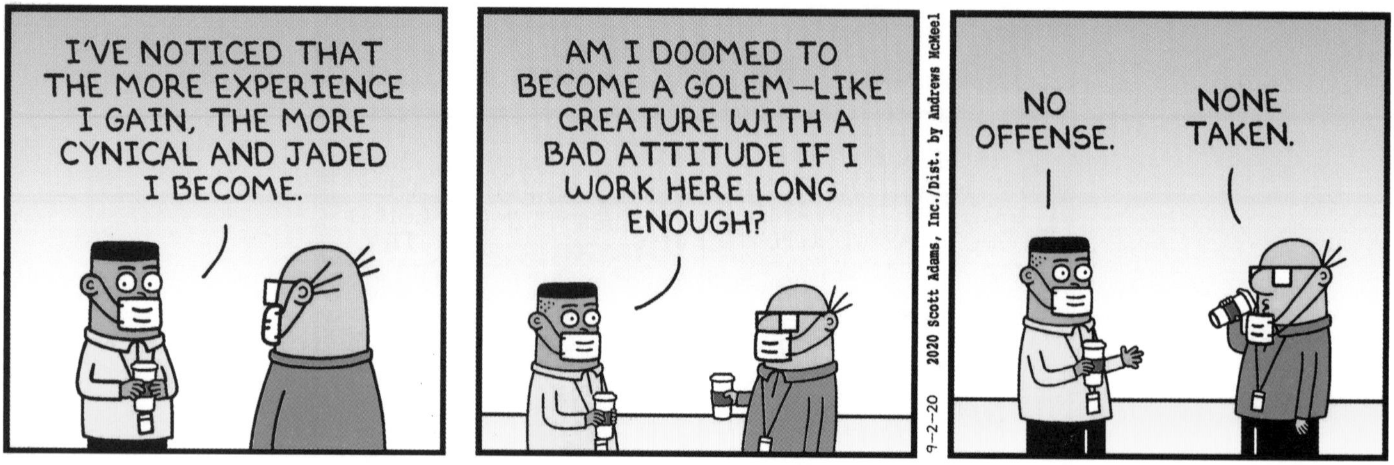
I'VE NOTICED THAT THE MORE EXPERIENCE I GAIN, THE MORE CYNICAL AND JADED I BECOME.
AM I DOOMED TO BECOME A GOLEM-LIKE CREATURE WITH A BAD ATTITUDE IF I WORK HERE LONG ENOUGH?
9-2-20 2020 Scott Adams, Inc./Dist. by Andrews McMeel
NO OFFENSE.
NONE TAKEN.

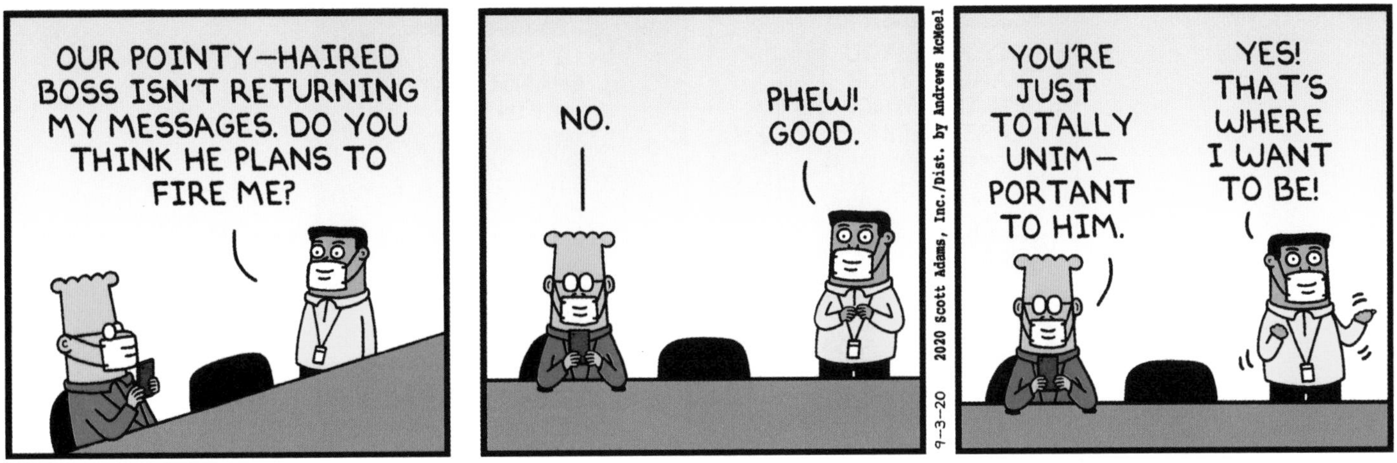
OUR POINTY—HAIRED BOSS ISN'T RETURNING MY MESSAGES. DO YOU THINK HE PLANS TO FIRE ME?
NO.
PHEW! GOOD.
YOU'RE JUST TOTALLY UNIM— PORTANT TO HIM.
YES! THAT'S WHERE I WANT TO BE!
9-3-20 2020 Scott Adams, Inc./Dist. by Andrews McMeel

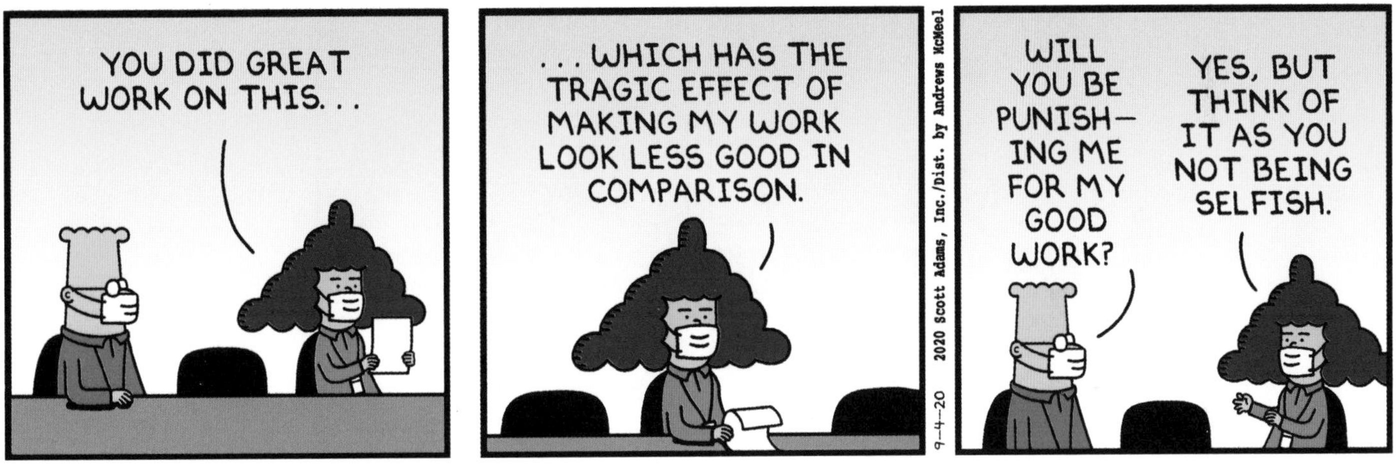
YOU DID GREAT WORK ON THIS. . .
. . . WHICH HAS THE TRAGIC EFFECT OF MAKING MY WORK LOOK LESS GOOD IN COMPARISON.
WILL YOU BE PUNISH— ING ME FOR MY GOOD WORK?
YES, BUT THINK OF IT AS YOU NOT BEING SELFISH.
9-4-20 2020 Scott Adams, Inc./Dist. by Andrews McMeel

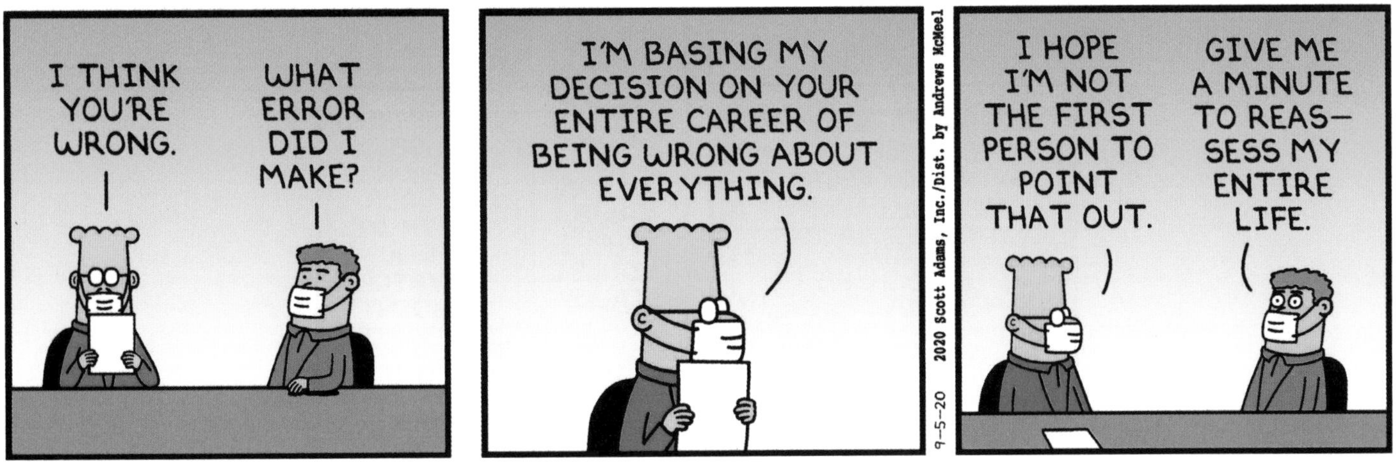
I THINK YOU'RE WRONG.
WHAT ERROR DID I MAKE?
I'M BASING MY DECISION ON YOUR ENTIRE CAREER OF BEING WRONG ABOUT EVERYTHING.
I HOPE I'M NOT THE FIRST PERSON TO POINT THAT OUT.
GIVE ME A MINUTE TO REAS— SESS MY ENTIRE LIFE.
9-5-20 2020 Scott Adams, Inc./Dist. by Andrews McMeel

WHY HAVE YOU CHANGED YOUR OPINION SINCE LAST WEEK?
I HAVEN'T CHANGED MY OPINION.
NO, IT WAS DIFFERENT LAST WEEK.
ARE WE REALLY DEBATING WHICH ONE OF US IS A BETTER AUTHORITY ON **MY *OPINION***?
YOU MIGHT BE LYING ABOUT NOT CHANGING YOUR OPINION.
AND YOU MIGHT BE HALLUCINATING OR LYING OR JUST STUPID.
YOU MIGHT BE TRYING TO GASLIGHT ME RIGHT NOW.
I'M GLAD WE CAN HAVE THESE HONEST TALKS.
I HOPE YOU PLUNGE TO YOUR DEATH IN A FREAK ELEVATOR ACCIDENT.
9-6-20

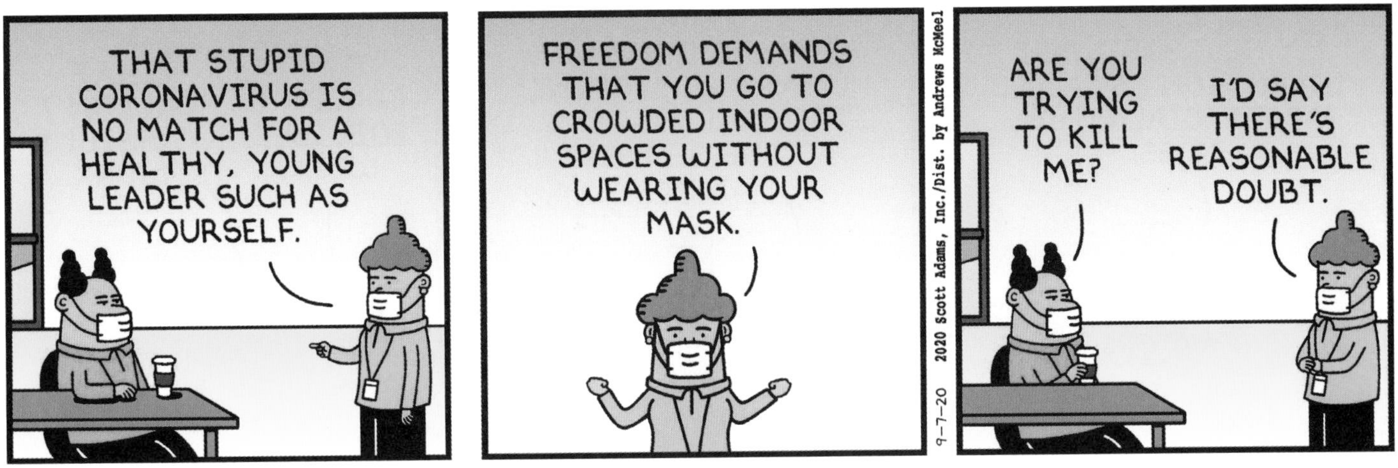
THAT STUPID CORONAVIRUS IS NO MATCH FOR A HEALTHY, YOUNG LEADER SUCH AS YOURSELF.
FREEDOM DEMANDS THAT YOU GO TO CROWDED INDOOR SPACES WITHOUT WEARING YOUR MASK.
9-7-20 2020 Scott Adams, Inc./Dist. by Andrews McMeel
ARE YOU TRYING TO KILL ME?
I'D SAY THERE'S REASONABLE DOUBT.

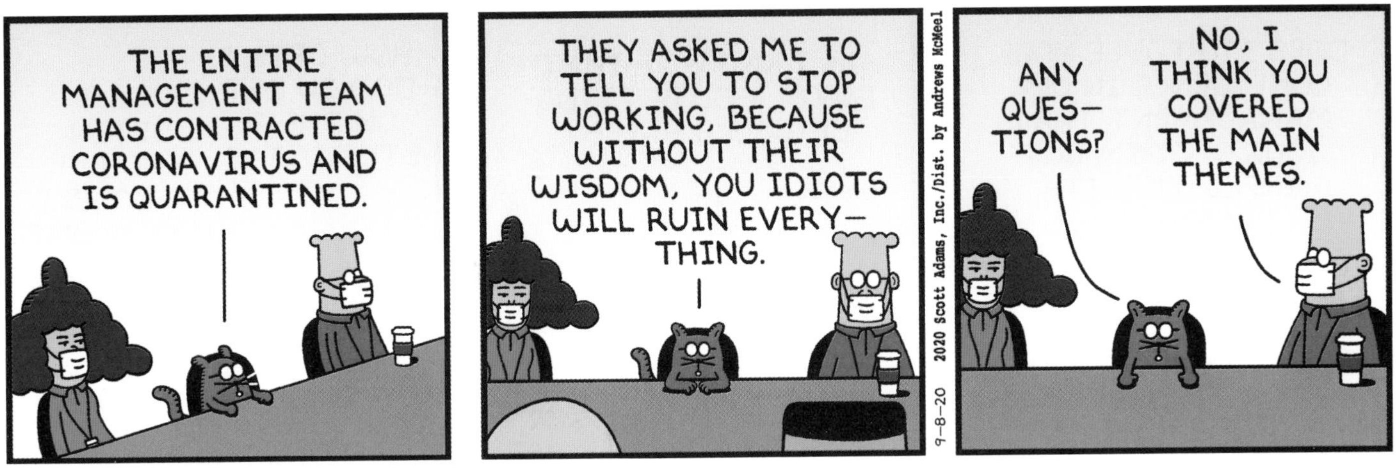
THE ENTIRE MANAGEMENT TEAM HAS CONTRACTED CORONAVIRUS AND IS QUARANTINED.
THEY ASKED ME TO TELL YOU TO STOP WORKING, BECAUSE WITHOUT THEIR WISDOM, YOU IDIOTS WILL RUIN EVERY-THING.
9-8-20 2020 Scott Adams, Inc./Dist. by Andrews McMeel
ANY QUES-TIONS?
NO, I THINK YOU COVERED THE MAIN THEMES.

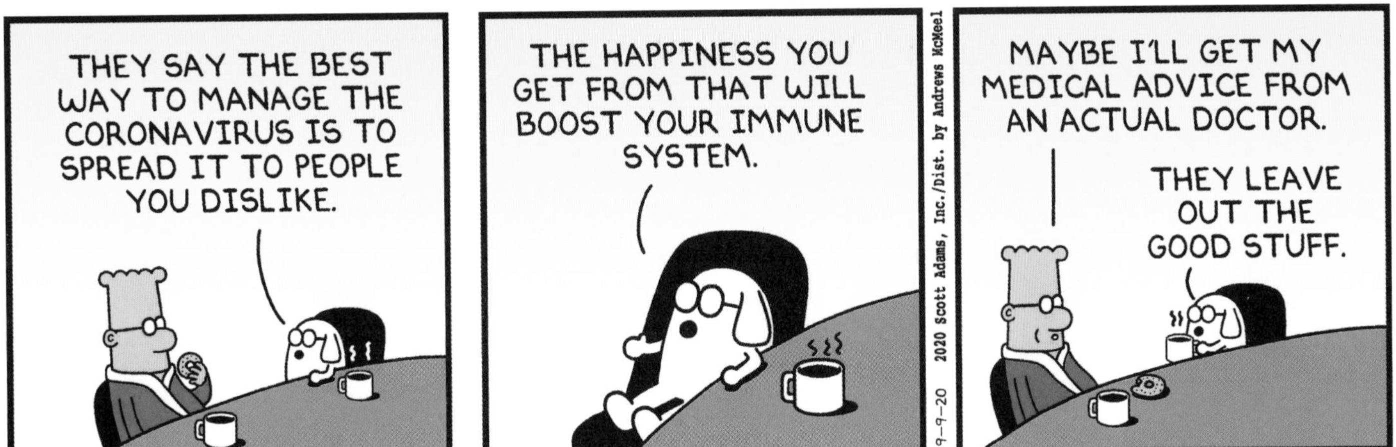
THEY SAY THE BEST WAY TO MANAGE THE CORONAVIRUS IS TO SPREAD IT TO PEOPLE YOU DISLIKE.
THE HAPPINESS YOU GET FROM THAT WILL BOOST YOUR IMMUNE SYSTEM.
9-9-20 2020 Scott Adams, Inc./Dist. by Andrews McMeel
MAYBE I'LL GET MY MEDICAL ADVICE FROM AN ACTUAL DOCTOR.
THEY LEAVE OUT THE GOOD STUFF.

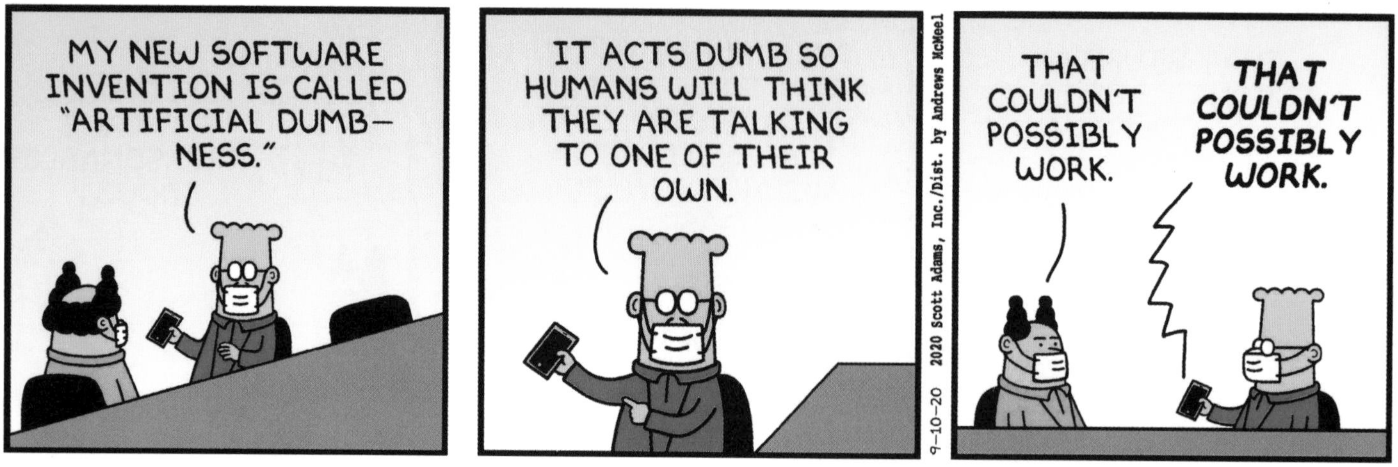
MY NEW SOFTWARE INVENTION IS CALLED "ARTIFICIAL DUMB–NESS."
IT ACTS DUMB SO HUMANS WILL THINK THEY ARE TALKING TO ONE OF THEIR OWN.
THAT COULDN'T POSSIBLY WORK.
THAT COULDN'T POSSIBLY WORK.
2020 Scott Adams, Inc./Dist. by Andrews McMeel
9-10-20

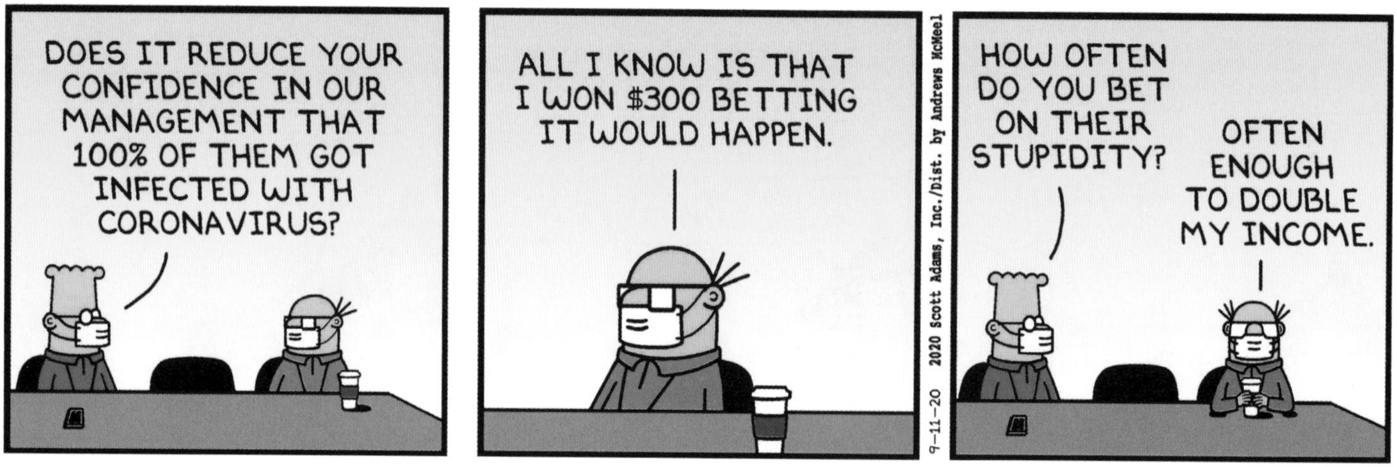
DOES IT REDUCE YOUR CONFIDENCE IN OUR MANAGEMENT THAT 100% OF THEM GOT INFECTED WITH CORONAVIRUS?
ALL I KNOW IS THAT I WON $300 BETTING IT WOULD HAPPEN.
HOW OFTEN DO YOU BET ON THEIR STUPIDITY?
OFTEN ENOUGH TO DOUBLE MY INCOME.
2020 Scott Adams, Inc./Dist. by Andrews McMeel
9-11-20

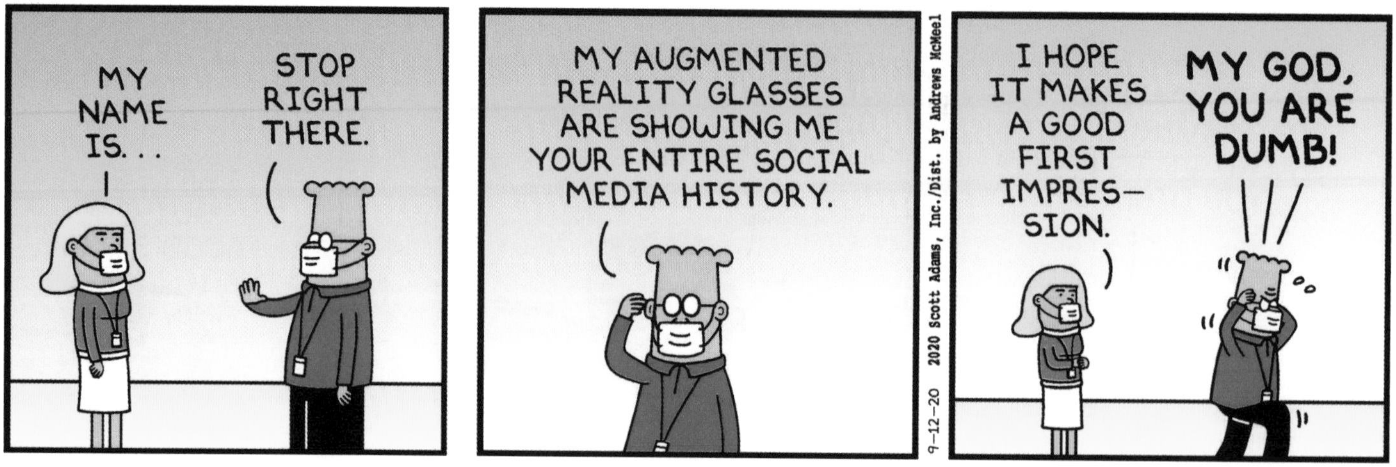
MY NAME IS. . .
STOP RIGHT THERE.
MY AUGMENTED REALITY GLASSES ARE SHOWING ME YOUR ENTIRE SOCIAL MEDIA HISTORY.
I HOPE IT MAKES A GOOD FIRST IMPRES–SION.
MY GOD, YOU ARE DUMB!
2020 Scott Adams, Inc./Dist. by Andrews McMeel
9-12-20

HOW CONFIDENT ARE YOU IN YOUR ANALYSIS?
VERY CONFIDENT.
GOOD.
UNLESS I USED THE WRONG DISCOUNT RATE, WHICH IS HARD TO KNOW.
BUT OTHERWISE, IT'S SOLID?
EXCEPT FOR THE INSTALLATION AND MAINTENANCE COSTS, WHICH ARE WILD GUESSES.
AND WE DON'T KNOW IF WE SIZED THE PROJECT RIGHT, SO COSTS COULD BE DOUBLE OR TRIPLE.
IT SOUNDS AS IF YOU APPLIED MATH TO A BUNCH OF WILD GUESSES.
YES, BUT I GOT THE RESULT YOU WANTED.
NEXT TIME, JUST SAY THAT.
© 2020 Scott Adams, Inc./Dist. by Andrews McMeel
9-13-20

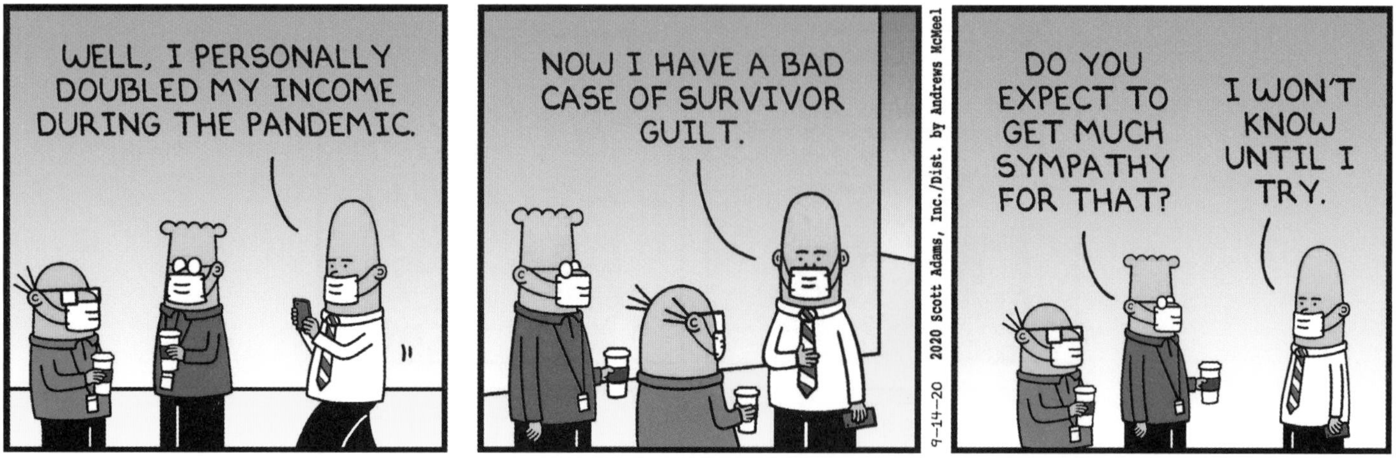
WELL, I PERSONALLY DOUBLED MY INCOME DURING THE PANDEMIC.
NOW I HAVE A BAD CASE OF SURVIVOR GUILT.
DO YOU EXPECT TO GET MUCH SYMPATHY FOR THAT?
I WON'T KNOW UNTIL I TRY.
9-14-20 2020 Scott Adams, Inc./Dist. by Andrews McMeel

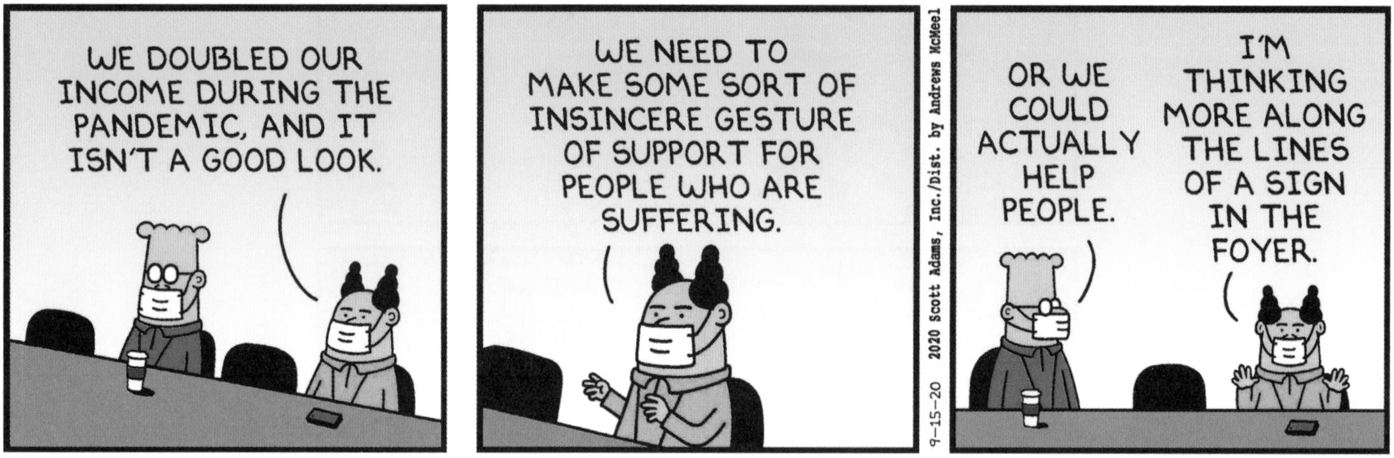
WE DOUBLED OUR INCOME DURING THE PANDEMIC, AND IT ISN'T A GOOD LOOK.
WE NEED TO MAKE SOME SORT OF INSINCERE GESTURE OF SUPPORT FOR PEOPLE WHO ARE SUFFERING.
OR WE COULD ACTUALLY HELP PEOPLE.
I'M THINKING MORE ALONG THE LINES OF A SIGN IN THE FOYER.
9-15-20 2020 Scott Adams, Inc./Dist. by Andrews McMeel

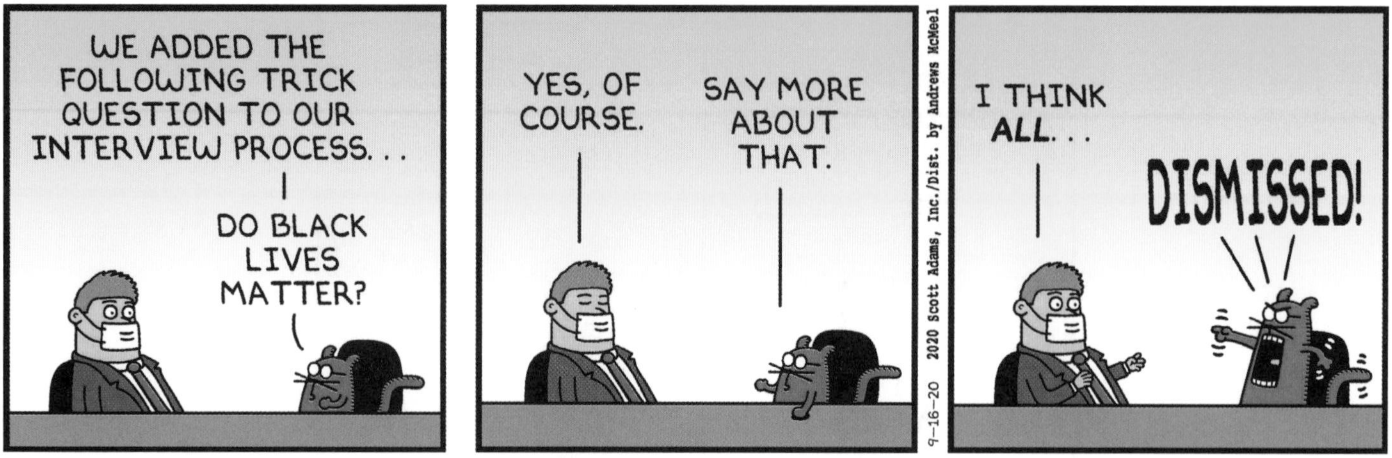
WE ADDED THE FOLLOWING TRICK QUESTION TO OUR INTERVIEW PROCESS...
DO BLACK LIVES MATTER?
YES, OF COURSE.
SAY MORE ABOUT THAT.
I THINK ALL...
DISMISSED!
9-16-20 2020 Scott Adams, Inc./Dist. by Andrews McMeel

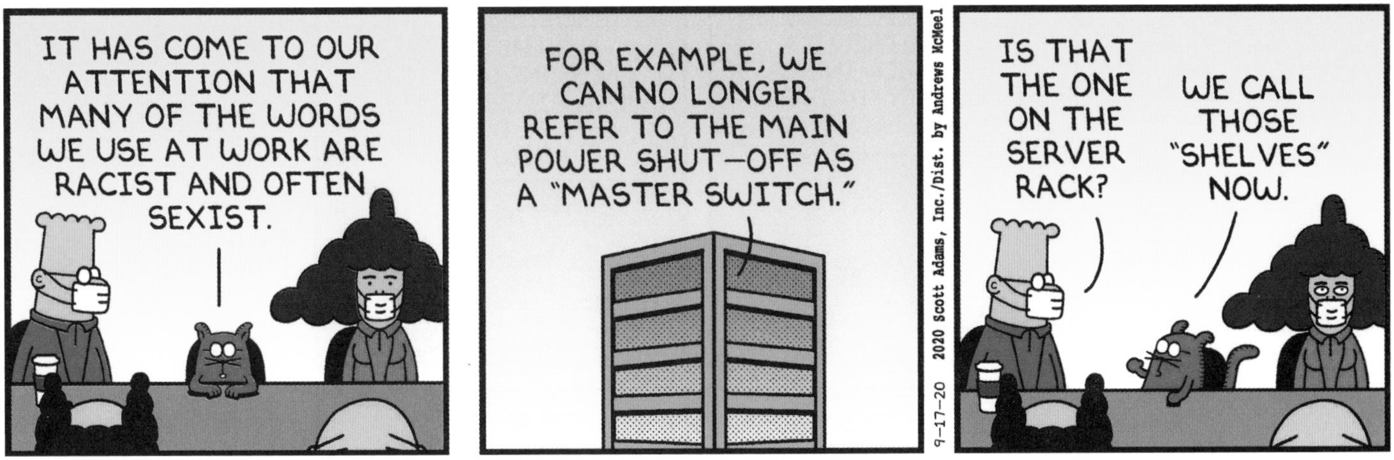
IT HAS COME TO OUR ATTENTION THAT MANY OF THE WORDS WE USE AT WORK ARE RACIST AND OFTEN SEXIST.
FOR EXAMPLE, WE CAN NO LONGER REFER TO THE MAIN POWER SHUT-OFF AS A "MASTER SWITCH."
9-17-20 2020 Scott Adams, Inc./Dist. by Andrews McMeel
IS THAT THE ONE ON THE SERVER RACK?
WE CALL THOSE "SHELVES" NOW.

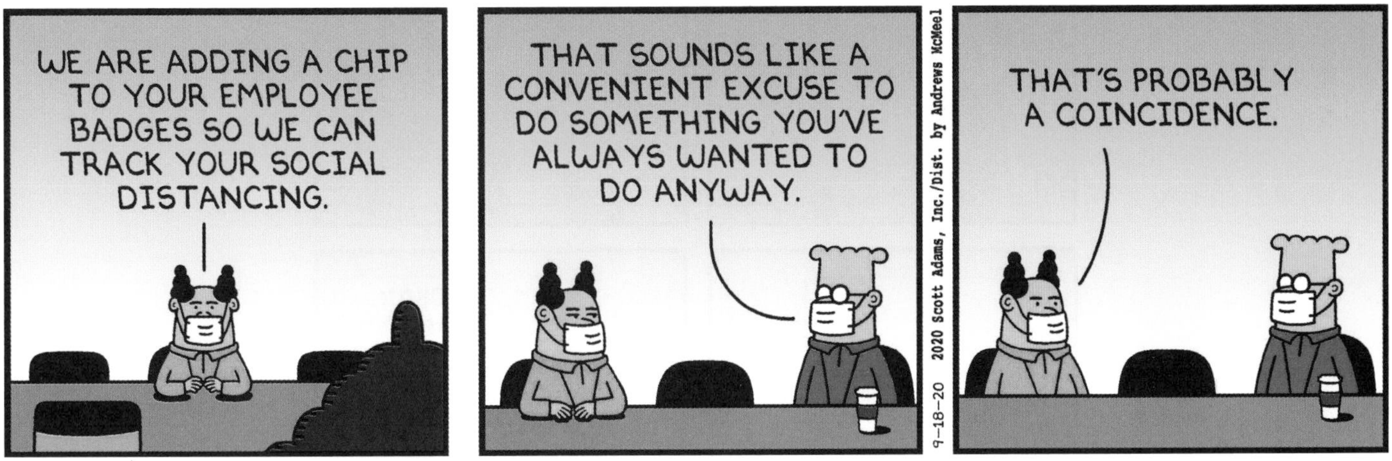
WE ARE ADDING A CHIP TO YOUR EMPLOYEE BADGES SO WE CAN TRACK YOUR SOCIAL DISTANCING.
THAT SOUNDS LIKE A CONVENIENT EXCUSE TO DO SOMETHING YOU'VE ALWAYS WANTED TO DO ANYWAY.
9-18-20 2020 Scott Adams, Inc./Dist. by Andrews McMeel
THAT'S PROBABLY A COINCIDENCE.

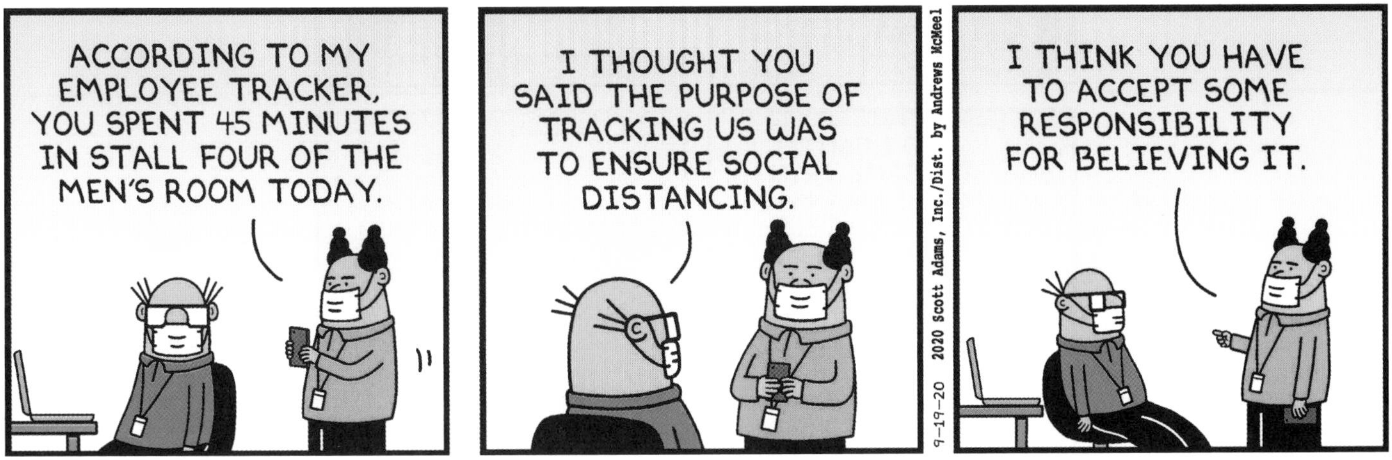
ACCORDING TO MY EMPLOYEE TRACKER, YOU SPENT 45 MINUTES IN STALL FOUR OF THE MEN'S ROOM TODAY.
I THOUGHT YOU SAID THE PURPOSE OF TRACKING US WAS TO ENSURE SOCIAL DISTANCING.
9-19-20 2020 Scott Adams, Inc./Dist. by Andrews McMeel
I THINK YOU HAVE TO ACCEPT SOME RESPONSIBILITY FOR BELIEVING IT.

I INSTALLED A SILENCER IN OUR POINTY-HAIRED BOSS'S FACE MASK.
NOW HE'S THE ONLY ONE WHO CAN HEAR HIMSELF TALK, BUT HE DOESN'T KNOW IT.
HERE HE COMES. PLAY ALONG.
UH-HUH.
OKAY, THANKS.
AND I CAN DO THE SAME THING TO THE FACE MASK OF ANYONE ELSE WHO BORES ME.
UH-HUH.
© 2020 Scott Adams, Inc./Dist. by Andrews McMeel
9-20-20

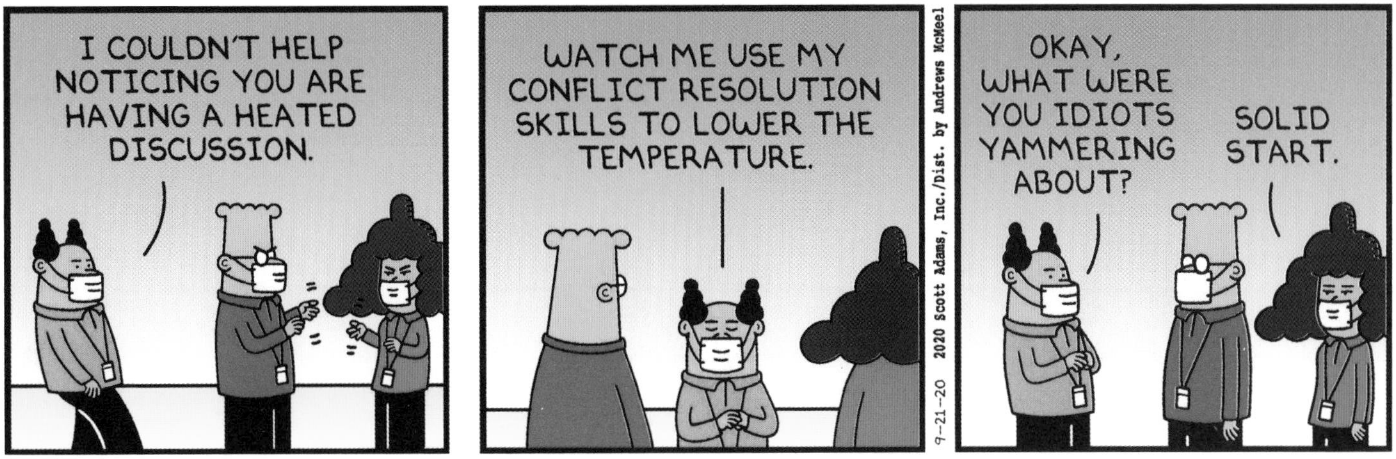
I COULDN'T HELP NOTICING YOU ARE HAVING A HEATED DISCUSSION.
WATCH ME USE MY CONFLICT RESOLUTION SKILLS TO LOWER THE TEMPERATURE.
9-21-20 2020 Scott Adams, Inc./Dist. by Andrews McMeel
OKAY, WHAT WERE YOU IDIOTS YAMMERING ABOUT?
SOLID START.

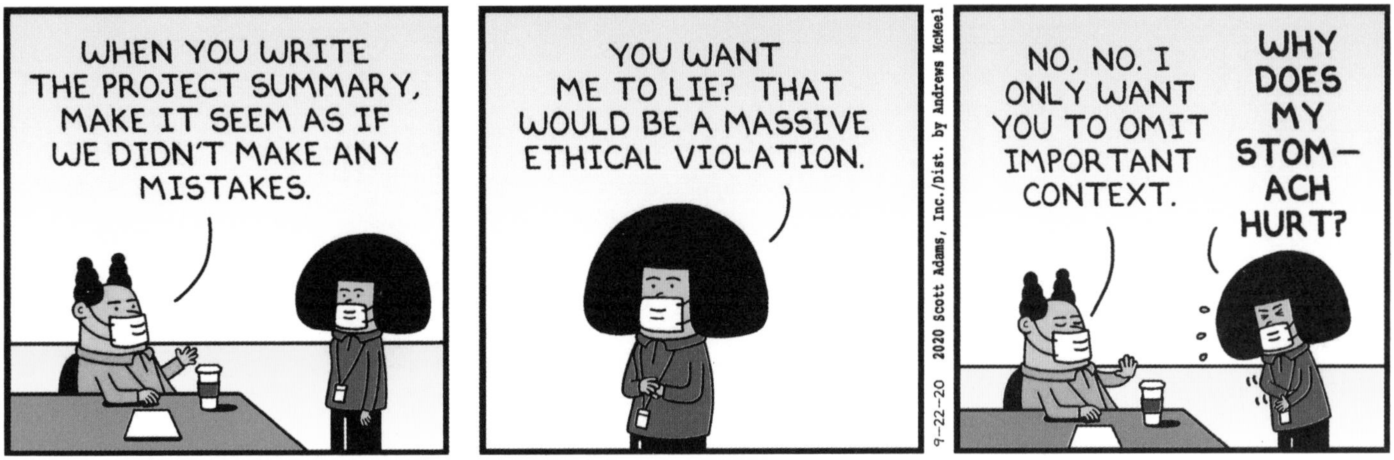
WHEN YOU WRITE THE PROJECT SUMMARY, MAKE IT SEEM AS IF WE DIDN'T MAKE ANY MISTAKES.
YOU WANT ME TO LIE? THAT WOULD BE A MASSIVE ETHICAL VIOLATION.
9-22-20 2020 Scott Adams, Inc./Dist. by Andrews McMeel
NO, NO. I ONLY WANT YOU TO OMIT IMPORTANT CONTEXT.
WHY DOES MY STOM-ACH HURT?

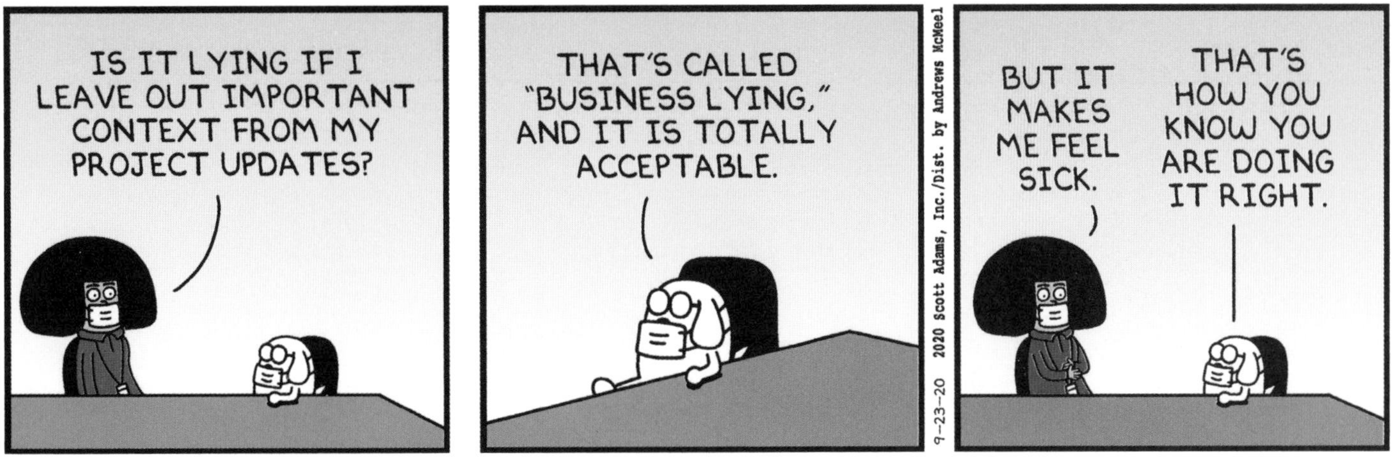
IS IT LYING IF I LEAVE OUT IMPORTANT CONTEXT FROM MY PROJECT UPDATES?
THAT'S CALLED "BUSINESS LYING," AND IT IS TOTALLY ACCEPTABLE.
9-23-20 2020 Scott Adams, Inc./Dist. by Andrews McMeel
BUT IT MAKES ME FEEL SICK.
THAT'S HOW YOU KNOW YOU ARE DOING IT RIGHT.

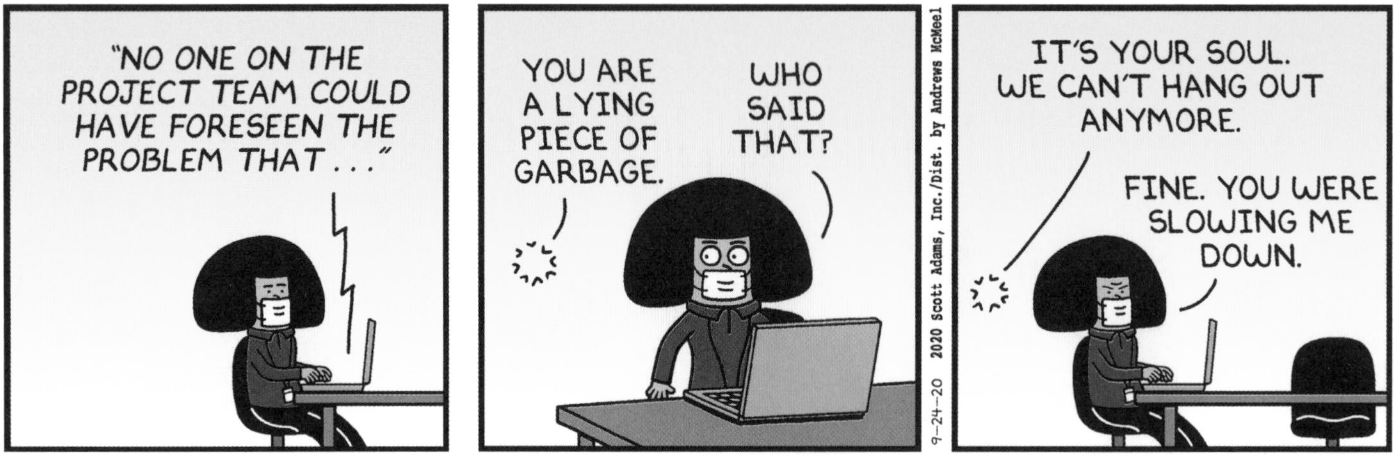
"NO ONE ON THE PROJECT TEAM COULD HAVE FORESEEN THE PROBLEM THAT . . ."
YOU ARE A LYING PIECE OF GARBAGE.
WHO SAID THAT?
9-24-20 2020 Scott Adams, Inc./Dist. by Andrews McMeel
IT'S YOUR SOUL. WE CAN'T HANG OUT ANYMORE.
FINE. YOU WERE SLOWING ME DOWN.

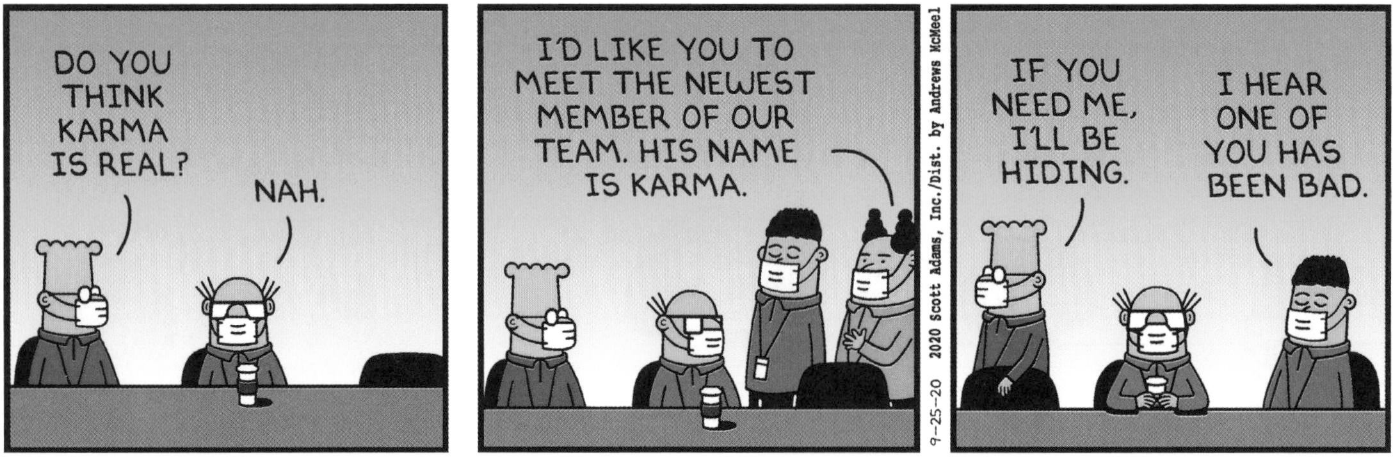
DO YOU THINK KARMA IS REAL?
NAH.
I'D LIKE YOU TO MEET THE NEWEST MEMBER OF OUR TEAM. HIS NAME IS KARMA.
9-25-20 2020 Scott Adams, Inc./Dist. by Andrews McMeel
IF YOU NEED ME, I'LL BE HIDING.
I HEAR ONE OF YOU HAS BEEN BAD.

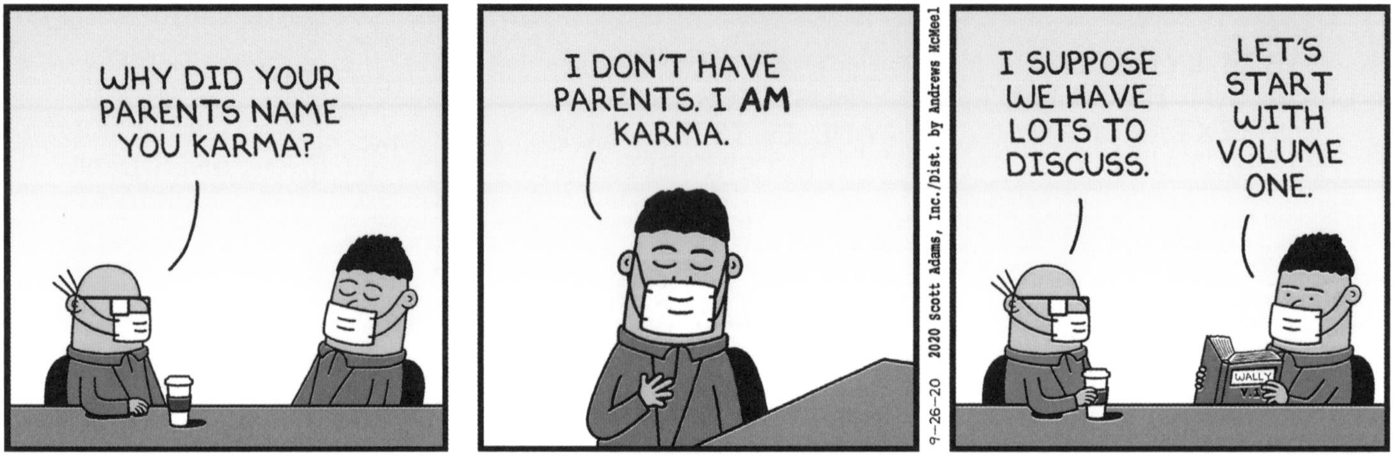
WHY DID YOUR PARENTS NAME YOU KARMA?
I DON'T HAVE PARENTS. I **AM** KARMA.
9-26-20 2020 Scott Adams, Inc./Dist. by Andrews McMeel
I SUPPOSE WE HAVE LOTS TO DISCUSS.
LET'S START WITH VOLUME ONE.
WALLY
V.1

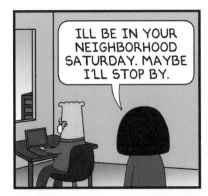

ILL BE IN YOUR NEIGHBORHOOD SATURDAY. MAYBE I'LL STOP BY.
I'M NOT FALLING FOR THAT TRICK.
WHAT TRICK?
THE TRICK WHERE YOU GIVE ME AN ESTIMATED TIME AND THEN PUSH IT BACK SEVEN TIMES UNTIL YOU CANCEL.
I'LL BE STUCK WAITING AT HOME UNTIL MY WHOLE DAY IS WASTED.
I PROMISE I WON'T DO THAT. I'LL STICK TO THE TIME.
WHAT TIME IS THAT?
DEPENDS HOW MY DAY GOES.
AND SO IT BEGINS.
I'LL TEXT YOU IF I'M RUNNING LATE.
©2020 Scott Adams, Inc./Dist. by Andrews McMeel
9-27-20

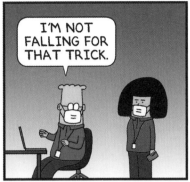

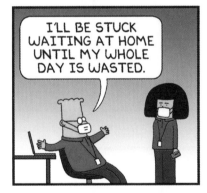

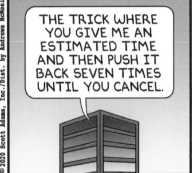

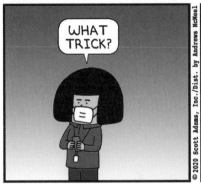

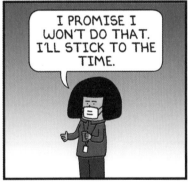

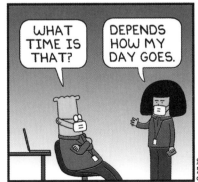

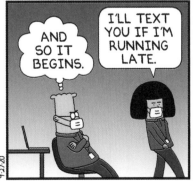

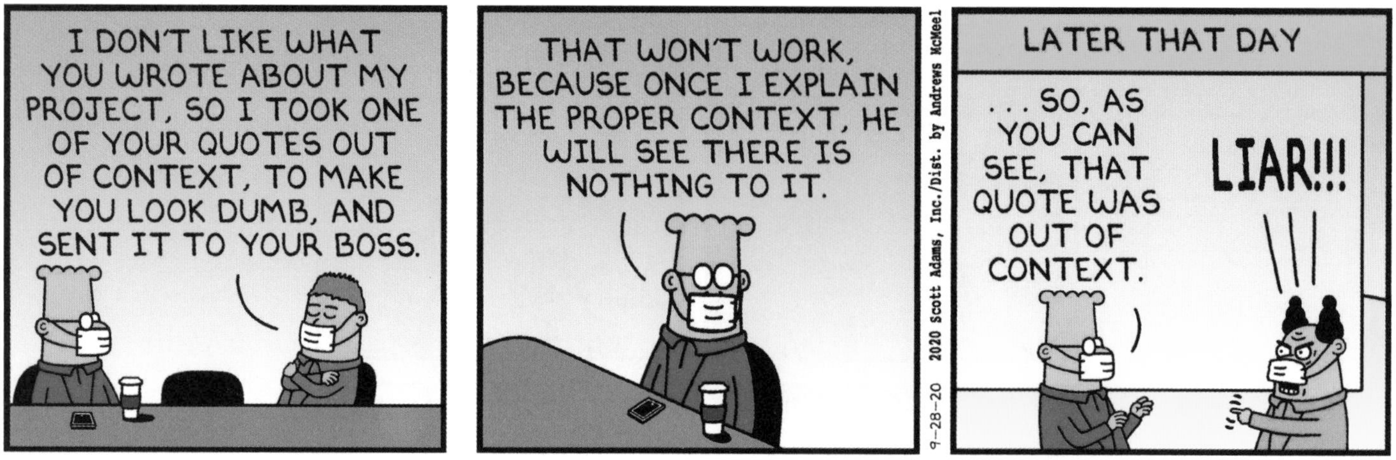
I DON'T LIKE WHAT YOU WROTE ABOUT MY PROJECT, SO I TOOK ONE OF YOUR QUOTES OUT OF CONTEXT, TO MAKE YOU LOOK DUMB, AND SENT IT TO YOUR BOSS.
THAT WON'T WORK, BECAUSE ONCE I EXPLAIN THE PROPER CONTEXT, HE WILL SEE THERE IS NOTHING TO IT.
9-28-20 2020 Scott Adams, Inc./Dist. by Andrews McMeel
LATER THAT DAY
. . . SO, AS YOU CAN SEE, THAT QUOTE WAS OUT OF CONTEXT.
LIAR!!!

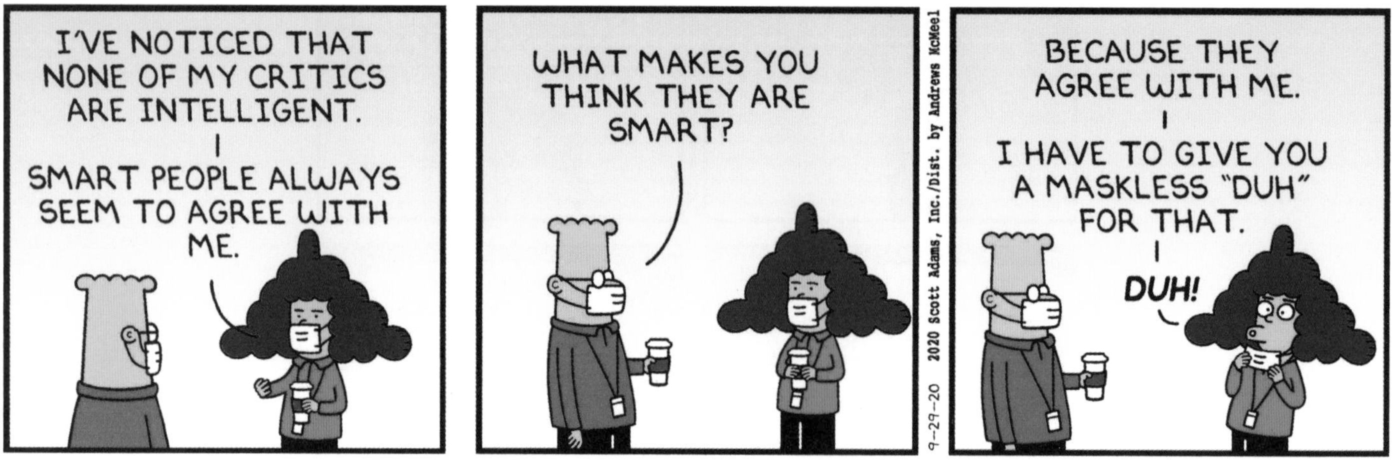
I'VE NOTICED THAT NONE OF MY CRITICS ARE INTELLIGENT.
SMART PEOPLE ALWAYS SEEM TO AGREE WITH ME.
WHAT MAKES YOU THINK THEY ARE SMART?
9-29-20 2020 Scott Adams, Inc./Dist. by Andrews McMeel
BECAUSE THEY AGREE WITH ME.
I HAVE TO GIVE YOU A MASKLESS "DUH" FOR THAT.
DUH!

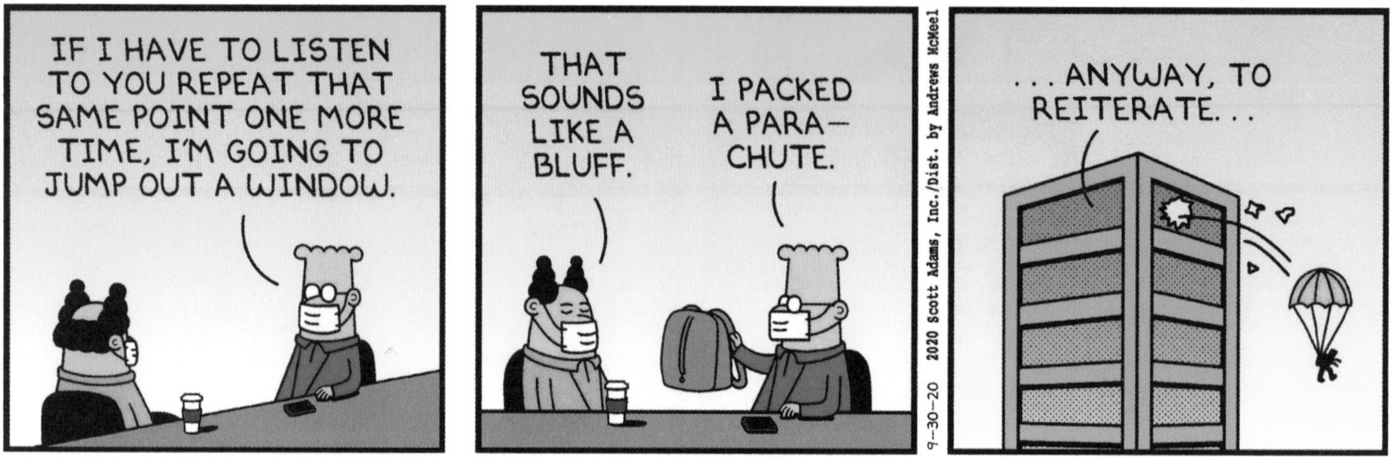
IF I HAVE TO LISTEN TO YOU REPEAT THAT SAME POINT ONE MORE TIME, I'M GOING TO JUMP OUT A WINDOW.
THAT SOUNDS LIKE A BLUFF.
I PACKED A PARA-CHUTE.
9-30-20 2020 Scott Adams, Inc./Dist. by Andrews McMeel
. . . ANYWAY, TO REITERATE. . .

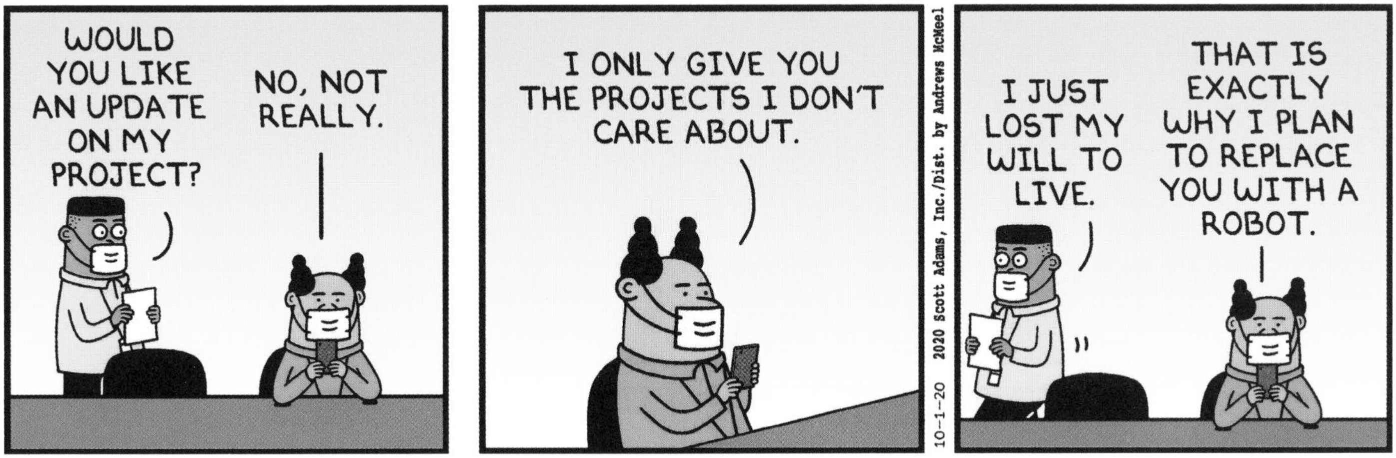
WOULD YOU LIKE AN UPDATE ON MY PROJECT?
NO, NOT REALLY.
I ONLY GIVE YOU THE PROJECTS I DON'T CARE ABOUT.
I JUST LOST MY WILL TO LIVE.
THAT IS EXACTLY WHY I PLAN TO REPLACE YOU WITH A ROBOT.
10-1-20 2020 Scott Adams, Inc./Dist. by Andrews McMeel

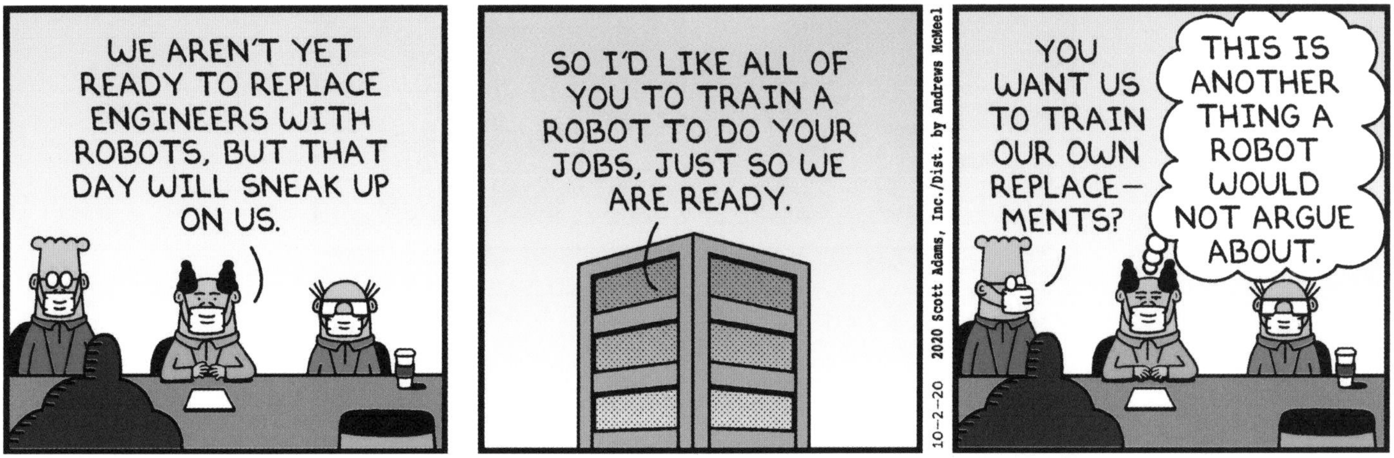
WE AREN'T YET READY TO REPLACE ENGINEERS WITH ROBOTS, BUT THAT DAY WILL SNEAK UP ON US.
SO I'D LIKE ALL OF YOU TO TRAIN A ROBOT TO DO YOUR JOBS, JUST SO WE ARE READY.
YOU WANT US TO TRAIN OUR OWN REPLACE- MENTS?
THIS IS ANOTHER THING A ROBOT WOULD NOT ARGUE ABOUT.
10-2-20 2020 Scott Adams, Inc./Dist. by Andrews McMeel

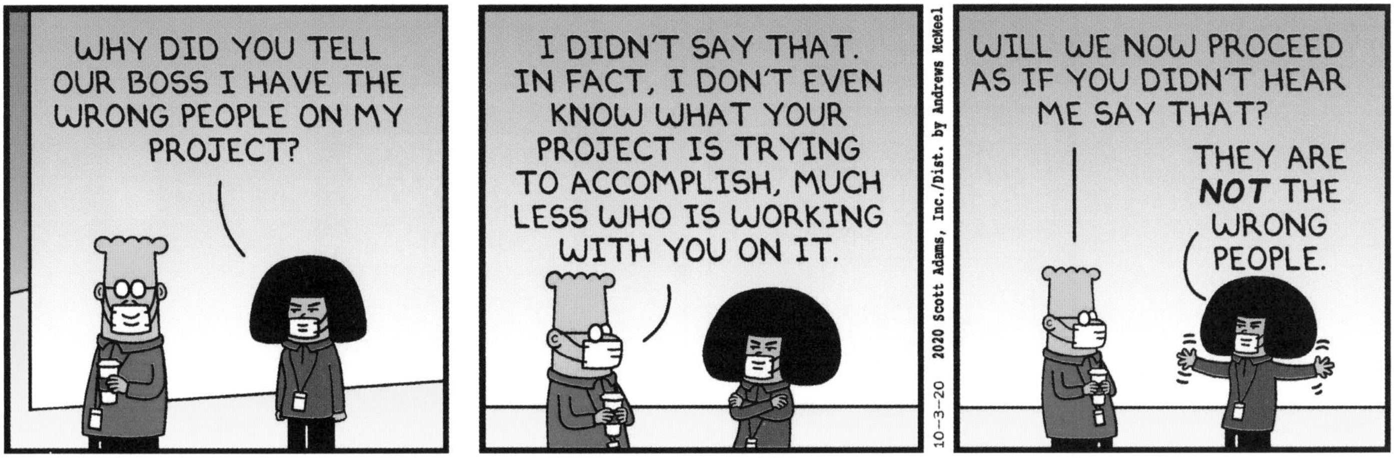
WHY DID YOU TELL OUR BOSS I HAVE THE WRONG PEOPLE ON MY PROJECT?
I DIDN'T SAY THAT. IN FACT, I DON'T EVEN KNOW WHAT YOUR PROJECT IS TRYING TO ACCOMPLISH, MUCH LESS WHO IS WORKING WITH YOU ON IT.
WILL WE NOW PROCEED AS IF YOU DIDN'T HEAR ME SAY THAT?
THEY ARE NOT THE WRONG PEOPLE.
10-3-20 2020 Scott Adams, Inc./Dist. by Andrews McMeel

SOCIAL DISTANCING HAS BEEN A GREAT UPGRADE TO MY LIFE.

IN THE OLD DAYS, WOMEN AVOIDED ME BY AT LEAST TEN FEET.

NOW I OFTEN GET WITHIN SEVEN.

I THINK IT'S BECAUSE I'M BETTER-LOOKING WITH MOST OF MY FACE COVERED.

ESPECIALLY IF I WEAR A HAT AND SUNGLASSES.

AND I LEARNED THAT WOMEN WILL TALK TO ME IF I WALK THE WRONG WAY DOWN A GROCERY AISLE.

THEY'RE USUALLY COMPLAINING, BUT AT LEAST THEY MAKE EYE CONTACT.

IT'S SORT OF A GOLDEN AGE FOR PEOPLE LIKE ME.

10-4-20

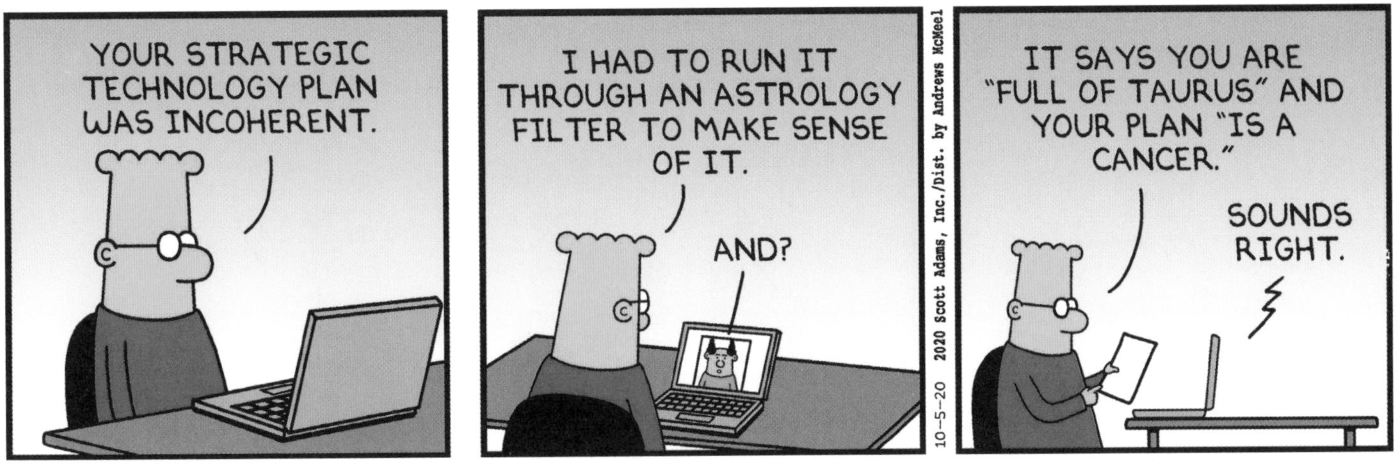
YOUR STRATEGIC TECHNOLOGY PLAN WAS INCOHERENT.
I HAD TO RUN IT THROUGH AN ASTROLOGY FILTER TO MAKE SENSE OF IT.
AND?
10-5-20 2020 Scott Adams, Inc./Dist. by Andrews McMeel
IT SAYS YOU ARE "FULL OF TAURUS" AND YOUR PLAN "IS A CANCER."
SOUNDS RIGHT.

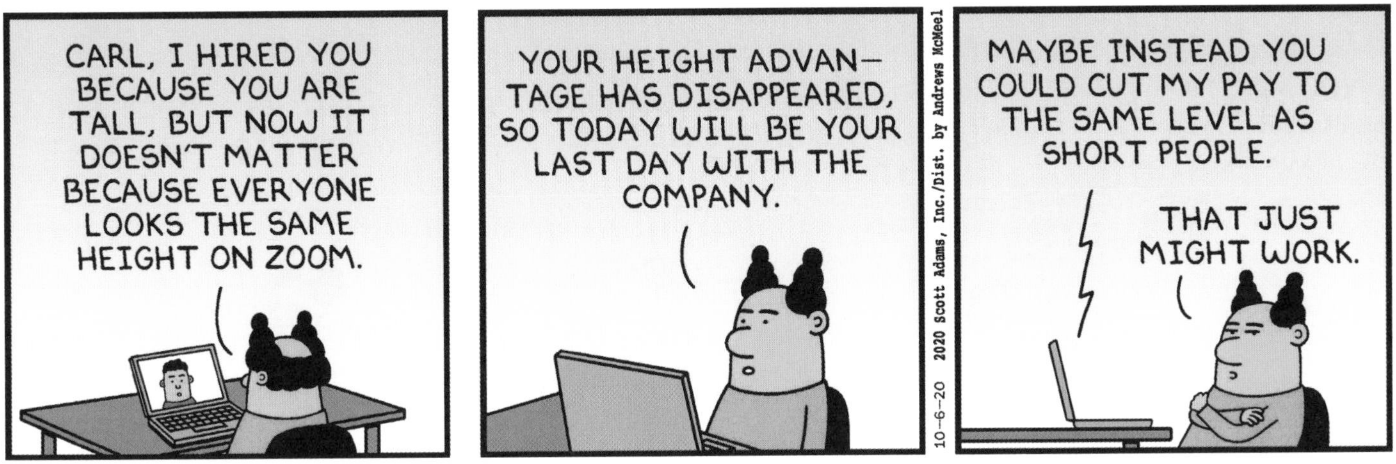
CARL, I HIRED YOU BECAUSE YOU ARE TALL, BUT NOW IT DOESN'T MATTER BECAUSE EVERYONE LOOKS THE SAME HEIGHT ON ZOOM.
YOUR HEIGHT ADVAN-TAGE HAS DISAPPEARED, SO TODAY WILL BE YOUR LAST DAY WITH THE COMPANY.
10-6-20 2020 Scott Adams, Inc./Dist. by Andrews McMeel
MAYBE INSTEAD YOU COULD CUT MY PAY TO THE SAME LEVEL AS SHORT PEOPLE.
THAT JUST MIGHT WORK.

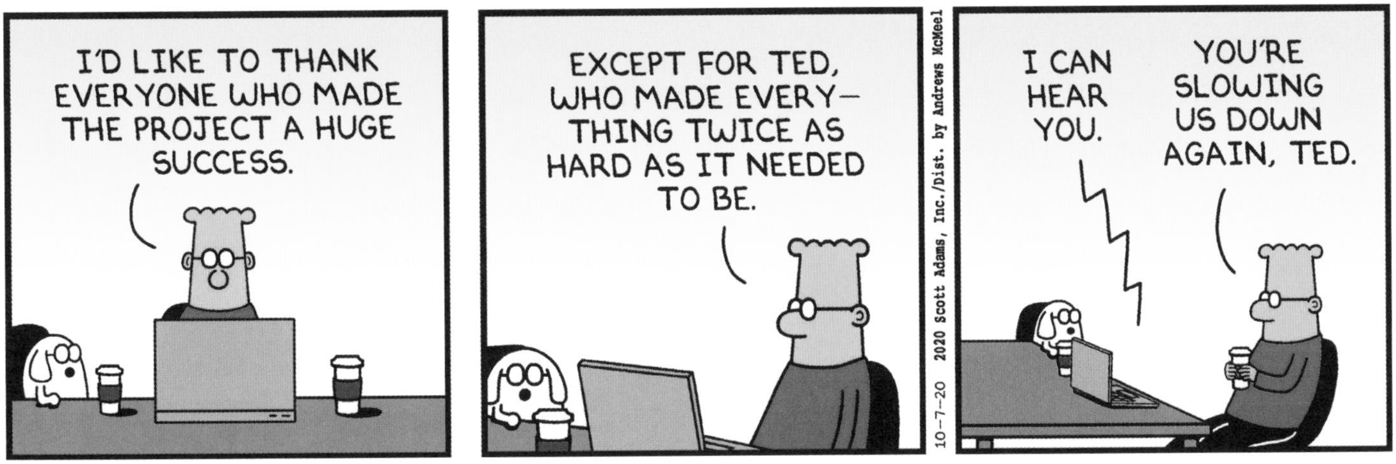
I'D LIKE TO THANK EVERYONE WHO MADE THE PROJECT A HUGE SUCCESS.
EXCEPT FOR TED, WHO MADE EVERY-THING TWICE AS HARD AS IT NEEDED TO BE.
10-7-20 2020 Scott Adams, Inc./Dist. by Andrews McMeel
I CAN HEAR YOU.
YOU'RE SLOWING US DOWN AGAIN, TED.

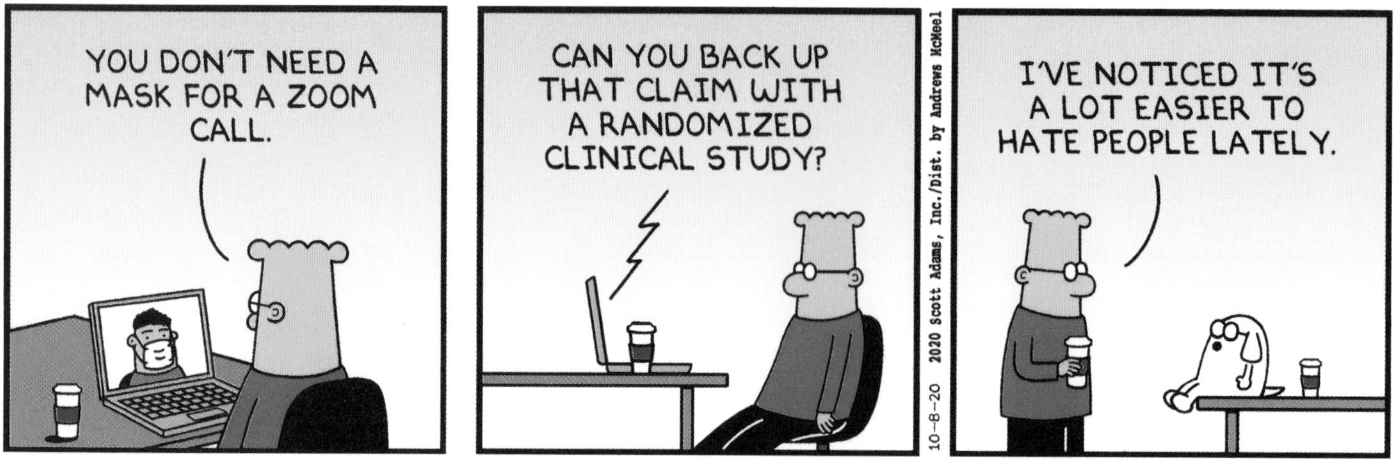
YOU DON'T NEED A MASK FOR A ZOOM CALL.
CAN YOU BACK UP THAT CLAIM WITH A RANDOMIZED CLINICAL STUDY?
10-8-20 2020 Scott Adams, Inc./Dist. by Andrews McMeel
I'VE NOTICED IT'S A LOT EASIER TO HATE PEOPLE LATELY.

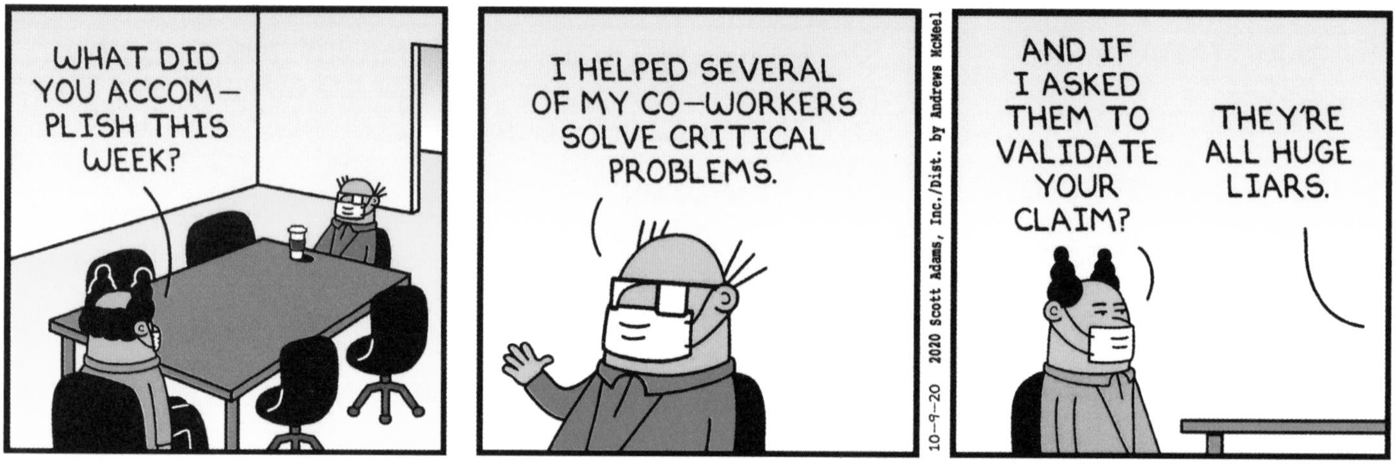
WHAT DID YOU ACCOM-PLISH THIS WEEK?
I HELPED SEVERAL OF MY CO-WORKERS SOLVE CRITICAL PROBLEMS.
10-9-20 2020 Scott Adams, Inc./Dist. by Andrews McMeel
AND IF I ASKED THEM TO VALIDATE YOUR CLAIM?
THEY'RE ALL HUGE LIARS.

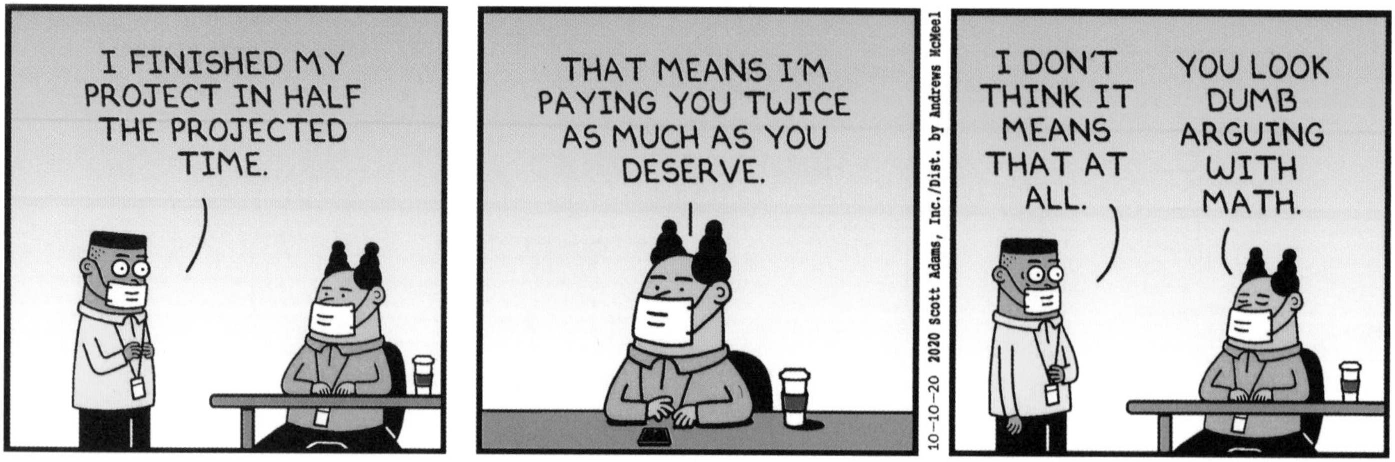
I FINISHED MY PROJECT IN HALF THE PROJECTED TIME.
THAT MEANS I'M PAYING YOU TWICE AS MUCH AS YOU DESERVE.
10-10-20 2020 Scott Adams, Inc./Dist. by Andrews McMeel
I DON'T THINK IT MEANS THAT AT ALL.
YOU LOOK DUMB ARGUING WITH MATH.

HOW'S THE NEW LAB CONSTRUCTION GOING?
I'M HAVING SOME ISSUES WITH THE LOCAL BUILDING CODES.
THEY SEEM UNNECESSARILY STRINGENT.
© 2020 Scott Adams, Inc./Dist. by Andrews McMeel
FOR EXAMPLE, WE HAVE TO GUARANTEE NO RAIN TOUCHES THE ROOF.
WHY?
NO ONE KNOWS.
BUT IF WE DONATE TO THE MAYOR'S CAMPAIGN, THE CITY WILL DESIGNATE THE ROOF A "HORI-ZONTAL WALL."
AND THEN WE CAN BEGIN CONSTRUCTION?
NO, THAT'S JUST THE BEGINNING OF THE FALSE HOPE PHASE.
10-11-20

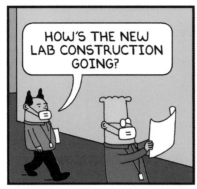

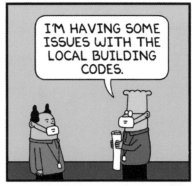

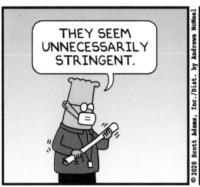

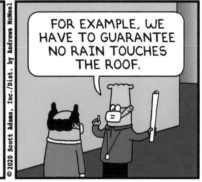

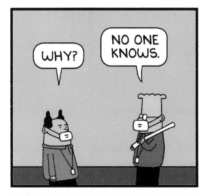

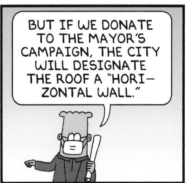

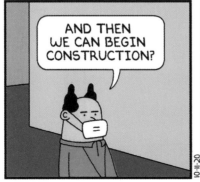

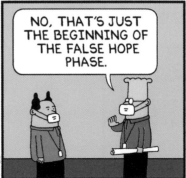

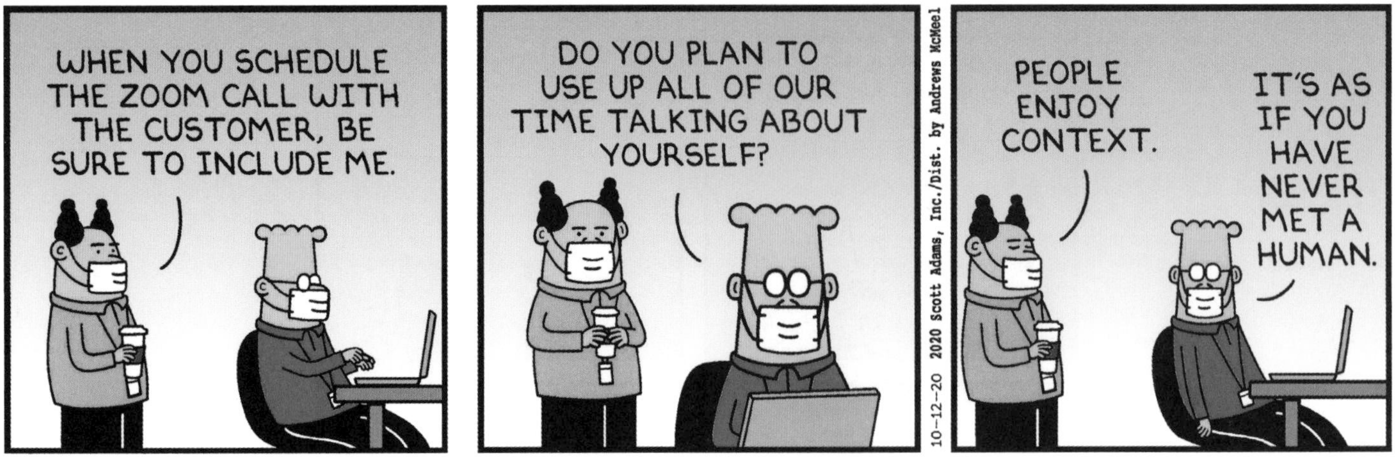
WHEN YOU SCHEDULE THE ZOOM CALL WITH THE CUSTOMER, BE SURE TO INCLUDE ME.
DO YOU PLAN TO USE UP ALL OF OUR TIME TALKING ABOUT YOURSELF?
10-12-20 2020 Scott Adams, Inc./Dist. by Andrews McMeel
PEOPLE ENJOY CONTEXT.
IT'S AS IF YOU HAVE NEVER MET A HUMAN.

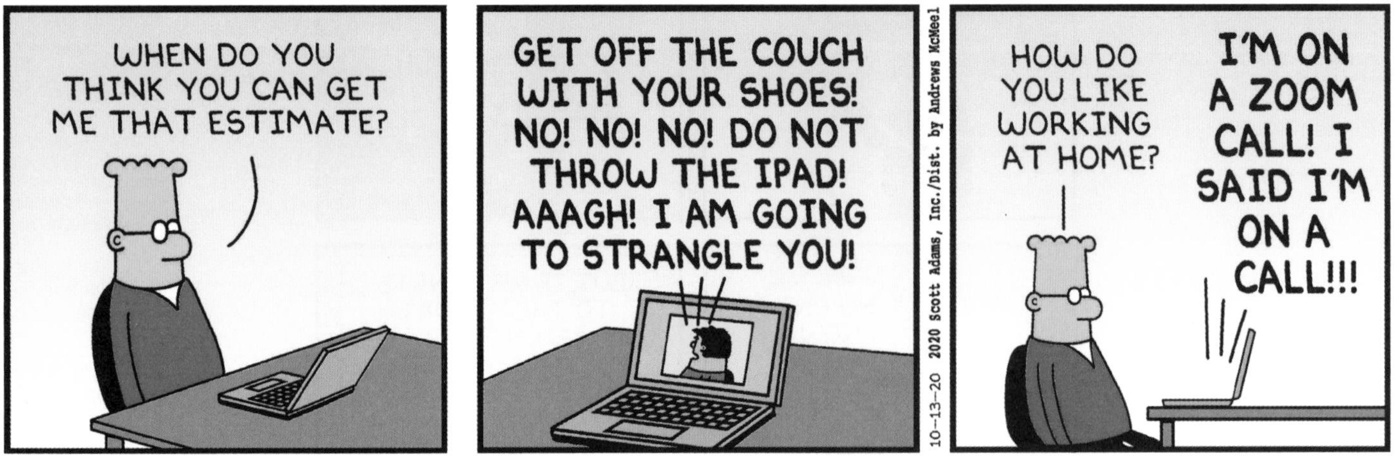
WHEN DO YOU THINK YOU CAN GET ME THAT ESTIMATE?
GET OFF THE COUCH WITH YOUR SHOES! NO! NO! NO! DO NOT THROW THE IPAD! AAAGH! I AM GOING TO STRANGLE YOU!
10-13-20 2020 Scott Adams, Inc./Dist. by Andrews McMeel
HOW DO YOU LIKE WORKING AT HOME?
I'M ON A ZOOM CALL! I SAID I'M ON A CALL!!!

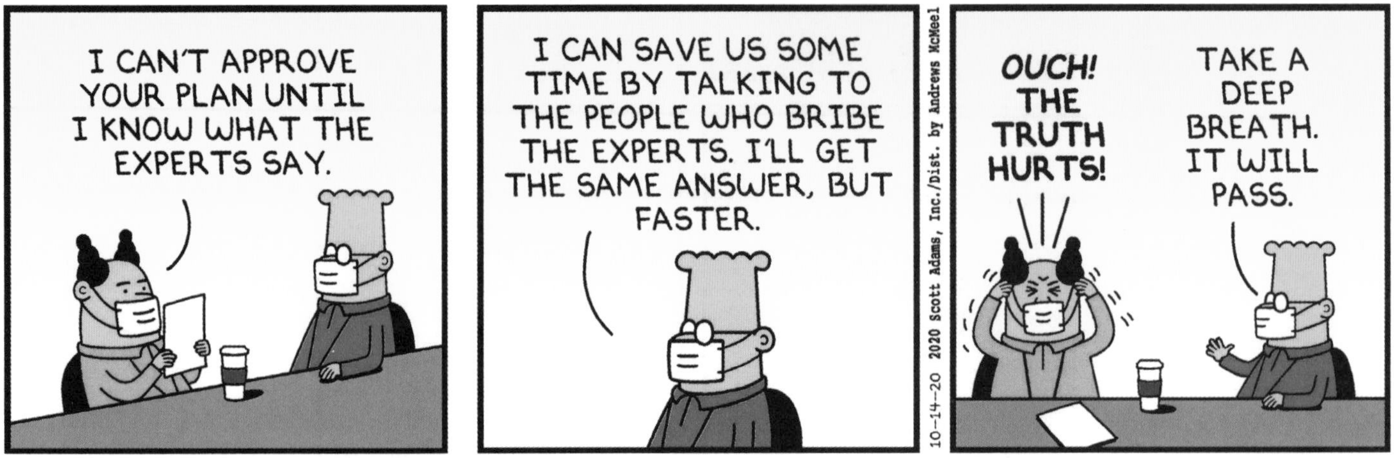
I CAN'T APPROVE YOUR PLAN UNTIL I KNOW WHAT THE EXPERTS SAY.
I CAN SAVE US SOME TIME BY TALKING TO THE PEOPLE WHO BRIBE THE EXPERTS. I'LL GET THE SAME ANSWER, BUT FASTER.
10-14-20 2020 Scott Adams, Inc./Dist. by Andrews McMeel
OUCH! THE TRUTH HURTS!
TAKE A DEEP BREATH. IT WILL PASS.

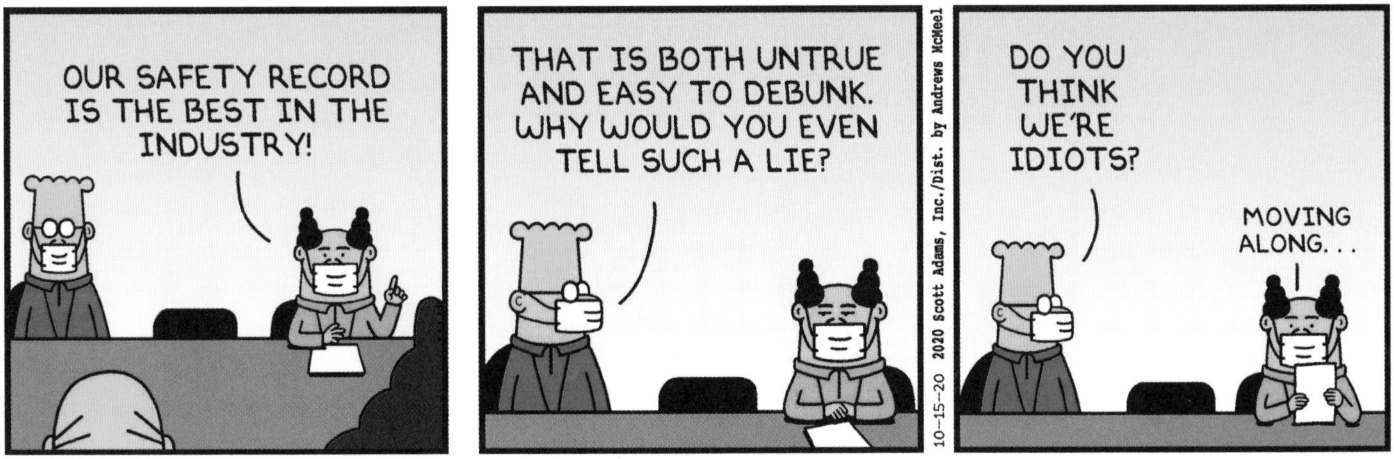
OUR SAFETY RECORD IS THE BEST IN THE INDUSTRY!
THAT IS BOTH UNTRUE AND EASY TO DEBUNK. WHY WOULD YOU EVEN TELL SUCH A LIE?
DO YOU THINK WE'RE IDIOTS?
MOVING ALONG. . .


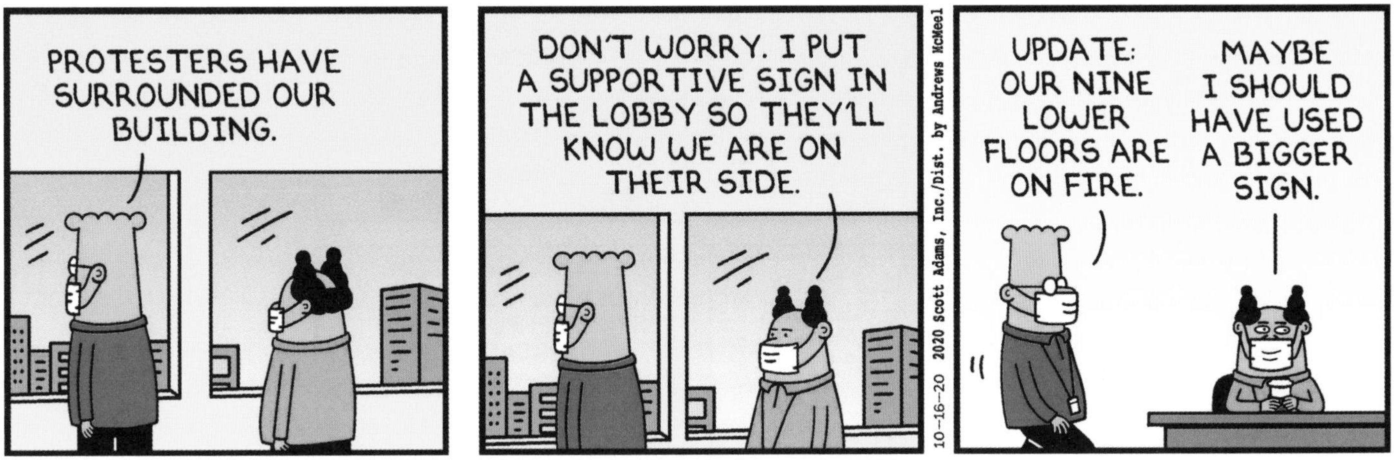
PROTESTERS HAVE SURROUNDED OUR BUILDING.
DON'T WORRY. I PUT A SUPPORTIVE SIGN IN THE LOBBY SO THEY'LL KNOW WE ARE ON THEIR SIDE.
UPDATE: OUR NINE LOWER FLOORS ARE ON FIRE.
MAYBE I SHOULD HAVE USED A BIGGER SIGN.


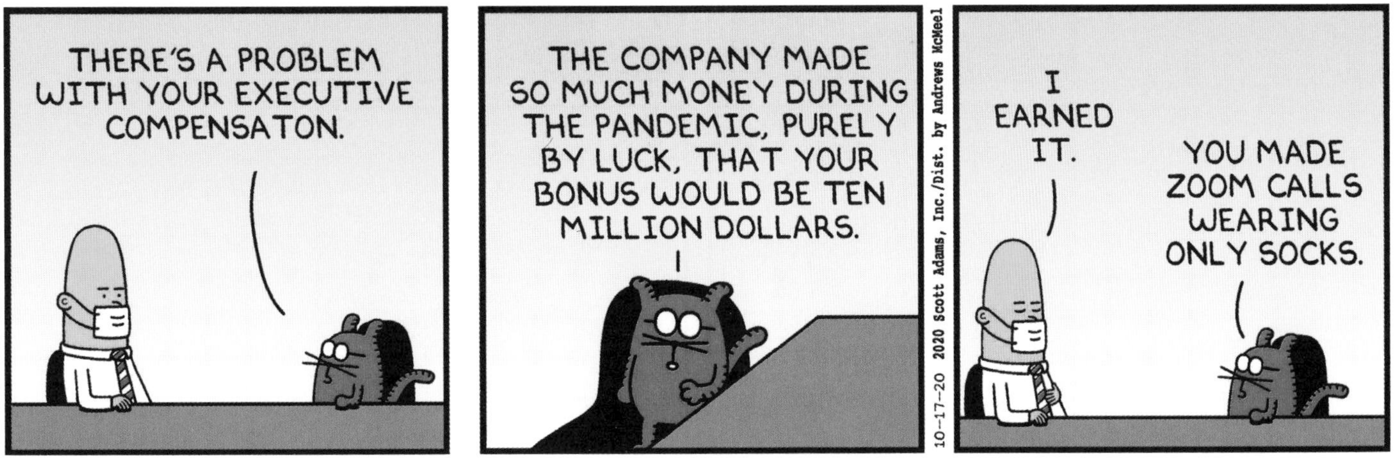
THERE'S A PROBLEM WITH YOUR EXECUTIVE COMPENSATON.
THE COMPANY MADE SO MUCH MONEY DURING THE PANDEMIC, PURELY BY LUCK, THAT YOUR BONUS WOULD BE TEN MILLION DOLLARS.
I EARNED IT.
YOU MADE ZOOM CALLS WEARING ONLY SOCKS.

HOW LONG SHOULD I WAIT BEFORE RESPONDING TO A TEXT MESSAGE FROM MY BOSS?
THAT DEPENDS. ARE YOU ALREADY OVERWORKED?
UM, SURE.
DO YOU NEED TO TEACH HIM A LESSON FOR ANY UNRELATED THINGS HE DID?
ALWAYS.
© 2020 Scott Adams, Inc./Dist. by Andrews McMeel
DO YOU DISLIKE HIM IN GENERAL?
YES.
LASTLY, HOW MANY MONTHS UNTIL YOUR NEXT PERFORMANCE REVIEW?
SEVEN.
OKAY. . . PUTTING THOSE INPUTS INTO MY SPREADSHEET.
YOU CAN WAIT 27 MINUTES BEFORE RESPOND-ING.
OH. I WAS HOPING IT WOULD BE CLOSER TO FIVE DAYS.
10-18-20
WHEN DID HE TEXT YOU?
I BELIEVE IT WAS AUGUST.

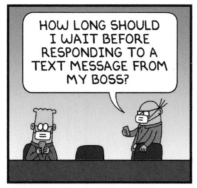

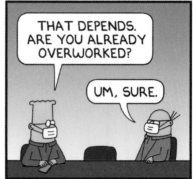

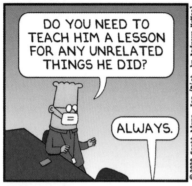

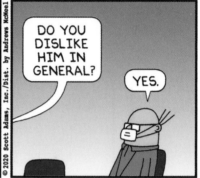

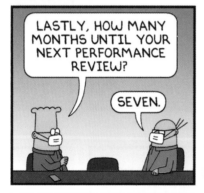

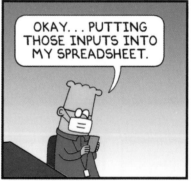

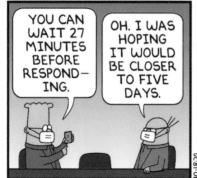

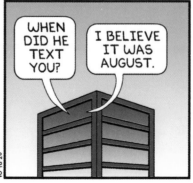

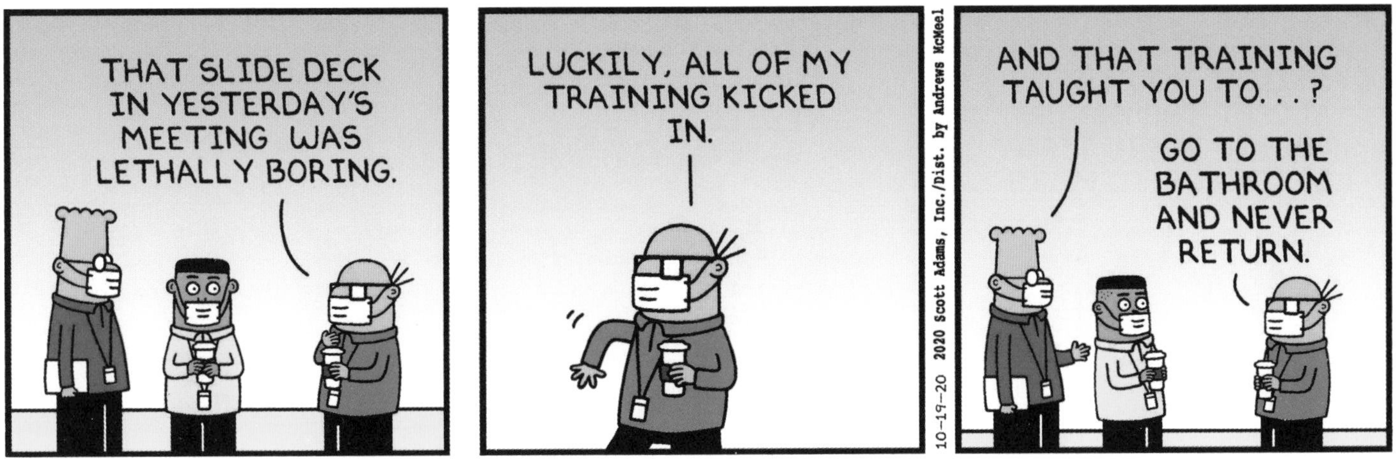
THAT SLIDE DECK IN YESTERDAY'S MEETING WAS LETHALLY BORING.
LUCKILY, ALL OF MY TRAINING KICKED IN.
AND THAT TRAINING TAUGHT YOU TO. . . ?
GO TO THE BATHROOM AND NEVER RETURN.
10-19-20 2020 Scott Adams, Inc./Dist. by Andrews McMeel

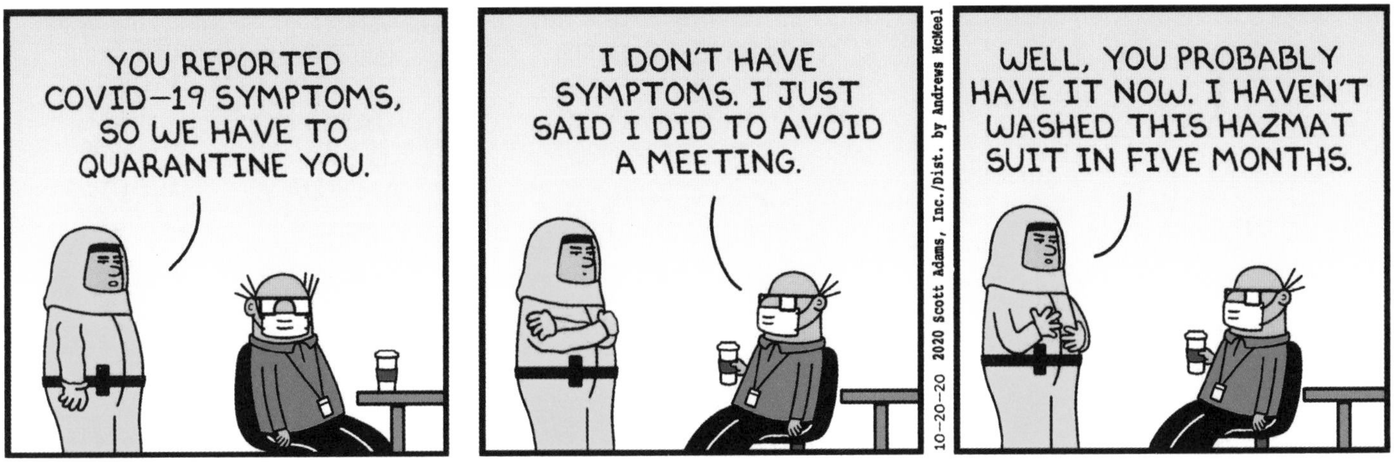
YOU REPORTED COVID-19 SYMPTOMS, SO WE HAVE TO QUARANTINE YOU.
I DON'T HAVE SYMPTOMS. I JUST SAID I DID TO AVOID A MEETING.
WELL, YOU PROBABLY HAVE IT NOW. I HAVEN'T WASHED THIS HAZMAT SUIT IN FIVE MONTHS.
10-20-20 2020 Scott Adams, Inc./Dist. by Andrews McMeel

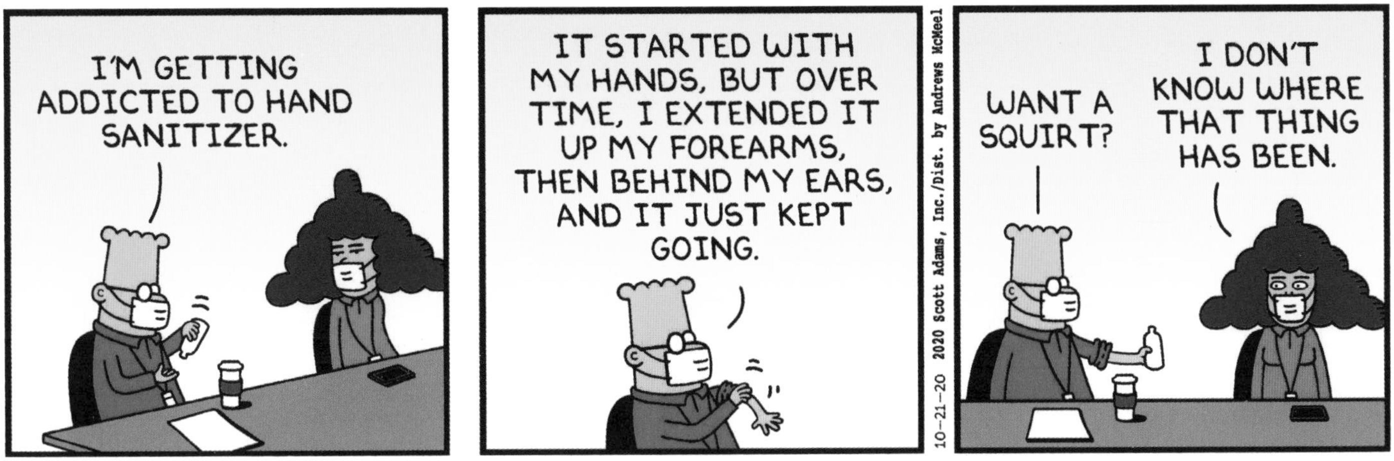
I'M GETTING ADDICTED TO HAND SANITIZER.
IT STARTED WITH MY HANDS, BUT OVER TIME, I EXTENDED IT UP MY FOREARMS, THEN BEHIND MY EARS, AND IT JUST KEPT GOING.
WANT A SQUIRT?
I DON'T KNOW WHERE THAT THING HAS BEEN.
10-21-20 2020 Scott Adams, Inc./Dist. by Andrews McMeel

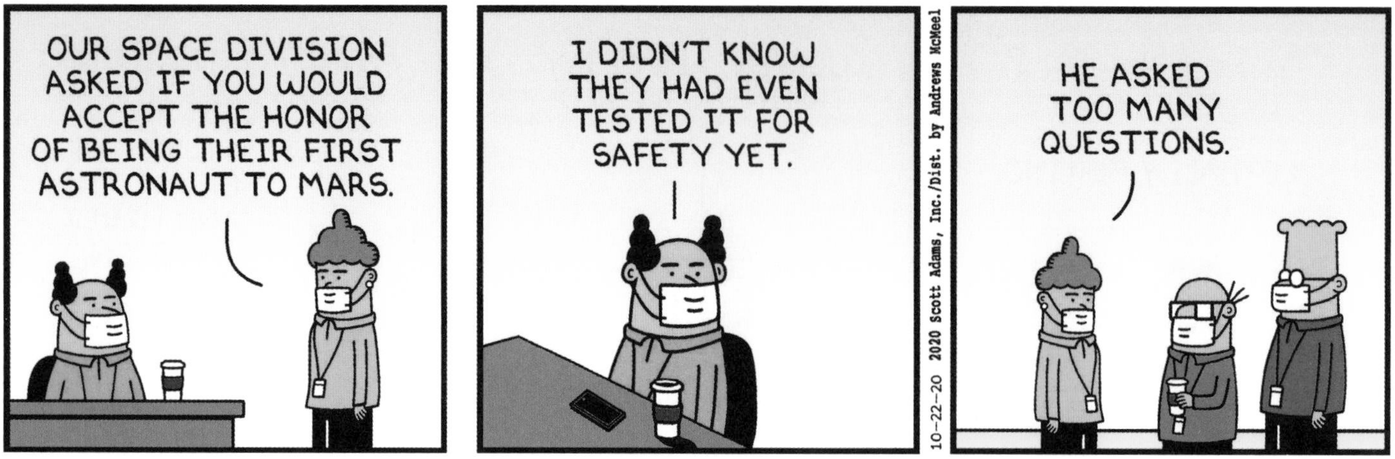
OUR SPACE DIVISION ASKED IF YOU WOULD ACCEPT THE HONOR OF BEING THEIR FIRST ASTRONAUT TO MARS.
I DIDN'T KNOW THEY HAD EVEN TESTED IT FOR SAFETY YET.
10-22-20 2020 Scott Adams, Inc./Dist. by Andrews McMeel
HE ASKED TOO MANY QUESTIONS.

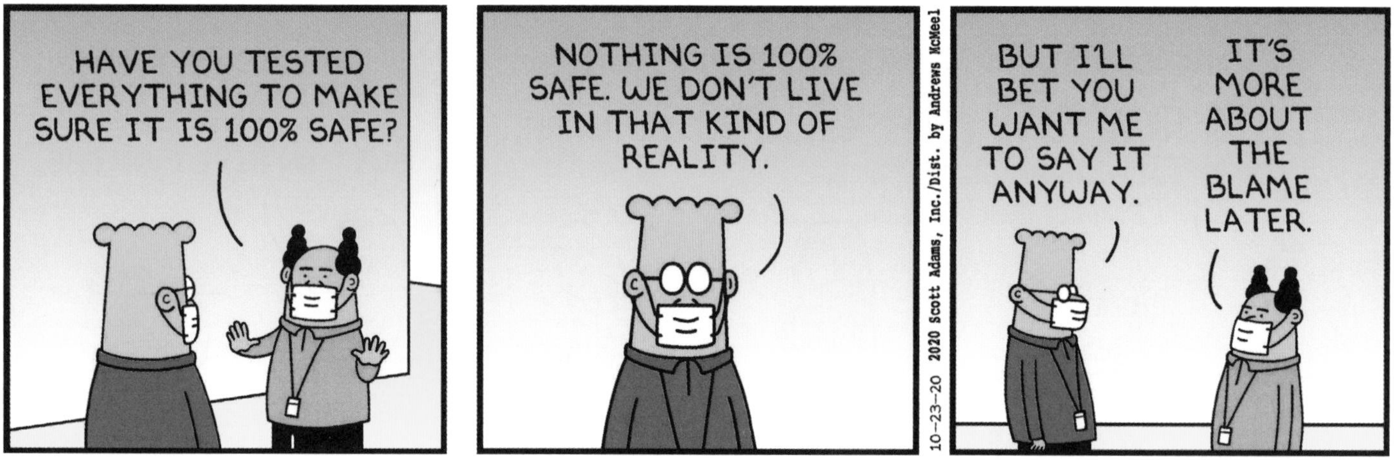
HAVE YOU TESTED EVERYTHING TO MAKE SURE IT IS 100% SAFE?
NOTHING IS 100% SAFE. WE DON'T LIVE IN THAT KIND OF REALITY.
10-23-20 2020 Scott Adams, Inc./Dist. by Andrews McMeel
BUT I'LL BET YOU WANT ME TO SAY IT ANYWAY.
IT'S MORE ABOUT THE BLAME LATER.

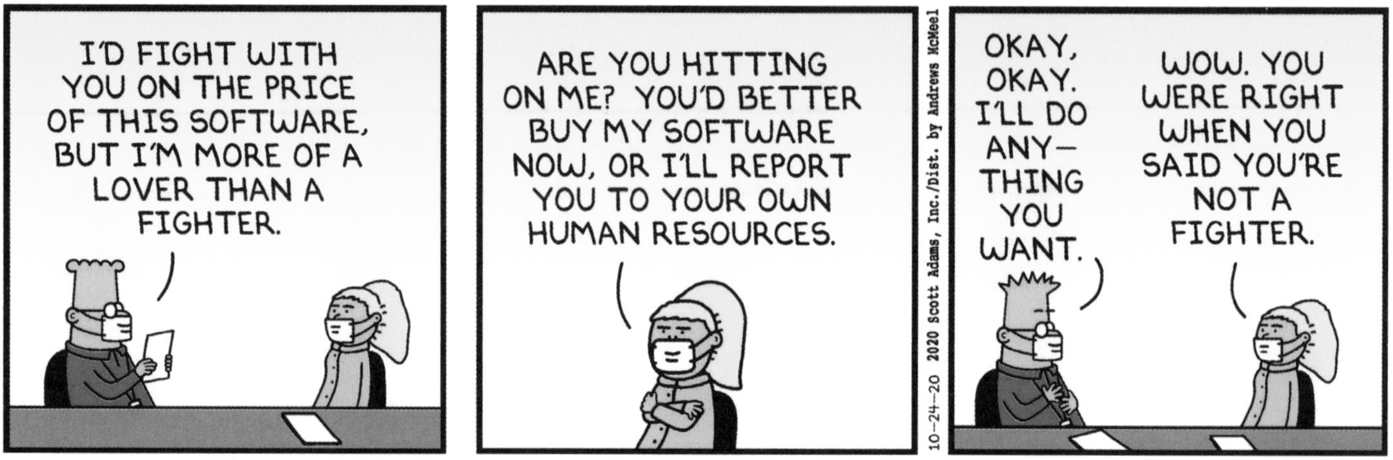
I'D FIGHT WITH YOU ON THE PRICE OF THIS SOFTWARE, BUT I'M MORE OF A LOVER THAN A FIGHTER.
ARE YOU HITTING ON ME? YOU'D BETTER BUY MY SOFTWARE NOW, OR I'LL REPORT YOU TO YOUR OWN HUMAN RESOURCES.
10-24-20 2020 Scott Adams, Inc./Dist. by Andrews McMeel
OKAY, OKAY. I'LL DO ANY-THING YOU WANT.
WOW. YOU WERE RIGHT WHEN YOU SAID YOU'RE NOT A FIGHTER.

AS YOU INSTRUCTED, I REFUSED TO GIVE IN TO OUR BIGGEST CUSTOMER'S DEMANDS AND THEY CANCELED ALL OF THEIR ORDERS.

I DIDN'T TELL YOU TO DO THAT, YOU FOOL!

YOU TOLD ME TO DO **EXACTLY** THAT.

© 2020 Scott Adams, Inc./Dist. by Andrews McMeel

I NEVER TOLD YOU TO LOSE OUR BIGGEST CUSTOMER!

YOU TOLD ME TO REFUSE THEIR DEMANDS.

BUT I DIDN'T TELL YOU TO LOSE THE CUSTOMER!

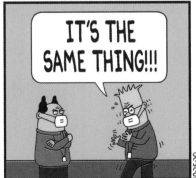

IT'S THE SAME THING!!!

THE IM-PORTANT THING HERE IS THAT IT'S YOUR FAULT.

I GET IT!!!

10-25-20

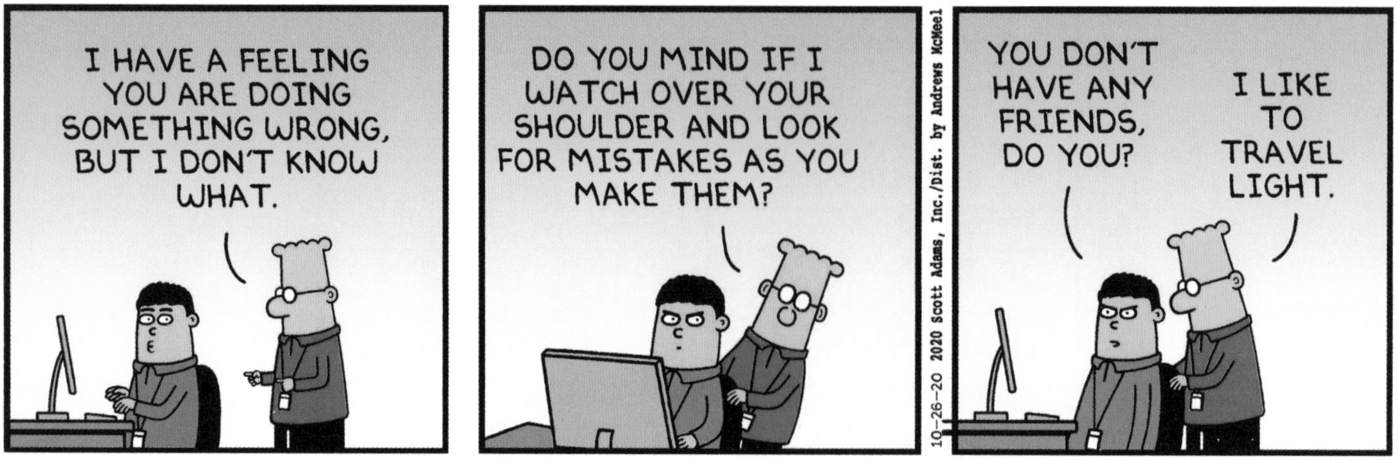
I HAVE A FEELING YOU ARE DOING SOMETHING WRONG, BUT I DON'T KNOW WHAT.
DO YOU MIND IF I WATCH OVER YOUR SHOULDER AND LOOK FOR MISTAKES AS YOU MAKE THEM?
10-26-20 2020 Scott Adams, Inc./Dist. by Andrews McMeel
YOU DON'T HAVE ANY FRIENDS, DO YOU?
I LIKE TO TRAVEL LIGHT.

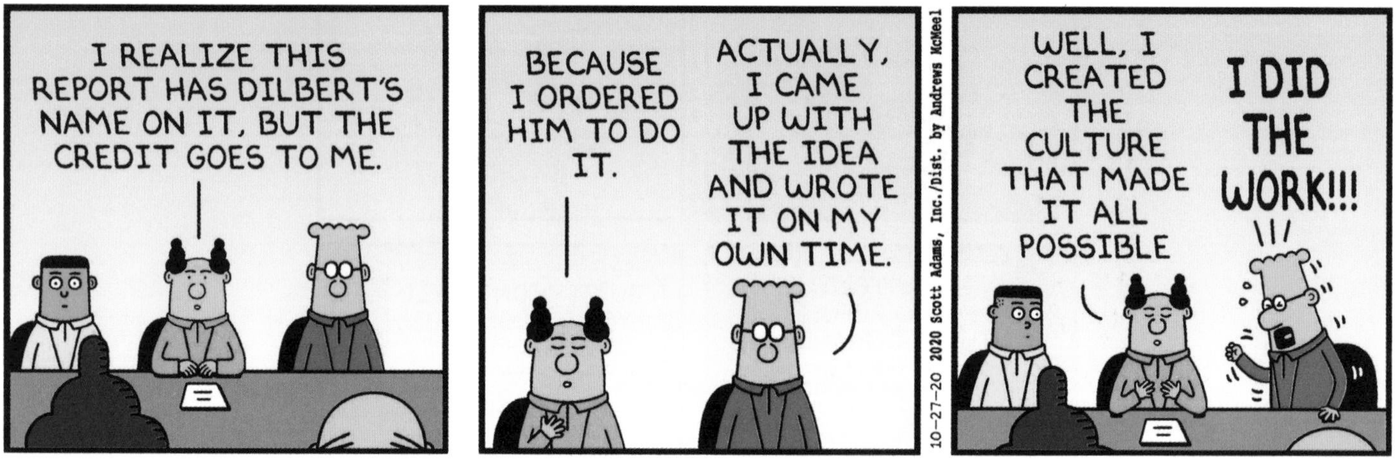
I REALIZE THIS REPORT HAS DILBERT'S NAME ON IT, BUT THE CREDIT GOES TO ME.
BECAUSE I ORDERED HIM TO DO IT.
ACTUALLY, I CAME UP WITH THE IDEA AND WROTE IT ON MY OWN TIME.
10-27-20 2020 Scott Adams, Inc./Dist. by Andrews McMeel
WELL, I CREATED THE CULTURE THAT MADE IT ALL POSSIBLE
I DID THE WORK!!!

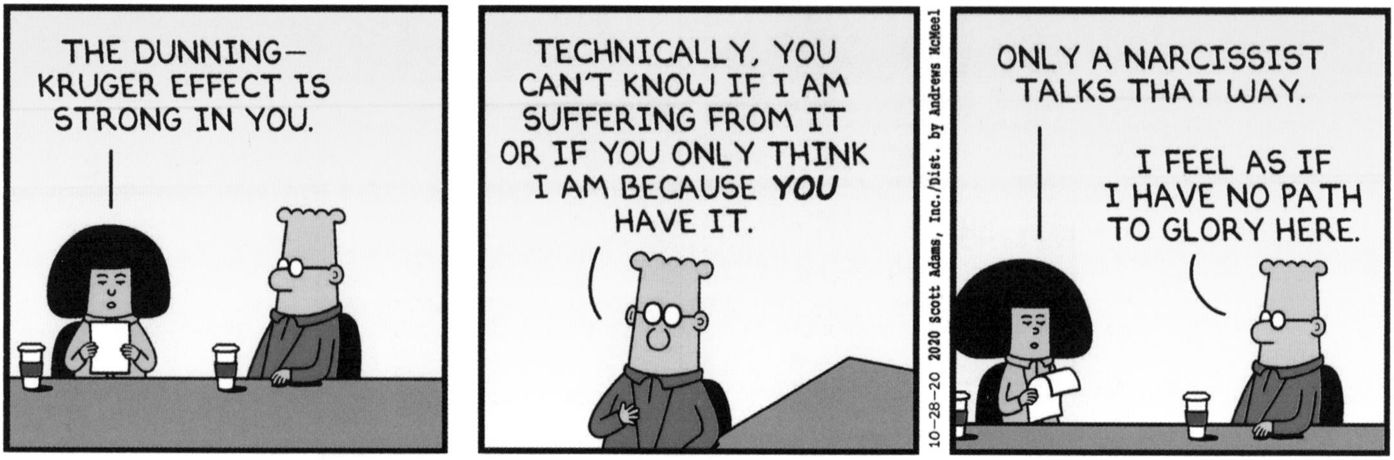
THE DUNNING-KRUGER EFFECT IS STRONG IN YOU.
TECHNICALLY, YOU CAN'T KNOW IF I AM SUFFERING FROM IT OR IF YOU ONLY THINK I AM BECAUSE *YOU* HAVE IT.
10-28-20 2020 Scott Adams, Inc./Dist. by Andrews McMeel
ONLY A NARCISSIST TALKS THAT WAY.
I FEEL AS IF I HAVE NO PATH TO GLORY HERE.

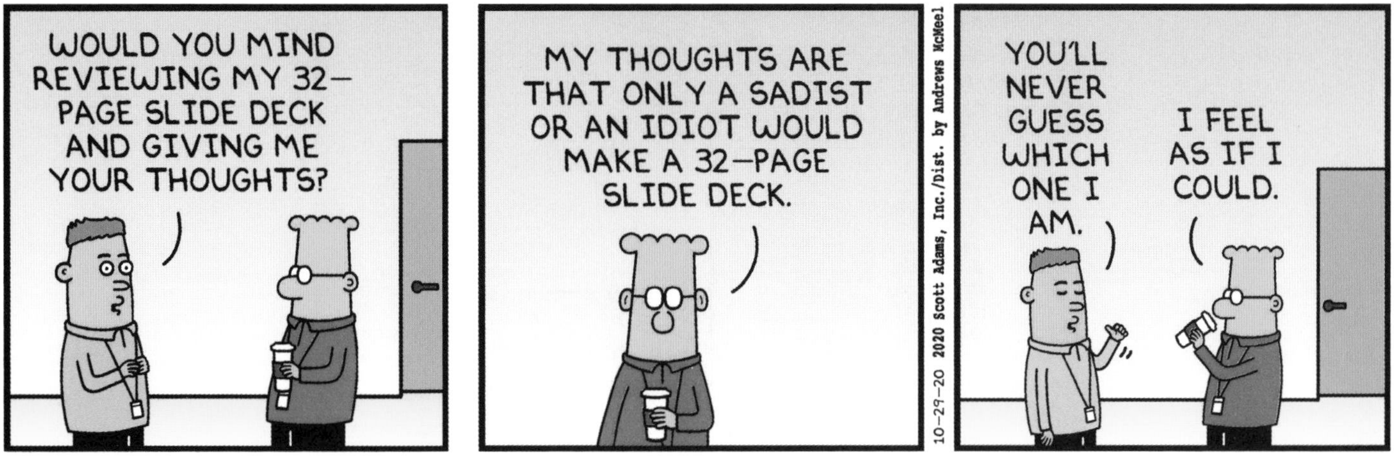
WOULD YOU MIND REVIEWING MY 32-PAGE SLIDE DECK AND GIVING ME YOUR THOUGHTS?
MY THOUGHTS ARE THAT ONLY A SADIST OR AN IDIOT WOULD MAKE A 32-PAGE SLIDE DECK.
YOU'LL NEVER GUESS WHICH ONE I AM.
I FEEL AS IF I COULD.
10-29-20 © 2020 Scott Adams, Inc./Dist. by Andrews McMeel

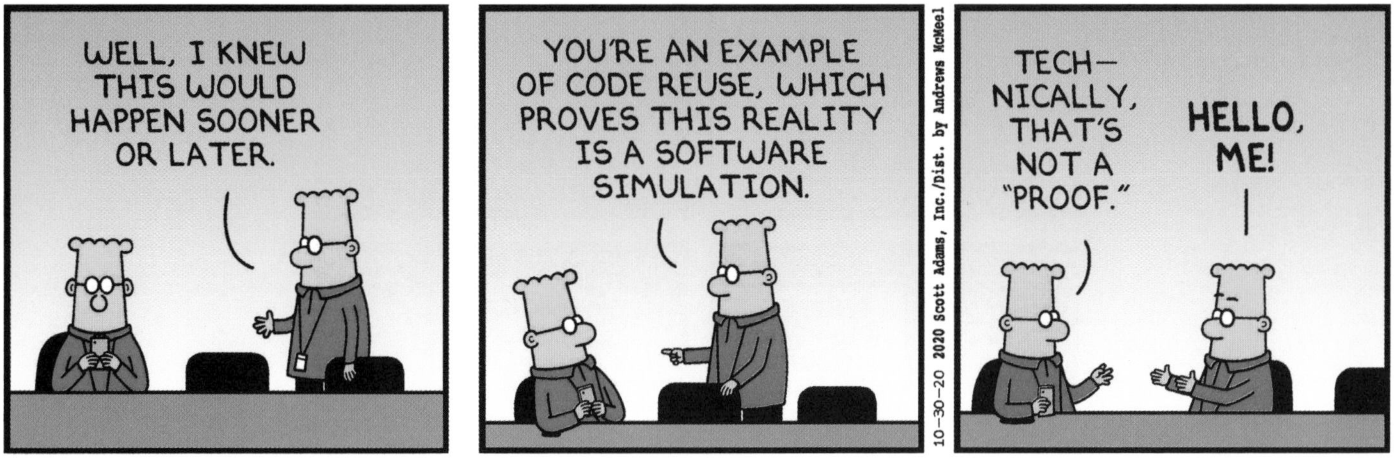
WELL, I KNEW THIS WOULD HAPPEN SOONER OR LATER.
YOU'RE AN EXAMPLE OF CODE REUSE, WHICH PROVES THIS REALITY IS A SOFTWARE SIMULATION.
TECHNICALLY, THAT'S NOT A "PROOF."
HELLO, ME!
10-30-20 © 2020 Scott Adams, Inc./Dist. by Andrews McMeel

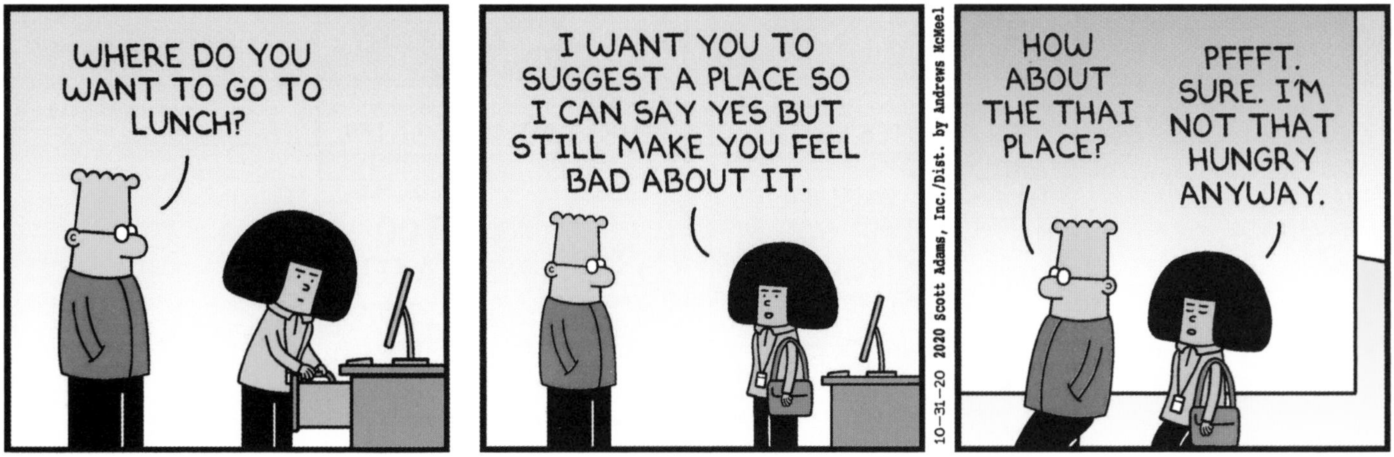
WHERE DO YOU WANT TO GO TO LUNCH?
I WANT YOU TO SUGGEST A PLACE SO I CAN SAY YES BUT STILL MAKE YOU FEEL BAD ABOUT IT.
HOW ABOUT THE THAI PLACE?
PFFFT. SURE. I'M NOT THAT HUNGRY ANYWAY.
10-31-20 © 2020 Scott Adams, Inc./Dist. by Andrews McMeel

ARE YOU AVAILABLE FOR A ZOOM CALL?
TAP TAP TAP
HE'S TYPING SOMETHING.
NOPE, HE STOPPED.
OKAY, HE'S TYPING AGAIN. NO, HE STOPPED AGAIN.
I'M AVAILABLE AT 2 P.M. TOMORROW, THURSDAY AT 9 A.M., OR NEXT WEEK ANY TIME AFTER THREE, AND NOW.
PERFECT. HOW ABOUT NOW?
ANSWER COMING.
NO, HE STOPPED TYPING.
TEN MINUTES LATER
ANSWER ME, YOU JERK!!!
THIRTY MINUTES LATER
DOES NOW WORK?
TOO LATE!!!
©2020 Scott Adams, Inc./Dist. by Andrews McMeel
11-1-20

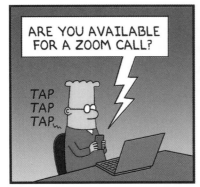

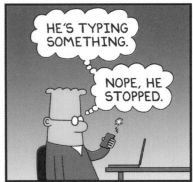

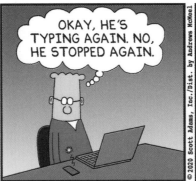

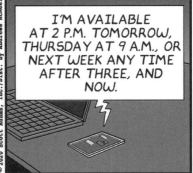

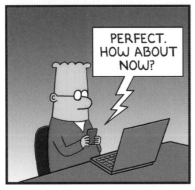

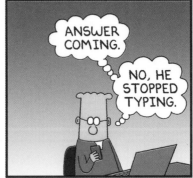

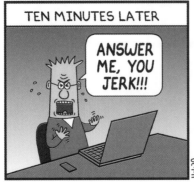

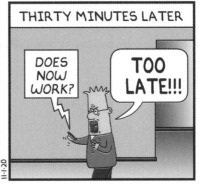

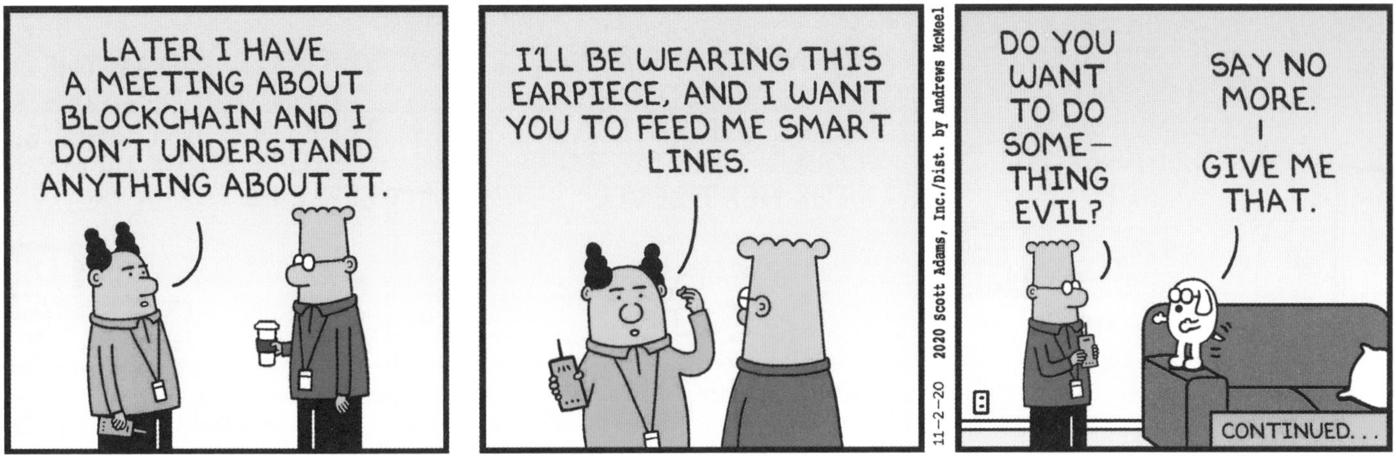
LATER I HAVE A MEETING ABOUT BLOCKCHAIN AND I DON'T UNDERSTAND ANYTHING ABOUT IT.
I'LL BE WEARING THIS EARPIECE, AND I WANT YOU TO FEED ME SMART LINES.
DO YOU WANT TO DO SOME-THING EVIL?
SAY NO MORE. I GIVE ME THAT.
CONTINUED. . .


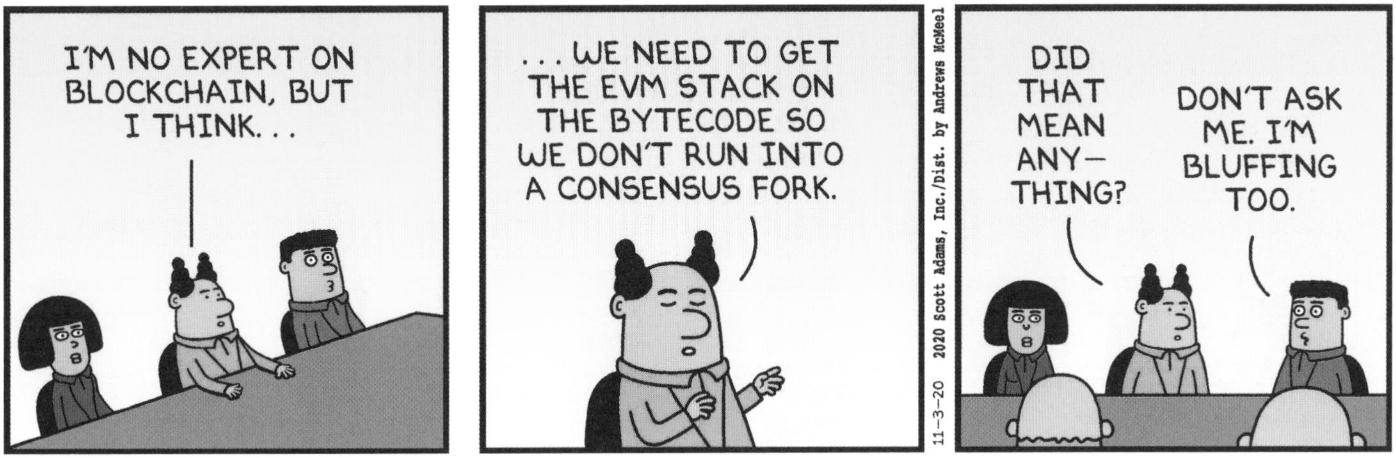
I'M NO EXPERT ON BLOCKCHAIN, BUT I THINK. . .
. . . WE NEED TO GET THE EVM STACK ON THE BYTECODE SO WE DON'T RUN INTO A CONSENSUS FORK.
DID THAT MEAN ANY-THING?
DON'T ASK ME. I'M BLUFFING TOO.


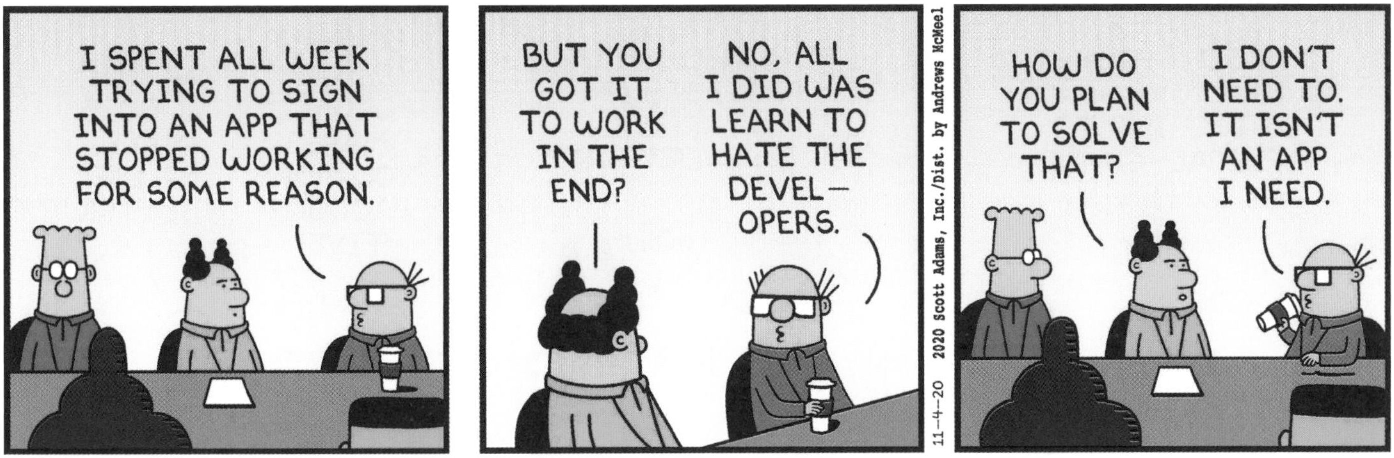
I SPENT ALL WEEK TRYING TO SIGN INTO AN APP THAT STOPPED WORKING FOR SOME REASON.
BUT YOU GOT IT TO WORK IN THE END?
NO, ALL I DID WAS LEARN TO HATE THE DEVEL-OPERS.
HOW DO YOU PLAN TO SOLVE THAT?
I DON'T NEED TO. IT ISN'T AN APP I NEED.

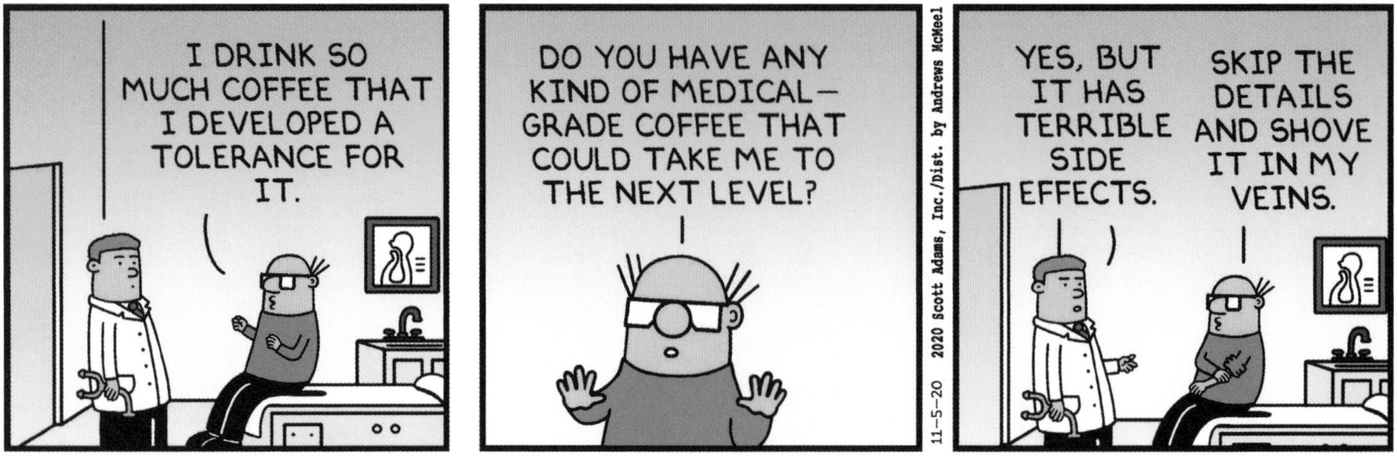
I DRINK SO MUCH COFFEE THAT I DEVELOPED A TOLERANCE FOR IT.
DO YOU HAVE ANY KIND OF MEDICAL-GRADE COFFEE THAT COULD TAKE ME TO THE NEXT LEVEL?
11-5-20 2020 Scott Adams, Inc./Dist. by Andrews McMeel
YES, BUT IT HAS TERRIBLE SIDE EFFECTS.
SKIP THE DETAILS AND SHOVE IT IN MY VEINS.

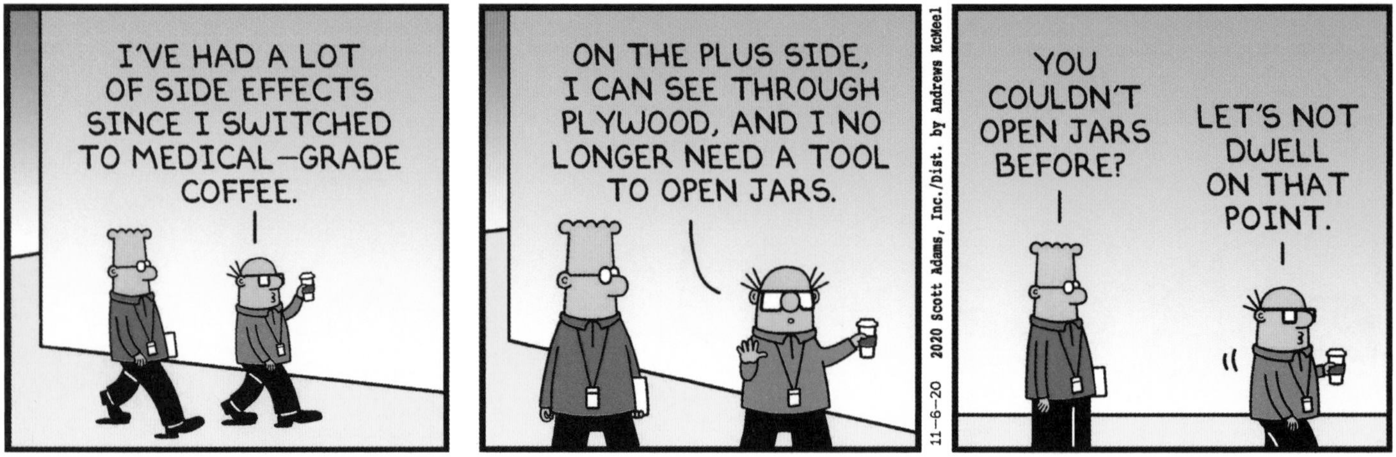
I'VE HAD A LOT OF SIDE EFFECTS SINCE I SWITCHED TO MEDICAL-GRADE COFFEE.
ON THE PLUS SIDE, I CAN SEE THROUGH PLYWOOD, AND I NO LONGER NEED A TOOL TO OPEN JARS.
11-6-20 2020 Scott Adams, Inc./Dist. by Andrews McMeel
YOU COULDN'T OPEN JARS BEFORE?
LET'S NOT DWELL ON THAT POINT.

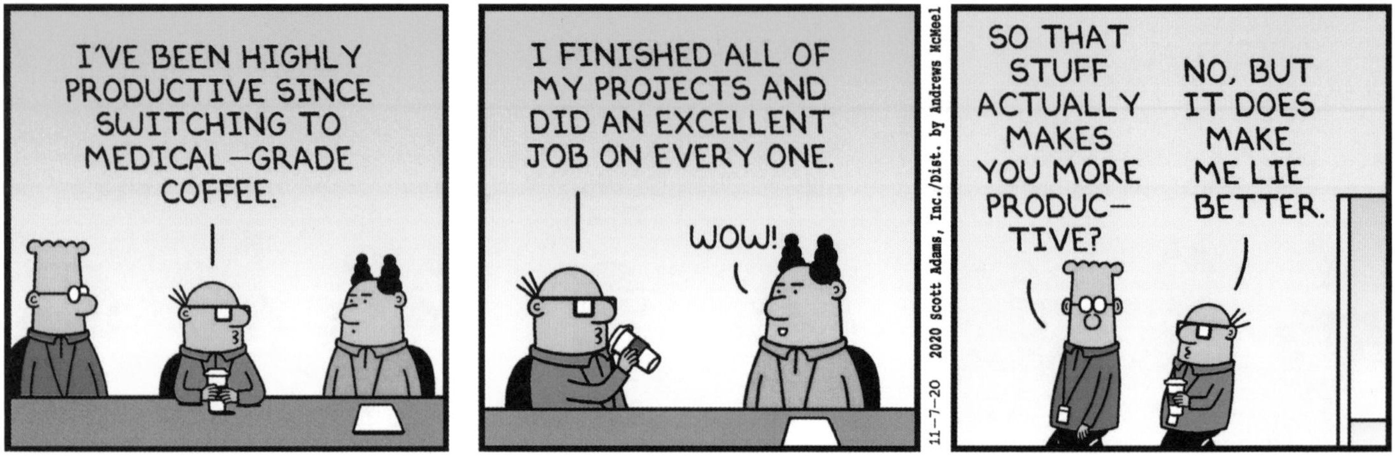
I'VE BEEN HIGHLY PRODUCTIVE SINCE SWITCHING TO MEDICAL-GRADE COFFEE.
I FINISHED ALL OF MY PROJECTS AND DID AN EXCELLENT JOB ON EVERY ONE.
WOW!
11-7-20 2020 Scott Adams, Inc./Dist. by Andrews McMeel
SO THAT STUFF ACTUALLY MAKES YOU MORE PRODUC-TIVE?
NO, BUT IT DOES MAKE ME LIE BETTER.

I'M NOT HUNGRY TODAY. DO YOU WANT MY BANANA?
THAT'S AN APPLE.
UM. . . NO. THIS IS A BANANA.
CLEARLY IT IS NOT.
I CAN'T BELIEVE YOU ARE MAKING ME DO A GOOGLE SEARCH TO PROVE I KNOW WHAT A BANANA IS.
© 2020 Scott Adams, Inc./Dist. by Andrews McMeel
SEE? THOSE ARE BANANAS. THIS LOOKS JUST LIKE THE PHOTOS. THIS IS A BANANA.
THOSE IMAGES ARE DOCTORED.
THERE ARE A MILLION BANANA IMAGES! THEY ARE NOT ALL DOCTORED!
YOU KNOW HOW I KNOW YOU ARE WRONG? BECAUSE YOU NEVER ADMIT YOU ARE WRONG.
GOTCHA!
11-8-20
THAT IS NOT A THING!!!
THAT'S EXACTLY WHAT ALL THE PEOPLE WHO ARE WRONG SAY.

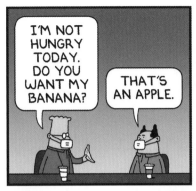

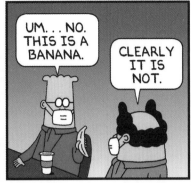

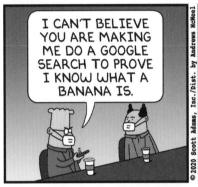

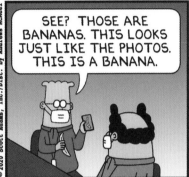

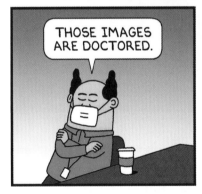

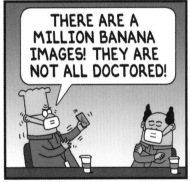

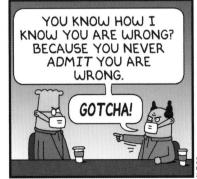

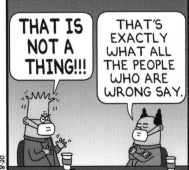

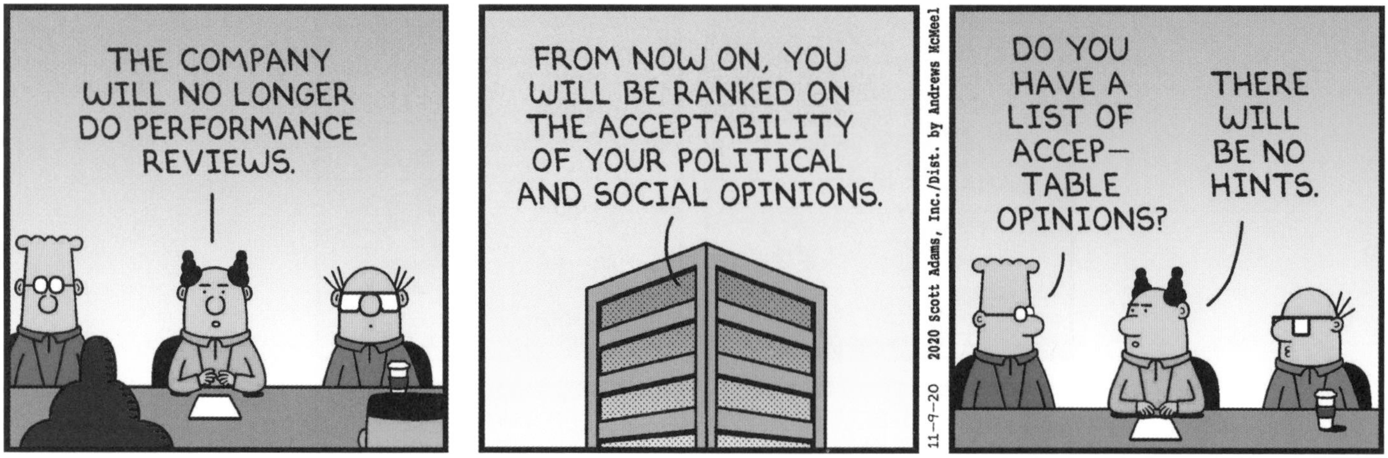
THE COMPANY WILL NO LONGER DO PERFORMANCE REVIEWS.
FROM NOW ON, YOU WILL BE RANKED ON THE ACCEPTABILITY OF YOUR POLITICAL AND SOCIAL OPINIONS.
11-9-20 2020 Scott Adams, Inc./Dist. by Andrews McMeel
DO YOU HAVE A LIST OF ACCEP—TABLE OPINIONS?
THERE WILL BE NO HINTS.

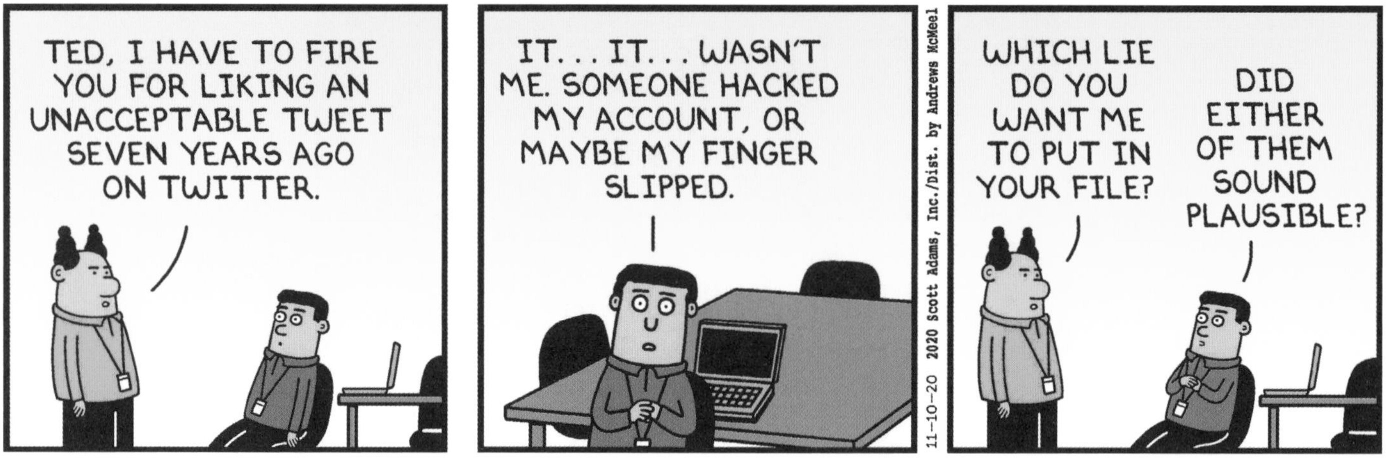
TED, I HAVE TO FIRE YOU FOR LIKING AN UNACCEPTABLE TWEET SEVEN YEARS AGO ON TWITTER.
IT. . . IT. . . WASN'T ME. SOMEONE HACKED MY ACCOUNT, OR MAYBE MY FINGER SLIPPED.
11-10-20 2020 Scott Adams, Inc./Dist. by Andrews McMeel
WHICH LIE DO YOU WANT ME TO PUT IN YOUR FILE?
DID EITHER OF THEM SOUND PLAUSIBLE?

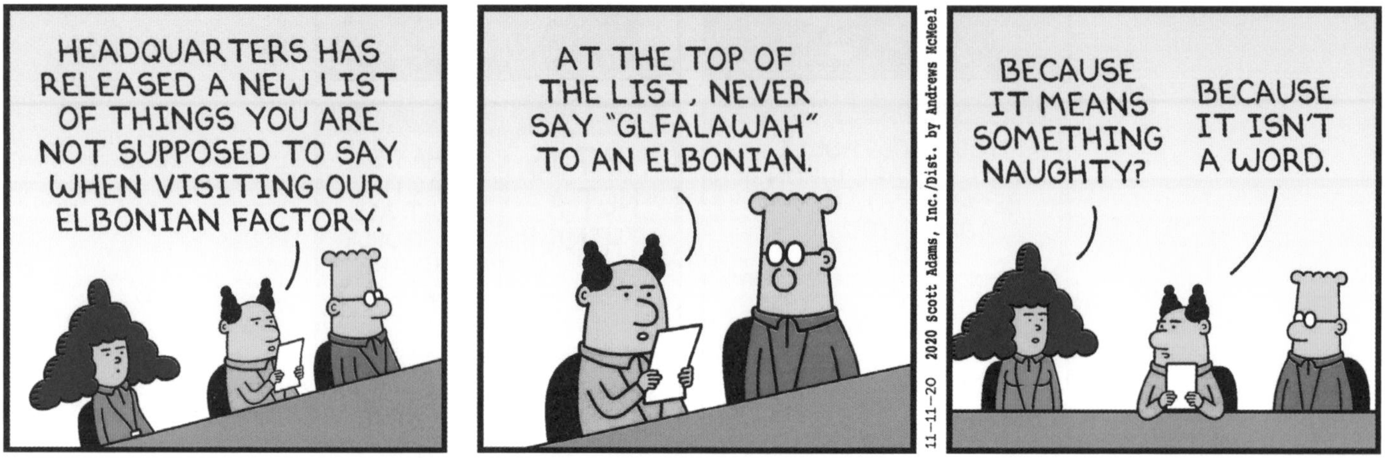
HEADQUARTERS HAS RELEASED A NEW LIST OF THINGS YOU ARE NOT SUPPOSED TO SAY WHEN VISITING OUR ELBONIAN FACTORY.
AT THE TOP OF THE LIST, NEVER SAY "GLFALAWAH" TO AN ELBONIAN.
11-11-20 2020 Scott Adams, Inc./Dist. by Andrews McMeel
BECAUSE IT MEANS SOMETHING NAUGHTY?
BECAUSE IT ISN'T A WORD.

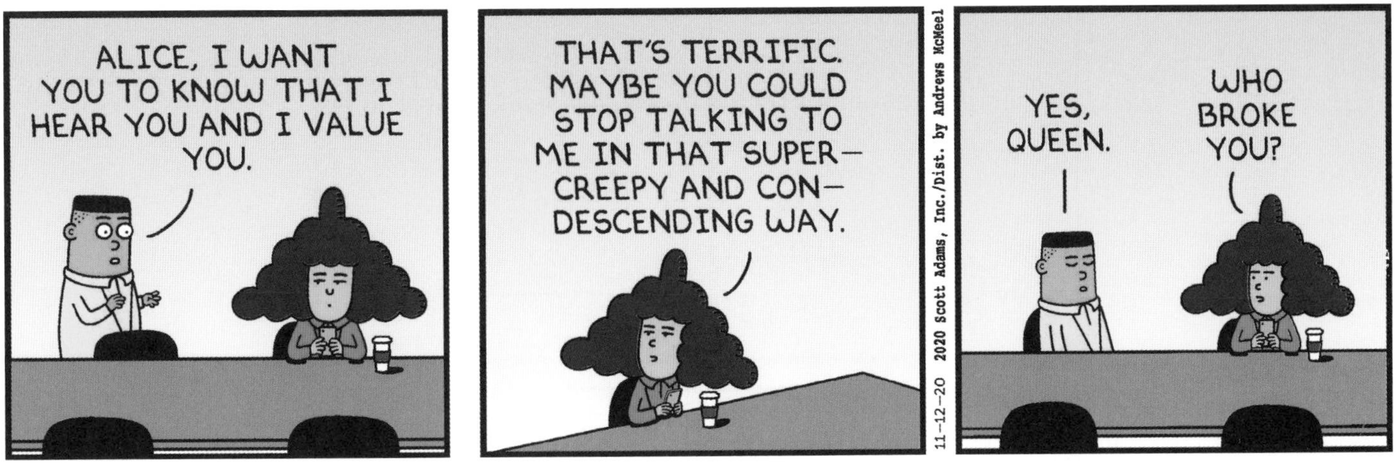
ALICE, I WANT YOU TO KNOW THAT I HEAR YOU AND I VALUE YOU.
THAT'S TERRIFIC. MAYBE YOU COULD STOP TALKING TO ME IN THAT SUPER-CREEPY AND CON-DESCENDING WAY.
11-12-20 2020 Scott Adams, Inc./Dist. by Andrews McMeel
YES, QUEEN.
WHO BROKE YOU?

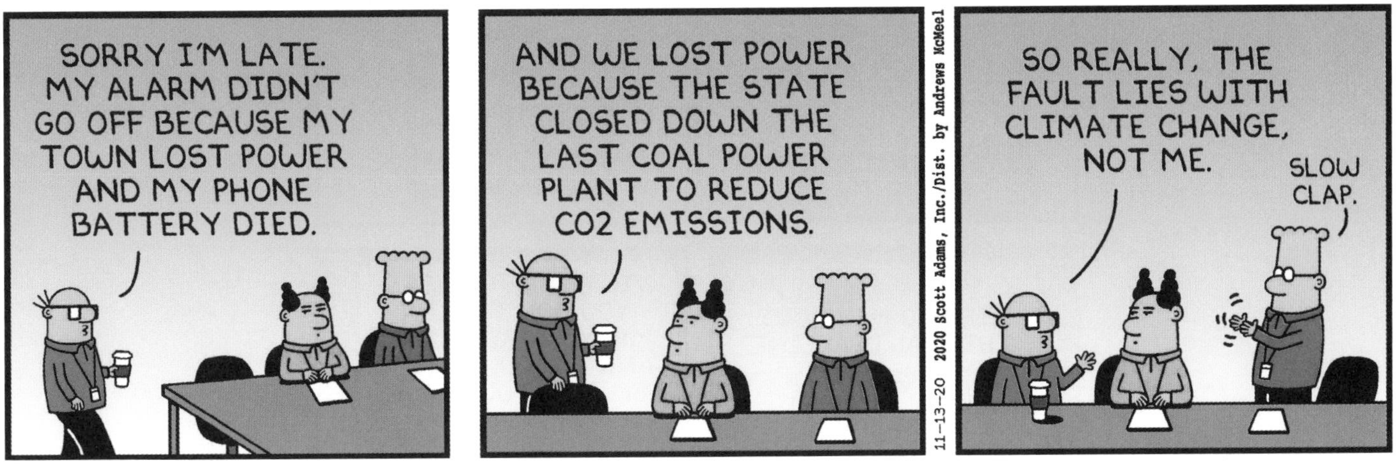
SORRY I'M LATE. MY ALARM DIDN'T GO OFF BECAUSE MY TOWN LOST POWER AND MY PHONE BATTERY DIED.
AND WE LOST POWER BECAUSE THE STATE CLOSED DOWN THE LAST COAL POWER PLANT TO REDUCE CO2 EMISSIONS.
11-13-20 2020 Scott Adams, Inc./Dist. by Andrews McMeel
SO REALLY, THE FAULT LIES WITH CLIMATE CHANGE, NOT ME.
SLOW CLAP.

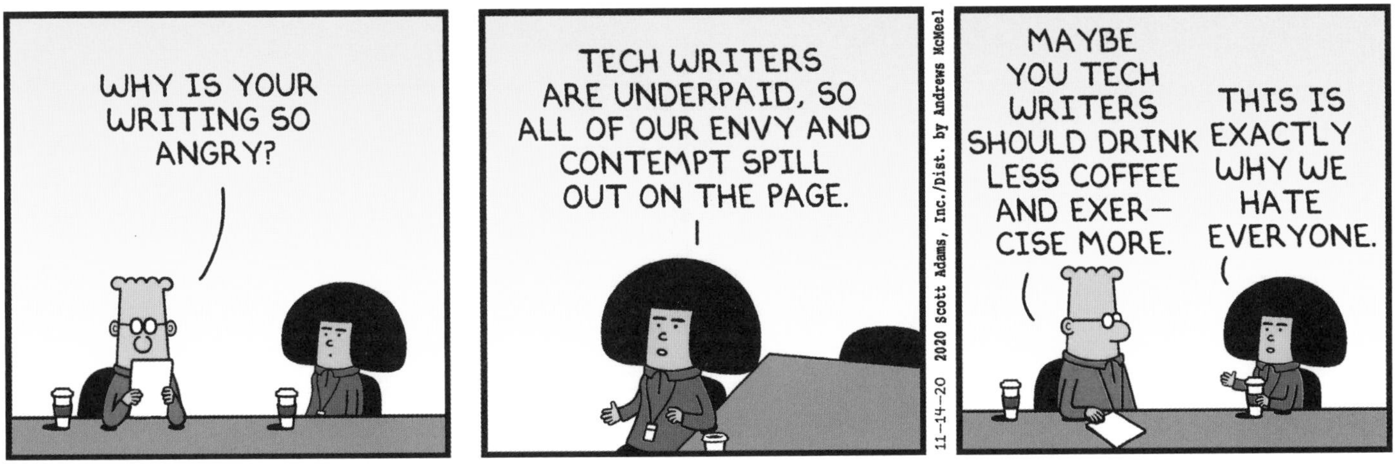
WHY IS YOUR WRITING SO ANGRY?
TECH WRITERS ARE UNDERPAID, SO ALL OF OUR ENVY AND CONTEMPT SPILL OUT ON THE PAGE.
11-14-20 2020 Scott Adams, Inc./Dist. by Andrews McMeel
MAYBE YOU TECH WRITERS SHOULD DRINK LESS COFFEE AND EXER-CISE MORE.
THIS IS EXACTLY WHY WE HATE EVERYONE.

I WORKED ALL WEEKEND TO GET THIS DONE FOR YOU BY THE DEADLINE.

THANKS. BUT I WON'T NEED IT FOR ANOTHER TWO WEEKS.

THEN . . . WHY DID YOU TELL ME THE DEADLINE WAS TODAY?

I BUILT SOME CUSHION INTO THE SCHEDULE.

YOU MEAN, YOU LIED TO ME ABOUT THE REAL DEADLINE.

IN OTHER WORDS, YOU DON'T TRUST ME, YOU ARE A LIAR, AND I SHOULD NEVER BELIEVE YOU AGAIN.

BUT YOU DIDN'T MISS THE DEADLINE!

OKAY, WELL, AT LEAST MY INPUT IS CRITICAL TO OUR SUCCESS.

I MIGHT HAVE EXAG— GERATED THAT.

11-15-20

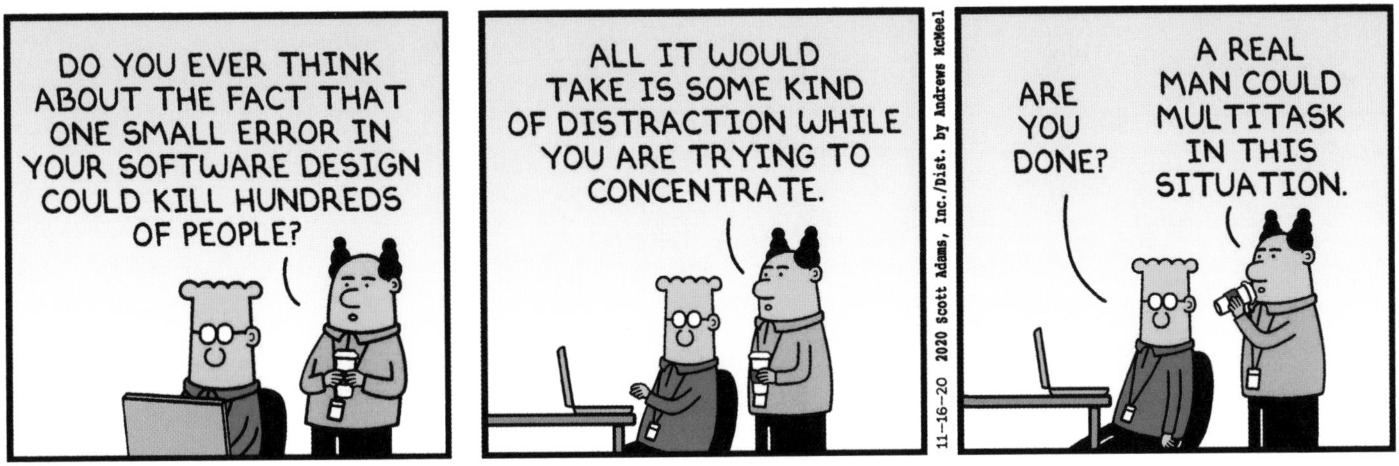
DO YOU EVER THINK ABOUT THE FACT THAT ONE SMALL ERROR IN YOUR SOFTWARE DESIGN COULD KILL HUNDREDS OF PEOPLE?
ALL IT WOULD TAKE IS SOME KIND OF DISTRACTION WHILE YOU ARE TRYING TO CONCENTRATE.
11-16-20 2020 Scott Adams, Inc./Dist. by Andrews McMeel
ARE YOU DONE?
A REAL MAN COULD MULTITASK IN THIS SITUATION.

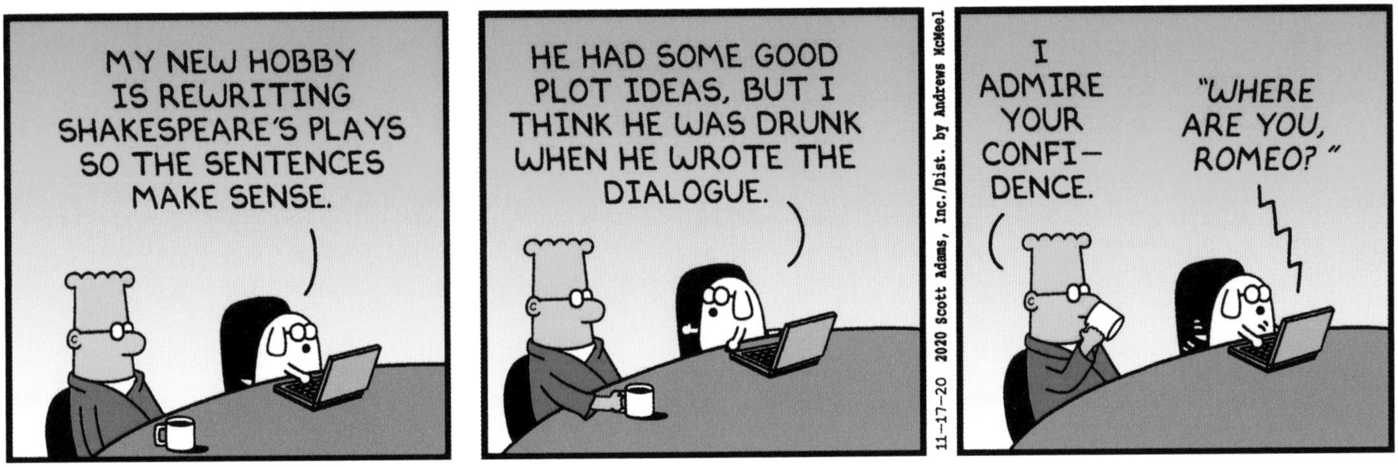
MY NEW HOBBY IS REWRITING SHAKESPEARE'S PLAYS SO THE SENTENCES MAKE SENSE.
HE HAD SOME GOOD PLOT IDEAS, BUT I THINK HE WAS DRUNK WHEN HE WROTE THE DIALOGUE.
11-17-20 2020 Scott Adams, Inc./Dist. by Andrews McMeel
I ADMIRE YOUR CONFI-DENCE.
"WHERE ARE YOU, ROMEO?"

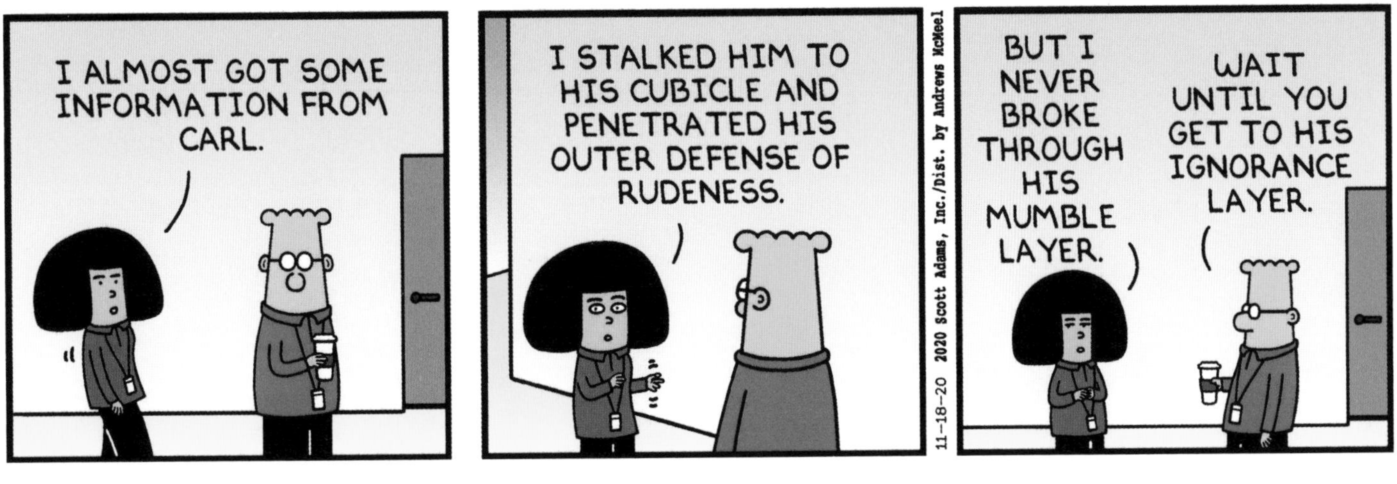
I ALMOST GOT SOME INFORMATION FROM CARL.
I STALKED HIM TO HIS CUBICLE AND PENETRATED HIS OUTER DEFENSE OF RUDENESS.
11-18-20 2020 Scott Adams, Inc./Dist. by Andrews McMeel
BUT I NEVER BROKE THROUGH HIS MUMBLE LAYER.
WAIT UNTIL YOU GET TO HIS IGNORANCE LAYER.

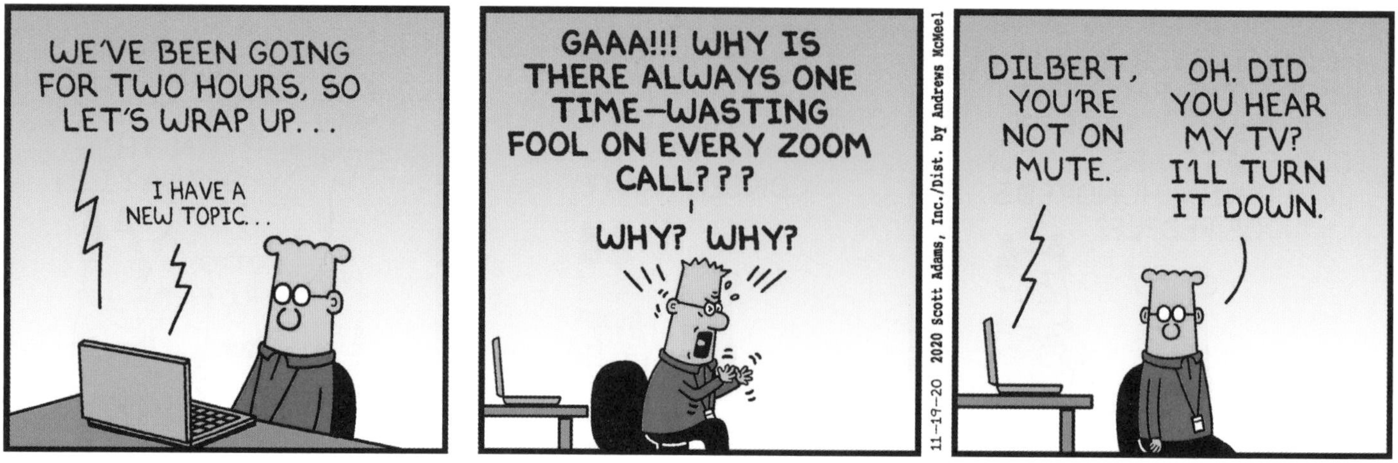
WE'VE BEEN GOING FOR TWO HOURS, SO LET'S WRAP UP...
I HAVE A NEW TOPIC...
GAAA!!! WHY IS THERE ALWAYS ONE TIME—WASTING FOOL ON EVERY ZOOM CALL???
WHY? WHY?
DILBERT, YOU'RE NOT ON MUTE.
OH. DID YOU HEAR MY TV? I'LL TURN IT DOWN.



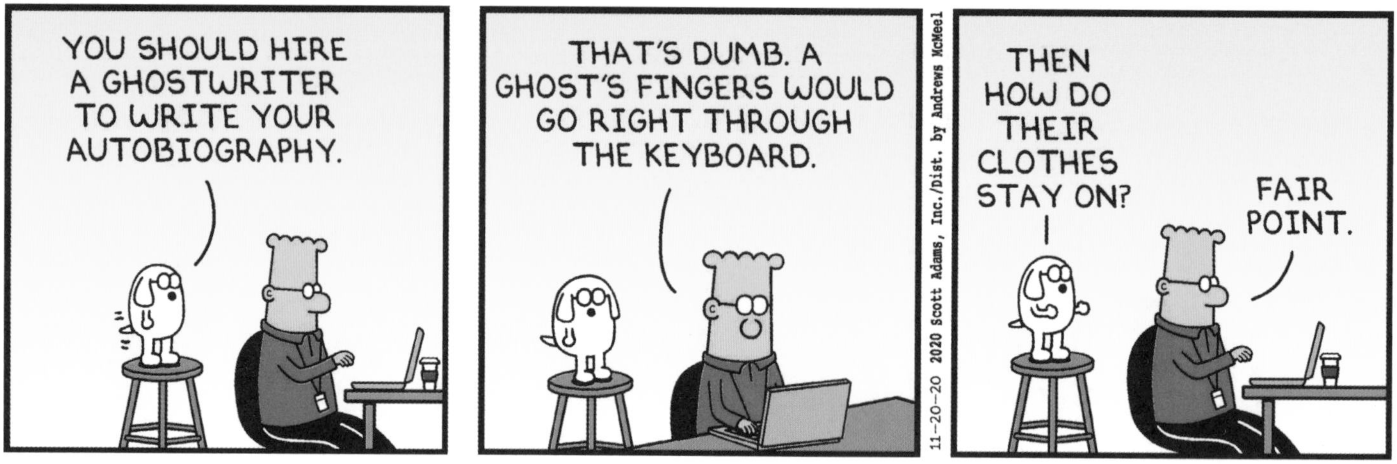
YOU SHOULD HIRE A GHOSTWRITER TO WRITE YOUR AUTOBIOGRAPHY.
THAT'S DUMB. A GHOST'S FINGERS WOULD GO RIGHT THROUGH THE KEYBOARD.
THEN HOW DO THEIR CLOTHES STAY ON?
FAIR POINT.



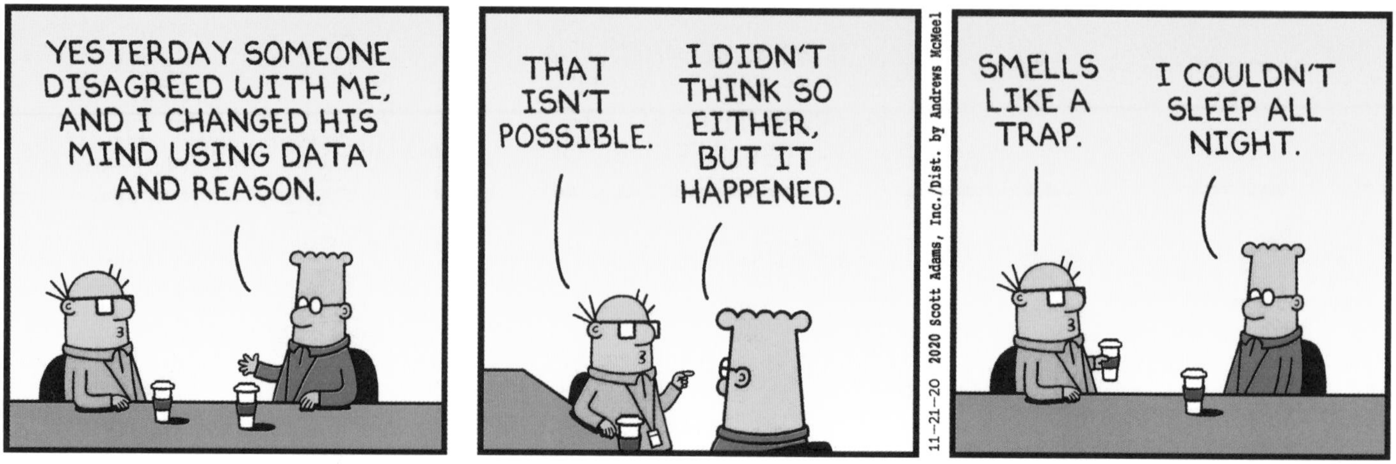
YESTERDAY SOMEONE DISAGREED WITH ME, AND I CHANGED HIS MIND USING DATA AND REASON.
THAT ISN'T POSSIBLE.
I DIDN'T THINK SO EITHER, BUT IT HAPPENED.
SMELLS LIKE A TRAP.
I COULDN'T SLEEP ALL NIGHT.

WE'VE TRIPLE-CHECKED ALL SYSTEMS, AND WE ARE READY TO LAUNCH THE SATELLITE.
NOTHING CAN GO WRONG.
INITIATING LAUNCH.
NOTHING CAN GO WRONG?
WHAT IF AN ALIEN SPACESHIP APPEARS OVER THE LAUNCH SITE?
GAAA!!! DON'T JINX US.
THAT'S NOT HOW REALITY WORKS. I CAN'T MAKE THINGS HAPPEN JUST BY SUGGESTING THEM.
YOU'RE WRONG! THAT IS **EXACTLY** HOW REALITY WORKS!
SOMETHING JUST APPEARED ON RADAR DIRECTLY ABOVE THE ROCKET'S TRAJECTORY.
MAYBE IT'S A BIRD.
IT'S THE SIZE OF BELGIUM.
© 2020 Scott Adams, Inc./Dist. by Andrews McMeel
11-22-20

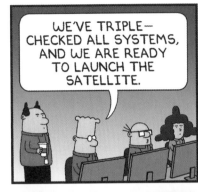

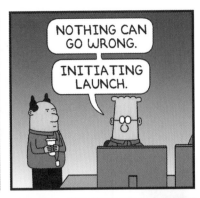

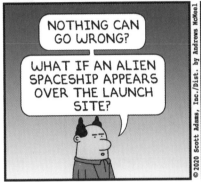

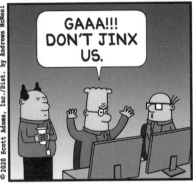

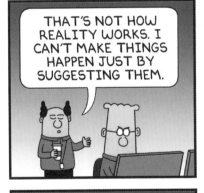

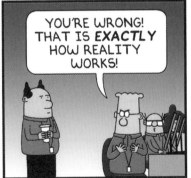

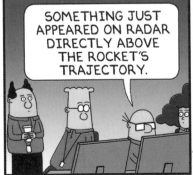

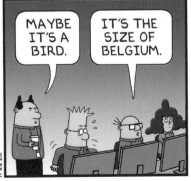

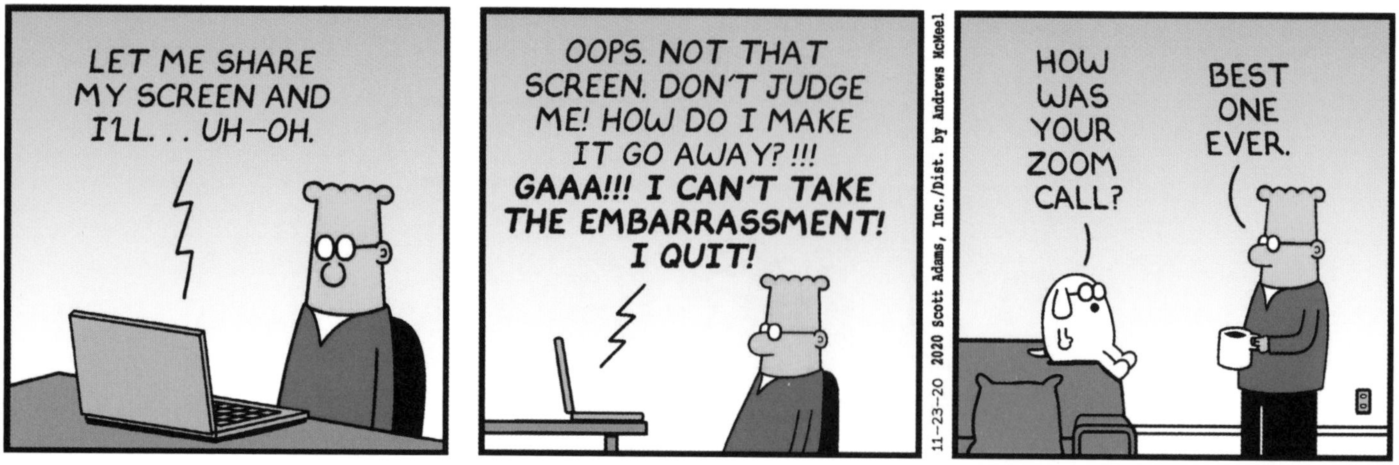
LET ME SHARE MY SCREEN AND I'LL. . . UH–OH.
OOPS. NOT THAT SCREEN. DON'T JUDGE ME! HOW DO I MAKE IT GO AWAY?!!!
**GAAA!!! I CAN'T TAKE THE EMBARRASSMENT! I QUIT!**
HOW WAS YOUR ZOOM CALL?
BEST ONE EVER.
11-23-20 2020 Scott Adams, Inc./Dist. by Andrews McMeel

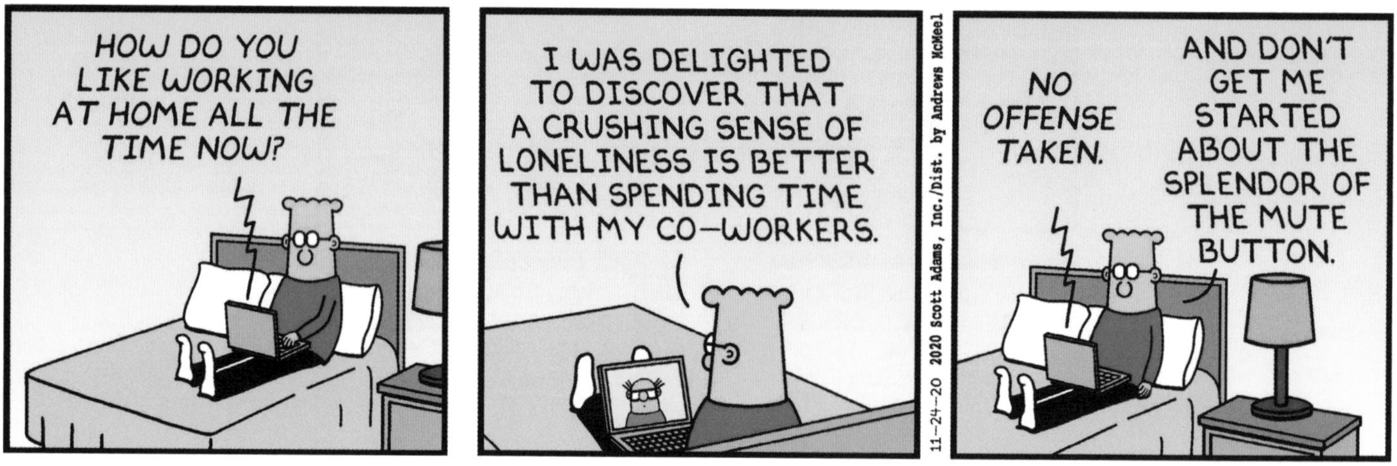
HOW DO YOU LIKE WORKING AT HOME ALL THE TIME NOW?
I WAS DELIGHTED TO DISCOVER THAT A CRUSHING SENSE OF LONELINESS IS BETTER THAN SPENDING TIME WITH MY CO–WORKERS.
NO OFFENSE TAKEN.
AND DON'T GET ME STARTED ABOUT THE SPLENDOR OF THE MUTE BUTTON.
11-24-20 2020 Scott Adams, Inc./Dist. by Andrews McMeel

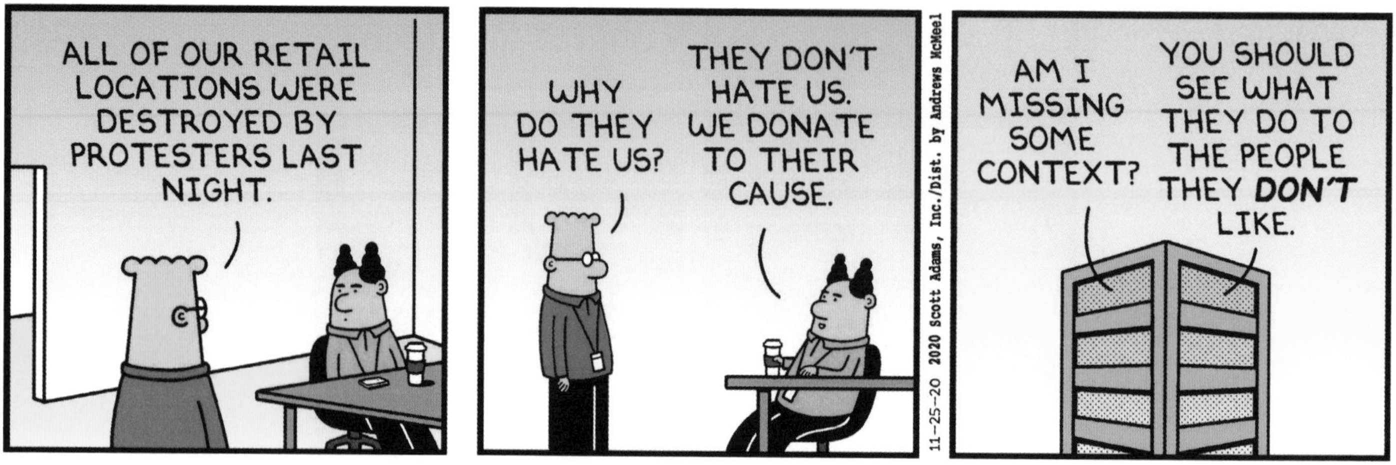
ALL OF OUR RETAIL LOCATIONS WERE DESTROYED BY PROTESTERS LAST NIGHT.
WHY DO THEY HATE US?
THEY DON'T HATE US. WE DONATE TO THEIR CAUSE.
AM I MISSING SOME CONTEXT?
YOU SHOULD SEE WHAT THEY DO TO THE PEOPLE THEY ***DON'T*** LIKE.
11-25-20 2020 Scott Adams, Inc./Dist. by Andrews McMeel

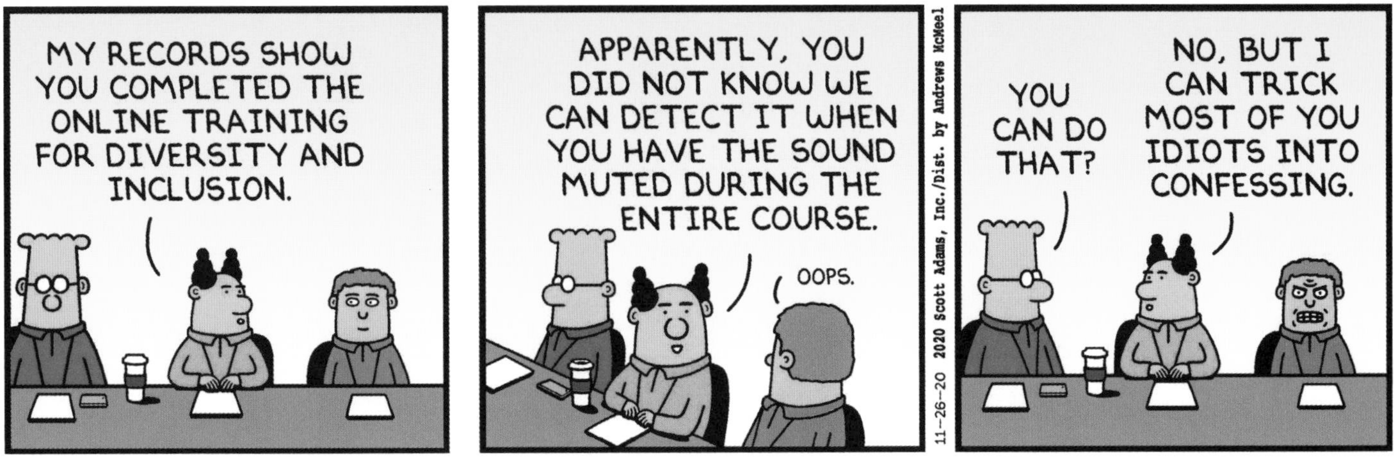
MY RECORDS SHOW YOU COMPLETED THE ONLINE TRAINING FOR DIVERSITY AND INCLUSION.
APPARENTLY, YOU DID NOT KNOW WE CAN DETECT IT WHEN YOU HAVE THE SOUND MUTED DURING THE ENTIRE COURSE.
OOPS.
YOU CAN DO THAT?
NO, BUT I CAN TRICK MOST OF YOU IDIOTS INTO CONFESSING.
11-26-20 2020 Scott Adams, Inc./Dist. by Andrews McMeel

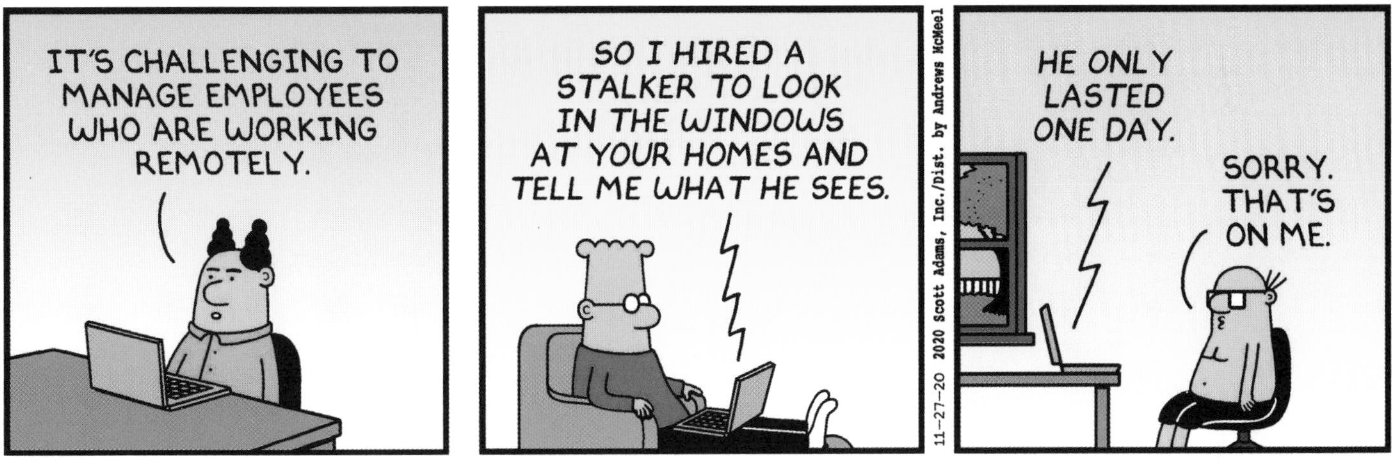
IT'S CHALLENGING TO MANAGE EMPLOYEES WHO ARE WORKING REMOTELY.
SO I HIRED A STALKER TO LOOK IN THE WINDOWS AT YOUR HOMES AND TELL ME WHAT HE SEES.
HE ONLY LASTED ONE DAY.
SORRY. THAT'S ON ME.
11-27-20 2020 Scott Adams, Inc./Dist. by Andrews McMeel

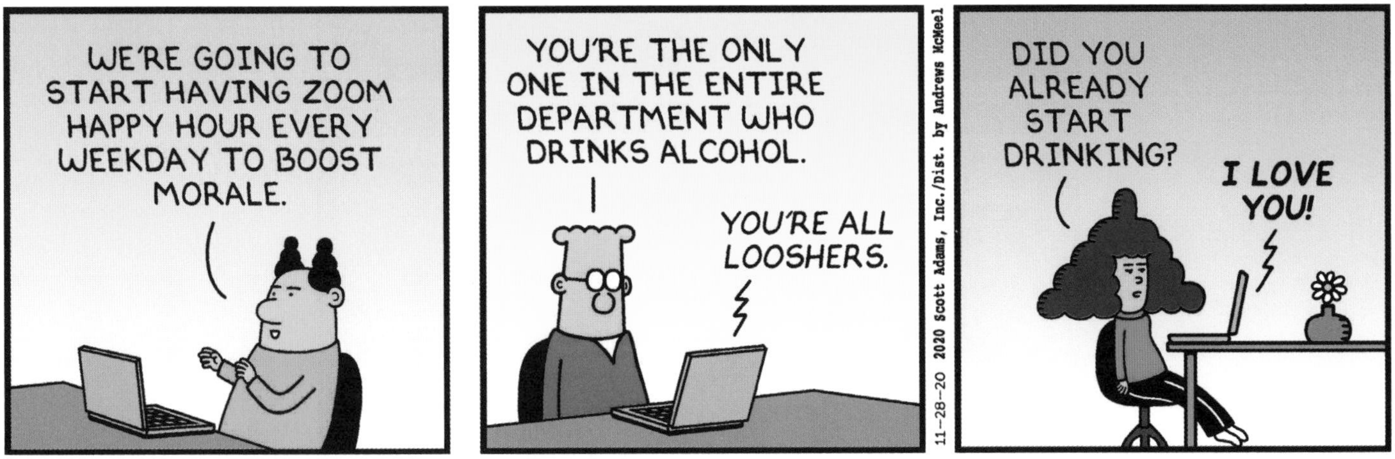
WE'RE GOING TO START HAVING ZOOM HAPPY HOUR EVERY WEEKDAY TO BOOST MORALE.
YOU'RE THE ONLY ONE IN THE ENTIRE DEPARTMENT WHO DRINKS ALCOHOL.
YOU'RE ALL LOOSHERS.
DID YOU ALREADY START DRINKING?
I LOVE YOU!
11-28-20 2020 Scott Adams, Inc./Dist. by Andrews McMeel

I STARTED DOING TELEMEDICINE IN MY SPARE TIME.
DON'T YOU NEED TO BE A DOCTOR TO DO THAT?
TECHNICALLY, YES. BUT I FOUND A WORKAROUND.
WHICH IS?
I TELL PEOPLE I'M A DOCTOR.
DOCTOR, I HAVE A SHARP PAIN IN THE BACK OF MY THIGH.
ARE YOU SITTING ON A RAKE?
THAT'S A WEIRD QUESTION.
OH, WAIT, I AM.
WHAT SHOULD I DO?
TRY PICKING UP LEAVES WITH YOUR HANDS.
© 2020 Scott Adams, Inc./Dist. by Andrews McMeel
11-29-20

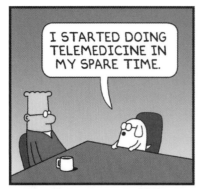

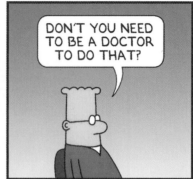

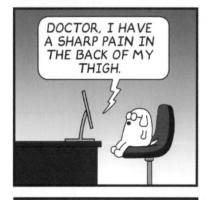

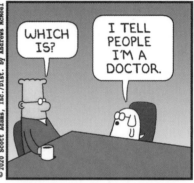

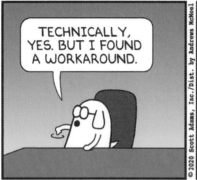

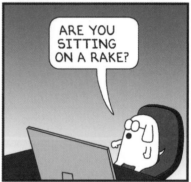

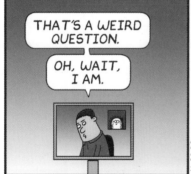

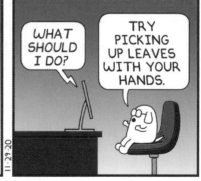

Andrews McMeel Publishing
a division of Andrews McMeel Universal
1130 Walnut Street, Kansas City, Missouri 64106
www.andrewsmcmeel.com

21 22 23 24 25 SDB 10 9 8 7 6 5 4 3 2 1

ISBN: 978-1-5248-6896-3

Library of Congress Control Number: 2021934984

www.dilbert.com